Human Biology
An activity approach

Pat Rowlinson,
formerly Head of Human and Social Biology,
Theale Green School,
Berkshire
and
Morton Jenkins,
Head of Science,
Howardian High School, Cardiff and
Chief Examiner CSE Biology, Welsh Joint Education Committee.

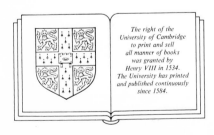

The right of the
University of Cambridge
to print and sell
all manner of books
was granted by
Henry VIII in 1534.
The University has printed
and published continuously
since 1584.

Cambridge University Press
Cambridge
London   New York   New Rochelle
Melbourne   Sydney

Preface

Human Biology – An Activity Approach is a main course book, suitable for students studying for C.S.E., 'O' level and 16+ examinations. The text has a completely new approach based on student involvement through practical activities in the laboratory, and writing and thinking activities at the desk. There are questions and exercises throughout, on the experiments, the text material itself, and also the photographs and line illustrations. This approach is designed to encourage careful observation and deductions.

Because this is a multi-purpose book which can be used by teachers in a variety of ways, it does not dictate a specific teaching style. Some teachers may want to teach a topic in their own way initially, and then allow the class to work through the appropriate sections in the book for reinforcement and revision. Others may decide that the thorough questioning approach presented by the book is a good way to introduce the topic to a class; and they can then add their own experiments, teaching aids and ideas as they work their way through the sections. Homeworks and extension material are suggested throughout the text.

Safety has been a major consideration in planning the activities. The recommendations of the A.S.E. in *Safeguards in the School Laboratory* have been followed carefully. Thus practical experiments on blood grouping involving students testing their own blood have been omitted from Unit 7, but work involving cultures of bacteria, sealed after innocula-tion and NEVER RE-OPENED in class, have been included in Unit 15 on diseases.

SI units have been used throughout, except in a few cases where other types of unit are so frequently used, and common values so widely known, that to introduce rigorous SI units would cause confusion. Thus blood pressure is given in mm Hg, and blood glucose level in mg/100ml, while food energy values are properly given in kJ.

The line illustrations have scale indicators wherever this is appropriate. The magnifications of histological photographs are not given in the captions, as these are often misunderstood and may impede interpretation of the photographs. In these cases, a list of magnifications is given after the index on p.284. It should be noted that all the histological photographs are of human tissues, unless otherwise indicated. This includes the selection showing mitotic division (p.20).

Special care has been taken with topics still the focus of research, and specialist advice has been sought where necessary. In this respect the authors and publisher are most grateful to Lord Adrian, FRS, Mr. John Bleach, Mr. Phillip Coffey (Jersey Wildlife Preservation Trust), Dr. J.A. Hardy, Mr. John Lewis, The Office of Population Censuses and Surveys, the Royal Society for the Prevention of Accidents, Miss Barbara Southworth (St. James' Hospital), the U.S. Department of Agriculture, and Dr. Paul Wheater.

Published by the Press Syndicate of the University of Cambridge
The Pitt Building, Trumpington Street, Cambridge CB2 1RP
32 East 57th Street, New York, NY 10022, USA
10 Stamford Road, Oakleigh, Melbourne 3166, Australia

First published 1982
Reprinted 1986

Printed in Great Britain at the University Press, Cambridge

British Library Cataloguing in publication data
Rowlinson, Pat
Human biology.
1. Human biology
I. Title   II. Jenkins, Morton
599.9   QP34.5
ISBN 0 521 28200 4

Contents

1 Man's position in the world

Ed Moses, the 400 m hurdles world record holder

1.1(a)

1.1(b)

1.1(c)

1.1(d)

1.1(e)

1.1(f) These five photographs are all of the same person

2

1 What is living?

Something which is living is able to carry out a number of activities. A non-living object cannot carry out all these. Fig 1.1 illustrates these activities of living organisms. Study each illustration carefully.

▶ **Questions**

1.1 What is the athlete on page 1 doing?
1.2 Using one word only, identify the life process illustrated by each of the other photographs and diagrams in Fig 1.1.
1.3 For each activity try to give an example of a non-living object which is able to carry it out.

These activities are called the characteristics of living things. Though non-living things may be able to carry out one or more of them, no non-living object can perform all of these characteristics. Each characteristic is discussed in detail in a later unit.

▷ **Homework**

Look at the relevant units in this book and write a brief description of each of the seven characteristics of living things.

2 Man in relation to other organisms

Living organisms are classified into two main groups called kingdoms: the **plant kingdom** and the **animal kingdom**. A basic difference between the two is the method of feeding. Most plants can produce their own food from simple materials such as water and carbon dioxide. Sunlight is necessary for this process, which is known as photosynthesis (see Unit 4). Animals cannot make their own food. They must obtain it from plants or other animals.

▶ **Questions**

1.4 Suggest two more differences between plants and animals apart from their method of feeding.
1.5 Why is man classified as an animal?

Table 1.1 lists a variety of animals. Some of these animals lack a backbone and are called invertebrates. Those which possess a backbone are called vertebrates.

Table 1.1 Some common animals

Animal	Vertebrate or invertebrate	Size measured by mass in kg
Amoeba	Invertebrate	0.000 000 1
Centipede	Invertebrate	0.002
Crab	Invertebrate	1
Deer	Vertebrate	100
Dog	Vertebrate	20
Earthworm	Invertebrate	0.02
Fish	Vertebrate	3
Frog	Vertebrate	0.5
Honey bee	Invertebrate	0.002
Hydra	Invertebrate	0.000 01
Man	Vertebrate	80
Millipede	Invertebrate	0.002
Parrot	Vertebrate	0.5
Roundworm	Invertebrate	0.000 5
Snail	Invertebrate	0.05
Snake	Vertebrate	2
Spider	Invertebrate	0.000 5

▶ **Questions**

1.6 Using the information in Table 1.1, make two lists, one of animals without a backbone and the other of animals with a backbone. Add any more examples you can think of to the lists.
1.7 What connection can you see between size and having or not having a backbone?

Vertebrates are divided into five classes: fishes, amphibians, reptiles, birds and mammals. An example of each class is shown in Fig 1.2.

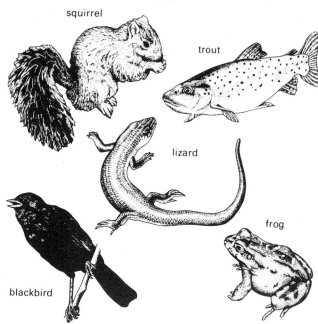

1.2 Vertebrates

▶ **Questions**

1.8 Which of the animals in Fig 1.2 most closely resembles man?

1.9 Which features of the animal of your choice are also found in man? Which of these features are not found in the other classes of vertebrates?

The young of mammals are born alive, and not as eggs, after a period of development inside the female in a muscular sac called the womb or uterus. Parental care of the young is well developed in all mammals and includes providing a home or nest, suckling of the very young by the mother, and training for adult life. Another feature of most mammals is that they have teeth which vary in form and function, and they often have two sets of teeth. The first set, or milk teeth, is not as sharp as the second set of permanent teeth. This is so that the milk teeth do not damage the mother's mammary glands during suckling. Mammals also maintain a constant body temperature – they are warm-blooded (see Unit 11). Birds are also able to maintain a constant body temperature.

There are many different types of mammal. Some of them are shown in Fig 1.3.

▶ **Questions**

1.10 Which of the mammals shown in Fig 1.3 most closely resembles man?

1.11 Give two reasons for your choice.

Monkeys, apes and man belong to a group called primates. Also included in this group are animals such as lemurs, lorises and tarsiers.

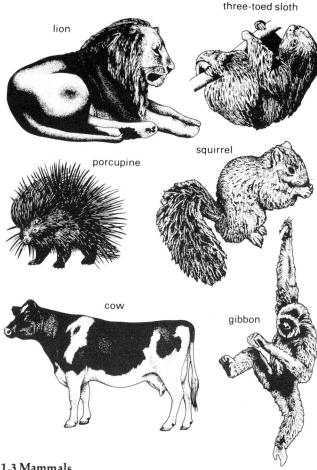

1.3 Mammals

▶ **Questions**

1.12 Select the primate in Fig 1.4 which you consider to be most like man.

1.13 In what ways are the other primates less like man?

▷ **Homework**

Construct a diagram to show the relationship between man and the rest of the animal kingdom. Your teacher will suggest how this should be laid out.

3 The uniqueness of man

Though man shares many features with other mammals, and particularly with other primates, in many ways he is different from all other animals. He is unique. Figs 1.5 – 1.7 illustrate some of the characteristics which make man different from the rest of the animal kingdom.

▶ **Questions**

1.14 Which skeleton in Fig 1.5 shows the larger cranium in comparison to the lower jaw?

1.15 What is the advantage of a larger cranium?

1.16 What is the difference in shape of the pelvises of the two skeletons? How will this difference affect their functions?

1.4 Primates **(a) Ring-tailed lemurs**

(b) Golden Lion tamarins

(c) Tarsiers

(d) A colobus monkey

(e) A chimpanzee

1.5 The skeletons of a chimpanzee and a man

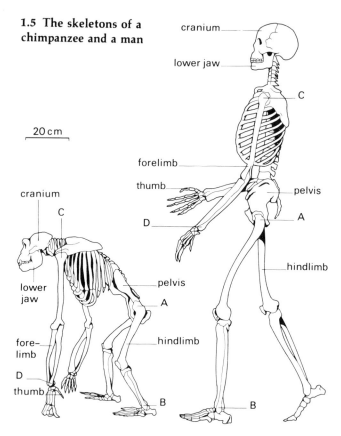

1.17 Using Fig 1.5, measure the lengths of each animal's hindlimb by measuring the distance between A and B. Using the scale indicated, estimate the lengths of a full size hindlimb of a chimpanzee and a man.
1.18 Repeat this for each forelimb, by measuring between C and D, and calculate the forelimb/hindlimb ratio for each animal.
1.19 How are these different ratios related to the ways of life of man and chimpanzees?

The foot bones and hand bones of chimpanzees and man also have differences. For example, the foot bones of a chimpanzee are more splayed out, and the big toe is separated which helps the chimpanzee to grip branches with its feet. Man's compact foot bones give better leverage for walking.

In a man's hand the thumb is opposable, that is, it can easily touch the tips of all the other fingers of the same hand. This enables man to grip objects carefully and delicately in a precision grip. Chimpanzees do not have such a large or easily opposed thumb, and therefore do not have such a good precision grip.

▶ Questions

1.20 As well as using a precision grip what other human traits are shown by the women in Fig 1.6?
1.21 In what way is the activity being performed by the man in Fig 1.7 unique amongst the animals?

This combination of features has contributed to the uniqueness of man. His totally upright posture allows complete freedom for use of the hands. His opposable thumb enables him to manipulate objects precisely.

1.6 Chemists at work. Notice the careful precision grip on the burette.

1.7 A local politician explains his point of view.

This ability, together with a relatively large brain, has accompanied the development of an inquiring mind. Language, culture and utilisation of the world's natural resources have been the result.

Research project

Investigate the extent of the use of language by animals other than man.

4 The evolution of man

The earth is estimated to be about 5000 million years old. We know that living things have existed for many

1.8 A cluster of fossilised ammonites

millions of years. Evidence for early life forms is to be found in sedimentary rocks. Records of the hard parts of animals and plants remain in the rock. These records are called fossils, and they have been shown to vary from one layer of rock to another. In general, smaller, more primitive forms are to be found in the layers of older rocks. Fig 1.8 shows some primitive animals which became fossilised in one of the oldest types of rock. Ammonites such as these are now extinct.

▶ Questions

1.22 Which animals alive today do you think are similar to an ammonite?
1.23 The animals in Fig 1.8 are invertebrates. Which parts of a vertebrate animal would you expect to find fossilised?

Recent techniques have enabled scientists to estimate the age of various rocks and the fossils they contain. These techniques depend on the gradual decay of radio-active elements.

A study of fossil remains often shows evidence for **evolution**. A series of fossils of a particular organism such as those of man illustrates changes in the form of the organism over long periods of time. Charles Darwin (1809–1882) made a detailed study of fossils and of living organisms. He was fascinated by the idea of evolution and eventually developed a theory to explain its mechanism – how a particular organism changes in time.

The graphs in Fig 1.9 show possible results of an experiment with shrews. Although Darwin did not actually carry it out, it does illustrate the type of observation Darwin made which led to his theory of natural selection. Graph (a) shows the possible increase in a population of shrews reared under laboratory conditions. They were given ample food, water and space. Graph (b) shows the possible increase in a population of shrews left in their natural environment over the same period of time.

▶ Questions

1.24 What is the population of shrews in graph (a) and graph (b) at the start of the fourteen week experiment?
1.25 What is the population of shrews in (a) and (b) at the end of the fourteen week experiment?
1.26 Suggest reasons for the difference in the results.

All living organisms have a tendency to over-reproduce. If all the offspring from one pair of starlings survived and reproduced over twenty-five years, there would be no perching room left in the world for any other species of bird. How, then, are numbers kept to a reasonable level and other species

1.9 (a) Laboratory shrew population

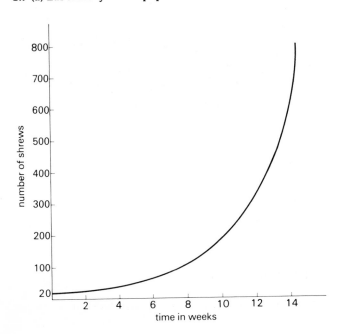

1.9 (b) Wild shrew population

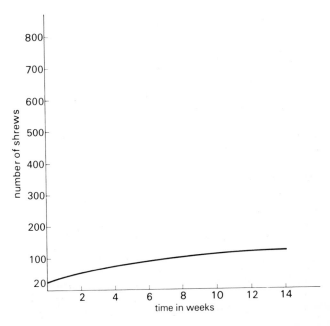

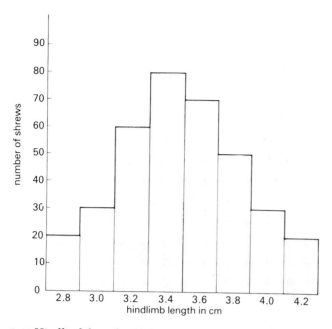

1.10 Hindlimb length of laboratory shrews

able to exist in the world? Examination of the shrews in the laboratory experiment would have shown a variation in the length of their hindlimbs. See Fig 1.10.

▶ **Questions**

1.27 What is the difference in centimetres between the longest and the shortest hindlimbs in the shrew population?
1.28 What difference could the possession of longer hindlimbs make to a shrew living in its natural environment?
1.29 What percentage of the total population has hindlimbs 4·0 cm long or longer?
1.30 Suggest another variation which could give a shrew an advantage over other shrews in its natural environment.

All the individuals in a population vary, even those in the same litter, and some variations do give an individual an advantage over the rest of the population. Such individuals are more likely to survive to reproduce. This means that their particular variation is more likely to be passed on to their offspring. For example, in a population of early man, an individual with particularly good eyesight could have been better able to find food. In such circumstances, he would have a better chance of a long reproductive life. He would have been selected by nature as the fittest to survive. Charles Darwin believed that this is how evolutionary change occurs.

This theory of natural selection can be applied to the evolution of man and apes from a common ape-like ancestor. Fossil remains are sometimes fragmentary, but there is a lot of evidence to show that man has evolved from earlier ape-like forms.

One difference between apes and man is that most apes live in trees whereas man lives on the ground. Early primates were also tree-dwelling. Therefore, early in man's evolution, any variations which helped him survive the unprotected life out of the trees were

advantages. These advantages would be naturally selected.

The common ancestor of a variety of forms of man, ape-man and ape is believed to be a small primate called *Ramapithecus* which existed about fifteen million years ago. Fossil remains of this animal consist mainly of lower jaws. These are intermediate in type between the massive square jaw of an ape and the smaller curved jaw of a man. A later intermediate type, shorter than modern man, but walking on two legs, has been named *Australopithecus* or southern ape-man.

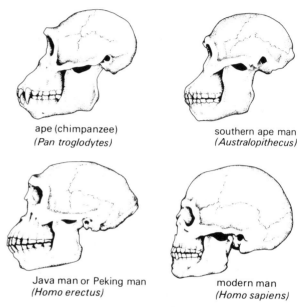

ape (chimpanzee)
(Pan troglodytes)

southern ape man
(Australopithecus)

Java man or Peking man
(Homo erectus)

modern man
(Homo sapiens)

1.11 Skulls of chimpanzee, *Australopithecus* **, Java man (an early form of man) and modern man**

▶ **Questions**

1.31 In what ways is the skull of *Australopithecus* more like modern man's than that of the chimpanzee?
1.32 List the ways in which the skull of *Homo erectus* is closer to modern man than that of *Australopithecus*.
1.33 Summarise the trends in the evolution of the skull of man.
1.34 Place the figures in Fig 1.12 in sequence, from the earliest to the most recent.

As man evolved, his precision grip was perfected and he was able to make and use more and more sophisticated tools. Many of the fossil remains of man have primitive tools associated with them. *Australopithecus* used pebbles for skinning animals. Actual manufacture of flaked tools is often taken as the hallmark of a 'true' man as opposed to an ape-man. Flaked tools were shaped by early man by chipping off parts of a flint to make a working edge.

▶ **Questions**

1.35 What do you think the man in the foreground of Fig 1.13 is doing?
1.36 What other skills does Fig 1.13 show that Peking man discovered apart from making tools?

1.12 Five stages in the possible evolution of man. The drawings are not in chronological order.

Homo neanderthalensis (neanderthal man)

Homo habilis (handy man)

Australopithecus (ape man)

Homo sapiens (modern man)

Homo erectus (Peking man or Java man)

From these early cultural beginnings a wealth of creativity has come from man – art, technology, music, writing and cultivation of the land and sea.

▶ **Questions**

1.37 What do the paintings in Fig 1.14 illustrate?

1.38 Suggest a reason for the subjects of the paintings.

Research project

Try to find references to the earliest paintings, pottery, sculpture, music, writing and agriculture, and construct a table giving the possible date of each and the part of the world in which they were found.

1.14 Very early cave painting at Altamira in Spain, probably done by Cro-Magnon man.

1.13 This drawing of Peking man, probably a contemporary of Java man, is based on fossil evidence.

Answers and discussion

1 What is living?

1.1 The athlete is running and jumping. He is moving.

1.2 (a) The baby is feeding. Feeding of living organisms is called nutrition. (b) The swimmer is breathing under water. Breathing is respiration. (c) excretion; (d) sensitivity; (e) reproduction; (f) growth.

1.3 (a) Feeding and (d) respiration are shown by boilers, cars, and aeroplanes which consume fuel to produce energy. (b) Locomotion is shown by cars, aeroplanes and trains. (c) The film in a camera is sensitive to light. (e) Waste products are produced and excreted during the manufacture of many chemicals, and by cars and trucks. (f) Growth can be shown by a crystal in a saturated solution. (g) A photocopying machine can reproduce duplicates of an original. This is a type of reproduction.

2 Man in relation to other organisms

1.4 (a) Plants and animals have generally different shapes. For example, plants have a branching form, and animals usually have a more compact form. (b) Plants generally cannot move from place to place as animals can.

1.5 Man cannot make his own food, he has a compact form, and he can move from place to place.

1.6 The following animals have a backbone: deer, dog, fish, frog, man, parrot, snake. The following animals do not have a backbone: *Amoeba*, centipede, crab, earthworm, honey bee, *Hydra*, millipede, roundworm, snail, spider.

1.7 Animals which have a backbone are able to grow to a larger size. None of the invertebrates listed is larger than 1 kg (the crab), and the *Amoeba* is microscopic.

1.8 The squirrel most closely resembles man.

1.9 Both squirrel and man have hairy skins, external ears and give birth to live young. The other vertebrates do not have hairy skins and they lay eggs.

1.10 The gibbon most closely resembles man.

1.11 The gibbon has an upright posture, that is, it can walk on two legs. Its eyes are directed forwards as in man, so stereoscopic vision is possible – see Unit 10. Both man and gibbon can grip objects with their hands.

1.12 The chimpanzee is most like man.

1.13 None of the other primates walks on two legs, and they all have long tails.

3 The uniqueness of man

1.14 The skull of man has a larger cranium.

1.15 It is able to contain a larger brain.

1.16 The pelvis of man is cradle-shaped to support the abdominal organs when he is walking upright. The pelvis of the chimpanzee is heavier, larger and more tilted. It will not support the abdominal organs.

1.17 On the page the hindlimb length is 28 mm on the chimpanzee and 52 mm on the man. These measurements represent real lengths of about 48 cm for the chimpanzee and 90 cm for the man.

1.18 The forelimb length CD is 33 mm on the chimpanzee and 40 mm on the man. The forelimb/hindlimb ratio for the chimpanzee is therefore 33/28 or 1·18/1 and the forelimb/hindlimb ratio for the man is 40/52 or 0·77/1.

1.19 The chimpanzee has longer forelimbs than hindlimbs. This is related to its tree-dwelling habit and helps it to swing from branch to branch. It walks using the knuckles of its forelimbs, which is not true bipedal walking. Man has longer hindlimbs than forelimbs. This is related to his upright walking habit.

1.20 These women are using purpose-built tools. Chimpanzees and one or two other animals sometimes use twigs or stones as tools to help them get food, but they cannot actually make tools and they do not have such a good precision grip. Fig 1.6 also shows that humans have inquiring minds. They are constantly, experimenting. No other animal has this ability so well developed.

1.21 This man is talking. No other animals have such a command of language as man. Human vocal cords are particularly well-developed and the large human brain makes complex communication by voice possible.

4 The evolution of man

1.22 Ammonites were simple forms of molluscs. Snails are their modern relatives.

1.23 The bones of a vertebrate are the most likely parts of the body to become fossilised.

1.24 (a) 20; (b) 20.

1.25 (a) 800; (b) 120.

1.26 The large population in the laboratory (graph (a)) has resulted from the provision of adequate food, water and space. In their natural habitat (graph (b)) the shrews probably had insufficient of these, so some of the young did not survive. The potential for reproduction of the shrew is enormous, but it is only apparent under laboratory conditions when the animals are protected and do not have to compete with each other for vital resources.

1.27 1.4 cm.

1.28 A shrew with longer hindlimbs than other shrews may be able to escape from a predator more swiftly.

1.29 14%.

1.30 There are many possibilities. A shrew with a coat of a colour which blended with its habitat better than that of the rest of the population might escape the notice of predators. More acute hearing might also be an advantage.

1.31 The *Australopithecus* skull has a smaller jaw in relation to its cranium than the chimpanzee. Its teeth are more like those of man – there are no large canines.

1.32 *Homo erectus* has a larger cranium and a smaller jaw than *Australopithecus*.

1.33 The evolutionary trends in the skull of man are towards a larger cranium and a smaller lower jaw with relatively small teeth.

1.34 1 *Australopithecus*; 2 *Homo habilis*; 3 *Homo erectus*; 4 *Homo neanderthalensis*; 5 *Homo sapiens*.

1.35 The picture shows Peking man using a pebble to flake a stone tool.

1.36 Peking man has discovered how to make fire, and how to use it. He will probably cook the deer.

1.37 The paintings show animals which Cro-Magnon man would hunt.

1.38 By painting the animals, Cro-Magnon man hoped to ensure a successful hunt.

2 Structural organisation of man

2.1 Dissection of a rat

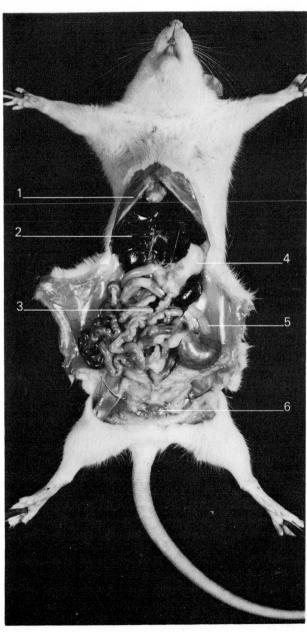

1 Systems and organs

Man is a highly complex organism. His anatomical structure is basically similar to that of other mammals. In common with rats, cows, cats and bats, he has a number of specialised **systems** which carry out particular activities: a digestive system for the digestion of food, a skeletal system for support and movement, a nervous system and a hormonal system for the co-ordination of body responses, a respiratory system for obtaining the oxygen required for respiration, a blood system for the transport of substances around the body, a urinary system for excreting urine and a reproductive system for producing sperms or ova (unfertilised eggs). These systems are made up of functional units called **organs** which may best be seen in the dissection of a small mammal such as a rat. You may have seen such a dissection demonstrated in class.

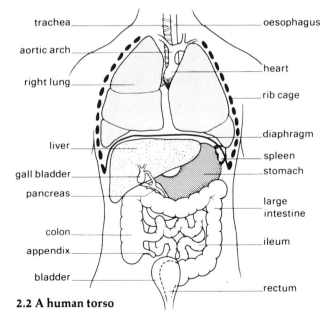

2.2 A human torso

▶ **Questions**

2.1 Using Fig 2.2 as a guide, identify the numbered organs in the dissected rat in Fig 2.1.

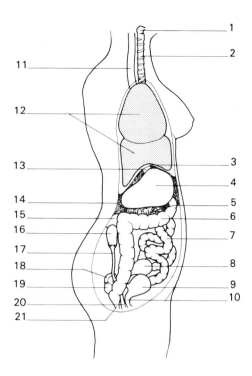

2.3 Lateral view of a human torso

2.2 Using Fig 2.2 and your own ideas and knowledge of your body, identify the numbered organs in Fig 2.3.

▷ **Homework**

Find out the functions of as many organs as you can which are illustrated in Figs 2.2 and 2.3.

2 Components of a system

▶ **Question**

2.3 List the organs shown in Figs 2.2 and 2.3 which make up the digestive system.

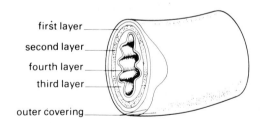

first layer
second layer
fourth layer
third layer
outer covering

2.4 Magnified view of the oesophagus showing the structure of its wall

2.5 Involuntary muscle cells

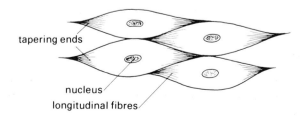

tapering ends
nucleus
longitudinal fibres

The oesophagus is composed of four layers. These layers are distinct because they contain different tissues. A **tissue** is a group of basic living units, usually similar in form, which we call cells, and they work together to perform a particular function. Fig 2.5 illustrates the structure of the two outer layers of the oesophagus shown in Fig 2.4 as they appear under a microscope. Though visible to the naked eye, it is not possible to see the details of this tissue unless it is very highly magnified. The cells which comprise the tissue taper and interlock with each other to produce a sheet. The cells contain minute fibres which can contract (shorten). The outer layer of tissue seen in Fig 2.4 has the cells and their fibres running the length of the oesophagus. The inner of these two layers of tissue has the cells and their fibres running around the circumference of the oesophagus.

▶ **Question**

2.4 Can you suggest a possible function of these two layers of tissue?

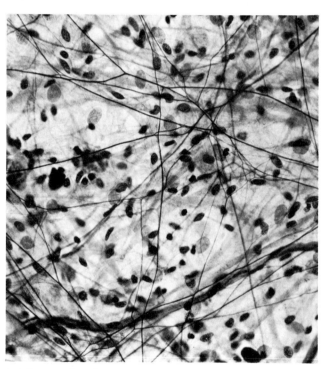

2.6 Connective tissue

Fig 2.6 illustrates the microscopic structure of the third layer of the oesophagus. The cells contained in this tissue produce a jelly-like background substance called a **matrix** in which they are suspended, and two kinds of fibres. These fibres are either formed from elastin, a protein which gives them an elastic property, or of collagen, a tough, fibrous non-elastic substance. This type of tissue, which is found in many other parts of the body, is called **connective tissue**.

▶ **Question**

2.5 Suggest the function of connective tissue in the body.

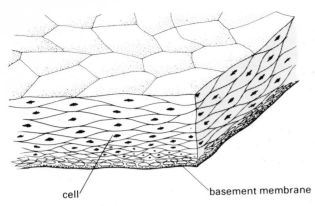

2.7 Stratified epithelium

Fig 2.7 illustrates the structure of the fourth and innermost layer of the oesophagus. The cells which comprise this tissue are closely packed, with very little matrix between them. The matrix in this tissue is firm and cement-like. Some of the cells, called goblet cells, produce a lubricating substance called mucus. This tissue is known as **epithelium**. In the oesophagus the cells, which arise from part of the matrix called the basement membrane, are flat and are known as stratified epithelium. In other parts of the body such as the liver, the cells are taller, when they are known as cubical epithelium. Sometimes they are noticeably flattened and are called pavement epithelium.

Epithelial tissues form the coverings and linings of the body. They are well adapted to this role since the cells which form them are closely packed. The columnar epithelium of the oesophagus produces mucus which lubricates the food and eases the passage of the food down the alimentary canal. In the stomach, specialised cells in the epithelium produce gastric juice, and in the respiratory system, the columnar epithelium has a border of hairs called cilia which waft particles out of the system. In the fallopian tube leading from the ovary, the ciliated epithelium helps to waft the egg cell towards the uterus (womb).

Connective tissue contains a high proportion of matrix to cells. In areolar connective tissue, the matrix is flexible and ideal for packing, in bone the matrix is hard and ideal for support and in the blood the matrix is the liquid plasma which is ideal for transporting substances.

Epithelium on the other hand, has a high proportion of cells to matrix, which is necessary to form complete coverings and linings.

▶ Question

2.6 Fig 2.8 illustrates the components of the digestive system. Label all the cells, tissues and organs numbered.

▷ Homework

Consider the structure of every part of your body and write a list of examples of epithelial tissue and a list of examples of connective tissue.

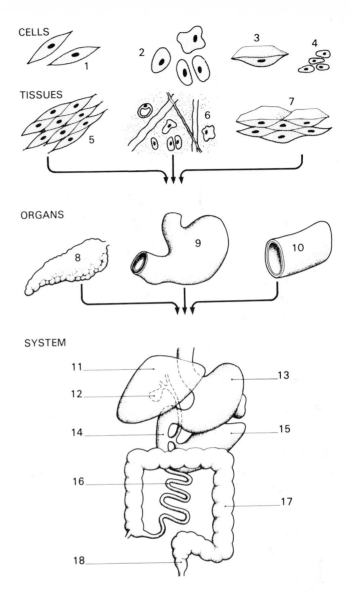

2.8 Components of the digestive system

3 Cells

The basic unit of living matter is called the cell. Certain organisms consist only of a single cell, but the vast majority of organisms are composed of many millions of cells. The tissues described in section 2 are all composed of cells and cell products. In general cells are very small and can only be seen with the aid of a microscope.

Activity 2.1   Examining cheek cells

1   Run a sterilised cotton wool bud along the inside of your cheek.
2   Draw the cotton wool bud across the centre of a clean microscope slide. The smear left on the slide will contain cheek cells.
3   Carefully add a drop of lactophenol blue to one side of the smear. This will make the cells easier to see.

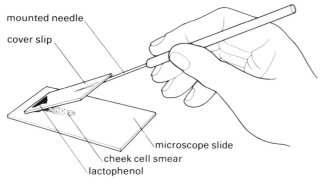

2.9

4 Gently lower a coverslip over the smear and the drop of dye as shown in Fig 2.9.
5 View the smear under the microscope first under low power, then under high power.
6 Using Fig 2.10 as a guide, identify the parts of the cells which you can see and make a drawing. Do not copy Fig 2.10.

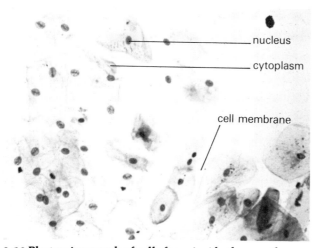

2.10 Photomicrograph of cells from inside the mouth

▶ Questions

2.7 Devise a method to estimate the approximate size of a cheek cell. What type of tissue do you think this cell has come from?
2.8 Why do you think the nucleus is darker than the cytoplasm?

School microscopes are not sufficiently powerful to show the detailed structure of a cell. Magnifications of above 400 are rarely achieved. However, an electron microscope can magnify an object hundreds of thousands of times. Scientists have learned a good deal about the minute structure of cells as a result of electron micrographs. An electron micrograph is a photograph of an object as seen under an electron microscope.

▶ Question

2.9 Study Fig 2.11 and Fig 2.12 carefully, and using the labelling of Fig 2.12, identify the numbered parts in Fig 2.11.

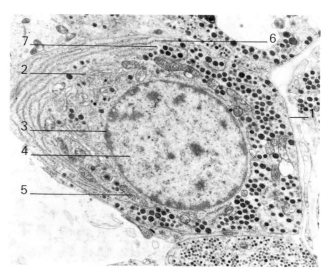

2.11 Electron micrograph of a cell from the pituitary gland

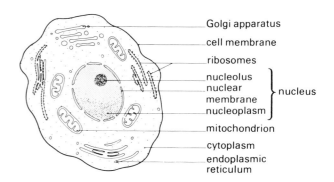

2.12 Diagram of a cheek cell as seen with an electron microscope

4 The parts of a cell

Protoplasm is the substance of living things. It is a colloid, which is a water-based jelly containing many substances in partial solution. All cells are made of protoplasm. It contains carbon, hydrogen, oxygen and nitrogen, and smaller amounts of phosphorus, sulphur and other elements are normally present. As seen in Figs 2.11 and 2.12, protoplasm also contains definite microscopic structures. Most conspicuous of these structures is the **nucleus**. The majority of cells contain a very distinct nucleus, surrounded by the clearer **cytoplasm**.

The nucleus

The nucleus contains a substance called chromatin. This is made of special proteins called nucleoproteins. These nucleoproteins are proteins associated with nucleic acids which control the activities of the cell. DNA (**deoxyribose nucleic acid**) is the active substance of the chromosomes. Chromosomes appear as twisted threads when the cell divides. See Fig 2.22.

Each type of living organism has a particular number of chromosomes in its cells. A human cell contains twenty-three pairs of chromosomes. These

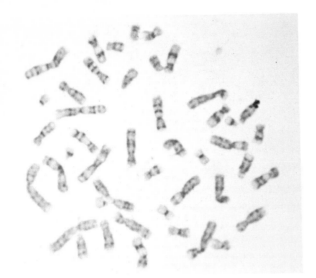

2.13 (a) Human chromosomes

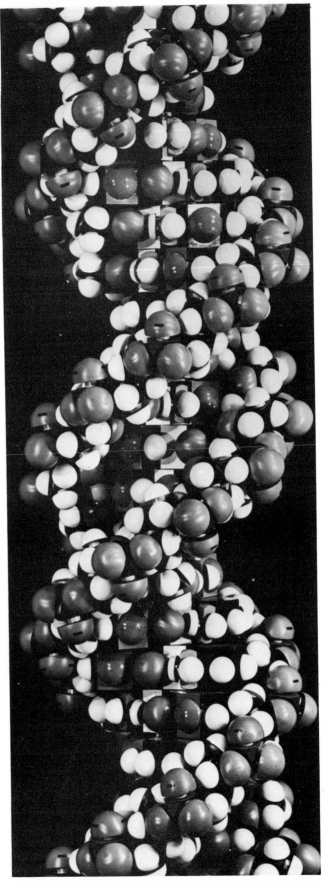

2.14 The DNA model devised by Watson and Crick

2.13(b) Human karyotype drawn from figure 2.13(a)

can be shown clearly when an electron micrograph of dividing cells such as that shown in Fig 2.13 (a) is cut up and the chromosomes are arranged regularly as shown in Fig 2.13 (b). This is called a karyotype.

▶ Question

2.10   What do you notice about the chromosome pairs illustrated in this karyotype?

DNA is a highly complex molecule, and its structure took many years to work out. Finally, in 1953, James Watson and Francis Crick were able to construct a model of its probable structure which was based on extensive research.

DNA carries the instructions for the functioning of the cell. A second nucleoprotein called RNA (**ribose nucleic acid**) is stored in the darkly staining nucleolus of a non-dividing cell. RNA is a messenger substance which relays the instructions from the DNA to the cytoplasm.

Endoplasmic reticulum

A thin membrane, the nuclear membrane, separates the nucleus from the surrounding cytoplasm. It can be seen from Figs 2.11 and 2.12 that there are minute pores in the membrane which allow the passage of substances in and out of the nucleus. The cytoplasm is not uniformly dense, but contains watery channels which form a network called the endoplasmic reticulum. Minute specks or granules can be seen along the edges of this reticulum. These are the ribosomes, and they help in making new proteins.

Golgi apparatus

The Golgi apparatus consists of globules. It is not visible in all cells, but is very easy to see in cells which secrete actively such as liver cells, cells of digestive glands and goblet cells in columnar epithelium.

▶ **Question**

2.11 Suggest the function of the Golgi apparatus.

Mitochondrion

Scattered throughout the cytoplasm are many cigar-shaped or spherical bodies called mitochondria (singular: mitochondrion). These structures contain enzymes. One function of enzymes is to speed up processes in the cell. Mitochondria are much more numerous in some cells than in others. They are numerous in very active cells such as kidney cells which are actively absorbing substances and glandular cells which are constantly producing substances. They are particularly numerous in nerve and muscle cells.

▶ **Question**

2.12 Suggest what process is speeded up by the enzymes present in the mitochondria.

Enzymes

All the activities of the cell are aided by protein substances produced by the cytoplasm in response to instructions by DNA. These helpers are the **enzymes** mentioned above. There are many thousands of them in the body. They are sometimes called biological catalysts. A catalyst is a substance which assists a reaction without being changed itself. In most reactions these enzymes help by speeding up the process. Every cell contains enzymes which speed up respiration. Some cells in our bodies contain enzymes not found in any other cells.

▶ **Question**

2.13 Suggest a reason why certain cells contain enzymes not found in other cells.

Activity 2.2 Investigating the action of catalase

Every cell contains an enzyme called catalase. Carry out the following simple investigation into the action of catalase.

1 Place a drop of hydrogen peroxide on a clean microscope slide (take care!).

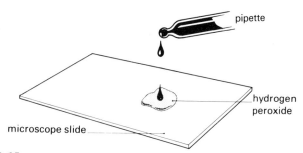

2.15

2 Obtain some blood from a freshly killed mammal.
3 Allow a drop of blood to fall on one side of the hydrogen peroxide drop and partially cover it.

▶ **Question**

2.14 What do you observe?

Cell membrane

The cytoplasm is bounded by a distinct layer called the cell or plasma membrane. The cell membrane acts as a barrier to keep valuable substances inside the cell and to keep unwanted substances out. It also permits the entry of vital substances such as water and food and the exit of toxic wastes. How is it able to do this? The following investigations will give a clue.

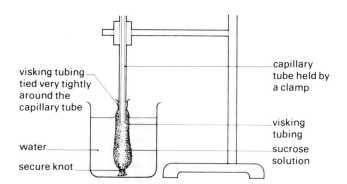

2.16

Activity 2.3 Investigating water uptake in a model cell

1 Take a 10 cm length of visking tubing to make the model cell. Wet it under a tap to make the material easier to use.
2 Tie a knot in one end of the tubing as shown in Fig 2.16.
3 Add enough 10% sucrose solution to half fill the visking tubing.
4 Take a length of capillary tubing, a clamp stand and a beaker and set up the apparatus as shown in Fig 2.16. Finally add water to the beaker so that the visking tubing is immersed in water.
5 Mark the level of the sucrose solution in the capillary tube and leave the apparatus to stand. Mark the level of water in the beaker.
6 Mark the level of the sucrose solution at ten minute intervals.

16

2.15 What height did the sucrose solution reach after forty minutes?
2.16 What has caused the level of the liquid in the tube to change? How can you support your idea?

The process which takes place in this experiment is called **osmosis**. It depends on the nature of the visking tubing as explained below. Where two solutions of differing concentrations are brought together, there is always a tendency for the concentrations to equalise.

Activity 2.4 Seeing what happens when ink is added to water

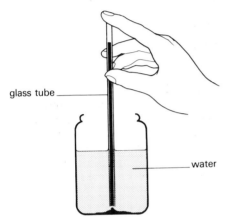

glass tube

water

2.17

1 Take a beaker of water and add a few drops of water-soluble dark blue ink on the bottom of the beaker as shown in Fig 2.17.
2 Leave for a few minutes, then observe the resultant liquid.

▶ **Question**

2.17 What do you observe? What do you think has happened?

The process demonstrated in Activity 2.4 is called **diffusion**. Provided there is no barrier to prevent it, particles (molecules) of a substance in solution will tend to disperse evenly throughout it. Movement of molecules will be equal in all directions when the concentration is constant throughout the solution. This is called **equilibrium**. Gas molecules behave in the same way.

2.18 Diagram to illustrate diffusion

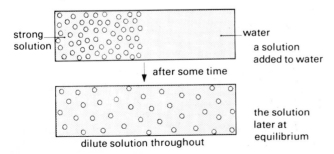

strong solution

water
a solution added to water

after some time

the solution later at equilibrium

dilute solution throughout

Where there is a barrier to movement of some molecules, then osmosis may occur. In Fig 2.19 water molecules pass from B to A tending to equalise concentrations. This is osmosis.

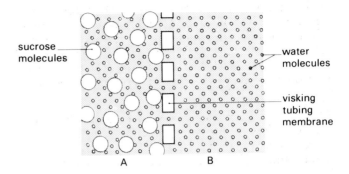

sucrose molecules

water molecules

visking tubing membrane

A   B

2.19 Diagram to illustrate osmosis

▶ **Question**

2.18 Why do the sucrose molecules not pass from A to B?

The visking tubing is called a **selectively permeable membrane**, that is a membrane which only allows the passage of some smaller molecules. Is the cell membrane similar in this respect to visking tubing? To find out, carry out Activity 2.5. You need to know that red blood cells contain a red pigment called haemoglobin in their cytoplasm.

Activity 2.5 Investigating osmosis in red blood cells

1 Take one test tube, labelled A, containing 2 cm³ of distilled water and a second test tube, B, containing 2 cm³ of 0.85% sodium chloride solution. (This is the concentration found in the blood plasma in which the red blood cells are bathed).
2 Use some blood from the same source as Activity 2.2.
3 Add a few drops of blood to both test tubes and gently shake the tubes to disperse the blood.
4 Leave for two or three minutes.
5 With a glass rod, remove a drop of liquid from both tubes and place the drop from tube A on a clean microscope slide labelled A and a drop from B on a similar slide labelled B.
6 Lower a coverslip carefully onto both drops and observe the appearance of the red blood cells in each, first under low power, then under the high power of the microscope.
7 Allow the test tubes to stand for a further thirty minutes, then compare the appearance of the liquids in the two tubes.

▶ **Questions**

2.19 Describe the appearance of the cells in drops A and B under the microscope.
2.20 How did the liquids compare at the end of the experiment? Suggest an explanation for your observations in this experiment.
2.21 What would happen if you put the red blood cells into a solution more concentrated than their cell content?

To summarise: diffusion is the movement of molecules of a liquid or gas from a high concentration to a lower concentration, leading to an equal concentration of molecules throughout. This state is called equilibrium. Osmosis is the movement of molecules of water from a low concentration of dissolved substances to a higher concentration of dissolved substances through a selectively permeable membrane, leading to equilibrium. The importance of both of these processes in the uptake and loss of substances by cells will be seen in later units.

▶ **Question**

2.22 Can you define osmosis in terms of the difference in concentration of water molecules in two solutions?

Diffusion of substances in and out of cells is possible where molecules are very small. In such cases the selectively permeable cell membrane will not present a barrier as the small molecules will be able to pass through the small pores. Thus glucose molecules may diffuse from a high concentration in the blood to a lower concentration in surrounding respiring cells because the molecules are small enough. Similarly, molecules of oxygen are able to diffuse from a high concentration in the air sacs to a lower concentration in the red blood cells (see Unit 6).

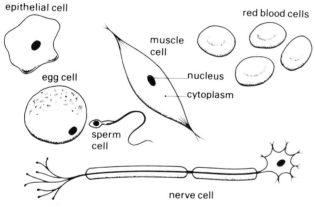

2.20 Some human cells

The variety of cells
Human cells are very diverse in size and form as illustrated in Fig 2.20. Carefully study the six types of cell shown. The muscle cell comes from a sheet of muscle in the oesophagus wall, the epithelial cell from the cheek lining. The nerve cell relays messages (impulses) from the spinal cord to the muscles. The egg cell will, after fertilisation, grow to produce the embryo. The sperm cell, after release into the womb, will swim up towards the egg cell in the liquid lining the womb. The red blood cells absorb oxygen from the lungs and transport it to the respiring cells in the form of oxyhaemoglobin.

▶ **Question**

2.23 In what ways are the cells illustrated well suited to their functions in the body?

Research project

Find out about the first scientists to see cells magnified as you have done. Write down who they were, when they lived, what kinds of cells they looked at and what particular problems they had with their work.

5 The division of cells

During growth, the cells of the body, with a few exceptions, are constantly dividing. Even when growth is complete, many body cells still actively divide to replace others which are worn out. This division is highly organised and always follows the same sequence. This sequence, called **mitosis**, is illustrated in Fig 2.22.

Each phase is given a name, but the important thing to remember is the sequence of events.
1 This is a non-dividing cell. The chromosomes are not visible in the nucleus. Only a tangle of threads called the chromatin network, and a dark-staining sphere called the **nucleolus**, are visible.
2 Here the chromosomes are becoming visible as mitosis begins. There are many more chromosomes in the human cell than shown here, but the number is reduced to four in these diagrams for the sake of simplicity. The chromosomes have split down their length to form two **chromatids**.
3 The chromosomes, each composed of two chromatids still joined at one point, become arranged across the 'equator' of the nucleus. A spindle is formed from the cytoplasm as the nuclear membrane disappears. This spindle is made of fibres along which the chromatids will move as if being pulled apart.
4 The chromatids become completely detached from each other and begin to move towards opposite ends of the cell along the spindle fibres.
5 The chromatids gather at their respective 'poles' of the cell and the cytoplasm begins to constrict in the region of the 'equator'. By this time the chromatids have become complete chromosomes.
6 The nuclear membrane has reappeared, the chromatin network has reformed and constriction of the cytoplasm is complete to form two daughter cells.

▶ **Question**

2.24 What has happened to the chromosome number in the daughter cells?

Activity 2.6   Making a model of mitosis
2.21

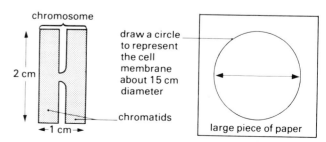

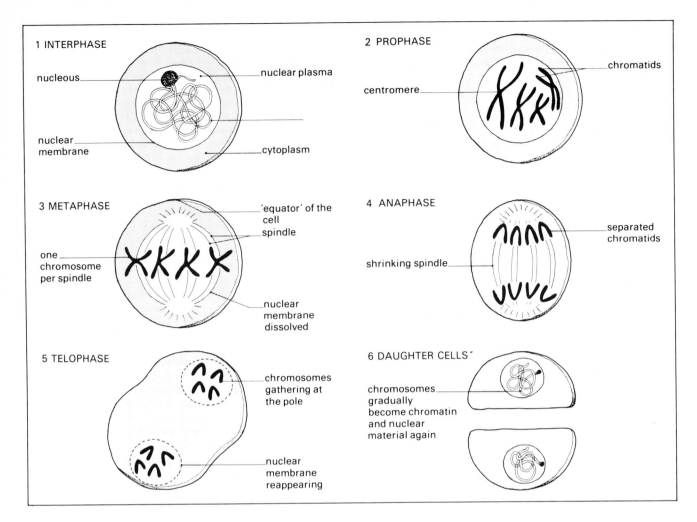

1 INTERPHASE

nucleous

nuclear plasma

nuclear membrane

cytoplasm

2 PROPHASE

centromere

chromatids

3 METAPHASE

one chromosome per spindle

'equator' of the cell

spindle

nuclear membrane dissolved

4 ANAPHASE

shrinking spindle

separated chromatids

5 TELOPHASE

chromosomes gathering at the pole

nuclear membrane reappearing

6 DAUGHTER CELLS

chromosomes gradually become chromatin and nuclear material again

2.22 Mitosis

1 Take a piece of clean paper (with a large circle drawn on it) and four pieces of different coloured card, the dimensions of which are shown in Fig 2.21. Almost bisect each piece of card as shown.

2 Place the four different coloured pieces of card in the centre of the piece of paper. Each strip represents a chromosome already split into chromatids.

3 Lay a piece of string in a circle around the chromosomes to represent the nuclear membrane.

4 Now remove the string. This represents the breakdown of the nuclear membrane. The chromosomes are now free to move into the cytoplasm. Move the strips into the cytoplasm.

5 Arrange the strips in a line along any diameter of the large circle. The chromatids are about to separate from each other.

6 Place two dots on the edge of the large circle, above and below the diameter on which the chromosomes are placed, so that a line through the dots will bisect the diameter.

7 Draw lines from each chromosome to the dot above and below the diameter.

8 Cut the connecting card between the pairs of chromatids, then replace them in the same position along the diameter.

9 Move each chromatid along its spindle fibre (line) so that one from each chromosome goes to opposite ends of the cell.

10 Cut the paper in the region of the diameter to obtain two daughter cells.

▶ **Questions**

2.25 What do the lines in step 7 represent?

2.26 How many chromosomes has each cell?

2.27 Apart from their size, are these chromosomes identical in every way with the original chromosomes of the parent cell?

2.28 Using the information you have gained in this section, suggest the correct sequence for the photographs of mitosis illustrated in Fig 2.23.

2.29 Why does the nucleus undergo such a complex process of division? What would happen if the chromosomes were split randomly into the two daughter cells?

Research project

You know that human beings have twenty-three pairs of chromosomes. Try to find out the chromosome number of six plants or animals.

2.23 The stages of mitosis in human bone marrow cells.
The pictures are out of order.

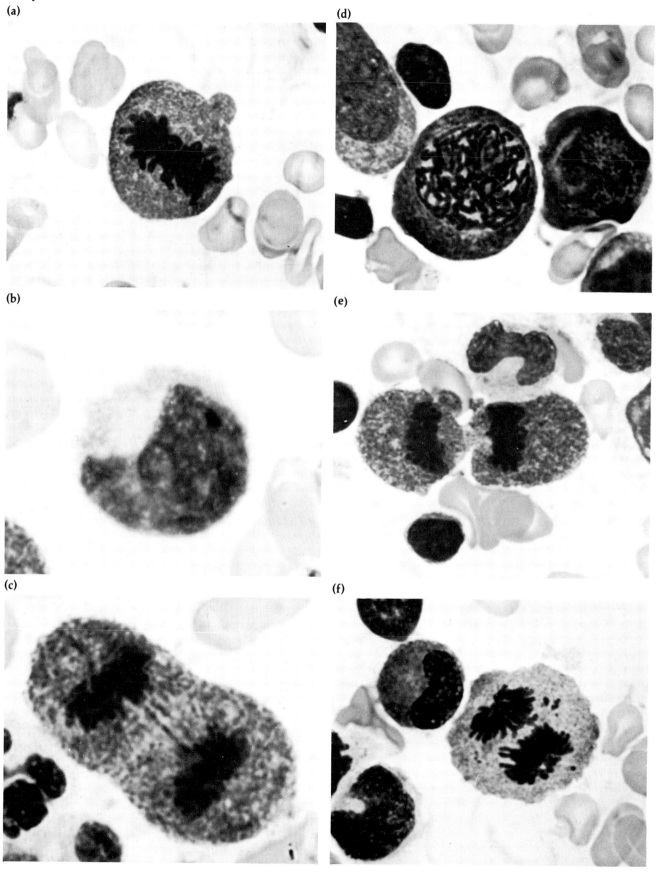

(a)

(b)

(c)

(d)

(e)

(f)

Answers and discussion

1 Systems and organs

2.1 1 rib cage; 2 liver; 3 ileum; 4 stomach; 5 large intestine; 6 bladder.

2.2 1 larynx; 2 trachea; 3 diaphragm; 4 stomach; 5 spleen; 6 colon; 7 ileum; 8 uterus (womb); 9 urinary bladder; 10 urethra; 11 oesophagus; 12 lobes of left lung; 13 oesophagus; 14 liver; 15 left adrenal gland; 16 left kidney; 17 ureter; 18 fallopian tube; 19 ovary; 20 vagina; 21 rectum.

2 Components of a system

2.3 Oesophagus, stomach, liver, gall bladder, pancreas, duodenum (not shown in Fig 2.2), ileum, colon, rectum.

2.4 These two layers of tissue are smooth (involuntary) muscle sheets (see Unit 3). The contractile fibres enable the tissue to alter the circumference of the oesophagus. The inner layer, with fibres running around the circumference, reduces the circumference when the fibres contract or shorten. The outer layer, with fibres running the length of the oesophagus, reduces this length when the fibres contract. This is important in the passage of food down the oesophagus, a movement known as peristalsis. The ball of food, called the bolus, is squeezed down the entire alimentary canal (food channel) in this way.

2.5 Connective tissue forms the packing material of the body. The inelastic fibres and gel matrix support other tissues, while the elastic fibres make the tissue flexible. The type of connective tissue illustrated in Fig 2.6 is called areolar connective tissue. Below the skin, fat cells are stored in the gel matrix and the tissue becomes known as adipose connective tissue. Other connective tissues are tendons, ligaments, cartilage, bone and blood, which will be discussed in Units 3 and 7.

2.6 1 smooth muscle cells; 2 connective tissue cells; 3 stratified cell; 4 young cell; 5 smooth muscle layer; 6 areolar connective tissue; 7 stratified epithelium; 8 pancreas; 9 stomach; 10 large intestine; 11 liver; 12 gall bladder; 13 stomach; 14 duodenum; 15 pancreas; 16 ileum; 17 colon; 18 rectum.

3 Cells

2.7 A rough estimate of the size of a cheek cell may be obtained by placing a hair beneath the coverslip, close to the smear. This will give an indication of the very small dimensions of such a cell. An accurate estimate of the size of a cheek cell can be obtained by using a measuring grid which can be placed in the eyepiece of the microscope. Such a grid is commonly marked in microns. One micron equals $\frac{1}{1000}$ of a millimetre. A very cheap grid on film, which can be fitted on the stage or into the eyepiece, is the Hillier graticule.

These cheek cells compose the pavement epithelium which lines the cheeks.

2.8 More lactophenol blue is retained by the nucleus because this part of the cell protoplasm attracts the stain more strongly than the surrounding cytoplasm.

2.9 1 cell membrane; 2 Golgi apparatus; 3 nuclear membrane; 4 nucleus; 5 mitochondria; 6 endoplasmic reticulum; 7 ribosome.

4 The parts of a cell

2.10 Twenty-two pairs of chromosomes are identical pairs, but X and Y are not identical: Y is much shorter than X. This karyotype is of a male human, and the X and Y chromosomes are the sex chromosomes which determine the sex of the individual. Females possess two identical X chromosomes.

2.11 The Golgi apparatus controls the production of useful substances which some cells pass out for use in the body. These substances are called secretions. An example is the secretion of mucus by goblet cells.

2.12 Energy is necessary for cells actively absorbing or manufacturing substances and mitochondria are present in large numbers particularly where energy production is necessary. They are concerned with respiration and actually contain the enzymes necessary for respiration (see Unit 6).

2.13 The various cells of the body have to perform a wide range of differing functions. Goblet cells have to produce mucus and they need an enzyme to speed up this process; liver cells produce bile and they need a different enzyme to speed up this process. Each enzyme will only aid one particular reaction. Enzymes are said to be specific.

2.14 A mass of bubbles are formed and a clear liquid flows along the slide. The millions of blood cells in the drop of blood contain catalase, which instantly assists in the breakdown of hydrogen peroxide to oxygen (seen as bubbles) and water (the clear liquid).

$$2H_2O_2 \xrightarrow{\text{catalase}} 2H_2O + O_2$$
$$\text{hydrogen peroxide} \qquad \text{water} \quad \text{oxygen}$$

In this way catalase assists all cells in the release of oxygen from various substances.

2.15 After forty minutes the level of the sucrose solution in the capillary tube will have risen considerably. The diameter of the capillary tube will determine the actual extent of the increased height, so it is not possible to state an exact figure here.

2.16 Water must have passed from the beaker into the sucrose solution contained in the visking tubing. It may be possible to check this by a drop in the level of the water in the beaker, though this will obviously only be a small drop in such a large volume and it may be difficult to detect.

2.17 The liquid in the beaker will appear pale blue throughout. The particles of ink will have dispersed evenly throughout the water.

2.18 The visking tubing contains small holes or pores which will allow only small molecules to pass through. The sucrose molecules are prevented from passing into the water. They would pass into the water in the absence of the visking tubing.

2.19 The liquid from test tube A contains no cells, the liquid from test tube B contains regular, biconcave discs (normal red blood cells).

2.20 The liquid from test tube A is a clear red, whereas that from test tube B is opaque red. The cells in test tube A have burst, releasing haemoglobin into the water, which appears clear red. In test tube B, the opaque red appearance is merely due to the presence of red blood cells. Water has been taken into the red blood cells in test tube A by osmosis through the selectively permeable cell membrane to such an extent that the membrane has burst. (Compare Activity 2.3 where the water which was taken into the sucrose solution was able to escape up the capillary tube. No strain was therefore put on the visking tubing.) The concentration of liquid in the red blood cells is much higher than that of distilled water, but no higher than that of the 0.85% sodium chloride solution in test tube B. Thus in B, no water was taken into the red blood cells, which retained their normal shape.

2.21 Red blood cells placed in a solution stronger than their cytoplasm would lose water to the stronger solution outside, and they would shrivel up and collapse. Cells in a collapsed state such as this are said to be plasmolysed.

2.22 In terms of water concentrations, osmosis is merely the diffusion of water from areas of high water concentration, for example, pure water, to areas of lower water concentration, such as a sugar solution.

2.23 (a) The muscle cell has a tapering shape enabling it to interlock with cells of a similar shape to form a complete sheet. It contains special fibres which enable it to shorten and consequently to bring about movement.

(b) The epithelial cell is flattened, with a crinkled edge which enables it to fit reasonably tightly with similar cells rather like a jigsaw, to form a tough lining sheet.

(c) The nerve cell has a very long process of cytoplasm for conducting a message at high speed. Certain of these nerve cells have processes up to 90 cm long. This enables uninterrupted passage of an impulse from the spinal cord as far as the foot.

(d) The egg cell contains yolk in the cytoplasm to nourish the very young embryo before it becomes implanted in the wall of the womb.

(e) The sperm cell has a long tail which enables it to swim quickly in the liquid lining the uterus. In fact a sperm can swim its own length as fast as a nuclear submarine can travel its own length!

(f) The red blood cells have no nucleus, so they are filled with the maximum amount of oxygen-carrying pigment (haemoglobin) possible. Also, the biconcave disc shape presents a very large surface area/volume ratio, enabling rapid absorption of oxygen from the surrounding plasma to occur.

5 The division of cells

2.24 There has been a duplication of chromosomes during mitosis, followed by a division into two daughter cells. Each cell, therefore, contains the same number of chromosomes as the parent cell.

2.25 The lines represent the fibres of the spindle formed by the cytoplasm.

2.26 The daughter cells have four chromosomes each.

2.27 The chromosomes in the daughter cells are identical in every way with those of the parent cell. As well as having the same number, it can be seen from this exercise that the actual chromosomes themselves are the same – one of each colour is still present. Thus mitosis maintains an identical set of chromosomes in dividing cells.

2.28 The correct sequence for Fig 2.23 is as follows: C (interphase), B (prophase), A (metaphase), F (anaphase), E (telophase), D (completed division).

2.29 The complex process of mitosis is necessary to ensure that the daughter cells acquire not only exactly the right number of chromosomes, but exactly one of each type that the parent cell had. If the chromosomes were split randomly, one of the daughter cells might get fewer chromosomes than the other, which would mean that it would be deficient and unable to carry out its proper functions.

3 The skeleton and movement

3.1 Model of a skeleton

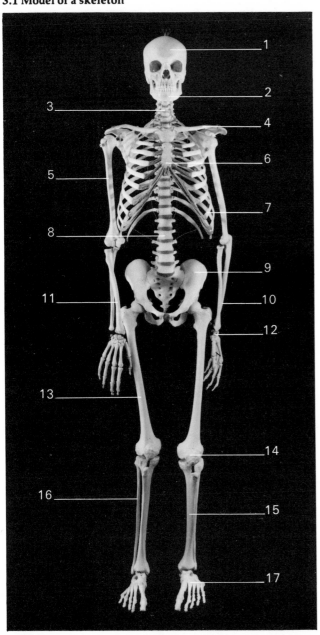

1 Structure and functions of the skeleton

In common with all other vertebrates, man possesses an internal framework or endoskeleton. This is constructed from a hard substance called bone. The skeleton of man is very complex and is composed of just over 200 individual bones. These bones may be closely joined together to form a structure such as the skull, or they may be only loosely joined as in the hand.

▶ Questions

3.1 Using Fig 3.2 as a reference, identify the structures and bones numbered on Fig 3.1.

3.2 Three types of bones occur in the skeleton: flat bones, long bones and short bones. Write down examples of each type of bone.

3.2 The human skeleton

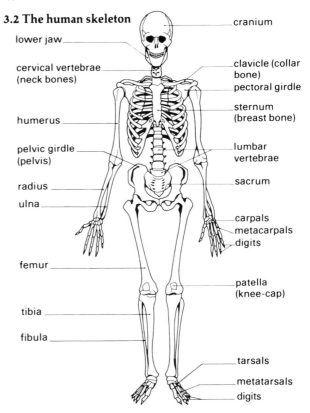

cranium
lower jaw
cervical vertebrae (neck bones)
clavicle (collar bone)
pectoral girdle
sternum (breast bone)
humerus
lumbar vertebrae
pelvic girdle (pelvis)
sacrum
radius
ulna
carpals
metacarpals
digits
femur
patella (knee-cap)
tibia
fibula
tarsals
metatarsals
digits

In general the main function of the skeleton is to support the tissues around it, but some bones have additional functions. Flat bones are protective. The skull protects the delicate brain, the sternum helps to protect the heart, and the pelvis helps to protect the abdominal organs. Also, the long bones in the limbs are concerned with movement. They act as levers when muscles move them and so help to move the limbs.

The skeleton is basically organised as an axis which supports more actively moving parts called appendages. When describing the skeleton it is convenient to refer to these components as the **axial skeleton** and the **appendicular skeleton**.

Research project

See if you can find out how a broken bone, for example a broken tibia, is treated medically. Explain the treatment as far as you can.

2 The axial skeleton

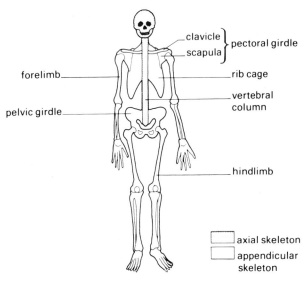

3.3 Axial and appendicular skeletons

▶ **Question**

3.3   Refer to Fig 3.3 and list the parts of the axial skeleton.

The skull consists of twenty-three bones. Eight of these are tightly fused to form the cranium, fourteen comprise the facial skeleton and one complex bone, the lower jaw or mandible, forms movable joints with the cranium.

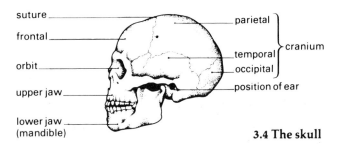

3.4 The skull

▶ **Question**

3.4   Using Fig 3.4 as a guide, study the form of the bones of the skull and suggest the functions of the cranium, the facial skeleton and the mandible.

The vertebral column is the main support of the body. The vertebrae are held together by flexible cartilage discs, thus allowing movement as well as support.

The vertebral column curves backwards (dorsally) in the thoracic region, so that the capacity of the lungs is increased by creating more space in the thoracic cavity. The forward (ventral) curve in the lumbar region offers support to the abdominal organs which are lacking a skeleton on the ventral side.

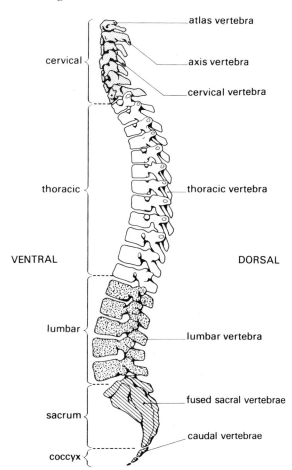

3.5 The vertebral column

▶ **Question**

3.5   There are thirty-three vertebrae altogether in the human vertebral column. How many vertebrae are found in each region shown in Fig 3.5 ?

Figs 3.6 and 3.7 illustrate the various types of vertebrae found in the different regions of the vertebral column. The structural differences are related to the different functions required. It will be very helpful if you can examine some actual vertebrae at this point. All vertebrae consist of a solid core, rather like a cotton reel, called the centrum. Arising

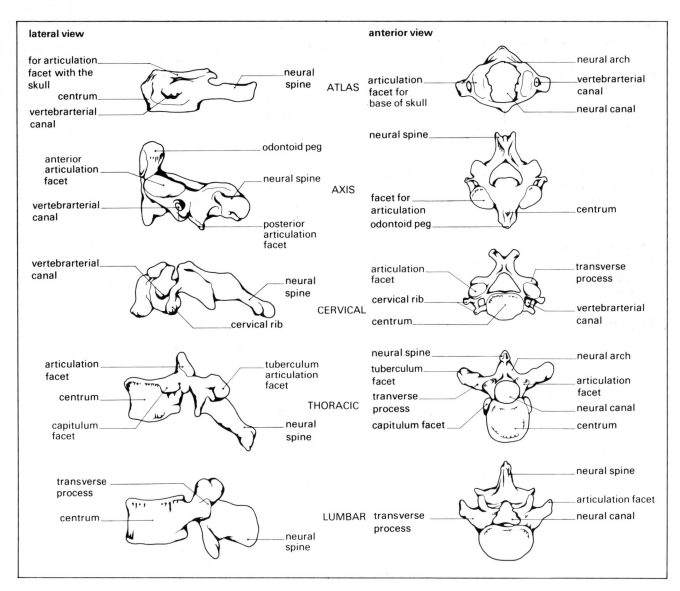

lateral view

for articulation facet with the skull
centrum
vertebrarterial canal
neural spine
ATLAS

anterior articulation facet
vertebrarterial canal
odontoid peg
neural spine
posterior articulation facet
AXIS

vertebrarterial canal
neural spine
cervical rib
CERVICAL

articulation facet
centrum
capitulum facet
tuberculum articulation facet
neural spine
THORACIC

transverse process
centrum
neural spine
LUMBAR

anterior view

neural arch
vertebrarterial canal
neural canal
articulation facet for base of skull

neural spine
centrum
facet for articulation odontoid peg

articulation facet
cervical rib
centrum
transverse process
vertebrarterial canal

neural spine
tuberculum facet
tranverse process
capitulum facet
neural arch
articulation facet
neural canal
centrum

neural spine
articulation facet
neural canal
transverse process

3.6 Different types of vertebra

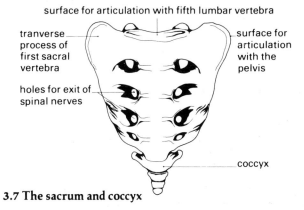

surface for articulation with fifth lumbar vertebra
tranverse process of first sacral vertebra
surface for articulation with the pelvis
holes for exit of spinal nerves
coccyx

3.7 The sacrum and coccyx

from this core is an arch of bone which encloses and protects the spinal cord. This is called the neural arch. Where the two sides of the arch meet, in the midline, there is a projection called the neural spine. This gives additional protection to the spinal cord. Arising from the sides of the vertebra are a pair of projections called the transverse processes. These form an area for attachment of muscles. The anterior and posterior facets of the vertebrae bear smooth surfaces which make contact with those of the vertebra immediately in front and immediately behind. These are called articular facets. These features may be reduced in some vertebrae. The caudal (tail) vertebrae which comprise the coccyx, only consist of a small centrum. Certain vertebrae may have additional features.

Study Figs 3.6 and 3.7 very carefully, then answer the following questions.

▶ **Question**

3.6 Why is the neural arch so large in the first neck (cervical) vertebra, the atlas vertebra ?
3.7 Can you think of a function of the odontoid peg on the second cervical vertebra, the axis ?
3.8 What are the vertebrarterial canals of the cervical vertebrae for?

3.9 Can you suggest the functions of the extra facets on the thoracic vertebrae? You may need to refer to Fig 3.2.

3.10 Why are the lumbar vertebrae so large and why do they have such stout transverse processes?

3.11 What is the advantage of having the sacral vertebrae fused together?

▷ **Homework**

Find out what happens when someone 'slips a disc' in their back.

3 The appendicular skeleton

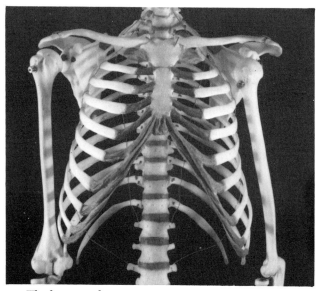

3.8 The human rib cage

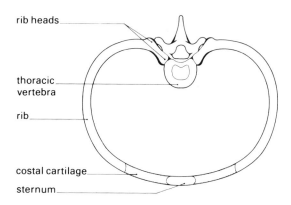

3.9 Sectional view of the rib cage showing a thoracic vertebra, a pair of ribs and part of the sternum

▶ **Questions**

3.12 List the parts of the skeleton which make up the appendicular skeleton.

3.13 Apart from protecting the heart and lungs, what is another function of the rib cage?

3.14 What are the component parts of the rib cage?

3.15 What is the purpose of the costal cartilages?

3.16 Do you think the rib heads are fixed rigidly to the thoracic vertebra? Give reasons for your answer.

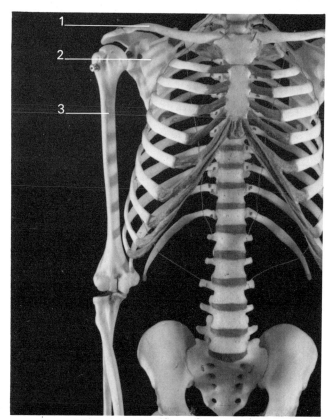

3.10 Part of the pectoral girdle and forelimb

▶ **Questions**

3.17 Using Fig 3.11 as a guide, identify the numbered parts on Fig 3.10.

3.18 Suggest reasons for the flat, triangular shape of the scapula.

3.19 Why do humans need clavicles?

3.20 Identify the numbered parts on Fig 3.12 using Fig 3.13 as a guide.

3.11 Dorsal view of the left side of the pectoral girdle and left forelimb. Note the scale.

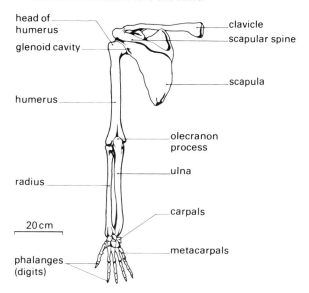

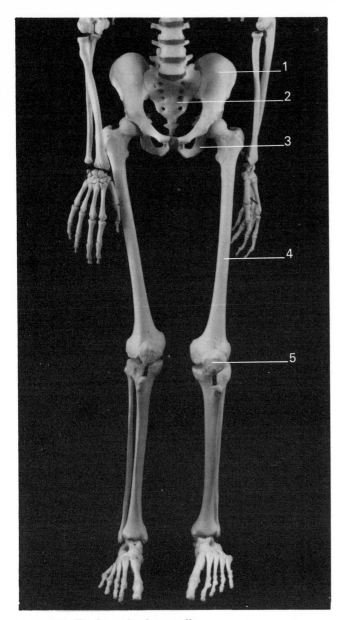

3.12 Hindlimbs and pelvic girdle

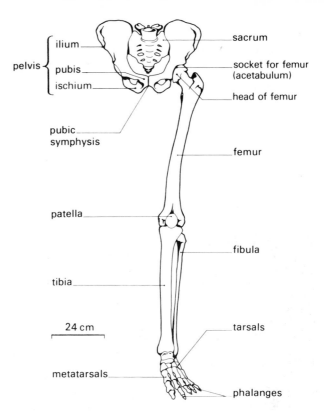

3.13 Ventral view of the pelvic girdle and left hind limb of the skeleton. Note the scale

The expanded ilia form a cradle which helps give the support needed for man's abdominal organs because of his upright posture. The pelvic girdle is a complete ring of bone, fused at front and back, and this gives it the strength to support the whole body through the vertebral column.

Using specimens of human bones, or the scaled drawings above, measure the length of the main bones in the fore and hindlimbs and complete the following table in your exercise book.

Forelimb bone	Length in cm	Hindlimb bone	Length in cm
Humerus		Femur	
Radius		Tibia	
Ulna		Fibula	

▶ **Questions**

3.21 Which is the longest limb bone?
3.22 Which limb is the longer, forelimb or hindlimb? Suggest a reason for this.
3.23 Which limb bones would you expect to be the thicker and why?

The limb bones of man are basically similar to those of a wide variety of mammals (see Unit 1). It is believed that early vertebrates possessed limbs built on the same pattern of bones. Such a limb, illustrated in Fig 3.14, is called a **pentadactyl** (five-digit) limb.

3.14 The pentadactyl limb

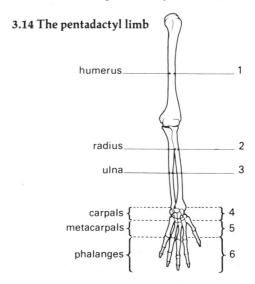

3.24 The fore and hindlimb bones both conform to the pentadactyl pattern. Label the numbered bones on the right of Fig 3.14 which represent the hindlimb bones.

The hand bones and foot bones of man are, however, different in detail. The hand bones have an opposable first digit which is much shorter than the other digits. This is important for grasping. The first digit of the foot (big toe) is large and unopposable. When walking, man pushes off with his big toe which gives greater impetus to the movement.

▷ **Homework**

The basis of all mammalian limbs is the pentadactyl limb. Write a list of examples where this basic pattern has been specially adapted.

4 The composition of the skeleton

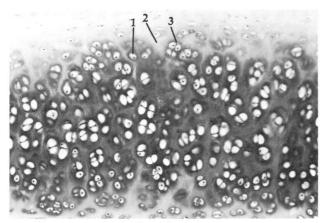

3.15 Photomicrograph of cartilage

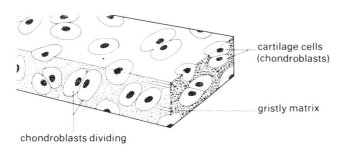

cartilage cells (chondroblasts)

gristly matrix

chondroblasts dividing

3.16 Cartilage

During the first four months of development in the womb, the skeleton of the foetus (unborn baby) is made of a hard, flexible, connective tissue called **cartilage** (gristle). At around four months, calcium salts, particularly calcium phosphate, are deposited in the cartilage and at the same time the cells in it are altered. The resulting very hard, inflexible tissue is called **bone**. The matrix of bone is packed with calcium salts and only about a quarter of the tissue is organic

material. Some cartilage persists until growth of the individual ceases. This allows for increase in length, girth and area of bones. This will be discussed more fully in Unit 12.

▶ **Questions**

3.25 Identify the numbered parts in Fig 3.15, using Fig 3.16 as a guide.
3.26 Some cartilage, called yellow elastic cartilage, has fibres of elastin running in the matrix. It is more flexible than ordinary cartilage. What structures, found on the head, are composed of this material?
3.27 Using Fig 3.18 as a guide, identify the numbered parts of Fig 3.17.
3.28 Osteoblasts are living cells which bring about the transformation of cartilage into bone. They are arranged in concentric circles around a system of canals in the hard matrix. These Haversian canals are in contact with the bone marrow. Suggest a reason for the arrangement of these cells around the canals.

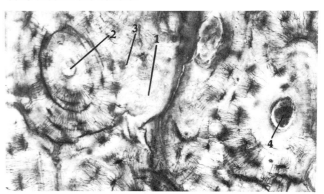

3.17 Photomicrograph of compact bone

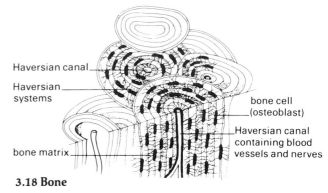

Haversian canal

Haversian systems

bone matrix

bone cell (osteoblast)

Haversian canal containing blood vessels and nerves

3.18 Bone

▷ **Homework**

Locate the gristle on a joint of meat and try to determine its position in the skeleton.

5 Joints

Every movement we make is made possible by the alteration of the position of various bones of the skeleton in relation to each other. Most bones are joined together in such a way that they can move against each other. The point at which two or more bones make contact is called a joint. Joints display a great variety of movement – from multidirectional to immovable. To illustrate this, carry out a variety of actions and classify them as freely movable, movable, partly movable and slightly movable. If a model skeleton is available, try moving the head, the shoulder, the elbow, the fingers, the wrist, the hip, the knee and the ankle and make a table of your results.

▶ **Question**

3.29 Classify the numbered joints in Fig 3.19 as freely movable, movable, partly movable etc. If it is difficult to classify some of those numbered, suggest another category.

Joints are also classified as follows: (a) ball and socket joints, (b) hinge joints, (c) pivot joints, (d) gliding joints, and (e) immovable joints. Using Fig 3.20, a model skeleton and your own body, answer questions 3.30 - 3.38.

▶ **Questions**

3.30 Which ball and socket joint allows the most universal movement?
3.31 Why do you think it is important to have free movement of this joint? Suggest a reason for the slightly restricted movement of the other ball and socket joint.
3.32 Describe the degree of movement possible in the hinge joints.

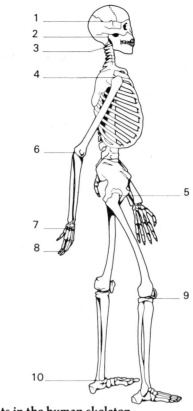

3.19 Joints in the human skeleton

3.20 Types of joints

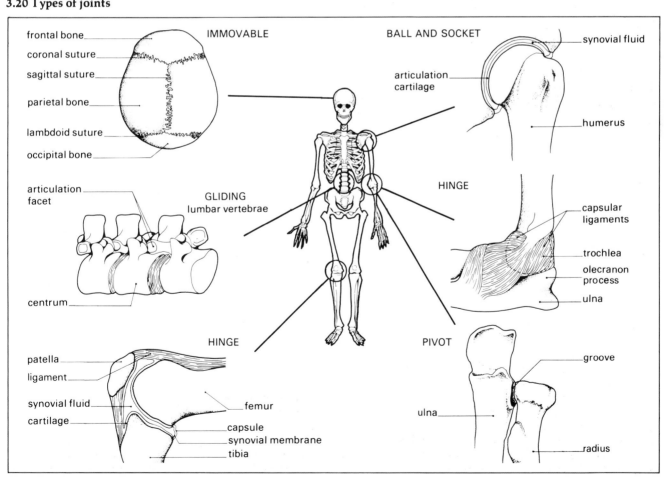

3.33 Which structures restrict movement in (a) the elbow and (b) the knee?
3.34 Which joint allows you to twist your forearm?
3.35 Name another pivot joint in the skeleton.
3.36 The gliding joints between the vertebrae only allow slight movement in one plane. How, then, are you able to touch your toes?
3.37 Name other groups of gliding joints in the body which combine to allow free movement.
3.38 What features of the skull sutures make them such tough, immovable joints?

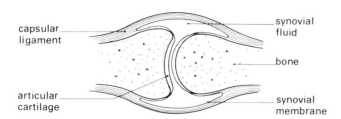

3.21 Section through a typical synovial joint

All ball and socket and hinge joints are **synovial joints**. Fig 3.20 shows synovial membranes. This thin membrane produces a fluid which bathes the articular surfaces of the bones.

▶ **Questions**

3.39 Name three synovial joints.
3.40 Suggest what the articulating surfaces of the bones are like.
3.41 Suggest the purpose of the production of synovial fluid.

▷ **Homework**

Discover all you can about the condition called 'tennis elbow'.

6 Bones as levers

Any movement we carry out, whether it is walking, lifting or grasping, requires **effort** to bring it about. This is because the natural state of any body is to be at rest. This inertia may be demonstrated by the following experiment.

Activity 3.1   Observing the inertia of a coin

3.22

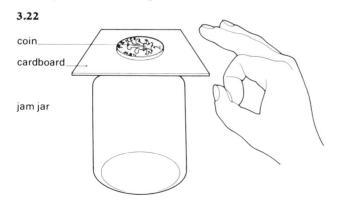

1   Place a coin in the centre of a square of cardboard as shown in Fig 3.22.
2   Flick the cardboard.

▶ **Question**

3.42 What happens to the coin? What does this suggest?

Activity 3.2   Measuring the forces exerted by the arm

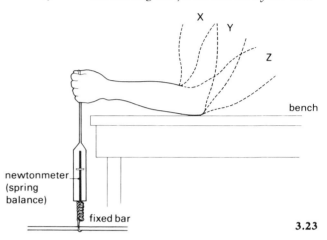

3.23

1   Place the forearm on a flat surface and move the upper arm to position X in Fig 3.23.
2   Attach the hand to a powerful spring balance, calibrated in newtons, which is anchored below bench level.
3   Record the force which the hand can exert in position X.
4   Rest the arm, then repeat steps 1–3 with the upper arm at position Y, then position Z.
5   Construct a table of your results.

▶ **Question**

3.43 What conclusions can you make from this experiment?

The force exerted by fingers, arms and legs requires effort. This effort is supplied by the muscles. These are mainly pulling forces. The ease with which the effort can bring about movement depends on the principle of moments.

Activity 3.3   Investigating the principle of moments

3.24 A balanced lever

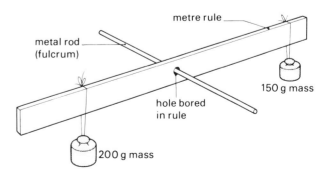

1 Construct the apparatus as shown in Fig 3.24. The 200 g mass represents a load which has to be lifted.
2 Take a 150 g mass and move it and the 200 g mass along the metre stick until the stick is level. The 150 g mass represents the effort.
3 Repeat step 2, using 100 g and 50 g masses for the effort.
4 Construct a table similar to the one below and enter your results.

Load	Distance from fulcrum	Effort	Distance from fulcrum
200 g		150 g	
200 g		100 g	
200 g		50 g	

▶ **Questions**

3.44 From your results, what can you deduce about the effect of applying less effort?
3.45 Why is the lever level when the mass at one end of it is greater than the mass at the other?

Bones act as levers in our bodies. Muscles supply the effort and usually the fulcrum is a joint. The load will vary depending upon the activity. As you have seen from Activity 3.4, provided the effort is further away from the fulcrum than the load, the lever system enables an effort to move a larger load. The example of a lever used in Activity 3.4 is a **first order lever**, with the fulcrum between the effort and the load. Other types of lever are **second** and **third order levers**. These are illustrated in Fig 3.25.

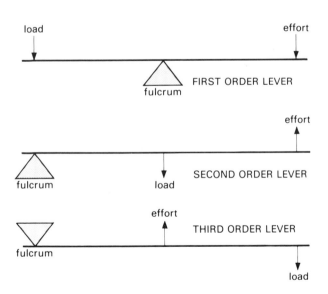

3.25 The three orders of lever

▶ **Questions**

3.46 (a) What is in the middle in a second order lever?
(b) What is in the middle in a third order lever?
3.47 Try to think of everyday examples of each order of lever.

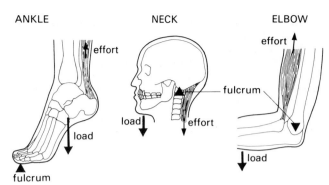

3.26 Different lever systems in the human body

▶ **Questions**

3.48 Work out which orders of lever the three examples in Fig 3.26 represent.
3.49 Which of the three orders of lever illustrated in Fig 3.26 would require the greatest effort to move a certain load?

▷ **Homework**

Record all the levers you use during one day and state whether they are examples of the first, second, or third order of levers.

7 The action of muscles on joints

When studying section 6 you may have thought that quite a lot of forces seem to be pushing forces rather than pulling forces. We do, of course, push as well as pull. Carry out the following activity, and decide whether or not our muscles can push.

Activity 3.4 Demonstration of the action of the muscles which raise and lower the forearm

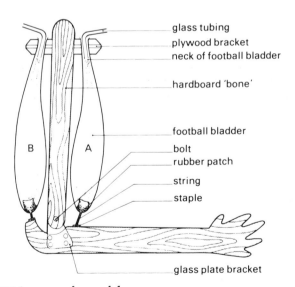

3.27 Arm muscles model

1 Construct the apparatus illustrated in Fig 3.27. The string must be firmly glued to the rubber patch and the ends of the string must be tightly stapled to the cardboard or plywood 'forearm'.

2 Inflate bladder A with a bicycle pump and observe the effect on the model.
3 Allow bladder A to deflate.
4 Inflate bladder B and observe the effect on the model.

▶ **Questions**

3.50 Describe the effect of inflation of first A, then B.
3.51 What do these bladders represent?

The muscle which begins the bending of the arm, the biceps, may be felt when you bend your forearm upwards. It feels like a hard bulge. The muscle is said to be contracting. When a muscle contracts, the individual fibres shorten, pulling a bone to which they are attached nearer to another bone. In the case of the biceps, the radius and ulna are pulled towards the humerus. Just as the football bladders only return to their original size, the muscle fibres can only regain their original length (relax). They are incapable of elongating. Thus a muscle cannot push a bone. In order for the arm to be straightened again after bending, an opposing or **antagonistic muscle** has to pull it back. The forearm is extended by the triceps muscle, which is attached to the opposite side of the

3.28 How the arm muscles straighten the arm

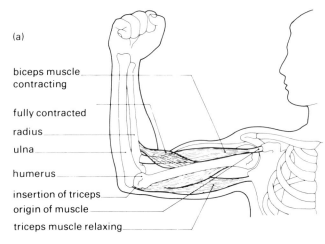

(a)

biceps muscle contracting
fully contracted
radius
ulna
humerus
insertion of triceps
origin of muscle
triceps muscle relaxing

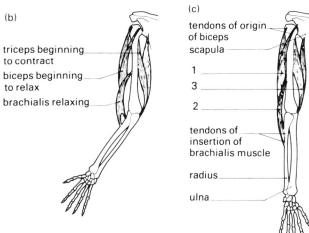

(b)

triceps beginning to contract
biceps beginning to relax
brachialis relaxing

(c)

tendons of origin of biceps
scapula
1
3
2
tendons of insertion of brachialis muscle
radius
ulna

forearm bones and humerus. Study Fig 3.28. The states of the muscles are labelled in the first two positions.

▶ **Questions**

3.52 Suggest the role of the additional muscle, the brachialis, in these diagrams.
3.53 Flexor muscles bend limbs, extensor muscles straighten them. Which are the flexor muscles and which the extensor muscles in these diagrams?
3.54 Identify the numbered muscles in (c) and state whether they are contracted or relaxed.

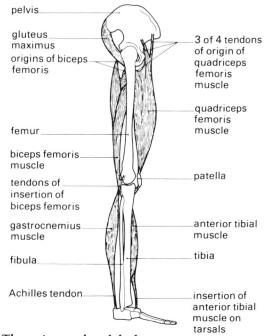

pelvis
gluteus maximus
origins of biceps femoris
femur
biceps femoris muscle
tendons of insertion of biceps femoris
gastrocnemius muscle
fibula
Achilles tendon

3 of 4 tendons of origin of quadriceps femoris muscle
quadriceps femoris muscle
patella
anterior tibial muscle
tibia
insertion of anterior tibial muscle on tarsals

3.29 The main muscles of the leg

▶ **Questions**

3.55 Look at Fig 3.29. What will be the effect on the leg or foot of contraction of the following muscles?
(a) biceps femoris   (b) quadriceps femoris
(c) gastrocnemius (calf)   (d) anterior tibial
3.56 By what means are muscles attached to bones?
3.57 What particular characteristic must this attaching tissue possess?

8 Tissues concerned with movement

3.30 Photomicrograph of tendon

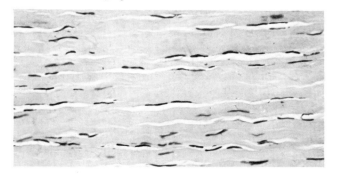

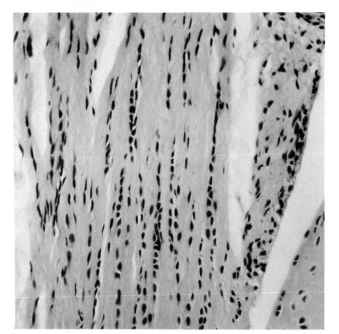

3.31 Photomicrograph of ligament

Tendons are the tough tissues which attach muscles to the bones they move. They are not elastic or flexible, and are made up of white collagen fibres. **Ligaments** are the more flexible tissues which join bones together (see Fig 3.20), and they are composed of yellow elastin fibres.

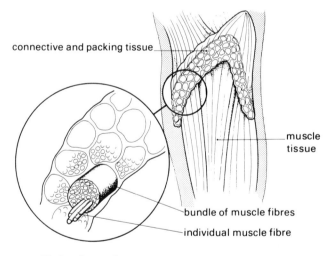

connective and packing tissue

muscle tissue

bundle of muscle fibres

individual muscle fibre

3.32 Skeletal muscle

Skeletal muscle is the flesh which we eat off a joint of meat. Skeletal muscle is also known as striated or striped muscle because of the alternate light and dark bands. It is called voluntary muscle because it is under the conscious control of the brain. We know when we pick something up or start to walk. We usually think about it beforehand. Some muscles found inside the body are not under the control of the will. We are not aware of peristalsis (passage of food) along the intestine. This is carried out by involuntary muscles, and their structure is discussed in Unit 2.

3.33 (a) Photomicrograph of skeletal muscle

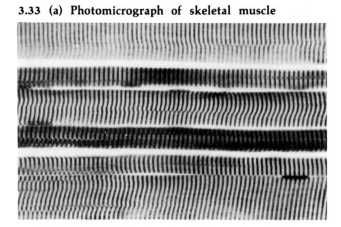

3.33 (b) Photomicrograph of smooth muscle

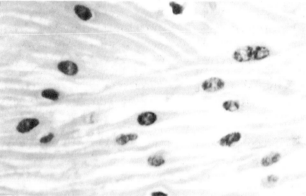

3.33 (c) Photomicrograph of cardiac muscle

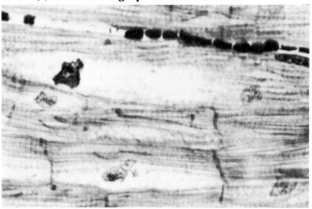

3.33 (d) Electron micrograph of skeletal muscle

3.58 How do involuntary muscles look different from voluntary muscles to the naked eye?

3.59 Why do you suppose involuntary muscle is sometimes called smooth muscle?

3.60 The heart consists mainly of cardiac muscle. What particular features would you expect cardiac muscle to possess?

▷ **Homework**

Write a list of as many involuntary muscles as you can think of and state their function in the body.

9 Muscles and energy

A muscle contracts in response to an electrical stimulus from the nerves. However, before a muscle can respond to a stimulus, it needs energy to enable it to contract.

► **Question**

3.61 What is the source of energy enabling an unfatigued muscle to respond to an electrical stimulus? (See Unit 6)

Activity 3.5 Investigating the source of energy for muscle contraction

1 Soak a small quantity of shin beef in Ringer's solution for fifteen minutes at 35–40°C.
2 Dissect a bundle of three or four fibres of beef about 20 mm in length.
3 Mount the fibres in a slide in Ringer's solution, and place the slide on a piece of graph paper. Measure the length by counting the squares, and record it in a table.
4 Mop up the excess Ringer's solution with filter paper. Place a few drops of dilute glucose solution on the fibres. Leave for five minutes.
5 Measure the length of the fibres again and record their length.
6 Repeat steps 1–5, using a solution of ATP, with a clean microscope slide and fresh fibres.

► **Questions**

3.62 What is the change in length when glucose solution is added? What can be deduced from this result?

3.63 By what percentage do the fibres shorten when ATP solution is applied?

3.64 From which of these solutions can a muscle best utilise the energy?

3.65 Suggest why Ringer's solution is used to soak the beef fibres during the experiment. Can you guess what Ringers' solution closely resembles?

Adenosine triphosphate (ATP) is the immediate source of energy utilised by muscles. When glucose is broken down in respiration to release energy, this energy is transferred to ATP molecules. The first step in the breakdown of a molecule of glucose can occur in the absence of oxygen. Enzymes bring about the breakdown. A substance called lactic acid is formed,

and two molecules of ATP are produced. This is called anaerobic respiration. See Unit 6.

If plenty of oxygen is present, pyruvic acid is produced instead of lactic acid, and this is further broken down to produce carbon dioxide and water when oxygen reacts with it. In this breakdown, called aerobic respiration, thirty-six molecules of ATP are produced for every original molecule of glucose.

If the muscles are subjected to a long period of vigorous activity, oxygen may not reach the muscles fast enough to keep pace with the rapid breakdown of glucose. The muscles therefore have to work without oxygen, and in doing so they build up an **oxygen debt**.

3.34 Sebastion Coe, the 1980 Olympic gold medal winner suffering an oxygen debt

► **Questions**

3.66 What substance accumulates in the absence of oxygen?

3.67 How may this substance be removed from the muscles after exercise?

3.35 Lactic acid concentration in the blood

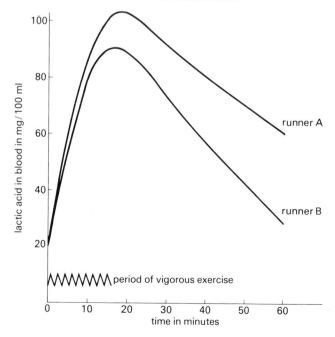

As oxygen is drawn in to pay the debt, the accumulated lactic acid is broken down. Fig 3.35 is a graph which illustrates the concentration of lactic acid in the blood of two subjects, A and B, during a period of strenuous exercise such as a race. Study the graph carefully before answering the following questions.

▶ **Questions**

3.68 In which subject is the accumulation of lactic acid greater? Suggest some reasons for this.
3.69 In which subject is the oxygen debt paid off more efficiently? What is the possible reason for this?
3.70 Why does the concentration of lactic acid in the blood continue to rise after the completion of exercise?

▷ **Homework**

Find out how athletic training can affect energy availability in the muscles.

10 Posture

A good posture is one of the attributes of a healthy person. It is maintained by the continuous contraction of individual muscle fibres working in turns to avoid fatigue. This is called muscle tone. Good muscle tone is also important for efficient exercise.

Fig 3.36 illustrates incorrect and correct standing postures. The numbers on (b) represent the features of a good posture. Study the figures carefully.

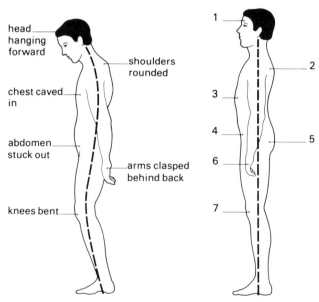

3.36 (a) Bad standing posture   **3.36 (b) Good standing posture**

▶ **Questions**
3.71 List the features of a good posture using the numbered order in Fig 3.36(b).
3.72 What are the adverse effects on the body of the incorrect posture illustrated in Fig 3.36(a)?
3.73 Explain why the posture illustrated in Fig 3.37(b) is bad for the body.
3.74 Which posture in Fig 3.38 is correct and why?

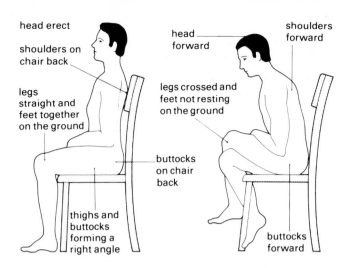

3.37 (a) Good sitting posture   **3.37 (b) Bad sitting posture**

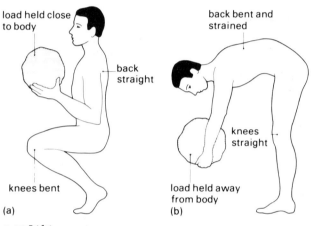

3.38 Lifting postures

▷ **Research project**

Observe the posture of all the people you meet in one day. Note whether they have a good or bad standing posture. Estimate the percentage of those who have a good posture.

Answers and discussion

1 Structure and functions of the skeleton

3.1 1 skull; 2 lower jaw (mandible); 3 cervical vertebra; 4 clavicle; 5 humerus; 6 sternum; 7 rib; 8 lumbar vertebra; 9 pelvis; 10 ulna; 11 radius; 12 carpals; 13 femur; 14 patella; 15 tibia; 16 fibula; 17 tarsals.

3.2 Flat bones: skull, scapula, pelvis.
Long bones: humerus, radius, ulna, femur, tibia, fibula.
Short bones: vertebrae, patella, clavicle, ribs, sternum.

2 The axial skeleton

3.3 Skull and vertebral column.

3.4 The flat bones of the cranium, tightly fused together, form a tough box to protect the delicate tissues of the brain. The bones of the facial skeleton form deep sockets, the orbits, which protect the eye balls. The upper jaw bones contain sockets for the teeth, which aid mastication of food. The nasal bones form the nasal passages. The shape of the face is mainly determined by the bone structure. The mandible contains sockets for the lower set of teeth and aids in mastication. Movement of the lower jaw is necessary for both mastication and speech.

3.5 Cervical, 7; thoracic, 12; lumbar, 5; sacral, 5 (fused); coccyx, 4 (fused).

3.6 The neural arch is especially large in the atlas vertebra because the spinal cord is widest at the base of the brain.

3.7 The odontoid peg on the anterior side of the axis vertebra makes a pivot joint with the atlas vertebra which allows movement of the skull on the vertebral column (see section 5).

3.8 The vertebrarterial canals of the cervical vertebrae house delicate arteries which pass up to the head.

3.9 The capitulum and tuberculum facets of the thoracic vertebrae form joints with the rib heads.

3.10 The lumbar vertebrae are very large because they are in a position in the lower back where there is a lot of strain. Their stout transverse processes give attachment to the very large, and powerful back muscles.

3.11 The sacral vertebrae are fused together to form a solid structure for the firm attachment of the pelvic girdle.

3 The appendicular skeleton

3.12 Two clavicles and two scapulae (pectoral girdle), forelimbs, pelvic girdle, hindlimbs and the ribs.

3.13 The rib cage is a moving structure which is necessary for the mechanism of breathing (see Unit 6)

3.14 The component parts of the rib cage are: twelve pairs of ribs (seven pairs of true ribs, attached directly to the sternum; three pairs of 'false' ribs, attached to the seventh pair of 'true' ribs and two tiny pairs of floating ribs); sternum; costal cartilages.

3.15 The costal cartilages are flexible, which aid movement of the rib cage.

3.16 The rib heads are not fixed to the thoracic vertebrae, but form gliding joints with them. If the rib heads were attached to the thoracic vertebrae, movement of the rib cage would be severely restricted.

3.17 1 clavicle; 2 scapula; 3 humerus.

3.18 The scapula has a large surface area for the attachment of the powerful shoulder muscles. Between them, the scapulae help to protect the dorsal part of the lungs.

3.19 The collar bones form struts which keep the shoulders apart and maintain an erect posture.

3.20 1 ilium; 2 sacrum; 3 ischium; 4 femur; 5 patella.

3.21 The femur is the longest limb bone.

3.22 The hindlimb is longer than the forelimb. This is an aid to walking. Longer limbs give a larger stride which increases the efficiency of walking.

3.23 The hindlimb bones should be thicker, since a thicker tube is a better supporting structure. The forelimbs are not weight supporting structures.

3.24 1 femur; 2 tibia; 3 fibula; 4 tarsals; 5 metatarsals; 6 phalanges.

4 The composition of the skeleton

3.25 1 chondroblasts; 2 matrix; 3 chondroblasts dividing.

3.26 The flexible structures on the head made of elastic cartilage are the ears and the tip of the nose. Another type of cartilage contains tough white fibres (collagen fibres) running in the matrix. This type of cartilage is tough and resistant to stretching and it acts as a shock absorber between bones for example between the vertebrae.

3.27 1 matrix; 2 Haversian canal; 3 osteoblast (bone cell); 4 blood vessels and nerve.

3.28 Osteoblasts are living and require food and oxygen. This is supplied by blood vessels in the Haversian canals.

5 Joints

3.29 4 is freely movable; 5 is movable; 2, 6, 8 and 9 are partly movable; 3, 7 and 10 are slightly movable; 1 is immovable.

3.30 The shoulder joints allow the most universal movement.

3.31 This enables the arms to be used for a very wide range of activities. Universal movement of the hip joint would be impractical since stability is necessary here for support of the body. The acetabulum is deeper than the glenoid cavity and the head of the femur is more complete than the head of the humerus. These facts, plus the presence of a ligament attaching the head of the femur to the centre of the acetabulum, restrict movement.

3.32 Movement in a hinge joint is restricted to almost 180° in one plane only.

3.33 (a) olecranon process (b) patella.

3.34 The gliding joint between the radius and the ulna allows this. The radius rotates over the ulna to bring the palm of the hand face downwards. The ability to move the palm upwards or downwards is important for many activities.

3.35 The joint between the atlas and axis vertebrae is a pivot joint.

3.36 In all there are twenty-four pairs of gliding joints in the vertebral column and it is possible to touch one's toes because the sum of slight movement at each of the joints yields sufficient mobility to allow this.

3.37 The carpals and tarsals have groups of gliding joints which together yield a considerable degree of mobility.

3.38 The white fibro-cartilage which attaches the bones of the skull to each other is very tough. Also, the very irregular edges of contact make an extremely stable joint.

3.39 A pale pink, tough but elastic tissue is attached near the articulating surfaces of the bones. This is ligament.

3.40 The articulating surfaces of the bones are covered with smooth cartilage. This smooth material reduces friction and allows easy movement.

3.41 The synovial fluid lubricates the joint and reduces friction. It also acts as a shock absorber should a blow be applied to the joint. This reduces the likelihood of the bones being chipped.

6 Bones as levers

3.42 The coin falls into the jar. It does not change its horizontal position even though the cardboard is moved. This suggests that an object tends to remain stationary. If the coin had been moved by flicking the cardboard, it would have fallen outside the jar. Falling is a movement, of course. This is due to a pull or force acting on an object. The force involved is gravity. Gravity overcame the inertia of the coin, pulling it downwards.

3.43 Since the force needed to pull on the spring balance is greater at Y and Z than at X, it is possible to conclude that less force has to be applied when it is in the direction of the movement concerned.

3.44 The greater the distance of the effort from the fulcrum, the less the mass (effort) required to lift the same load.

3.45 The lever is balanced because the distances between the fulcrum and the load and the fulcrum and the effort are not equal. 200 g mass × 10 cm distance = 100 g mass × 20 cm distance. This is the principle of moments whch applies to all levers.

3.46 (a) the load; (b) the effort.

3.47 First order levers: scissors; pincers; a crowbar.
Second order levers; wheelbarrow, the oar of a boat.
Third order levers: fishing rod; sugar tongs.

3.48 First order: skull nodding on vertebral column.
Second order: lifting foot.
Third order: lifting an object with the hand.

3.49 Lifting an object with the hand would require the greatest effort. In third order levers, the distance between the effort and the fulcrum is always less than the distance between the load and the fulcrum.

7 The action of muscles on joints

3.50 When the football bladder A is inflated, the forearm is pulled upwards. When bladder B is inflated, the forearm is pulled straight again.

3.51 Bladder A represents the biceps muscles and bladder B the triceps muscle.

3.52 The brachialis muscle is necessary to help the contraction of the biceps to obtain position a. This action is an example of the third order of levers, so a lot of effort is necessary to lift the load. Position c does not require so much effort. Extension of the arm is an example of the first order of levers.

3.53 The biceps and brachialis are flexor muscles, the triceps is an extensor muscle.

3.54 1 biceps relaxed; 2 brachialis relaxed; 3 triceps contracted.

3.55 (a) flexes leg; (b) extends leg; (c) raises heel; (d) flexes foot.

3.56 Muscles are attached to bones by tendons. The origin of a muscle is where it is attached to a bone which it cannot move and the insertion of a muscle is onto a bone it can move. Hence these tendons are called tendons of origin and tendons of insertion.

3.57 A tendon should be inelastic. If it could stretch it would diminish the effect of the muscle contracting.

8 Tissues concerned with movement

3.58 Involuntary muscles appear as smooth, pink sheets, whereas voluntary muscles appear as bundles of fibres.

3.59 Involuntary muscle is referred to as smooth muscle because it lacks striations and appears smooth when seen under the microscope.

3.60 Cardiac muscle will need to go on contracting continuously without us thinking about it. It also needs to be very tough. The striations and permanent joining of cells enable it to be particularly strong.

9 Muscles and energy

3.61 Energy used in the body comes from the breakdown of the carbohydrate glucose which is in many of the foods we eat. It is stored in the form of an insoluble carbohydrate called glycogen in the liver and skeletal muscles.

3.62 There is no change in the length of the muscle fibres when glucose solution is added. Immediate energy for muscle contraction cannot be obtained from dilute glucose solution.

3.63 The fibres treated with ATP are reduced in length by about 30% (20 mm to 14 mm).

3.64 A muscle can utilise energy instantly from ATP, but not from glucose solution.

3.65 Ringer's solution stops the fibres from drying out. It must have the same concentration as the inside of the fibres to avoid osmosis in either direction. It closely resembles the body fluid in which the muscle is normally bathed.

3.66 Lactic acid accumulates in the muscles in the absence of oxygen. This eventually builds up and prevents the muscles from contracting. The muscles are then said to be in a state of fatigue.

3.67 At the end of a race an athlete suffers from oxygen debt and extra oxygen is needed to break down the accumulated lactic acid. You will have seen sprinters gulping for air at the end of a race. The extra oxygen taken in helps convert the accumulated lactic acid back to pyruvic acid, which then provides more ATP molecules to replenish those used up.

3.68 Subject A has a greater accumulation of lactic acid in the blood than B. This could be because A was already active before the race or A could be anaemic. In anaemia there are fewer red blood cells per millilitre of blood to carry oxygen.

3.69 B pays the oxygen debt off more quickly than A. It is advisable to rest after exercise to help to pay off the debt. A may not have done this.

3.70 There will be a time lag before oxygen to pay off the debt reaches the tissues to break down the lactic acid, hence the lactic acid concentration will continue to rise after exercise.

10 Posture

3.71 1 head erect; 2 shoulders back; 3 chest out; 4 abdomen in; 5 hips slightly forward; 6 arms held loosely; 7 knees straight.

3.72 (a) A drooping head contributes to rounded shoulders which make an individual appear unhealthy and unattractive.
(b) A caved-in chest restricts breathing movements.
(c) A protruding abdomen will produce displacement of the abdominal organs as the abdominal muscles lose their tone.

(d) Bent knees contribute to the entire unbalanced stance of the body. (Note the curved line.) Under these circumstances certain muscles are overworked and become fatigued, while other muscles are underworked.

3.73 The posture illustrated in Fig 3.37(b) is bad for the body since breathing is restricted, only certain groups of muscles are in use and the circulation may be impeded by the crossed legs.

3.74 Fig 3.38(a) illustrates the correct lifting posture. With the back straight, the knees bent and the load held close to the body, there is far less strain on the vertebral column and back muscles. A slipped disc could result from the posture shown in Fig 3.38(b). Sometimes one of the cartilage discs which form immovable joints between the centra of the vertebrae is pulled out of alignment as a result of undue strain.

4 The need for food

4.1 Judo experts

1 Why do we need food?

We must have food in order to survive. After a severe drought which caused crop failure, twelve million people, mainly children, died from starvation in Africa in 1980. Why did they die? Why could they not survive without food? Study Figs 4.1 – 4.4 carefully, then answer the questions.

▶ **Questions**

4.1 What do the judo experts in Fig 4.1 need to enable them to keep fighting for some time without getting tired?

4.2 Fig 4.2 shows two photographs of the same person, one taken some years ago, the other recently. What process has taken place over the period between?

4.3 Fig 4.3 shows a badly wounded arm. What will happen to this wound in the next few months?

4.4 Describe the appearance of the children in Fig 4.4(a). How does it compare with the appearance of the children in Fig 4.4(b)? Suggest a reason for the differences you describe.

▷ **Homework**

Find out why children are the main victims of starvation in Africa.

4.2 (a) The Princess of Wales as a child ...

4.2 (b) ... and as an adult

40

4.3 A wounded arm

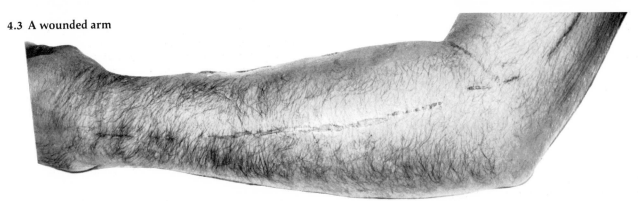

4.4 (a) Karamajong children from East Africa

4.4 (b) Some children at play

2 The source of all our food

Green plants are the ultimate source of all our food. Even meat comes from cows or other animals which themselves ate green plants. Green plants are capable of **photosynthesis**. Photosynthetic literally means light-made, so photosynthesis means making something, such as food, in the presence of light. Because they can trap sunlight, green plants can use simple inorganic chemicals such as water and carbon dioxide, and combine them to make organic food materials such as carbohydrates. This may be shown by the following experiment.

Activity 4.1   Is starch produced by green leaves?

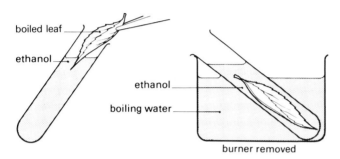

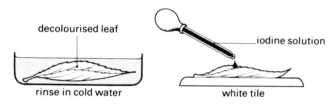

4.5

1   Take a soft, medium-sized leaf which has been exposed to sunlight and place it in a beaker of gently boiling water for about one minute. This will kill the cells and soften the cell walls.
2   Place the leaf in a boiling tube containing ethanol. Turn off the bunsen. Place the boiling tube in the beaker of boiling water.
3   Observe the ethanol boiling. (Take care. Ethanol has a lower boiling point than water and is inflammable.)
4   Dip the decolourised leaf into cold water to wash out the ethanol.
5   Place the leaf on a white tile and cover it with iodine solution using a dropper pipette.
6   Examine the leaf after a few minutes.

▶ Questions

4.5   What effect does the ethanol have on the leaf?
4.6   What do you observe after the leaf has been soaked in iodine solution? Suggest an explanation of your observation.
4.7   It is possible to use this experiment to show that light is necessary for photosynthesis. Describe how you would do this.

The first carbohydrate formed is a simple, soluble sugar called glucose. This is quickly converted into insoluble starch inside the leaf which can be stored more easily.

Activity 4.2   Is light necessary for starch production?

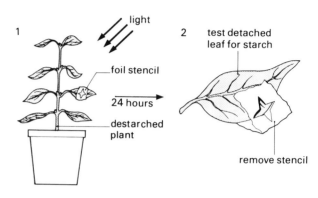

4.6

1   Place a potted plant in a dark cupboard for twenty-four hours.
2   Place the same plant in a light place and attach an aluminium foil stencil to a leaf as shown in Fig 4.6.
3   Leave the plant for twenty-four hours.
4   Detach the leaf with the stencil, remove the stencil and test the leaf for starch as in Activity 4.1.
5   Draw the result of the starch test.

▶ Questions

4.8   What do you conclude from your result?
4.9   Why is the potted plant placed in a dark cupboard at the start of the experiment?

What are the materials used by green plants to manufacture carbohydrates? Carry out the following experiment.

Activity 4.3   Is carbon dioxide necessary for photosynthesis?

4.7

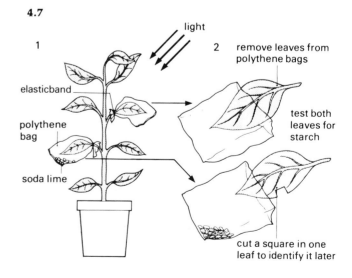

1   Place a potted plant in a dark cupboard for twenty-four hours.
2   Place the same plant in the light with two leaves enclosed in transparent bags as shown in Fig 4.7. Ensure that the elastic bands make an airtight seal. One of the bags should contain some soda lime.
3   Leave the plant for two or three days in the light.
4   Detach the leaves which were contained in the polythene bags. Nick the margin of the leaf from the soda lime bag so that you will not confuse them.
5   Test both leaves for starch as in Activity 4.1.

▶ Questions

4.10   Suggest the purpose of the soda lime in one of the polythene bags.
4.11   What is the result of the starch test? What is your conclusion?

Carbon dioxide is one of the substances used by green plants for the manufacture of carbohydrate. The other substance is very difficult to test for in a leaf. Carbohydrates contain carbon, hydrogen and oxygen in the following proportion: $C H_2 O$.

▶ Question

4.12   Can you suggest what this other substance might be?

These two substances and light alone will not produce carbohydrates. A fourth factor is necessary since it absorbs the light and makes it available for photosynthesis.

Activity 4.4   Discovering the substance which absorbs light

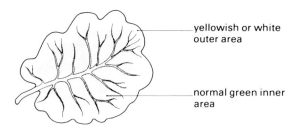

yellowish or white outer area

normal green inner area

4.8

1   Take a variegated (green and white) leaf, as illustrated in Fig 4.8, from a potted geranium plant which has been exposed to light.
2   Make a careful drawing of the leaf to show the two distinct areas.
3   Apply the starch test as in Activity 4.1.

▶ Question

4.13   What do you conclude from this result?

The following equation summarises the process of photosynthesis. The importance of the production of oxygen as a by-product of photosynthesis will be discussed in Unit 20.

$$CO_2 + H_2O \xrightarrow{\text{light energy absorbed by chlorophyll}} CH_2O + O_2$$

carbon dioxide   water   carbohydrate   oxygen

As well as carbohydrates, all the other chemicals which make up our food (see section 4) are available from green plants. Fig 4.9 summarises the nutrition of a green plant.

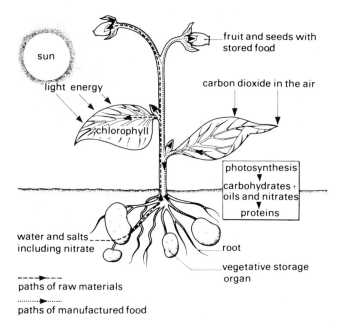

sun

light energy

chlorophyll

fruit and seeds with stored food

carbon dioxide in the air

photosynthesis
▼
carbohydrates + oils and nitrates
▼
proteins

water and salts including nitrate

root

vegetative storage organ

- - - ▶ paths of raw materials

········▶ paths of manufactured food

4.9 Green plant nutrition

▶ Question

4.14   From what substances are proteins made by a green plant?
4.15   Where do the mineral salts come from?

▷ Homework

Write a short essay explaining to a non-scientist why we are all dependent on green plants.

3 Food chains and webs

All living creatures are ultimately dependent on green plants. Aquatic organisms are dependent on water weeds or algae. Many algae are minute plants which float on the surface of the water. These plants, together with microscopic animals, comprise the plankton.

   Some animals eat green plants directly. These are called **herbivores**. Many animals eat other animals. These are called **carnivores**.

▶ Questions

4.16   List six herbivorous animals.
4.17   List six carnivorous animals.

4.18 Briefly describe the human diet and indicate whether humans are examples of herbivores, carnivores, or another category of animal.

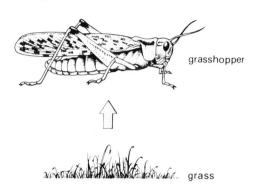

grasshopper

grass

4.10 A simple food chain

It is possible to trace the diet of any animal back to a green plant by means of a **food chain**.

▶ **Questions**

4.19 How many links are there in the chains in Figs 4.10 and 4.11?
4.20 Using Fig 4.12 construct (a) a two link, (b) a three link and (c) a four link food chain.

4.11 A food chain with a carnivore

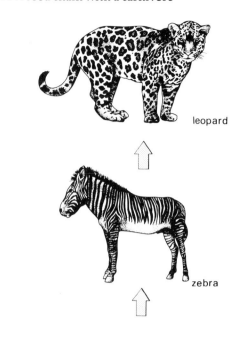

leopard

zebra

4.12 Organisms in an oak woodland

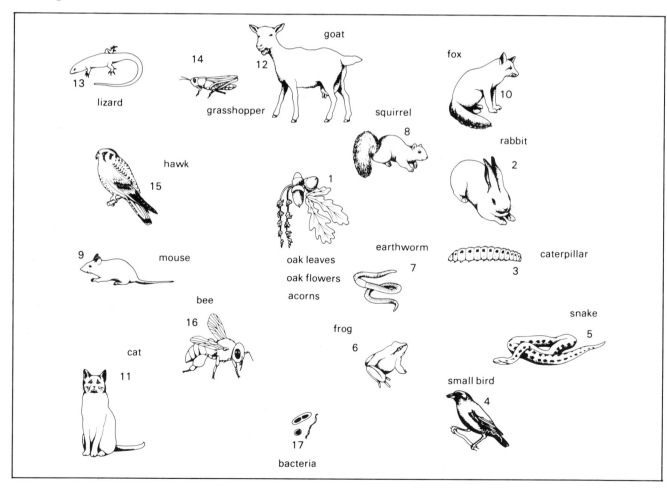

13 lizard

14 grasshopper

goat 12

fox 10

squirrel 8

rabbit 2

hawk 15

1 oak leaves / oak flowers / acorns

earthworm 7

caterpillar 3

9 mouse

bee 16

frog 6

snake 5

cat 11

small bird 4

17 bacteria

Relationships between living organisms are very complex, and usually there are a number of animals competing for the same food. Fig 4.12 forms the basis of a **food web**. A food web shows the feeding links between a group of animals and plants living in a particular environment.

▶ **Question**

4.21 Take a piece of tracing paper and trace the numbers only from Fig 4.12 into your exercise book. Then write the name of each organism in a box by each number. Insert arrows to indicate which organism is consumed by another.

Green plants are frequently called producers, since they produce the food used throughout food chains and food webs. Herbivores are called primary consumers, and carnivores secondary consumers. A carnivore which feeds on another carnivore (for example, a fish consuming a water boatman) is called a tertiary consumer. In any community, the number of organisms decreases as you go up the chain, forming a pyramid of numbers.

4.13 Pyramid of numbers

▶ **Questions**

4.22 Identify the producers, primary consumers, secondary consumers and tertiary consumers in Fig 4.13.

4.23 Why are there fewer hawks than grasshoppers? Can you suggest a reason for the pyramid of numbers?

4.24 What can you learn from the figures in Fig 4.14? What happens to the energy between each feeding level?

4.25 From these facts, state which of the following one hectare fields would yield more available energy for human consumption and explain why: (a) a field of maize; (b) a field of grazing cattle.

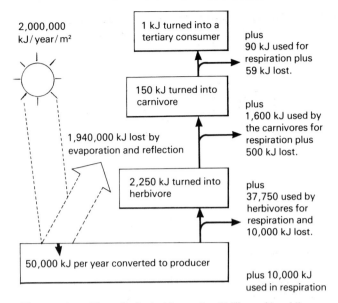

2,000,000 kJ/year/m²

1 kJ turned into a tertiary consumer — plus 90 kJ used for respiration plus 59 kJ lost.

150 kJ turned into carnivore — plus 1,600 kJ used by the carnivores for respiration plus 500 kJ lost.

1,940,000 kJ lost by evaporation and reflection

2,250 kJ turned into herbivore — plus 37,750 used by herbivores for respiration and 10,000 kJ lost.

50,000 kJ per year converted to producer — plus 10,000 kJ used in respiration

(Figures adapted from *Ecological Energetics,* Phillipson (Arnold), and given in kJ per m² per year.)

4.14 Energy available at each level of a feeding community

▷ **Homework project**

Construct a web to illustrate the feeding relationships between pond organisms.

4 The composition of food

All food contains one or more of these substances: carbohydrates, fats, proteins, minerals, vitamins, fibre and water.

4.15 Foods with a high proportion of carbohydrates or fats

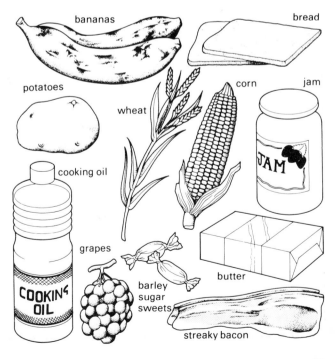

bananas · bread · potatoes · wheat · corn · jam · cooking oil · grapes · barley sugar sweets · butter · streaky bacon

Carbohydrates and fats – energy foods

All the foods in Fig 4.15 contain the elements carbon, hydrogen and oxygen. In carbohydrates the hydrogen and oxygen are in the same proportion as they are in water. Fats contain proportionately less oxygen.

Three classes of carbohydrate are found in foods. The simplest are soluble sugars which consist of a single molecular unit. An example is glucose. Next come the soluble sugars which consist of two molecular units. Examples are sucrose, which is our ordinary white sugar, and maltose which is found in malt. (See Unit 5.)

Finally there is a group of insoluble, non-sweet carbohydrates which have complex molecules comprising many units. An example of this class is starch.

▶ **Questions**

4.26 Identify the foods in Fig 4.15 as sweet carbohydrate foods, starchy foods or fats.
4.27 Can you suggest a difference between plant fats and animal fats?

4.16 Foods rich in protein

Proteins – body building foods

All the protein foods in Fig 4.16 contain the elements carbon, hydrogen, oxygen and nitrogen. Phosphorus and sulphur are also usually present. Proteins are formed from molecular units called **amino acids** (see Unit 2). There are over twenty different amino acids, nine of which are essential in the diet of man. These are leucine, isoleucine, tryptophan, valine, threonine, phenylalanine, cystine, methionine and lysine. Most plant sources of protein do not contain all these essential amino acids. They are therefore termed second class proteins. Most animal sources of protein

do contain all the essential amino acids. These are called first class proteins. A notable exception to this rule is soya bean which is a first class protein.

▶ **Question**

4.28 Construct a table with two columns, one headed 'first class protein' and the other 'second class protein', and classify the foods illustrated in Fig 4.16 under these two headings.

Proteins are also essential for the repair of damaged tissues. In the absence of available carbohydrate or fat, protein may be used as an energy source.

▶ **Question**

4.29 Under what circumstances is it likely that protein will be used as an energy source?

Minerals and vitamins

Fish, fruits, green vegetables, liver and milk are often said to be good for you. This idea is quite sound because these are foods which are rich in minerals and vitamins. Minerals and vitamins are essential for maintaining the various tissues of the body in good working order. A deficiency of these substances, as you will see in Unit 16, can lead to serious diseases.

Mineral elements such as iron, calcium, sodium, chlorine, phosphorus, sulphur, iodine and fluorine are mainly available combined as salts such as calcium phosphate and sodium chloride. Vitamins are a collection of unrelated organic substances which have been found in recent years to be essential in trace quantities in the diet. The following graph shows the results of some experiments carried out by Sir Frederick Gowland Hopkins on the growth of rats. The rats' diet consisted of pure protein, carbohydrate, minerals, fat and water.

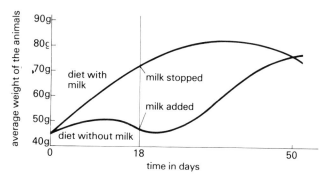

4.17 Graph to illustrate Gowland Hopkins' results

▶ **Question**

4.30 What does this graph demonstrate?

Vitamins are known by letters of the alphabet. The most important are A, B (a complex of several substances), C, D, E and K. Vitamins A, D, E and K are fat-soluble; vitamins B and C are water-soluble. To some extent this determines the food in which they are found.

Table 4.1 Sources and functions of minerals

Mineral element	Food source	Function in the body
Calcium	Milk, cheese, green vegetables	Formation of bones and teeth. Necessary for muscle contraction and blood clotting
Phosphorus	Protein foods: lean meat, fish, eggs, milk	Formation of bones and teeth. Synthesis of proteins and protoplasm. Formation of ATP
Nitrogen	As for phosphorus	Formation of proteins and protoplasm
Sulphur	As for phosphorus	As for nitrogen
Iron	Liver, kidney, lean meat, green vegetables, yeast, eggs	Formation of the oxygen carrier, haemoglobin, in in the blood
Potassium	Vegetables	Transmission of nerve impulses
Sodium	Table salt, green vegetables	Maintains blood and lymph. Transmission of nerve impulses
Chlorine	Table salt, seafoods	Maintains blood and and lymph
Iodine	Seafoods, cheese, iodised table salt	Needed to form thyroxin, the hormone which controls mental and physical growth
Fluorine	Water supply	Makes strong tooth enamel

Table 4.2 Sources and functions of vitamins

Vitamin	Sources	Function in the body
A Retinol	Liver, egg yolk, butter, margarine, fish liver oils, green vegetables	Keeps the mucous membranes healthy. Necessary for visual purple formation in the eye (this absorbs light)
B_1 Thiamine	Cereals, bread, Marmite, milk, kidney, lean meat, egg yolk	Forms a respiratory coenzyme, keeps nervous system healthy
B_2 Riboflavin	As for B_1 plus green vegetables	Keeps skin healthy
Niacin	As for B_2	Keeps nervous system healthy
B_{12} Cyanocoba-lamin	As for B_1 but especially liver	Necessary for proper development of red blood cells
C Ascorbic acid	Blackcurrants, citrus fruits, raw vegetables	Keeps the blood vessels supple
D Calciferol	Liver, butter, margarine, fish liver oils, egg yolk. Formed from ergosterol in the skin by sunlight	Necessary for the combination of and phosphorus to to make bone and tooth enamel
E Tocopherol	Green vegetables, vegetable oils, egg yolk, liver	Necessary for the development of the reproductive organs
K	Liver, green vegetables, egg yolk, cereals	Essential for blood clotting

▶ **Questions**

4.31 Study Table 4.1 carefully and then suggest the possible results of a deficiency of calcium, iron, iodine and fluorine.

4.32 Study Table 4.2 carefully and then suggest the possible results of a deficiency of vitamin A, vitamin C and vitamin D.

Water

Over 60% of our body weight consists of water. Even bone, one of the densest of our tissues, contains a large percentage of water. We contain about eight pints of blood, which is nearly 90% water, and our tissues are bathed in tissue fluid. Whereas we can survive for sixty days or more without food, even the hardiest among us would be unlikely to survive a week without water.

▶ **Question**

4.33 Apart from the obvious role of water as the major component of the body, in what other respects is water essential to us?

Food testing

It is possible to detect components in a sample of food by chemical tests. A selection of the simpler tests is suggested here. Suitable foods for testing include bread, sugar, milk, egg, peas or beans, orange juice, iodised table salt, cheese, lean meat or liver. Solid foods such as peas, beans or meat should be ground up in a pestle and mortar. Cheese should be grated and the egg yolk must be separated from the egg white. In order to display the results, construct a table such as the one shown overleaf.

Test Food	1 Starch	2 Reducing sugar	3 Non-reducing sugar	4 Fats	5 Protein	6 Vitamin C	7 Iron	8 Calcium	9 Potassium	10 Phosphorus	11 Sulphur	12 Chlorine	13 Iodine
Bread													
Sugar													
Milk													
Cheese													
Egg yolk													
Egg white													
Peas													
Orange juice													
Iodised table salt													
Lean meat													
Liver													

Activity 4.5 Testing food for starch

1 Place a small quantity of the food to be tested on a white tile.
2 Using a dropper pipette, add a drop of iodine solution.
3 Enter your results in the table.

▶ **Question**

4.34 What will happen if starch is present?

Activity 4.6 Testing food for reducing sugars (simple sugars)

4.18

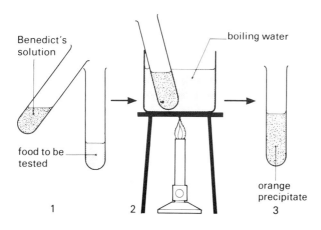

Activity 4.7 Testing food for non-reducing sugars (such as sucrose)

1 Take 1 cm³ of the prepared food and place it in a test tube.
2 Add 2 cm³ of Benedict's solution.
3 Place the test tube in a water bath of boiling water for about five minutes.
4 Look for an orange precipitate which is a positive result for the presence of a reducing sugar such as glucose.
5 Enter the result in the table.

4.19

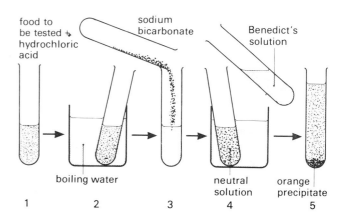

48

1 Take 1 cm³ of a sample of food which gave a negative result to Activity 4.6.
2 Add three drops of dilute hydrochloric acid.
3 Place in a water bath and boil for two or three minutes.
4 Cool in a beaker of cold water, then add sodium bicarbonate until the fizzing stops. The solution is now neutralised and if there was a non-reducing sugar present, it will have been converted to a reducing sugar.
5 Add 2 cm³ of Benedict's solution and place in a water bath of boiling water for about five minutes.
6 Enter the result in the table.

▶ Question

4.35 What result will you expect to see if the food originally contained a non-reducing sugar?

Activity 4.8   Testing food for fats and oils

4.20

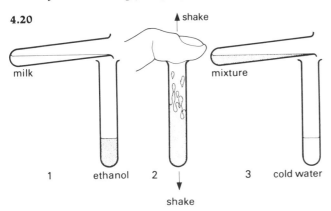

1 Test milk first in this experiment.
2 Take 2 cm³ of ethanol in a test tube and add to it a small quantity of milk.
3 Shake thoroughly, keeping your thumb over the end of the test tube.
4 Pour the mixture into a second test tube containing about 2 cm³ of water.
5 Enter the result in the table. Then test one other food.

▶ Question

4.36 What do you observe when adding the mixture to water?

Activity 4.9   Testing food for protein (Biuret test)

4.21

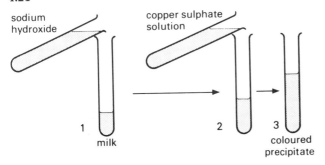

1 Test milk first in this experiment.
2 Place 2 cm³ of milk into a test tube and add 1 cm³ of sodium hydroxide solution.
3 Add 1% copper sulphate solution slowly, drop by drop, shaking at each drop.
4 Enter the result in the table. Then test one other food.

▶ Question

4.37 What colour changes do you observe?

Activity 4.10   Testing food for vitamin C

This is a very precise experiment which depends on the bleaching property of vitamin C (ascorbic acid). An indophenol known as DCPIP, a blue dye, is used to test for vitamin C. Vitamin C decolourises it.
1 Place 2 cm³ of 0.1% DCPIP solution into a clean test tube. Use a syringe to measure the exact quantity required.
2 Measure 2 cm³ of fruit juice, for example orange juice into another syringe.
3 Add the fruit juice one drop at a time to the DCPIP solution and notice how many drops it takes before the dye is decolourised.
4 Indicate either a positive or a negative result in your table.

▶ Question

4.38 It is possible to compare the amount of vitamin C in different fruit juices. Suggest how this could be done.

Activity 4.11   Testing food for some minerals

It will be necessary for your teacher to prepare the food extracts to be tested in these experiments. Group work is best for these experiments. Each group of six pupils should be given 12 cm³ of food extract which they divide equally between six test tubes.

Testing for iron
1 To 2 cm³ of food extract add 6 drops of ammonium thiocyanate (3M) solution and 2 cm³ 3M hydrochloric acid.
2 Gently shake the mixture.
3 A faint pink colour indicates the presence of iron ions.

Testing for calcium
1 To 2 cm³ of food extract add 6 drops of 0.25M ammonium oxalate.
2 Shake the mixture.
3 A fine white precipitate indicates the presence of calcium ions.

Testing for potassium
1 To 2 cm³ of food extract add 6 drops of freshly prepared 0.08M sodium cobalinitrite.
2 Gently shake the mixture.
3 Add 2 cm³ of 95% ethanol.

4 A yellow precipitate indicates the presence of potassium ions.

Testing for phosphate
1 To 2 cm³ of food extract add 10 drops of freshly prepared 0.5M ammonium molybdate solution.
2 Shake the mixture well.
3 Add a small piece of metallic tin.
4 A blue colour around the tin indicates the presence of phosphate ions.

Testing for sulphate
1 To 2 cm³ of food extract add 3 drops of 0.25M barium chloride.
2 A white precipitate indicates the presence of sulphate.

Testing for chloride and iodide
1 To 2 cm³ of food extract add 2 drops of silver nitrate.
2 A white precipitate indicates the presence of chloride or iodide.

Testing for iodine in sea salt
This is a simple alternative method of testing for the presence of iodine in food.
1 Fill half a test tube with coarse crystal sea salt.
2 Add 3 cm³ of 20 vol hydrogen peroxide to the sea salt.
3 Shake the contents of the tube vigorously to ensure complete mixing.
4 Add a few drops of a suspension of starch in distilled water.

▶ **Question**

4.39 What colour change would you expect to see if iodine is present?

Enter your results for all the mineral tests in the table. Collect results for foods you have not tested from other members of the class.

▷ **Homework**

Which of the foods tested by your class contained the greatest variety of nutrients?

5 Food and energy

We obtain energy from food for every living activity. It is possible to measure the energy available from a given mass of food by determining the amount of heat energy it will produce when ignited. Heat is one form of energy.

The unit of heat used in the past has been the calorie (cal). A calorie represents the amount of heat required to raise the temperature of 1 gram of water by 1°C. More frequently used was the kilocalorie (Cal). A kilocalorie represents the amount of heat required to raise the temperature of 1 litre (1 kilogram) of water

by 1°C. Since the introduction of SI units, the **joule** (J) and the larger **kilojoule** (kJ) and **megajoule** (MJ) have come into current use. Table 4.3 illustrates the relationships between all these units.

Table 4.3 Conversion table

Old units	New units
1 calorie (cal)	= 4.2 joules (J)
1 kilocalorie (Cal)	= 4200 joules (J)
	= 4.2 kilojoules (kJ)
239 kilocalories	= 1 megajoule (MJ)
1 MJ = 1000 kJ = 1 000 000 J	

▶ **Question**

4.40 (a) How many kilojoules are required to heat 100 g of water through 1°C?
(b) How many kilojoules are required to heat 50 g of water from 20°C to 30°C?

Activity 4.12   Measuring the heat energy produced by burning foods

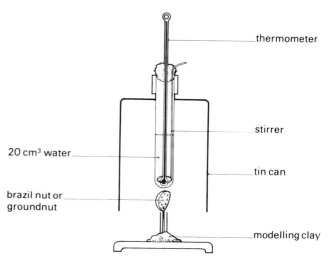

4.23 **Simple apparatus for measuring energy in foods**

1 Weigh a large peanut, mount it on a pin and fix it vertically on the table, using modelling clay, as shown in Fig 4.23.
2 Place 20 cm³ of water in the test tube.
3 Read the temperature on the thermometer.
4 Ignite the peanut with a bunsen burner, but do not let the burner heat the test tube and water.
5 As soon as the peanut is burning, place the test tube over it so as to catch as much of the heat as possible.
6 Stir the water to distribute the heat evenly.
7 Read the temperature as soon as the peanut has finished burning.
8 Record the temperature increase, and work out the number of joules of heat the water has received.

Remember that 4.2 J are required to raise 1 g of water 1 °C.

▶ **Questions**

4.41 How many kilojoules per gram (kJ/g) did the peanut release as it burned?

4.42 What are the main sources of error in this experiment? Can you suggest ways in which it could be made more accurate?

More sophisticated experiments show the following results:

protein foods (e.g. egg albumen)	– about 16 kJ/g
carbohydrate (e.g. sugar)	– about 16 kJ/g
animal fats (e.g. lard)	– about 38 kJ/g

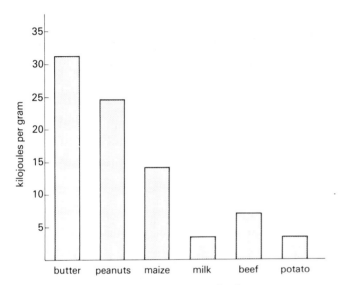

4.24 Energy content of some common foods

▶ **Questions**

4.43 Which class of foods yields the most energy per gram?

4.44 What can you conclude about the classes of foods contained in those shown in Fig 4.24?

Table 4.4 Kilojoule requirements according to age

Age in years	Amount in kJ per day
2 – 5	4 200 – 5 460*
6 – 12	7 140 – 8 400*
12 – 16+	8 400 – 10 920*
Adult women	8 400 – 10 080
Adult men	12 600 – 21 000

* higher for boys

▶ **Questions**

4.45 Why do infants need less energy than older people?

4.46 Why do teenagers need more energy than other groups?

4.47 Can you suggest a reason why men require more energy than women, assuming that they have similar occupations?

4.48 From the histogram in Fig 4.25 work and how many kilojoules are required per day by (i) a female artist, (ii) a male bank clerk, (iii) a lady doctor, (iv) a busy male shop assistant, (v) a top tennis coach

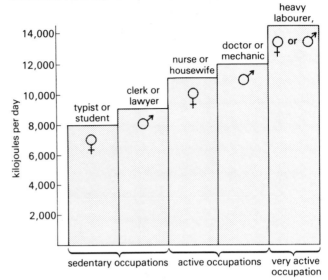

4.25 Energy requirements for people of different occupations

It is possible to work out the amount of energy, in kilojoules, required to carry out certain tasks, such as climbing a staircase. It is known that 9·8 joules are required to lift a weight of 1 kilogram through a vertical distance of 1 metre. If we know the height of the staircase and the mass of the individual, the energy requirement for the task can be calculated.

▶ **Question**

4.49 Work out the number of kilojoules which a child with a mass of 60 kg uses in climbing a staircase with a vertical height of 3 m.

▷ **Homework**

Work out the number of kilojoules you need to climb the stairs in your home and the energy required to carry a 10 kg television set upstairs.

6 A balanced diet

Some people eat unwisely. They eat far too many sweet foods and not enough fresh fruit and vegetables. Such a diet is unbalanced.

▶ **Question**

4.50 Explain why you think such a diet is unbalanced.

A balanced diet contains all the classes of food, to ensure that enough energy is available, that sufficient protein is present for growth and that enough vitamins and minerals are available to maintain the tissues in a healthy condition.

Table 4.5 An ideal balance of nutrients

55% carbohydrates 15% fats and oils	Energy giving
20% protein	Body-building
10% water, minerals, vitamins and fibre	To maintain health

4.26 Nutrients in soya beans, eggs, milk and meat

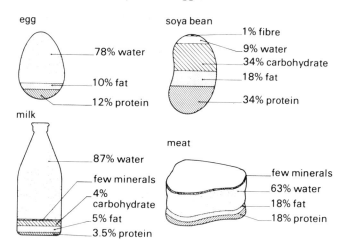

▶ Questions

4.51 Select the food in Fig 4.26 which you consider to be the most useful in a normal diet and state your reasons.
4.52 What is fibre? Can you suggest why we need fibre, otherwise known as roughage, in our food?
4.53 Fig 4.27 shows a party spread. Select food from this spread which will give you a good, balanced meal. Give reasons for your choice.

4.27 A party spread

N.B. Vitamins A and D are shown in international units (i.u.)

Table 4.6 Analysis of some common foods

Food	Composition in grams per 100 g food (edible portion)										
	Carbohydrate	Fat	Protein	Calcium	Iron	Vitamin A	Vitamin B₁	Vitamin C	Vitamin D	MJ	kJ
	g	g	g	mg	mg	i.u.	mg	mg	i.u.		
White bread	52.7	1.4	7.8	92.0	1.80	0	0.18	0	0	1.03	1030
Brown bread	47.1	2.0	8.2	26.0	2.88	0	0.20	0	0	0.96	960
Fresh milk	4.8	3.7	3.4	120.0	0.08	125	0.04	2	1	0.28	280
Cheese	Trace	34.5	25.4	810.0	0.57	1400	0.04	0	14	1.79	1790
Butter	Trace	85.1	0.4	15.0	0.16	3500	Trace	Trace	40	3.17	3170
Egg	0.0	12.3	11.9	56.0	2.53	1000	0.10	0	170	0.68	680
Bacon	0.0	53.4	24.6	11.5	2.80	Trace	0.40	0	Trace	2.50	2500
Lean beef	0.0	12.3	26.8	6.5	5.30	Trace	0.05	0	Trace	0.95	950
Liver	2.4	14.5	29.0	8.8	21.70	5000	0.30	20	10	1.10	1100
Cod	0.0	0.9	18.0	14.6	0.50	Trace	0.09	Trace	0	0.35	350
Herring	1.5	15.1	21.8	38.6	1.90	150	0.03	Trace	900	0.99	990
Potato	19.7	Trace	1.4	4.3	0.48	0	0.10	20	0	0.34	340
Orange	10.0	Trace	0.8	30.0	0.5	60	0.08	45	0	0.18	180
Raw carrot	5.4	Trace	0.7	48.0	0.56	0	0.06	6	0	0.10	100
Peas	6.0	0.2	2.0	65.0	2.0	180	0.08	15	50	0.14	140
Lettuce or Cabbage	3.0	0	1.5	40.0	0.5	150	0.10	30	60	0.08	80

4.54 Select four foods from Table 4.6 which you consider to be particularly valuable in any diet and give reasons for your choices.

4.55 100 g of white bread yields 1030 kJ and 100 g of fresh milk yields 280 kJ. What proportion of the kilojoules in each case are contributed by carbohydrate, fat and protein?

4.56 Using Tables 4.4 and 4.6, work out a diet for yourself for one day. This diet must include a balance of all the nutrients, and sufficient kilojoules.

Special diets

Certain categories of people require special diets.

Table 4.7 Six recommended diets

Key number	Recommended diet
1	High proportion of lean meat, liver, eggs, milk, cheese and green vegetables Limited amount of bread, cakes, potatoes Kilojoule requirement: 10 000 – 11 000 per day
2	Moderate amount of lean meat, liver, eggs, milk, green vegetables, bread, cakes and potatoes Kilojoule requirement: 8500 – 11 000 per day
3	Balanced amount of lean meat, liver, eggs, milk and green vegetables Very limited amount of bread, cakes, potatoes Kilojoule requirement: 4000 – 5 000 per day
4	High proportion of lean meat, liver, eggs, milk and green vegetables Balanced amount of bread, cakes, potatoes High liquid (water) intake Kilojoule requirement: 10 500 – 11 500 per day
5	High proportion of milk, limited amount of cereal Kilojoule requirement: 3000 – 3500 per day
6	Balanced amount of lean meat, milk, vegetables, grapes, liver, eggs Limited amount of bread, cakes and potatoes Kilojoule requirement: 4500 – 5500 per day

▶ **Question**

4.57 Select a recommended diet for each person illustrated in Fig 4.28. Match each number with a letter and then explain why the diet you chose is particularly suitable in each case. D, E and F are on page 54.

4.28 People requiring special diets

(a) (b)

(c)

(d)

(e)

(f)

Several categories of people, suffering from rare diseases, are unable to exist on a diet of familiar food. One such category is PKU sufferers. PKU stands for phenylketonuria. In this disease the liver lacks an enzyme which metabolises the amino acid phenylalanine. Large quantities of phenylalanine circulate in the blood, and when this reaches the head, it damages neurons in the brain. An untreated phenylketonuriac becomes mentally retarded (see Unit 14). Now, babies are tested at the age of six weeks. Phenylalanine in the urine indicates PKU. Babies who give a positive result are immediately put on a diet in which the level of phenylalanine is kept to a minimum. This involves very complex preparation, and does not include ordinary food like sausages and potatoes.

▷ **Homework**

Write a shopping list to include all the food items you consider a normal, healthy family would require during one week.

7 Food: old and new

Nearly every day we are reminded of the fact that in many parts of the world, thousands of people are dying from lack of food.

4.29 World grain consumption and production

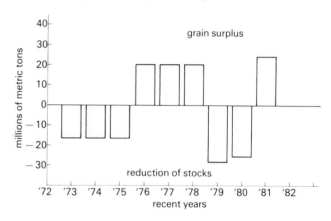

4.30 A pilot plant growing single cell protein (SCP)

4.58 Fig 4.29 shows the production and consumption of world grain, the staple diet of a majority of the world population. What do you conclude from a study of this graph?

4.59 Suggest ways in which world grain production could be increased.

In many parts of the world, such as India, Ethiopia and Latin America, the most acute shortage is of protein foods. Animals are difficult to rear in tropical countries, especially where water is short and tsetse flies attack the cattle. Many children suffer from the protein deficiency disease, kwashiorkor (see Unit 14).

Many new sources of protein are being currently investigated. In this country it is now possible to buy 'meat' pies and 'mince' made from soya beans, and not containing any meat at all. Fig 4.30 shows a scheme which uses bacteria or yeast which can grow in sugar and by their own growth, convert the sugar to protein. This SCP (single cell protein) is then dried and used to feed animals. Eventually such SCP may be used to feed humans!

▶ **Question**

4.60 Why should plant proteins be more suitable for helping out the world protein shortage than animal proteins?

4.31 Shows a modern method of producing animal protein. This oyster farm is one of thousands of seafood and fish farms which are gaining in popularity over conventional fishing.

▶ **Question**

4.61 List the advantages of fish farming over sea fishing. Are there any disadvantages?

▷ **Research project**

Write to some of the major international aid organisations. Try to find out about projects they are funding which are especially designed to improve food production. Ask about better fertilisation, better irrigation and about projects developing new types of farming and food production, such as fish farming.

Answers and discussion

1 Why do we need food?

4.1 Judo experts can keep on fighting for long periods because they have energy. This energy comes from food. Food is man's fuel – it gives him energy. The fuel of a car is petrol. It is burned in the engine to produce the energy to drive it. The fuel of a man, food, is 'burned' or broken down slowly in the body to produce the energy we need for every activity.

4.2 The child has grown into an adult. This involves the formation of more protoplasm and cells. The material for the production of more protoplasm comes from food.

4.3 The badly wounded arm will heal. New tissue will form to repair the wound. The material for the formation of this new tissue has come from food.

4.4 The children in Fig 4.4(a) look very unhealthy. They are thin, with dull eyes and faded hair. The children in Fig 4.4(b) by comparison, look extremely healthy. They are well-built, with shining eyes and healthy hair. The difference arises from the food they eat. The unhealthy children are almost starving, while the healthy group feed well. Food is necessary to keep people healthy and free from disease.

2 The source of all our food

4.5 Ethanol is a solvent for chlorophyll, the green pigment in green plants. All the pigment dissolves into the ethanol, leaving the leaf colourless so that the result of the starch test may be seen.

4.6 After a few minutes the brownish orange of the iodine solution is replaced by a dark blue-black colour. A blue-black colour indicates that starch is present. Starch is always turned blue-black by iodine solution.

4.7 In order to show that starch is only produced in a green leaf which has been exposed to light, you should test a second leaf from a similar plant which has been kept in a dark cupboard for twenty-four hours. Any starch formed earlier by the plant in the dark would have been used up in that time. Therefore, when the iodine solution is added, you should expect to see no change in its brownish orange colour, as there would be no starch present.

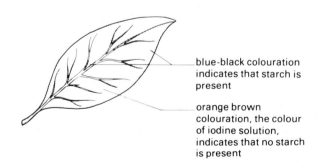

blue-black colouration indicates that starch is present

orange brown colouration, the colour of iodine solution, indicates that no starch is present

4.32 A typical leaf test result

4.8 Since the areas of the leaf exposed to the light go blue-black showing the presence of starch, and the areas covered by the foil remain brownish orange, showing that there is no starch there, it follows that light must be necessary for starch formation.

4.9 The plant is placed in a dark cupboard for twenty-four hours before the experiment in order to destarch it, that is in order to enable it to use up all the starch it had made before the experiment so that this does not confuse the results.

4.10 Soda lime absorbs carbon dioxide. The leaf in this bag will therefore be in an atmosphere free of carbon dioxide.

4.11 No starch is formed in the leaf kept in the carbon dioxide-free atmosphere. The iodine solution remains brownish orange. A blue-black colouration indicates that starch is formed in the leaf kept in the normal atmosphere. Carbon dioxide must therefore be necessary for the formation of starch.

4.12 Since hydrogen and oxygen are present in carbohydrates in the same proportion as they are in water, it is possible that water is the other substance used to make carbohydrates.

4.33 A typical leaf test result

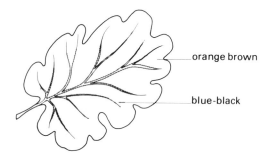

orange brown

blue-black

4.13 Starch is only formed in the green areas of the leaf. This suggests that the green pigment must be the substance which absorbs light. This substance, chlorophyll, is the key to photosynthesis.

4.14 Proteins are made in a green plant by the combination of carbohydrate molecules with nitrates and other minerals from the soil. All proteins contain nitrogen, so nitrates are particularly involved in their formation.

4.15 All the mineral salts are taken up by the root hairs of the plant from the soil water.

3 Food chains and webs

4.16 Herbivorous animals include rabbits, cows, guinea pigs, grasshoppers, caterpillars, deer and so on.

4.17 Carnivorous animals include cats, dogs, lions, tigers, hawks, owls, water boatmen, frogs, some snakes and so on.

4.18 Humans eat a variety of plant material such as fruit, vegetables, mushrooms and nuts in addition to animal food such as milk, butter, cheese, meat and eggs. They are neither pure herbivores nor pure carnivores. They are omnivores – they eat a bit of everything. Another group of organisms does not fit into any of these three categories. These organisms feed on the decaying tissues of other organisms. They are called decomposers. Examples are mushrooms, moulds and bacteria.

4.19 (a) two links; (b) three links.

4.20 (a) caterpillar ← leaves
    (b) frog ← caterpillar ← leaves
    (c) hawk ← frog ← caterpillar ← leaves

4.21 See Fig 4.34.

4.34 A food web

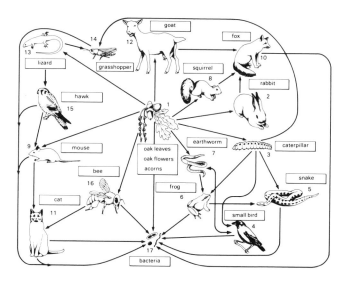

4.22 Grass is the producer, grasshoppers are primary consumers, frogs and snakes are secondary consumers and the hawk is a tertiary consumer. A snake may also be a tertiary consumer if it eats a frog.

4.23 The mass of the individual organisms tends to increase at each level. A grasshopper must consume a lot of blades of grass in order to survive. A frog needs to eat a large number of grasshoppers, and a hawk needs to consume a lot of frogs and snakes. Thus there must be fewer grasshoppers than blades of grass, and fewer frogs than grasshoppers. A population of, say, a hundred frogs will only yield enough food to satisfy ten hawks for ten days.

4.24 There is a significant loss of available energy from one feeding level to another. Of 2 million kJ available to the producers, only 50 000 kJ are available to the primary consumers and only 2250 kJ to the secondary consumers. Only about 4.5% of the energy available from the producers is used in growth to produce new tissue in the primary consumers. The rest is used up in respiration to produce energy for heat production and daily activity and in excretion.

4.25 The field of maize will yield more energy for human consumption than a field with grazing cattle. The cattle will use 95% of the energy they receive from the grass in respiration and excretion, leaving only 5% available for man. It is thus more economical for man to eat a diet of mainly plants than a diet of mainly animal foods.

4 The composition of foods

4.26 The sweet carbohydrates are grapes, bananas, jam, and sweets. The starchy foods are bread, maize, wheat and potato. The fatty foods are butter, bacon and oil.

4.27 Animal fats are solid at room temperature; plant fats are liquid at room temperature. Fats with a lower melting point are usually unsaturated which means that they contain relatively fewer hydrogen atoms than saturated fats and they do not contain cholesterol. Cholesterol and saturated fats are sometimes thought to contribute to thickening of the artery walls which can cause coronary thrombosis. For these reasons, many people prefer to use vegetable oils in cooking.

4.28

First class protein	Second class protein
Meat	Peas
Fish	Nuts
Egg	Broad beans
Cheese	
Milk	
Poultry	

4.29 If there is an extreme shortage of food, the body will begin to break down its own tissues to obtain energy. Wasted muscles are one of the first effects of starvation. Also people living on a high protein diet will use the protein to obtain energy.

4.30 Gowland Hopkins' graph demonstrates that milk contains something other than carbohydrate, fat, protein, minerals or water, which is essential for a good rate of growth in rats. He named this something 'accessory factors'. Today we call these 'accessory factors' vitamins.

4.31 Calcium deficiency results in poor development of the bones and teeth, underdevelopment of the muscles and nerves, and reduced ability of the blood to clot. This may cause internal bleeding and painful joints. Iron deficiency can prevent proper formation of haemoglobin in the blood causing the paleness and weakness called anaemia. Iodine is necessary for one of the hormones, thyroxin (see Unit 9), so a deficiency of iodine causes swelling of the thyroid gland (goitre) and disturbance of the body's metabolism. Fluorine deficiency allows the more rapid development of tooth decay and dental caries.

4.32 Vitamin A deficiency can prevent proper formation of visual pigments and give rise to night-blindness. It also causes a very dry skin. Vitamin C deficiency causes scurvy, a disease which sailors used to suffer from on long trips at sea with no fresh fruit. It causes damage to the skin and brittle blood vessels which bleed easily, and do not heal. Deficiency of vitamin D can result in brittle bones, a condition called rickets and in soft enamel which may cause tooth decay.

4.33 Water is essential for the following reasons. (a) Sweat is mainly water. If we did not sweat, we could not keep cool. (b) Urine is mainly water. We must excrete urine to rid the body of toxic wastes. (c) Synovial fluid is basically water. This is necessary to lubricate joints and absorb shock. (d) The inner ear is filled with fluid. We could not hear without water. (e) Water is essential for all chemical processes in the body. One example is the chemical breakdown of foods by hydrolysis (see Unit 5).

4.34 A blue-black colouration will indicate the presence of starch.

4.35 An orange precipitate should result if non-reducing sugar was originally present.

4.36 A ring of emulsion forms between the water and the milk. This indicates the presence of fat in the milk.

4.37 After a few moments a violet colouration appears. This probably indicates the presence of protein.

4.38 A count of the number of drops of the test sample of food needed to decolourise DCPIP gives an indication of the amount of vitamin C contained. The more drops it takes, the lower the ascorbic acid content. It should be possible to assess the quantity of vitamin C in a known volume of test fruit juice by comparing it with a known standard. A commercial vitamin C tablet of quoted strength may be dissolved in 2 cm³ of distilled water. A comparison of the number of drops it takes the fruit juice to decolourise the dye, with the number of drops the commercial vitamin C tablet takes, will indicate the strength of the vitamin C content of the fruit juice.

4.39 If iodine is present, a blue-black colouration will be produced on the addition of starch.

5 Food and energy

4.40 (a) 0.42 kJ; (b) 2.1 kJ.

4.41 Work out your results as follows:
temperature increase = Y °C mass of peanut = Xg
heat gained by water = 20 g (mass of water) × Y °C × 4.2 J
heat produced by 1 g of sample = $\dfrac{20 \times Y\,°C \times 4.2}{1000 \times Xg}$ kJ/g

Possible results are in the region of 15 – 35 kJ/g.

4.42 Sources of error include (a) heat loss around the sides of the test tube, (b) heat loss raising the temperature of the thermometer, the test tube, the stirrer and so on, (c) incomplete burning of the peanut (a shell of carbon is often left unburnt), (d) inaccurate measurements of temperature and (e) extra heat supplied by using the bunsen to ignite the peanut, though this in fact may help to offset some of the heat losses. Improvements should include enclosing the food to avoid heat losses, burning in oxygen to ensure complete combustion, improving the heat collecting apparatus, electrical ignition of the food to avoid using a bunsen and improving the accuracy of the measurements.

4.43 Fats yield over twice as many kilojoules per gram as carbohydrates and proteins.

4.44 Butter and peanuts are probably rich in fats, maize, potato, milk and meat in carbohydrates and/or protein.

4.45 Infants are very much smaller than all the other classes of people listed. The amount of energy needed actually depends on the basal metabolic rate of the individual. This is the rate at which all body reactions occur, and it is influenced by the rate of respiration. Infants have a higher basal metabolic rate per unit mass than adults, but as their mass is very much smaller, they require less energy.

4.46 Teenagers have a higher metabolic rate than adults and their unit mass is often similar to that of an adult.

4.47 Since the energy requirement of men carrying out the same activities as women is higher than that of the females, they must have a higher basal metabolic rate than women.

4.48 (i) 8000 kJ per day; (ii) 9000 kJ per day; (iii) 11 000 kJ per day; (iv) 12 000 kJ per day; (v) 15 000 kJ per day.

4.49 Work out the child's energy requirement for climbing the stairs as follows:
9.8 J are required to raise 1 kg through 1 m.
Therefore 3 × 9.8 J are required to raise 1 kg through 3 m.
Therefore 3 × 9.8 × 60 J are required to raise 60 kg through 3 m.
Therefore the number of joules required is 3 × 9.8 × 60
= 1764 J.

6 A balanced diet

4.50 A diet of sweet foods and little fresh fruit and vegetables will consist mainly of carbohydrate. This could cause an overweight problem, and lack of fruit and vegetables will mean a shortage of vitamins and minerals which will reduce the individual's resistance to disease.

4.51 Soya bean is the most useful food illustrated. It contains a good balance of carbohydrate, fat and protein.

4.52 Fibre is the fibrous parts of vegetables and meat. Vegetable fibre is made of undigestible cellulose and it has no nutritional or energy-giving value. This roughage passes unchanged through the alimentary canal, but it is necessary to enable the bowel muscles to work. Absence of fibre can cause constipation. Prolonged absence of fibre in the diet is considered to be a factor contributing to cancer of the bowel.

4.53 Meat loaf (protein and carbohydrate); rice (carbohydrate); vegetables (fibre, minerals and vitamins); corn (fibre, carbohydrate, vitamins and protein). Fat will be available in the bacon, and the butter consumed with the corn.

4.54 Four particularly valuable foods in Table 4.6 are: fresh milk, liver, herring and peas. These foods contain a proportion of all the food classes listed. Milk is obviously a very valuable food. All humans survive on milk alone for the first few weeks of life, during which time growth is at a maximum.

4.55 White bread: $52 \cdot 7\,g \times 16 = 843 \cdot 2\,kJ$ carbohydrate
$1 \cdot 4\,g \times 38 = 53 \cdot 2\,kJ$ fat
$7 \cdot 8\,g \times 17 = 132 \cdot 6$ protein

Milk: $4 \cdot 8\,g \times 16 = 76 \cdot 8\,kJ$ carbohydrate
$3 \cdot 7\,g \times 38 = 140 \cdot 6\,kJ$ fat
$3 \cdot 4\,g \times 17 = 57 \cdot 8\,kJ$ protein

4.56 Sample daily balanced diet

Breakfast:		Lunch:		Dinner:	
Eggs	680	Beef	950	Herrings (2)	1980
Brown bread	960	Potatoes (2)	680	Raw Carrot	100
Butter (5 g)	158	Peas	140	Lettuce	80
Tea or coffee		Cheese	1790	Orange	180
		Butter (5 g)	158	Milk	280
		Brown bread	960		
		Tea or coffee			
Total:	1798	Total:	4678	Total:	2620

Day total = 9096 kJ plus tea or coffee

4.57
A – 5 Babies need a high protein diet to sustain growth. Milk provides this, plus essential vitamins A and D and calcium and phosphorus for bone and teeth growth. Cereal provides additional carbohydrate, vitamin B for healthy growth and roughage.
B – 4 General requirements are similar to C, but even more kilojoules are required to satisfy the appetite of the baby. A high liquid intake is necessary to help to make milk.
C – 1 A pregnant woman must consume a lot of protein foods, since the embryo is growing rapidly. Dairy products provide calcium, phosphorus and vitamin D for the formation of embryonic bones. Shortage of calcium in the diet leads to withdrawal of calcium from the mother's teeth and bones. Vitamin C and iron are important for a healthy placenta and the extra blood required. Excess carbohydrate can cause toxaemia and dangerous overweight of both mother and foetus. The kilojoule requirement is very high despite this.
D – 2 Adolescents require a diet with a balance of body building, energy giving and protective nutrients. They have a high kilojoule requirement since they are undergoing rapid growth and are usually energetic.
E – 6 Emphasis here is on protective foods and body-building foods. Energy foods should be kept to a minimum since energy expenditure is low. Invalids easily become

overweight due to lack of exercise.
F – 3 Overweight people should limit their intake of carbohydrates and fats, but eat sufficient protective foods to keep healthy during the slimming process.

7 Food: old and new

4.58 World grain consumption overtook grain production in 1979 and 80. There was a shortfall of 55 million metric tons in those years. 1981 helped to restore stocks but unless production can be increased or consumption decreased, there will be famine in many parts of the world.

4.59 World grain production could be increased by growing better strains of grain. These grains could yield more per hectare by having better heads, or by being more resistant to pests, or by being more hardy (tolerant of poor soil and climatic conditions). Use of pesticides to reduce the incidence of pests which reduce yield per hectare is another method of increasing production.

4.35 The strain of grain on the left is an improved variety which will not fall over when fertilisers are used to improve growth

4.60 Plant proteins are more economical to produce. A field of soya beans yields far more protein than an identical field used for raising cattle. A lot of the grass grazed is not converted to flesh, so there is a net loss of available protein.

4.61 Fish farming yields a larger amount of protein per unit area than sea fishing. The available water is very heavily stocked with fish. A harvest is more certain. Predators are kept away from fish or seafood raised in ponds. It is also easier to control the fish population, and catching them is easier and less hazardous.
A disadvantage of fish farming is that if a fish becomes diseased, the other fish will quickly be infected and all stocks may be lost. To guard against this, many fish farmers include antibiotics in the feed they supply.

5 Utilisation of food

1 Complex food made simple

The food we eat is not in a form which can be immediately used by the body. It consists of bite-sized pieces of solids which are chemically complex. Before the cells can use the nutrients contained in the food, it must undergo a process of breaking up or **digestion**. The food is broken into smaller pieces mechanically by the teeth, and is broken chemically in the alimentary canal, where insoluble compounds are changed into soluble compounds.

▶ Question

5.1 Why must insoluble compounds be broken down to soluble compounds?

Chemical digestion is brought about by the action of water aided by enzymes. This process is called **hydrolysis**. The following equation represents the hydrolysis of a typical starch molecule. Starch molecules vary in size, but most of them are about the size shown.

$$C_{3000}H_{5000}O_{2500} + 500\ H_2O \longrightarrow 500\ C_6H_{12}O_6$$

| starch molecule (large and insoluble) | water | sugar molecules (small and soluble) |

The soluble molecules formed are molecules of a simple sugar called glucose. Maltose is first produced as an intermediate in this hydrolysis, but it is then converted to glucose. When cane sugar (sucrose) is broken down, one of the molecules formed is glucose and the other is a similar sugar called fructose. Thus we can write:

starch ⟶ maltose ⟶ glucose,

sucrose ⟶ glucose and fructose.

Hydrolysis without the aid of enzymes is a very slow process. Our food would not reach the individual cells fast enough if the process was not speeded up by the enzymes of the digestive system. The following activities demonstrate the action of different enzymes on starch, protein and fat.

Activity 5.1   Investigating the action of amylase on starch

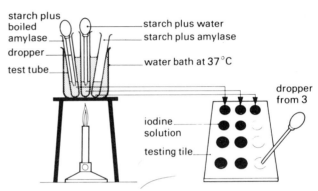

5.1

1 Take three test tubes labelled 1, 2 and 3 and add $2\ cm^3$ of 1% starch solution to each.
2 Boil $2\ cm^3$ of 1% amylase and add it to test tube 1.
3 Add $2\ cm^3$ of distilled water to test tube 2.
4 Add $2\ cm^3$ of unboiled 1% amylase to test tube 3.
5 Using dropper pipettes and a white tile, test one drop of mixture from each of 1, 2 and 3 with iodine solution.
6 Record your results in a table.
7 Place the three test tubes in a water bath maintained at 37 °C.
8 Test one drop of each mixture at five minute intervals up to twenty minutes.
9 Record these results in the table used for step 6.

▶ Questions

5.2 What can you conclude from these results?
5.3 Why are the test tubes put in a water bath at 37° C? How could you show that it is necessary to do this?
5.4 What test could be used to discover the substance produced by starch breakdown?
5.5 What can you conclude about the action of amylase from this activity?

Activity 5.2   Investigating the action of lipase

1 Pour agar into a Petri dish to a depth of 0·5 cm.
2 Add about $2\ cm^3$ of salad cream.
3 Stir to ensure an even distribution.

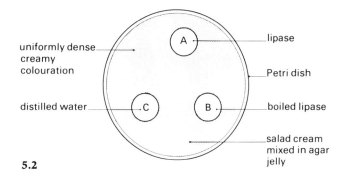

uniformly dense creamy colouration

distilled water

A — lipase

Petri dish

B — boiled lipase

C

salad cream mixed in agar jelly

5.2

4 On cooling, scoop out three holes in the jelly with a cork borer.
5 Mark the bottom of the Petri dish A, B and C, using a chinagraph pencil, to distinguish the holes.
6 Add lipase to A, boiled lipase to B and distilled water to C.
7 Incubate the Petri dish with the lid on for twelve hours at 37 °C.
8 Observe the appearance of the agar.

This technique of using agar jelly may also be used as an alternative to the method described in Activity 5.1 for investigating the action of amylase, by adding iodine solution to starch agar before it sets and adding the amylase preparations to the holes in the jelly.

▶ **Questions**

5.6 Explain what you see after twelve hours incubation. What do you think happened?
5.7 What particular ingredient of the salad cream has been digested?

Activity 5.3   Investigating the action of pepsin

5.3

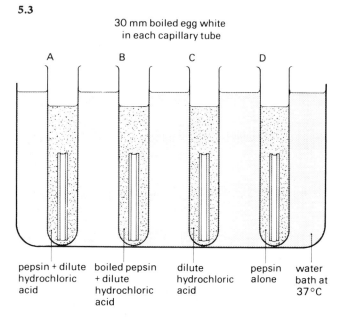

30 mm boiled egg white in each capillary tube

A   B   C   D

pepsin + dilute hydrochloric acid   boiled pepsin + dilute hydrochloric acid   dilute hydrochloric acid   pepsin alone   water bath at 37 °C

1 Take four pieces of capillary tubing 4 cm in length which contain uncooked egg albumen (egg white).
2 Place the tubes in a beaker of water and boil for five minutes.

3 Measure the length of each egg white accurately. Record the lengths in a table.
4 Place the capillary tubes with their egg whites in the following test tubes:
A – with 4 cm³ 1% pepsin and 2 drops dilute hydrochloric acid
B – with 4 cm³ boiled 1% pepsin and 2 drops dilute hydrochloric acid
C – with 4 cm³ dilute hydrochloric acid
D – with 4 cm³ 1% pepsin
5 Place them in a water bath at 37 °C for one hour.
6 Record the lengths of egg white in each tube in a table.

An alternative method of investigating the action of pepsin is to add some milk powder to some agar, pour it into a dish, make three marked holes and add the pepsin preparation, dilute acid plus pepsin, and dilute acid alone to the three holes. Incubate for twelve hours at 37 °C and then observe the results.

▶ **Questions**

5.8 What can you conclude from your results?
5.9 What is the purpose of tube C?
5.10 Why is there a change in tubes B and C?
5.11 What other control could be included?
5.12 Can you suggest the class of food which pepsin acts on?
5.13 Using the information you have gained from Activities 5.1 to 5.3, compile a list of the properties shared by the enzymes tested.

Characteristics of enzymes

1 Enzymes are specific substances which will only act on one type of substance or **substrate**. For example, lipase only acts on fats and oils.

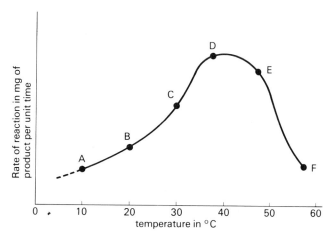

5.4 How reaction rate of an enzyme varies with temperature

Fig 5.4 is a graph constructed from results obtained from an experiment carried out on salivary amylase. The amylase was added to starch solution in a number of test tubes which were placed in waterbaths of differing temperatures. After a set time the degree of starch digestion was noted in each case.

5.14 What is the effect on rate of starch digestion of an increase of 10° C between A and B? How does this compare with the effect of 10° C increase between B and C?

5.15 At which point does starch digestion take place most quickly: C, D or E? What is the most effective temperature (optimum temperature) for starch digestion?

5.16 Over what range of temperature is amylase active or fairly active?

5.17 Suggest a reason for the low rate of activity at F.

2   Human enzymes work best at body temperature. Their optimum temperature is 37 °C.

3   Enzymes are destroyed at high temperatures.

4   Enzymes act only when the pH medium is right. For example, pepsin works only in an acid medium.

5   Only very small quantities of an enzyme are required.

6   All reactions catalysed by enzymes are reversible.

▷ **Homework**

Enzymes are used for a variety of domestic and industrial purposes. List the enzymes used in your home and explain what they do.

2 Mechanical digestion

Solid food reaches the ileum in a liquid form called **chyle**. The change from solid to liquid is largely a mechanical process. In the mouth, teeth masticate the food, that is they break it up into small pieces. The stomach muscles later churn these pieces together with gastric juice and the semi-liquid product leaving the stomach is known as **chyme**. Peristalsis (see Unit 2) in the duodenum helps to convert the chyme into chyle. Food must be broken down into a liquid form early in digestion to enable the enzymes to gain access to all the molecules. The surface area to volume ratio of a large piece of solid food will make it difficult for an enzyme to act on molecules in the centre of the solid. Breaking food down increases its surface area and reduces the volume of the component pieces. The total volume remains the same.

Activity 5.4   Observing and drawing your own teeth

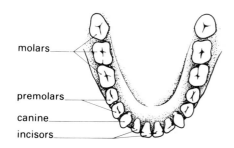

5.5 Teeth in an adult's lower jaw

1   Open your mouth, take a mirror (a concave one is best), and observe your lower set of teeth. They should appear basically similar to Fig 5.5.

2   Study Fig 5.5 and then identify the different types of teeth in your lower jaw.

3   Make a labelled drawing of your lower teeth.

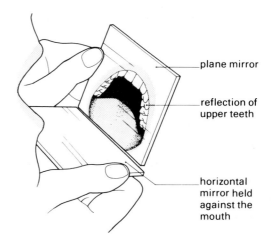

5.6 How to use two mirrors to view your upper teeth

4   Take a second mirror and hold it at right angles to the first mirror as in Fig 5.6. This will enable you to view your upper set of teeth.

5   Record the numbers of teeth in your upper jaw.

▶ **Questions**

5.18 How many incisors, canines, premolars and molars have you? How does this compare with Fig 5.5?

5.19 Does the number of your teeth vary in the upper and lower jaws?

Construct a **dental formula** of your teeth. A dental formula is based on the fact that the left and right sides of the jaw are identical. You count the teeth on one side of your jaw and record the numbers. Below is an example made by an adult.

Upper jaw	i	$\frac{2}{2}$	c	$\frac{1}{1}$	p	$\frac{2}{2}$	m $\frac{3}{3}$
Lower jaw							

Total number of teeth in this formula = 16
Total number of teeth on both sides = 2 × 16 = 32

If you have had any teeth extracted, try to work out what type they were and where they were positioned, and include them.

5.7 Human teeth

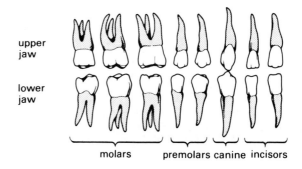

5.20 Eat a quarter of a slice of bread slowly. Think about every action of the teeth. Record which teeth bite the bread, which teeth cut the bread and which teeth chew the bread. Fig 5.7 should help you since it shows the working edges of the teeth.

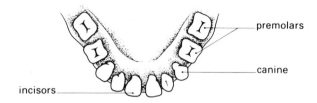

5.8 Milk teeth in the lower jaw

The milk teeth shown in Fig 5.8 are gradually replaced from the age of five or six by the permanent teeth.

▶ **Questions**

5.21 Which teeth present in the permanent dentition are missing in the milk dentition?
5.22 What other differences can you see?
5.23 Try to account for these differences.

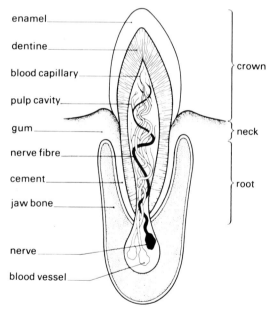

5.9 Internal structure of a canine tooth

In Fig 5.9 the part of the teeth above the gum, the crown, is covered with **enamel**. Enamel is the hardest substance in the body and contains calcium and phosphorus. The root, embedded in a bony socket in the jaw, is covered in **cement**. Cement is less hard, but gives attachment to fibrous tissue known as the periodontal membrane. The body of the tooth is packed with **dentine**, a greyish substance which is less hard than enamel. It contains protoplasm in channels between the hard material. The centre of the tooth forms the pulp cavity, in which a blood capillary and a nerve fibre are found. Tooth decay and care of teeth will be discussed in Unit 17.

▶ **Questions**

5.24 Why does the crown of the tooth require a harder covering than the root?
5.25 Suggest the function of the periodontal membrane.
5.26 Why do teeth require a blood capillary and a nerve fibre?

▷ **Homework**

Find out why certain groups of people such as the Eskimoes, never normally suffer from tooth decay.

3 The digestive system, digestion and absorption

The digestive tract, or alimentary canal, is basically a tube about 820 cm long, extending from the mouth to the anus. Opening into this long tube are a number of small ducts which bring the products of various digestive glands to act on the food. The general structure of the digestive system is discussed in Unit 2.

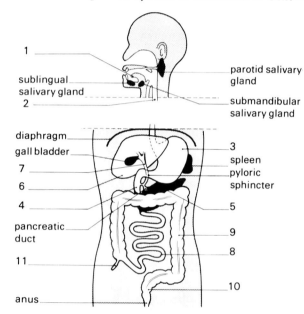

5.10 The human alimentary canal

▶ **Question**

5.27 Study Fig 5.10 and 5.11. Using the labels of the equivalent structures in rat, and your knowledge of the digestive system gained from Unit 2, identify the numbered organs in Fig 5.10.

Note that man has no caecum. The appendix is all that remains of that part of the intestine. Cellulose-digesting bacteria which digest plant cell walls live in the caecum of a rat. This releases the protein from inside the cells. Man eats a mixed diet, so he does not require cellulose-digesting bacteria.

The internal walls of the alimentary canal are specialised for different functions. The longitudinal muscles (see Fig 5.12 and 5.13) contract regularly to move the canal back past the food and the circular muscles contract to squeeze it further down. This wave of contraction of the longitudinal muscles

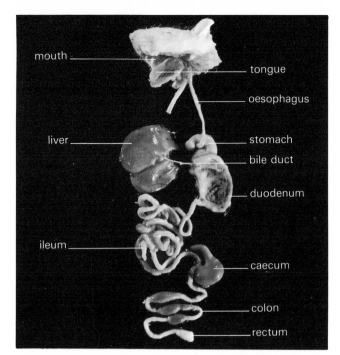

5.11 Dissection showing the alimentary canal of a rat

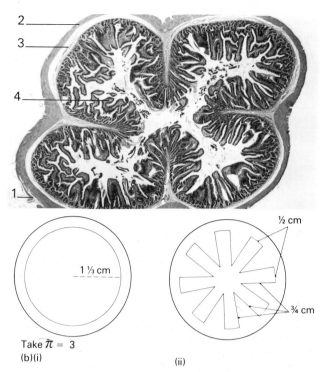

Take $\pi = 3$
(b)(i)   (ii)

5.13 Transverse section of the ileum

followed by contraction of the circular muscles continues down the digestive tract. It is called **peristalsis**. The gastric pits (see Fig 5.12) contain special secretory cells which comprise the gastric glands. Some cells produce pepsinogen and others produce hydrochloric acid. These substances make up the gastric juice.

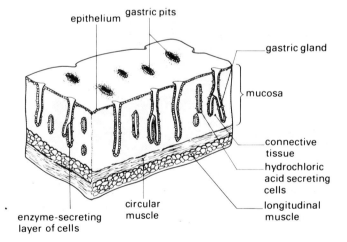

5.12 A portion of the stomach wall

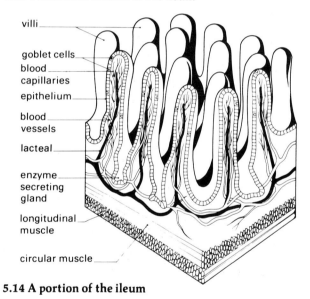

5.14 A portion of the ileum

5.15 Photomicrograph of the ileum wall

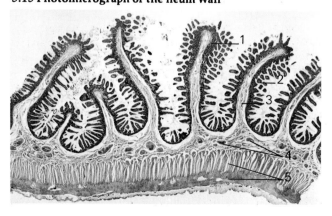

▶ **Questions**

5.28 By referring to Fig 5.12 and to the work on the oesophagus in Unit 2 identify the numbered tissues and structures in Fig 5.13.

5.29 Describe the internal lining of the ileum.

5.30 Calculate the lengths of the inside lines in Fig 5.13(b) (i) and (ii). If the diagrams represent cross-sections of cylinders 100 cm long, calculate the internal surface area of each cylinder.

5.31 Using Fig 5.14 as a reference, identify the parts numbered in Fig 5.15.

5.32 Explain why you think the epithelial lining of the ileum is so deeply folded.

Let us consider the fate of a meal of bacon, egg, wholemeal toast and milk. While the teeth cut and chew the bacon, egg and toast, a digestive juice, saliva is poured onto the food from the salivary glands (see Fig 5.10).

► **Questions**

5.33 What are the main food constituents of bacon, egg and wholemeal toast which need digestion?

5.34 What is the enzyme present in saliva? Which constituent of the meal, or substrate, does this enzyme act on and what is the product of digestion?

Saliva also moistens the foods, and together with the rolling action of the tongue, fashions the masticated food into a ball. This ball or **bolus** is about the right size for swallowing.

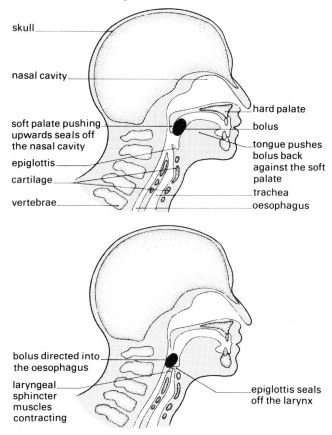

skull

nasal cavity

soft palate pushing upwards seals off the nasal cavity

epiglottis

cartilage

vertebrae

hard palate

bolus

tongue pushes bolus back against the soft palate

trachea

oesophagus

bolus directed into the oesophagus

laryngeal sphincter muscles contracting

epiglottis seals off the larynx

5.16 Swallowing

► **Question**

5.35 Study Fig 5.16 carefully and feel your Adam's apple as you swallow. Describe the methods used to ensure that the bolus does not go down the wrong way into the trachea, nor up into the nasal cavity.

Digestion of starch in toast to maltose is continued by ptyalin during the passage of the bolus down the oesophagus. In the stomach, a second digestive juice, gastric juice, is poured onto the food.

► **Questions**

5.36 What substances are present in gastric juice?

5.37 Which components of the meal are acted upon by pepsin?

5.38 Suggest a reason why pepsin is present in its inactive form, pepsinogen, in the absence of food.

5.39 Why is dilute hydrochloric acid produced in the gastric juice?

In addition to pepsin, gastric juice contains a second enzyme called rennin. Rennin coagulates the milk protein casein to form the insoluble caseinogen.

► **Question**

5.40 How does the clotting of milk help its digestion?

Gastric juice is thoroughly mixed with the food as it is churned up by the stomach muscles. The food remains in the stomach for an hour or two before it is released into the duodenum as chyme. The cardiac and pyloric sphincters are bands of circular muscle which close the entrance and exit of the stomach when they contract. This keeps the chyme in the stomach when it is churning. When digestion in the stomach is complete, the pyloric sphincter relaxes for short intervals, allowing small quantities of chyme to enter the duodenum. This ensures that digestion in the duodenum is thorough.

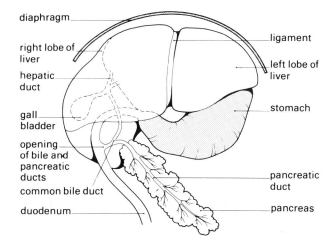

diaphragm

right lobe of liver

hepatic duct

gall bladder

opening of bile and pancreatic ducts

common bile duct

duodenum

ligament

left lobe of liver

stomach

pancreatic duct

pancreas

5.17 Bile duct and pancreatic duct entering the duodenum

The bile duct pours a secretion of the liver called **bile** onto the chyme. Bile is a greenish, alkaline fluid which contains the bile salts sodium taurocholate and sodium glycocholate. These salts act on fats in the chyme, breaking them into tiny droplets of fat, which form an emulsion.

► **Question**

5.41 How does the emulsifying of fats help in their digestion?

The pancreas is a delicate, leaf-shaped gland which produces a number of enzymes in the alkaline pancreatic juice. The enzymes contained in it are pancreatic amylase, pancreatic lipase and trypsinogen. Like pepsinogen, trypsinogen is an inactive form of a protein splitting enzyme. If the active form, trypsin, was produced in the absence of food, it would digest the duodenum. A substance called enterokinase activates trypsinogen to form trypsin in the presence of food. Trypsin converts polypeptides to dipeptides and amino acids.

▶ **Questions**

5.42 In what pH medium will the enzymes in the duodenum function best?
5.43 (a) What does pancreatic amylase act on?
(b) What does pancreatic lipase act on?

The chyle formed in the duodenum now contains maltose and some glucose from the toast, fatty acids and glycerol from the bacon, egg yolk and milk, and dipeptides and some amino acids from the lean part of the bacon, egg white, milk and wholemeal bread. In addition, undigested fibre from the wholemeal toast is present.

In the ileum the chyle is further acted upon by enzymes produced in the intestinal juice. This alkaline juice is produced in the walls of the ileum. It contains the following enzymes: intestinal lipase, maltase, lactase, sucrase and erepsin (also called endopeptidase). Maltase converts any remaining maltose to glucose. Lactose, or milk sugar, is converted to the simple soluble sugars glucose and galactose by lactase, and sucrose is converted to glucose and fructose by sucrase (also called invertase).

▶ **Questions**

5.44 What do intestinal lipase and erepsin act on and what are the products of the reactions?
5.45 Construct a summary table of the chemical digestion of carbohydrates, fats and protein.

Intestinal juice is only produced when it is activated by a chemical messenger substance called secretin. Secretin is a hormone (see Unit 9). Secretin is released from glands in the ileum wall when food is released from the stomach into the duodenum. When the meal is in the ileum it is in a form ready for absorption into the blood circulatory system.

▶ **Questions**

5.46 Suggest a reason for the control of intestinal juice production by secretin.
5.47 What are the end products available for absorption from the digestion of bacon, eggs, toast and milk?
5.48 Fig 5.18 is an X-ray photograph of a special barium meal used to check a patient's digestive system. The X-ray photograph was taken at midday. The patient had had the meal at 6:00 am. What can you deduce from this?
5.49 By what process are the products of digestion absorbed into the blood and lymph?

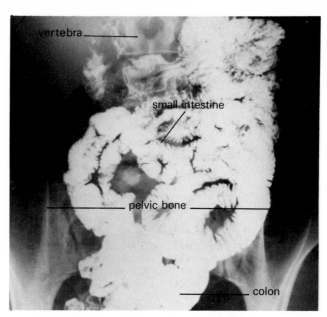
5.18 X-ray photograph after a barium meal

Activity 5.5 Diffusion of glucose through a selectively permeable membrane

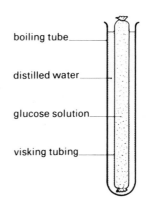
5.19

1 Set up the apparatus as shown in Fig 5.19.
2 Test the distilled water with Benedict's solution at the beginning of the experiment.
3 Repeat the test at two minute intervals for ten minutes.
4 Record your results in a table.

▶ **Questions**

5.50 What part of the digestive system does the visking tubing represent? Which liquids do the glucose solution inside the tubing, and the distilled water outside the tubing represent?
5.51 How do the results of the experiment illustrate the action of the digestive system?
5.52 What happens to the components of the meal which are not absorbed into the blood?

▷ **Homework**

List the enzymes which would be needed to digest the following: a piece of cake, a peanut, a green pea, some spaghetti.

4 Fate of the absorbed nutrients

Substances absorbed into the blood and lymph in the ileum are put to use or assimilated in the body in a number of ways.

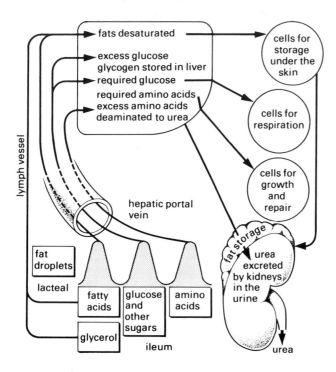

5.20 Summary of nutrient absorption

▶ **Questions**

5.53 From Fig 5.20 describe what happens to fatty acids and glycerol after absorption.
5.54 Describe the fate of glucose after absorption.
5.55 What happens to amino acids after absorption?

▷ **Homework**

Write a brief essay to explain the steps involved in the utilisation of a slice of beef.

Answers and discussion

1 Complex food made simple

5.1 Insoluble compounds must be made soluble so that the molecules of the food can diffuse through the walls of the digestive system into the blood and be carried in solution throughout the body.

5.2 Results table for Activity 5.1

	0 min	5 min	10 min	15 min	20 min
1 *Starch and boiled amylase*	Black	Black	Black	Black	Black
2 *Starch and distilled water*	Black	Black	Black	Black	Black
3 *Starch and amylase*	Black	Orange	Orange	Orange	Orange

Digestion of starch only occurs in tube 3 which contained unboiled amylase. Therefore starch digestion requires amylase. Boiling destroys the activity of the amylase.

5.3 Normal human body temperature is 37 °C. This experiment assumes that enzymes only act at body temperature. This could be shown by setting up a fourth test tube, containing starch and amylase, which is left at room temperature and then tested with the others.

5.4 Sugar is a simpler carbohydrate than starch, so it is possible that sugar is the breakdown product formed in Activity 5.1. This may be tested by applying the Benedict's test described in Unit 4. Use the method for testing for reducing sugars first, then if that is negative, carry out the procedure for non-reducing sugars.

5.5 Activity 5.1 shows that starch is broken down with the help of salivary amylase and that boiling the enzyme destroys its activity.

5.6 After twelve hours' incubation, a clear circle appears around A. This suggests that lipase has broken down an ingredient of salad cream in hole A only.

5.7 Oil is the main ingredient of salad cream which could have been digested. Lipase is an enzyme which digests fats and oils.

5.8 Results table for Activity 5.3.

Tube	A	B	C	D
Original length of egg white	30 mm	30 mm	30 mm	30 mm
Length of egg white after one hour	15 mm	29 mm	29 mm	30 mm

From these results it can be seen that pepsin and hydrochloric acid digests half of the egg white in one hour. Boiled pepsin is ineffective.

5.9 Tube C shows that it is not hydrochloric acid alone which digests the egg white.

5.10 A slight erosion of the egg white occurs with acid, but this is not digestion, only simple acid destruction.

5.11 To show that pepsin is only active at 37 °C, a control tube E, containing pepsin and hydrocloric acid could be set up and left at room temperature for one hour.

5.12 The food class which pepsin acts on is protein. Both egg albumen and milk are examples of foods rich in protein.

5.13 1 Enzymes work best at body temperature, 37 °C.

2 Enzymes are inactivated by boiling.

3 Enzymes need a particular pH medium of acidity or alkalinity to work in.

4 Enzymes speed up digestion.

5.14 An increase of temperature from 10 °C to 20 °C does not appreciably increase the rate of reaction of amylase. Between 20 °C and 30 °C there is a considerable increase in the rate of reaction of amylase.

5.15 Starch digestion is most complete at D. The optimum temperature is around 37 °C.

5.16 Amylase is quite active between 30 °C and 50 °C.

5.17 At F the temperature is 60 °C. This relatively high temperature could destroy amylase, which is a protein, making it inactive.

2 Mechanical digestion

5.18 In Fig 5.5 there are four incisors, two canines, four premolars and six molars. You will probably have fewer molars than this. Molar teeth are the last to erupt. The very back molars, called the wisdom teeth, often do not appear until the late teens or early twenties and may in fact, in some individuals, never erupt at all.

5.19 The number of your teeth may differ in upper and lower jaws because not all your teeth may have erupted yet. You may have had teeth extracted to make room for others if your jaw is small.

5.20 Incisors bite the bread, canines cut and tear it, and premolars and molars chew it up as they grind together.

5.21 There are no molars in the milk dentition.

5.22 The canines are less well defined in the milk dentition.

5.23 The differences arise because the diet of infants is less varied than that of adults. Infants are unable to cut tough meat with their canines or to chew it with their premolars.

5.24 The crown of the tooth is subject to constant wear from mastication, so it must be extremely hard wearing.

5.25 The fibres of the periodontal membrane hold the tooth in its bony socket. Slight movement of the tooth within its socket is possible due to the periodontal membrane. This enables the tooth to give a little when chewing something hard. An immobile tooth would be more likely to break under such conditions.

5.26 Teeth are living structures which are constantly renewing the inorganic materials in the enamel. The protoplasm in the dentine requires food and oxygen from the blood capillary. The nerve fibre relays stimuli of pain, pressure, heat or cold which indicate the state of the tooth.

3 The digestive system, digestion and absorption.

5.27 1 tongue; 2 oesophagus; 3 stomach; 4 duodenum; 5 pancreas; 6 liver; 7 bile duct; 8 ileum; 9 colon; 10 rectum; 11 appendix.

5.28 1 outer protective membrane; 2 longitudinal muscles; 3 circular muscles; 4 villi.

5.29 The internal lining of the ileum is very deeply folded to form long finger-like structures called villi.

5.30 Length of internal line (i) = $2 \pi r = 2 \times 3 \times 1\frac{1}{3}$ = 8cm

Length of internal line (ii) = $(8 \times \frac{1}{2}) + (16 \times \frac{3}{4})$ = 16cm

Internal surface area of cylinder (i) = 8 × 100 = 800 cm²

Internal surface area of cylinder (ii) = 16 × 100 = 1600 cm²

5.31 1 epithelium; 2 villus; 3 blood capillary and lymph vessel; 4 blood vessels; 5 muscle layers.

5.32 The deep folding of the epithelial lining of the ileum provides a greatly increased surface area (refer to question 5.30). This increased surface area makes more rapid and efficient absorption of digested foods possible.

5.33 The main constituents of bacon are protein, in the lean part, and fat. Egg is mainly protein and fat (in the yolk) and wholemeal toast is mainly starch with some protein. The fibre in wholemeal toast is not a nutrient.

5.34 Ptyalin (salivary amylase) is the enzyme in saliva. It acts on starch to produce maltose.

5.35 As swallowing begins, the larynx is raised to meet the epiglottis, thus sealing off the trachea. This stops the bolus from entering the windpipe. At the same time, the tongue pushes the bolus against the soft palate (uvula), which is pushed into position to seal off the nasal cavity.

5.36 Pepsinogen and hydrochloric acid are present in gastric juice. Pepsinogen is an inactive form of the enzyme pepsin. It becomes active when food enters the stomach.

5.37 Pepsin acts on proteins. They are broken down into substances called polypeptides. In this case it will act on the lean bacon and the egg.

5.38 Pepsin is present in an inactive form in the absence of food, otherwise it would begin to digest the stomach walls, which are made of protein.

5.39 Hydrochloric acid is produced to create the acid medium necessary for the action of pepsin.

5.40 Liquid milk would pass quickly through the stomach. This would not allow pepsin enough time to act on the milk protein.

5.41 Emulsification of fats increases the surface area available to the enzymes so that lipase can act more quickly on them.

5.42 Bile and pancreatic juice are both alkaline to neutralise the gastric acid and to ensure an alkaline medium in the small intestine. All the enzymes in the small intestine require an alkaline medium.

5.43 (a) Pancreatic amylase acts on starches, changing them to maltose.

(b) Lipase acts on fats. Fatty acids and glycerol, which are soluble products, are produced.

5.44 Intestinal lipase converts any remaining fats to fatty acids and glycerol. Erepsin converts any remaining dipeptides into amino acids which are generally soluble.

5.45 Summary table of chemical digestion

Part of alimentary canal	Digestive gland and juice	Enzymes produced	pH medium	Substrate	End product(s)
Mouth	Salivary glands Saliva	Salivary amylase	Slightly acid	Cooked starch	Maltose
Stomach	Gastric glands Gastric juice	Pepsinogen Pepsin Rennin	Acid	Proteins Casein (milk protein)	Polypeptides Caseinogen (coagulated)
Duodenum	Liver	No enzymes, bile salts	Alkaline	Fats	Emulsified fats
	Pancreas Pancreatic juice	Amylase Lipase Trypsinogen Trypsin	Alkaline	All starch Fats Polypeptides	Maltose, some glucose Fatty acids and glycerol Dipeptides, some amino acids
Ileum	Intestinal glands Intestinal juice	Maltase Lactase Sucrase Lipase Erepsin	Alkaline	Maltose Lactose Sucrose Fats Dipeptides	Glucose Glucose and galactose Glucose and fructose Fatty acids and glycerol Amino acids

5.46 If intestinal juice was not controlled by secretin, and was produced in the absence of food, the protein splitting enzyme erepsin, which does not have an inactive form, would digest the small intestine.

5.47 The end products available for absorption from a meal of bacon, eggs, toast and milk are glucose, galactose, fructose, fatty acids, glycerol and amino acids.

5.48 From the X-ray photograph, which shows the barium meal to be in the colon, it can be deduced that it takes about six hours for the food consumed by the patient to reach the colon. Therefore it can be assumed that the digestion of food, which is completed in the ileum, takes about six hours.

5.49 Products of digestion pass into the villus and then into the blood and lymph by diffusion.

5.50 The visking tubing represents the selectively permeable walls of the villi and the blood capillaries. The glucose solution represents the liquid chyme containing products of digestion, and the distilled water represents the blood ready to absorb these products.

5.51 The results show that progressively more glucose has diffused through into the water, just as the products of digestion in the ileum diffuse through into the blood.

5.52 Undigested parts of the meal which remain in the ileum after absorption are passed by peristalsis to the large intestine. In the colon, most of the water is re-absorbed into the blood, together with any remaining vitamins and mineral ions. Roughage, in this case fibre, passes together with rubbed off epithelial cells, bacteria and mucus along the colon to the rectum. This matter, called faeces, is then ejected through the anus at regular intervals by peristalsis of the rectal muscles. The process is called defaecation.

4 Fate of the absorbed nutrients

5.53 Fatty acids and glycerol pass into the lacteal (lymph capillary) and blood capillaries, where they recombine to form fats. Droplets of fat reach the liver, where animal fats are desaturated (have some hydrogen removed) before being transported to storage areas. The main storage areas are beneath the skin and around the kidneys.

5.54 Glucose diffuses into blood capillaries in the villi which join up to form the hepatic portal vein. This vein takes the glucose to the liver. In the liver, any glucose not immediately required is converted to insoluble glycogen and stored until it is needed. The remaining glucose is passed by the blood system to all the cells where it is used for respiration.

5.55 Amino acids are also taken to the liver in the hepatic portal vein. In the liver, some amino acids are broken down if they are in excess into two products, a carbohydrate form which is used in respiration, and urea which is transported to the kidneys and excreted in urine. The remaining essential amino acids are transported to all the cells, where they are used for production of protoplasm in growth and repair.

6 Respiration

6.1 A climber with special breathing apparatus. Suggest the gas contained in the gas cylinder

1 The purpose of respiration

In Unit 1 the process of respiration in living things was illustrated, Fig 1.1, by a diver breathing out the waste products of respiration. But what is the vital product of respiration? You may be able to answer this question after doing the following experiments.

Activity 6.1 Can a human being affect the air temperature?

A

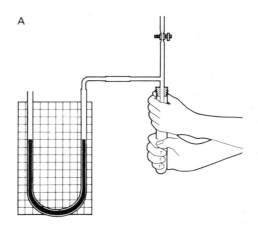

B

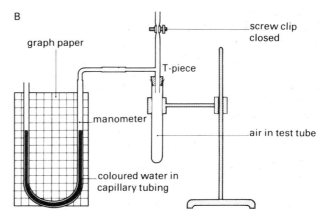

graph paper

screw clip closed

T-piece

manometer

air in test tube

coloured water in capillary tubing

6.2

1 Set up the two manometers and test tubes as shown in Fig 6.2.
2 Open the screw clips of both A and B to equalise the pressures; then close the clips. The liquid levels in both manometers should be level. Mark the levels.

3 Grasp the test tube of apparatus A with your hands for one minute.
4 Observe the levels in both manometers.

▶ **Questions**

6.1 What changes, if any, do you observe in the manometers?
6.2 Why does the level of the liquid in the right limb of the manometer A fall?
6.3 What is the purpose of manometer B?
6.4 What can you deduce from this experiment?

Activity 6.2 The effect of burning glucose in air, oxygen and carbon dioxide-rich air

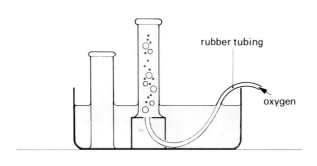

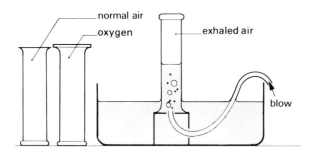

6.3 Collecting exhaled air

1 Obtain three gas jars and label them A, B and C. Fill A with oxygen from an oxygen cylinder. Your teacher must supervise this. Fill B with exhaled (carbon dioxide-rich) air as shown in Fig 6.3. Leave jar C open to obtain ordinary atmospheric air.
2 Fill a deflagrating spoon with glucose.
3 Apply a burning splint to the glucose to ignite it, and then plunge the spoon into jar A.
4 Repeat steps 2 and 3, plunging the spoon into jar B and then jar C.

▶ **Questions**

6.5 Describe what happens in steps 3 and 4 of Activity 6.2.
6.6 What do you infer from this experiment?

Glucose is a carbohydrate which acts as a food for cells. In living cells, glucose is broken down slowly by oxygen into carbon dioxide and water (as in Activity 6.2). During the breakdown, potential **energy** stored in the glucose molecule is liberated. This liberated energy can be detected as warmth of the hands in Activity 6.1, and heat of the jar in Activity 6.2. Most of the energy released is put to active use by living organisms, and all life processes such as movement, growth, repair and reproduction require energy.

Respiration can be summarised by the following equation:

$$6 \; O_2 + C_6H_{12}O_6 \longrightarrow 6 \; CO_2 + 6 \; H_2O + ENERGY$$

enzymes controlling
the rate of respiration

The amount of energy stored in a food is measured in joules (J) or kilojoules (kJ), as was explained in Unit 4.

Some plants respire without oxygen, using only enzymes to break down the carbohydrates. This process, called **anaerobic** respiration as distinct from the aerobic respiration outlined above, does not produce so much energy. In animals, including man, glucose is broken down by enzymes alone to form pyruvic acid, and then, if there is still no oxygen available, lactic acid, but no further. Oxygen is necessary for the further release of energy.

▷ **Homework**

Suggest occasions other than climbing when special breathing apparatus may be required.

2 How energy is released from a molecule of glucose

▶ **Questions**

6.7 Glucose is a soluble substance not suitable for storage. Can you recall from Unit 5 how the body is able to keep glucose constantly available?
6.8 In Unit 2 you learned about mitochondria. Where are mitochondria found, and what is their function?

6.4 Electron micrograph of mitochondria in cardiac muscle

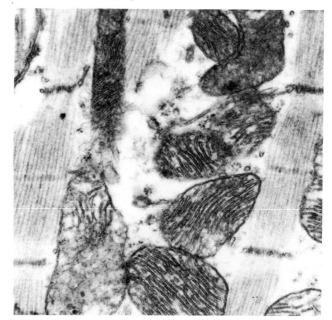

The release of energy from a molecule of glucose involves many chemical steps. Glucose is broken down without the use of oxygen to form pyruvic or sometimes lactic acid (see Unit 3). Oxygen initiates the further breakdown to carbon dioxide and water, during which process a great deal of energy is released. Seven enzymes at least are necessary to aid the process, part of which is known as the Krebs' cycle, named after the German scientist who discovered how it works. The process is a relatively slow one.

Immediate energy does not come directly from the Krebs' cycle. It comes from ATP molecules. The energy released from glucose is transferred to molecules of adenosine diphosphate (ADP), which in the presence of phosphate ions is converted to ATP.

$$ADP + P + ENERGY \longrightarrow ATP$$
$$\text{(with stored energy)}$$

Now you can see the importance of phosphate ions in the mitochondria. Steady amounts of energy released from glucose are stored in ATP molecules from which they can be released very quickly when required.

▶ Question

6.9 By referring to the paragraphs above, name the substances numbered in Fig 6.5 as accurately as you can.

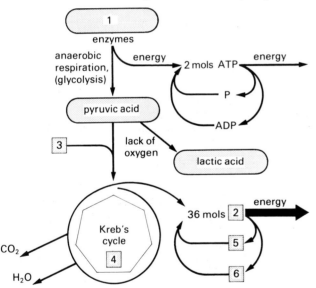

6.5 Energy production by respiration

▷ Homework

Describe and explain your physical condition at the end of a hard race.

3 Obtaining oxygen

Some animals experience more difficulty in obtaining oxygen than others, and some require special breathing organs while others can manage without any. For example mammals and birds have complex lungs, but smaller animals such as earthworms have no special structures. The reason for this is demonstrated below.

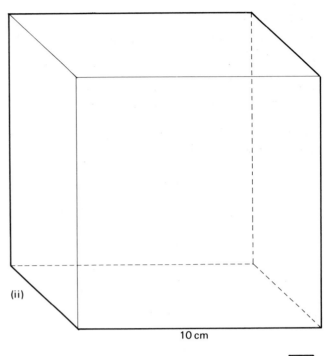

6.6

▶ Questions

6.10 For each of the cubes in Fig 6.6, work out the following.
(a) The area of one side in cm^2.
(b) The total surface area of each cube in cm^2.
(c) The volume of each cube in cm^3.
(d) The ratio of cm^2 of surface area to cm^3 of volume. To get this, divide your answer to (b) by your answer to (c) for each cube.
(e) Which cube has the larger surface area to volume ratio?

6.11 Why does this difference in ratios mean that smaller animals often do not need special breathing structures, while larger animals generally do ?

Activity 6.3 Investigating the rate of diffusion into cubes of differing size

6.7

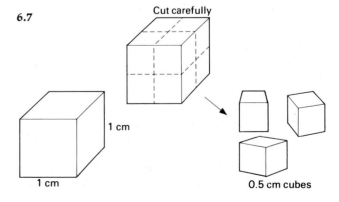

1 Pour agar solution into a tin lid or other suitable rectangular container to a depth of 1 cm and allow it to solidify.
2 Using a centimetre rule and a fine knife or scalpel, divide the agar into as many 1 cm cubes as possible.
3 Cut one of the cubes as shown in Fig 6.7 to obtain eight 0.5 cm cubes.
4 Place four cubes of each size into a beaker containing eosin or any other water-soluble dye.
5 Remove one cube of each size every two minutes and compare the colour penetration in each case.

▶ Question

6.12 What observation can you make about colour penetration in the two sizes? What can you infer about the relationship between surface area to volume ratio and diffusion?

6.8 Air passages in a cow's lungs shown by injecting rubber solution into the lungs which then hardens. The lung tissue is then digested away to leave the rubber showing the air passages.

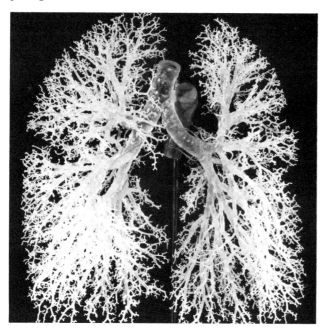

6.9 Lungs in the thoracic cavity

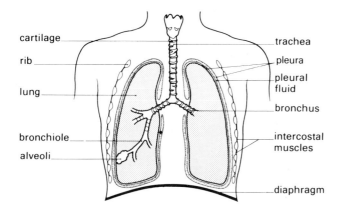

Lungs

The lungs are massively branched infoldings of the body surface, which represent a huge surface area for the absorption of oxygen. Each lung, if flattened out, would occupy the area of a tennis court.

The lungs are pink, with a spongy texture, overlaid by a thin, glistening membrane. The organs are lobed and are wider at the base than at the apex. Lungs are pink because they are covered by a network of blood capillaries which link the pulmonary artery with the pulmonary vein. The spongy texture is due to the clusters of **alveoli** or air sacs at the terminus of each bronchiole. The glistening covering is the pleural membrane, which also lines the thoracic cavity. Each lung is thus contained in a separate cavity called the pleural cavity. These membranes produce pleural fluid which lubricates the lungs and aids inflation and deflation. (See Fig 6.9.)

The **trachea** is a tube which runs from the cartilaginous larynx or voice box and which divides at the base to form the right and left bronchi. Hoops of cartilage are present in the walls of both the trachea and bronchi.

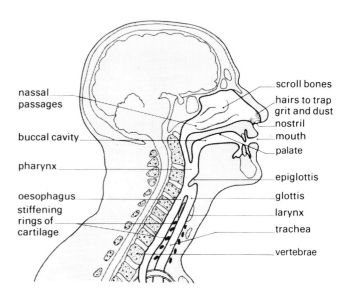

6.10 Section through the head showing the air passages

▶ Questions

6.13 What is the purpose of the cartilage hoops in the wall of the trachea and bronchi? Why are they incomplete at the back of the trachea?
6.14 Looking at Fig 6.9, describe the branching of each bronchus within the lungs.
6.15 From Fig 6.10 suggest the functions of the following: (a) hairs and mucus in the nasal passage (b) scroll bones (c) palate (d) epiglottis
6.16 Using information gained from Figs 6.8, 6.9 and 6.10 and 6.12, summarise the route of air passing from the atmosphere to the alveoli.

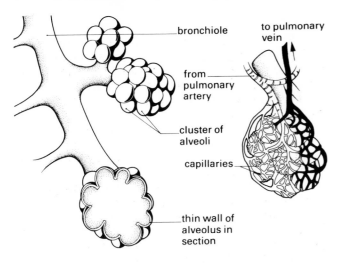

6.11 Structure of the alveoli

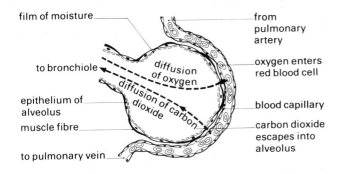

6.12 Gas exchange in the alveoli

► **Questions**

6.17   Why are the walls of the alveoli elastic ?

6.18   List the features of the alveoli shown in Figs 6.11 and 6.12 which make them extremely efficient as sites of gaseous exchange.

6.13 Photomicrogragh showing alveoli in lung tissue

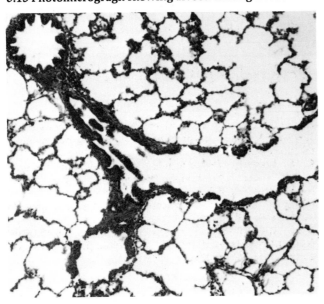

Oxygen dissolves in the film of moisture in the alveoli and diffuses from the high concentration in the alveoli to the lower concentration in the blood plasma and from there to the even lower concentration in the red blood cells. Here it combines with the carrier substance haemoglobin to form oxyhaemoglobin, in which form it is transported throughout the blood to the tissues.

Carbon dioxide, in the form of carbonic acid and bicarbonates, is in a higher concentration in the blood plasma than in the alveoli. It therefore diffuses across the alveolar walls into the lower concentration inside the lung and is breathed out.

▷ **Homework**

Consult Unit **17** and read about the effects of smoking on the lungs.

4 Expired air and inspired air

A number of simple experiments can be carried out to compare the temperature, carbon dioxide content and water content of the air we breathe in with the air we breathe out.

Activity 6.4   Comparing the temperature of inspired and expired air

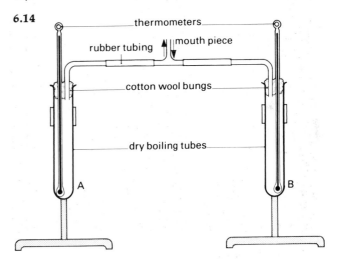

6.14

1   Set up the apparatus as shown in Fig 6.14. Ensure that the cotton wool bungs are secure and that the bulbs of the thermometers are not touching the sides of the boiling tubes.
2   Note the temperature in each boiling tube.
3   Close the entry into tube B by pinching the rubber tubing and draw in air through tube A by gently drawing on the mouthpiece about ten times. Record the temperature in boiling tube A.
4   Close the entry into tube A, then breathe out gently through tube B about ten times. Record the temperature in boiling tube B.
5   Compare your results with those of other class members.

▶ Questions

6.19 What can you deduce from this experiment?
6.20 Why is the apparatus supported by retort stands?

Activity 6.5 Comparing the carbon dioxide content of inspired and expired air

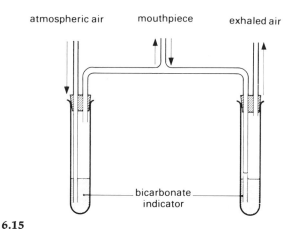

6.15

1 Set up the apparatus as shown in Fig 6.15. Note the arrangement of the tubes.
2 Breathe in and out gently through the mouthpiece about ten times and watch for any change in the purple bicarbonate indicator as atmospheric air is bubbled through it in boiling tube A and expired air is bubbled through it in boiling tube B.
3 Compare your results with those of other class members.

▶ Question

6.21 What can you infer from the results of this experiment?

Activity 6.6 Comparing the water content of inspired and expired air
1 Replace the bicarbonate indicator in the apparatus in Fig 6.15 with blue cobalt chloride paper. Ensure that the cobalt chloride paper is completely blue by using totally dry boiling tubes and removing the indicator papers from the desiccator only at the last moment.
2 Breathe in and out gently ten times and note any change in the indicator paper in boiling tubes A and B.
3 Compare your results with those of other class members.

▶ Questions

6.22 What do you conclude from the results of this experiment?
6.23 Summarise the differences you have detected between inspired (atmospheric) air and expired air.

Except under certain circumstances, the percentages of oxygen and carbon dioxide are virtually constant in the atmosphere.

Table 6.1 The differences between inspired and expired air.

Component	Inspired air	Expired Air
Oxygen	20%	16%
Carbon dioxide	0.03%	4.03% (about)
Nitrogen	79%	79%
Other inert gases	0.97% (about)	0.97% about)
Water vapour	Variable	Saturated
Temperature	Variable	Body temperature

▶ Questions

6.24 Suggest some of the circumstances which could affect the percentage of atmospheric oxygen and carbon dioxide.
6.25 In Table 6.1 water vapour and temperature are stated to be variable in inspired air. Explain why this is so.

▷ Research Project

Deep sea divers and mountaineers both use gas cylinders. Find out exactly what gases are in these cylinders, and why these gases are used.

5 How we breathe

Normally we take breathing for granted, but if you stop and think about breathing – 'listen' to your breathing – you will become aware of it as a very active process.

Activity 6.7 Discovering the effect of breathing on the chest circumference

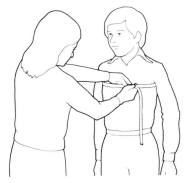

6.16 Measuring chest circumference

1 Work in pairs, using a tape measure marked in centimetres.
2 Measure your partner's chest near the base of the rib cage as shown in Fig 6.16 immediately after an exhalation and before the next inhalation. Record the measurement.
3 Repeat, keeping the tape measure loosely in position in readiness, and measure at the peak of your partner's next inhalation. Record the circumference.
4 Repeat steps 2 and 3 at least five times, and then take the average measurements for 2 and 3 and record the difference.

▶ **Question**

6.26 What do you learn from this experiment?

Activity 6.8 Observing a model of the thoracic cavity

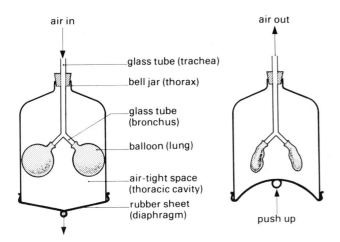

6.17 Thoracic cavity model

1 Observe the condition of the balloons which represent the lungs, in the model when the rubber sheet, which represents the diaphragm, is in the resting position (domed).
2 Observe the condition of the balloons when the rubber sheet is pulled down.

▶ **Questions**

6.27 What is the effect on the balloons of pulling the rubber sheet down? What happens to the balloons when the sheet is pushed back up?
6.28 What particular property must lungs have in common with balloons for the model to be an effective comparison?
6.29 What effect has the movement of the rubber sheet on the volume (capacity) of the simulated thoracic cavity?
6.30 Relate inspiration and expiration to the movements of the rubber sheet.

When we breathe in, the capacity of the thoracic cavity is increased in circumference as the rib cage moves upwards and outwards, and in depth as the diaphragm moves down. This creates a partial vacuum or reduced pressure inside the chest cavity, resulting in air rushing into the lungs to fill the space and equalise the air pressures. When we breathe out, the circumference and depth of the thoracic cavity are reduced as the ribs move inwards and downwards and the diaphragm moves up. This creates a higher pressure which forces the air out of the lungs, causing them to deflate.

▶ **Question**

6.31 Study Figs 6.18, 6.19 and 6.20 carefully and explain what happens when the outer intercostal muscles shown in Fig 6.19 contract.

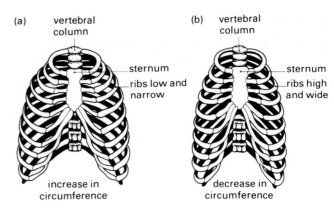

6.18 (a) The rib cage after inspiration (b) The rib cage after expiration

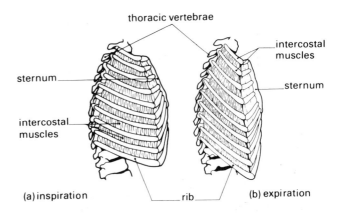

6.19 Lateral view of the rib cage during (a) inspiration and (b) expiration

6.20 How the thoracic cavity volume changes

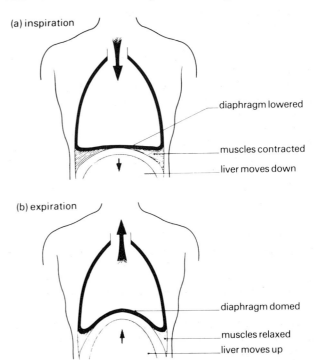

▷ **Research Project**

You will probably be familiar with the pain in the chest you sometimes get from breathing hard when running or exercising. It is often called 'getting a stitch'. Find out what a stitch is, what causes it, and what can make it go away.

6 How oxygen consumption varies

6.21 Allan Wells, the 100 m Olympic champion

▶ **Question**

6.32 Look at the two men shown in Figs 6.21 and 6.22. Which one do you think is consuming more oxygen?

Differing oxygen consumption can be determined experimentally in a number of ways. The simplest way is to compare rates of breathing under different conditions. If one person is breathing more rapidly than another person, it can be reasonably assumed that he is using more oxygen in a given period of time.

Activity 6.9   Comparing breathing rates at rest and following strenuous activity

1   Sit quietly for a few moments, then place your hands on the lower part of your rib cage. Feel the rising and falling of the rib cage.
2   Set a stop clock and count the total number of inspirations over a period of thirty seconds. Do not force your breathing – breathe naturally.
3   Repeat step 2 at least four times. Note the average number of inspirations in thirty seconds and double it to give your breathing rate per minute.
4   Run on the spot vigorously for one minute, sit down and repeat step 2.
5   Repeat step 4 at least four times (if you have the stamina!) Note the average number of inspirations in thirty seconds and double it to give your breathing rate in one minute.
6   Compare your results with those of other class members.

▶ **Questions**

6.33 What is your breathing rate at rest and after exercise?
6.34 Draw a bar chart to show the increases in breathing rates of the class after exercise. What deductions can be made from this experiment?

6.22 Meditation requires a deep relaxation of as many of the body muscles as possible.

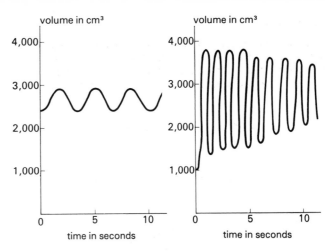

6.25 Spirometer graphs

▶ **Questions**

6.35 Can you suggest which of the graphs in Fig 6.25 was produced by the subject after exercise?

6.36 Apart from the rate of breathing recorded in (a) and (b) being different, what else is different? What is the significance of this?

The fact that the depth of breathing can vary implies that under normal conditions the lungs are not using their full capacity. This may be investigated by the following experiments.

Activity 6.10   Estimating the volume of air inspired in a normal breath

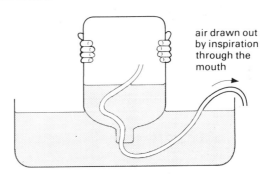

6.26

1   Pass a length of wide rubber tubing through the neck of a 5 l polythene bottle until it nearly reaches the bottom.

2   Invert the bottle and place it under water in a very large bowl as shown in Fig 6.26.

3   Hold your nose tightly and practise breathing in and out through the mouth.

4   Breathe in air from the inverted bottle through the rubber tubing. Repeat three or four times.

5   After breathing in, quickly remove the rubber tubing, insert a stopper in the bottle neck and remove the bottle from the water.

6   Measure the volume of water contained in the bottle using a measuring cylinder.

7   Repeat several times and take the average volume.

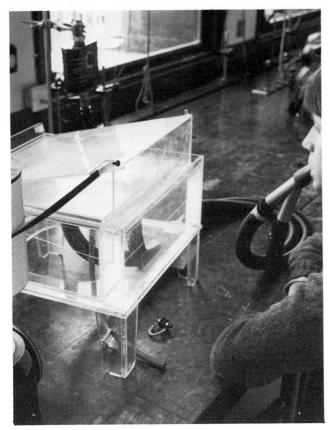

6.23 A student uses a spirometer

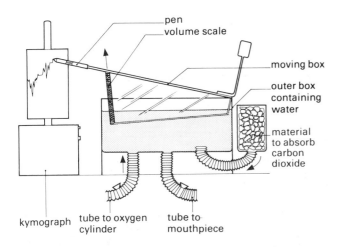

6.24 A spirometer

The apparatus shown in Fig 6.23 and 6.24 is a **spirometer**. As a subject breathes out, the carbon dioxide in their exhaled air is absorbed, so that differences in volume due to oxygen consumption cause the suspended box to rise and fall. The moments of the box are recorded on a rotating drum called a kymograph. The graphs shown in Fig 6.25 were obtained from one subject during an experiment similar to Activity 6.9, but where he breathed into a spirometer instead of noting the movements of his rib cage.

6.37 What is the volume of the water and what does it represent?

Activity 6.11 Estimating the largest possible volume of air expired in one breath

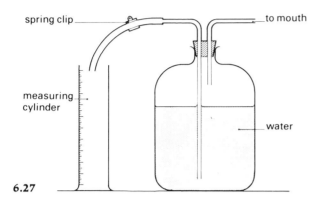

6.27

1 Set up the apparatus as shown in Fig 6.27.
2 Practise deep breathing a few times, then, after a best effort, blow out through the mouth into the apparatus.
3 Collect the displaced water. Warning: you will need a very large collecting cylinder!
4 When you can blow out no more, measure the volume of displaced water.
5 Repeat several times and take the largest reading as your vital capacity.

► **Questions**

6.38 What is your vital capacity? How does it compare with others in your class?
6.39 Construct a bar chart of the vital capacities of all the members of your class. How does this compare with the bar chart of the breathing rates?

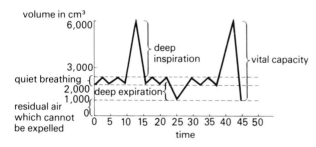

6.28 Spirometer graph

Fig 6.28 is a spirometer reading which illustrates all the various volumes of air which may be exchanged in the lungs.

► **Questions**

6.40 How much air can be obtained in a deep intake of breath?
6.41 How much air can be forcibly expelled?
6.42 How much air remains in the lungs and is not expelled?

6.43 What is the total capacity of the lungs?
6.44 How would you define the vital capacity of the lungs from this graph?

Using the facts in this section and in section 4, it should be possible for you to calculate your oxygen consumption at rest and after exercise. You need to know your breathing rate at rest and following exercise, the volume of inspired tidal air, the volume of deep inspiration (you can use Fig 6.28 for this) and the percentage of oxygen in inspired air.

▷ **Homework**

Calculate your oxygen consumption at rest and after running up and down a flight of stairs for one miniute. Then calculate your oxygen demands when at rest for one hour and for one day.

Answers and discussion

1 The purpose of respiration

6.1 The liquid in the right limb of the manometer of apparatus A has fallen. In manometer B, the levels of liquid remain the same.

6.2 The liquid in the right limb of manometer A has been pushed down by the air in test tube A. The test tube is a closed container, so that the enclosed air must have expanded. Heat is necessary for this.

6.3 Manometer B is a control to show what happens if the test tube is not held by hands.

6.4 The air in apparatus A expanded because it was heated. The heat to do this must have come from the hand of the human subject. Humans therefore produce heat. Heat is one form of energy. The immediate origin of this energy will be demonstrated in Activity 6.2.

6.5 In gas jar A, the glucose burns with a fierce flame and turns brown, the gas jar feels warm and droplets of moisture colllect in the jar. Testing with blue cobalt chloride paper will show the moisture to be water. In jar B the glucose will not burn at all, while in jar C the glucose burns very briefly and most of it is left unburnt.

6.6 Oxygen supports the combustion (burning) of glucose, carbon dioxide does not, and ordinary air supports combustion to a limited extent only. Heat is produced during the burning of glucose. A liquid is produced, which turns blue cobalt chloride paper pink, indicating that it is water.

2 How energy is released from a molecule of glucose

6.7 When glucose is absorbed into the blood, any excess not immediately needed by the body is converted into insoluble glycogen and stored in the liver and skeletal muscles. When the blood glucose falls below 0.1% some of the stored glycogen is reconverted into glucose. The hormones insulin and adrenalin play a part in this (see Unit 11). Thus glucose is constantly available.

6.8 Mitochondria are to be found in living cells. They contain the enzymes required for respiration and phosphate ions necessary for the production of adenosine triphosphate (ATP).

6.9 1 glucose; 2 ATP; 3 oxygen; 4 seven enzymes; 5 phosphate ions; 6 ADP.

3 Obtaining oxygen

6.10

	(i)	(ii)
(a)	$1\,cm^2$	$100\,cm^2$
(b)	$6\,cm^2$	$600\,cm^2$
(c)	$1\,cm^3$	$1\,000\,cm^3$
(d)	$6:1$	$0.6:1$

(e) The small ($1\,cm^3$) cube has the larger surface area to volume ratio.

6.11 Smaller animals have a relatively large surface area compared with their volume through which to absorb the oxygen they need. Many animals are small enough to get all the oxygen they need straight through their surface. Larger animals need more oxygen, but they have a relatively smaller surface area compared with their volume. Thus special breathing structures, such as lungs, are necessary for larger animals to help them get enough oxygen.

6.12 Colour penetration is much more rapid in the 0.5 cm cube and there is even distribution of colour throughout within two minutes. The centre of the 1 cm cube is still clear after eight minutes. Diffusion is therefore much more efficient in objects with a large surface to volume ratio.

6.13 The cartilage hoops ensure that the trachea and bronchi are constantly open. If air could not reach the lungs, suffocation and death would result in a short time. The hoops are incomplete at the back of the trachea because they would interfere with peristalsis of the oesophagus in that region.

6.14 The bronchi divide up into similar tubes called bronchioles, the larger of which have cartilage hoops. These in turn branch to form smaller bronchioles which do not require cartilage hoops to keep them open. They contain elastic fibres in their walls. They terminate in clusters of thin-walled swellings called alveoli.

6.15 (a) The cilia lining the nose and upper parts of the respiratory tract are to trap dust particles, bacteria and viruses which enter with the air. These particles become entangled with the mucus secreted by the goblet cells, and the cilia then waft them towards the nostrils. This mechanism reduces respiratory infections.

(b) The scroll bones increase the surface area in the nasal cavities and as air circulates around them, it is warmed by contact with the blood capillaries which run between the bones. Warmer air will diffuse more rapidly in the lungs.

(c) The palate separates respiratory and digestive tracts making simultaneous breathing and eating possible.

(d) The epiglottis is a cartilaginous flap which covers the larynx and trachea during swallowing, so preventing food from entering the lungs.

6.16 Nostrils ⟶ nasal cavity ⟶ pharynx ⟶ larynx ⟶ trachea ⟶ bronchi ⟶ bronchioles ⟶ alveoli.

6.17 The lungs are stretched as air inflates them, and the elastic walls help to reduce the resistance to air flow. Deflation is assisted by the recoil of the alveoli walls.

6.18 (a) The single-celled thin walls reduce resistance to diffusion to a minimum.

(b) The film of moisture lining the walls of the alveoli accelerates diffusion through the cells by dissolving the gases.

(c) The rich, fast-moving blood supply facilitates rapid diffusion.

(d) The enormous surface area of the alveoli is another aid to rapid diffusion of gases.

4 Expired air and inspired air

6.19 The temperature in boiling tube A remains the same. In B it rises by 2–3 °C. Expired air is therefore warmer than inspired air.

6.20 The boiling tubes must be supported, because if they were held in the hands, body heat would affect the temperature in the tubes (see Activity 6.1).

6.21 The bicarbonate indicator in boiling tube A remains the same (purple), while that in B changes to yellow. This change occurs only in the presence of carbon dioxide in higher concentration than that found in the atmosphere. Therefore expired air contains more carbon dioxide than inspired air.

6.22 The cobalt chloride paper in boiling tube A remains blue. In B it changes to pink. This indicates water; therefore expired air contains more water than inspired air.

6.23 From these experiments it is evident that expired air contains more carbon dioxide and is warmer and more moist than inspired air.

6.24 Where there is a restricted flow of air for long periods, it is possible for oxygen levels to fall. For example, mine shafts and tunnels must have special ventilation, otherwise oxygen shortages could occur. Firemen working inside a burning building also require special breathing apparatus, as much of the oxygen is used up by the fire itself. In a badly ventilated room, in extreme circumstances the oxygen percentage could fall and the carbon dioxide percentage rise, though the latter would have to rise a great deal before it caused discomfort to humans.

6.25 Climatic conditions will inevitably effect temperature and humidity, so there will be wide variations between the Poles and the Tropics and between deserts and swamps. The adverse effects felt in a crowded, badly ventilated room are principally related to excesses of heat and moisture produced by expired air. As the heat rises, sweat will not evaporate because the air is already saturated with water vapour. Cooling thus becomes impossible and fainting is a possible result.

5 How we breathe

6.26 The circumference of the chest is between 5 cm and 6 cm greater during inhalation than exhalation. When we breathe in the volume of the thoracic cavity, which is a sealed space, increases.

6.27 When the rubber sheet is pulled down, the balloons inflate, and when the sheet is pushed back up, the balloons deflate.

6.28 Lungs must be elastic in order to inflate without resistance and to recoil on deflation, a characteristic shared with balloons.

6.29 When the sheet is pulled down, the volume is increased from top to bottom and when the sheet is returned, the volume is reduced again.

6.30 Inflation of the balloons (lungs) with depression of the rubber sheet (diaphragm) and consequent increase of the capacity of the thoracic cavity is equivalent to inspiration; deflation of the balloons, raising of the rubber sheet and decrease of the thoracic cavity capacity is equivalent to expiration.

6.31 Movement of the rib cage is brought about by the intercostal muscles which contract, pulling it upwards and outwards, and the diaphragm muscles pull the normally domed diaphragm flat. This produces inspiration and is an active movement. The rib cage moves in and down passively as the intercostal muscles relax and the diaphragm relaxes into a domed position during expiration.

6 How oxygen consumption varies

6.32 The sprinter would be expected to consume more oxygen than the meditating man because he is using more energy and therefore needs more oxygen to liberate more energy from glucose.

6.33 At rest, the average breathing rate for a teenager is around eighteen breaths per minute, and after exercise it is around thirty-six breaths per minute.

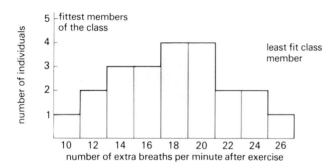

6.29 Chart showing increase in breathing rates in a class after exercise

6.34 The experiment shows that the rate of breathing is greatly increased with exercise. The wide variation in the increase of the breathing rates of class members demonstrates individual variations in oxygen demands. A bar chart shows this clearly. The more athletic members of the class probably had a smaller increase in breathing rate than the less athletic members. The reasons for this are complex, but it will be partly explained in question 6.39.

6.35 Fig 6.25(b) represents the breathing rate after exercise, which is approximately twice that shown in Fig 6.25(a).

6.36 The depth of breathing recorded in Fig 6.25 (b) is about four times that illustrated by Fig 6.25(a). Thus the

amount of oxygen consumed in a given time during exercise is approximately eight times that during rest in the case of the subject used in Fig 6.25.

6.37 The volume of water displaced is about 500 cm³. This represents 500 cm³ of air inspired. This volume is known as tidal air. During normal breathing at rest, the air change in the lungs is of the order of 500 cm³ per breath.

6.38 Unlike the tidal air, the vital capacity varies enormously from one individual to another. In a really fit person it is around 5000 cm³.

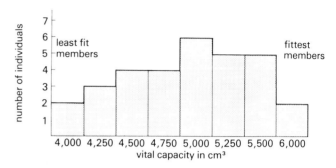

6.30 Vital capacities of healthy young adults

6.39 A bar chart of vital capacities will look very similar to that of breathing rate increase, but in this case the less athletic individuals will be at the beginning of the graph instead of at the end. From this you can see that one reason why athletes do not have the rapid increase in breathing rate experienced by non-athletes during exercise is that they are able to obtain more oxygen per breath.

6.40 4000 cm³ of air can be obtained by deep inspiration.

6.41 1500 cm³ of air can be expelled by forced expiration.

6.42 1000 cm³ of air remains in the lungs as residual air.

6.43 The total capacity of the lungs is 6000 cm³.

6.44 The vital capacity of the lungs is the maximum volume of air which can be exchanged, that is the volume of air which can be expelled by forced expiration following deep inspiration.

Homework

In this example, let us assume that the breathing rate at rest is fifteen breaths per minute, and after exercise it is thirty per minute. Tidal air is 500 cm³ and deep inspiration is 4000 cm³. The percentage of oxygen in the air is assumed to be 20%.

(a) Consumption at rest for one minute:
Oxygen in 500 cm³ of air = 100 cm³. Multiply 100 cm³ by 15 breaths per minute = 1500 cm³ = 1.5 litres.
(b) Consumption during one minute of exercise:
Oxygen in 4000 cm³ of air = 800 cm³. Multiply 800 cm³ by 30 breaths per minute = 24 000 cm³ = 24 litres.
(c) Consumption at rest for one hour = 1.5 l × 60 = 90 litres.
(d) Consumption at rest for 24 hours = 90 l × 24 = 2160 litres.

7 Internal transport

1 The blood circulatory system

Man possesses a very complex network of transporting channels to convey substances around the body. This enables these substances to reach all the parts of the body as quickly as possible.

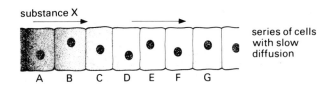

7.1 (a) Distribution by diffusion

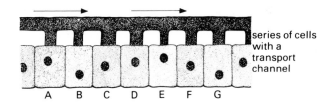

7.1 (b) Use of a transport channel

▶ Questions

7.1 Which cell G receives more of the substance X more quickly, the one in Fig 7.1(a) or the one in Fig 7.1(b)? Explain your answer.

7.2 Suggest another important factor which makes a transport system in man a necessity (remember Unit 6 section 3).

Until the seventeenth century there were many theories about the way blood moves round the body. The most popular theory was that the blood ebbs and flows from the heart like waves on the beach. Then in 1628 William Harvey (1578–1657), during a number of dissections of the heart and the blood vessels, discovered a series of valves which suggested that the blood could only flow in one direction. He concluded from this that the blood **circulates** around the body.

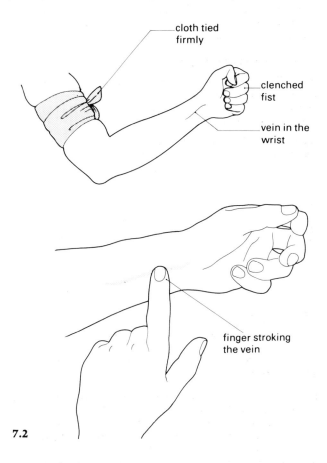

7.2

Activity 7.1   Observing blood flow in veins in the arm

1   Tie a piece of cloth (not too tightly) around your partner's upper arm as in Fig 7.2.
2   Tell him to close his fist tightly. This should make the veins of his arm stand out.
3   Press a finger against a large vein, slide it with light pressure a few centimetres along the vein in the direction of the wrist, and continue to hold your finger on the vein. Observe the appearance of the vein.
4   Repeat step 3, but this time sliding your finger towards the elbow.

7.3 Describe the appearance of the vein after sliding the finger towards the wrist in step 3.
7.4 Describe the difference made by changing the direction of sliding the finger. What can you conclude from this?

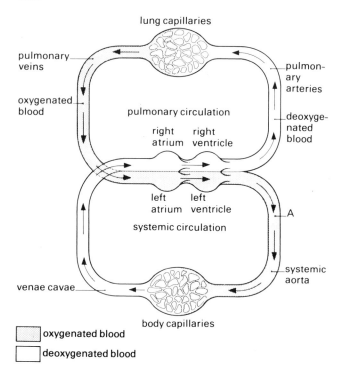

7.3 A double circulation

Fig 7.3 shows the double circulatory system found in man. To see why it is called a double circulatory system, start at point A and trace a path right around the system until you return to point A again.

► **Questions**

7.5 How many times does the trace pass through the heart in making one complete circulation? Can you now explain why it is called a double circulation?
7.6 Other animals such as fish have a single circulatory system, where the blood is pumped through the heart only once as it travels to the gills and the rest of the body. Can you suggest any advantages man's double circulatory system might have over the fishes' system?

▷ **Research project**

Find out all you can about the work of William Harvey.

2 The heart

The heart is a bag of cardiac muscle about the size of a clenched fist. It is situated to the left of centre in the thoracic cavity, between the left and right lungs. It is a twin pump which maintains the double circulation of blood around the body. The heart is composed of four chambers. If possible, examine a sheep's heart.

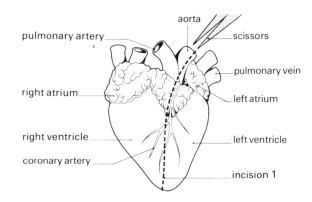

7.4 External view of the heart

Activity 7.2   Observing a dissected heart

1   Take a sheep's heart, and locate and name its four chambers.
2   Locate the aorta (a big artery arising from the left ventricle), and cut into it as shown on Fig 7.4.
3   Open out the aorta and left ventricle, and then cut into the left atrium as shown in Fig 7.5(a). This displays the left side of the heart.
4   Make a third incision into the pulmonary artery (arising from the right ventricle) as shown in Fig 7.5(b). This will open up the right side of the heart.

7.5 Dissection of a sheep's heart

(a)

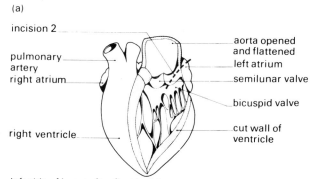

left side of heart after first incision
Incision 2 cuts through the bicuspid valve into left atrium

(b)

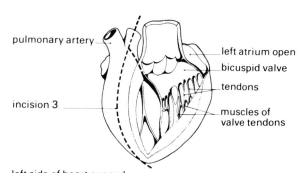

left side of heart opened
incision 3 cuts through the pulmonary artery and right ventricle

(c)

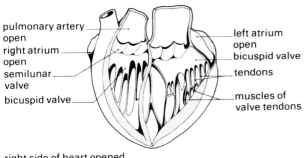

pulmonary artery
open
right atrium
open
semilunar
valve
bicuspid valve

left atrium
open
bicuspid valve
tendons
muscles of
valve tendons

right side of heart opened

▶ Questions

7.7 Apart from the atria and ventricles, what other structures are visible inside the heart?

7.8 Suggest the function of these structures in the passage of blood through the heart. Refer to William Harvey's work in section 1.

The **ventricles** have thicker muscular walls than the **atria**. The atria, when they contract, only have to force blood into the ventricles. The ventricles have to force blood round the body. The left ventricle is larger than the right ventricle because it pumps blood to all parts of the body except the lungs. The right ventricle only pumps blood to the lungs.

Blood flowing through the left side of the heart comes from the lungs and is well oxygenated. This blood leaves the left ventricle via the aorta which distributes oxygenated blood to all the tissues. See Fig 7.6. Blood flowing through the right side of the heart is deoxygenated blood returned from the body tissues, via the venae cavae, into the right atrium. This blood passes from the right ventricle into the pulmonary arteries and to the lungs for re-oxygenation.

Blood is pumped through the heart constantly throughout life. The regular rhythm of blood being forced through the heart is called a heartbeat. Fig 7.7 shows one side of the heart during the active phases of a heartbeat. The other side works in exactly the same way at exactly the same time.

7.7 (a) Atrial contraction

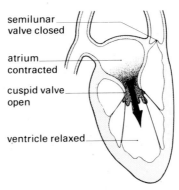

semilunar
valve closed

atrium
contracted

cuspid valve
open

ventricle relaxed

7.7 (b) Ventricular contraction

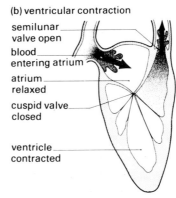

(b) ventricular contraction

semilunar
valve open

blood
entering atrium

atrium
relaxed

cuspid valve
closed

ventricle
contracted

7.6 Vertical section through a human heart showing direction of blood flow

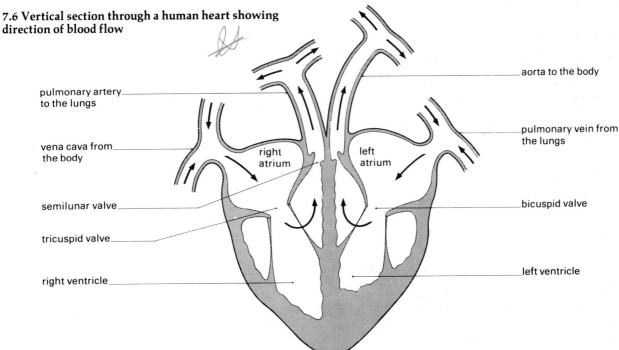

pulmonary artery
to the lungs

vena cava from
the body

right
atrium

left
atrium

aorta to the body

pulmonary vein from
the lungs

semilunar valve

tricuspid valve

right ventricle

bicuspid valve

left ventricle

▶ **Question**

7.9 Fig 7.7(a) represents atrial systole, the phase of contraction of the atrium. Describe the state of the ventricle, the state of the atrium and the position of the valves during this phase of a heartbeat.

(b) represents ventricular systole. Describe the state of the ventricle, the state of the atrium and the position of the valves during this phase of a heartbeat.

Systole is followed by a short inactive phase called diastole when neither the atria nor the ventricles are contracting and the main veins are filling with blood awaiting entry into the heart.

▶ **Question**

7.10 Try to explain how the cuspid and semi-lunar valves prevent backflow of blood in the heart.

Activity 7.3   Investigating heartbeat

1   Take a stethoscope or construct a simple one using a filter funnel, rubber tubing and a glass tubing T-piece.
2   Place the stethoscope in your ears and put the end of it to the left of centre of the thorax of your partner. It will be best to remove any outer woollen garments first. Listen to the sounds of the heart.
3   Remove the stethoscope. If a tape-recorder is available, place a microphone against a partner's chest. Hold the microphone and its cord quite still to avoid introducing unwanted sounds. Record the heartbeats and play the recording back.
4   Estimate the number of your heartbeats per minute at rest.
5   Construct a bar chart to show the range of heartbeat rates in your class.

7.9 A heart-lung machine in use during an operation

▶ **Question**

7.11   Describe the sounds you heard in step 2. What do they represent?

Hospitals use more accurate methods to record heart activity. The machine used is an **electrocardiograph**. An electrical circuit amplifies changes in voltage during a heartbeat and this produces tracings on paper or on a television screen. Fig 7.8 shows the electrical pattern of one normal heartbeat.

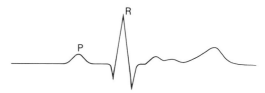

7.8 Electrocardiogram of a normal heart

▶ **Question**

7.12   Suggest what the peaks of electrical activity labelled P and R represent.

The rate of heartbeat can be altered to meet the requirements of the body. During exercise the heart beats faster to direct more blood to the muscles. It also expels more blood per stroke, that is it has a greater stroke volume. Alterations in heartbeat rate and stroke volume are controlled by a knot of nervous tissue situated in the right atrium called the **pacemaker**.

▶ **Question**

7.13   Some individuals have a defective pacemaker and their heart often beats more quickly than it should. This may be so serious that an artificial pacemaker has to be fitted. Suggest how an artificial pacemaker works.

Open heart surgery is now a common procedure. Some babies are born with a hole in the heart between the ventricles so that oxygenated and deoxygenated blood mix, but this can be dealt with surgically. Damaged valves can also be replaced by plastic ones or by those of a pig. These methods of surgery have been made possible by the **heart-lung machine** which enables the patient to survive for several hours without the pumping action of their own heart.

A heart-lung machine takes over the functioning of the heart and lungs. Deoxygenated blood from the body tissues is diverted into it. The machine removes carbon dioxide and adds oxygen to the blood through a very large, folded surface area. It then pumps this oxygenated blood back into the aorta for distribution throughout the tissues.

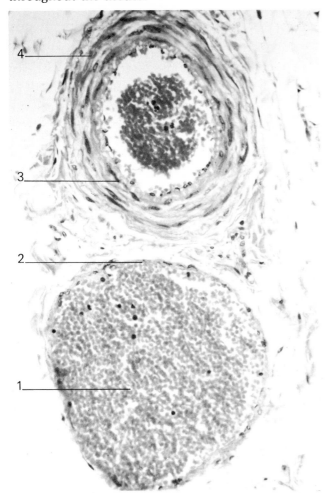

7.10 Artery and a vein in cross-section

▶ **Question**

7.14 How would mixing of oxygenated and deoxygenated blood affect the individual with a hole in the heart?

▷ **Homework**

Try to make an improvised stethoscope at home and compare the rate of your own heartbeat when under-going different activities. List two things which change your heartbeat rate apart from exercise and rest.

3 The blood vessels

Blood is taken away from the heart in vessels called arteries and returned to the heart in vessels called veins. There are certain differences between arteries and veins which are related to their functions.

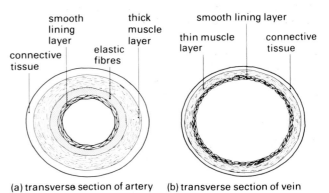

(a) transverse section of artery   (b) transverse section of vein

7.11 Transverse section of an artery and a vein

Questions

7.15 Using Fig 7.11 as a guide, identify the numbered parts of Fig 7.10.
7.16 List the differences in the walls of the artery and vein.
7.17 Explain why arteries have such a thick muscle layer.
7.18 Suggest the function of the elastic fibres in the wall of the artery.
7.19 Why do veins need pocket valves as shown in Fig 7.12?

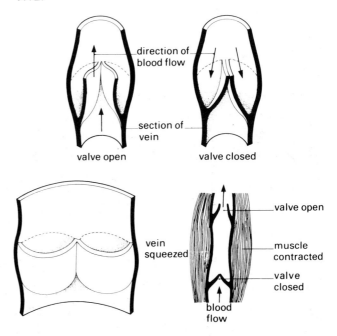

7.12 Pocket valves in a vein

Arteries are usually more deep-seated than veins. If they are cut, the blood, under high pressure, spurts out. Veins when cut only release a slow trickle of blood. It is less dangerous for them to be near the surface. Where an artery does flow close to the

85

surface, over a bone, a wave of blood may be felt pulsating as it passes along the artery. This pulse reflects ventricular systole (see section 2). It may be detected at particular areas in the body called pressure points.

Activity 7.4   Investigating the pulse

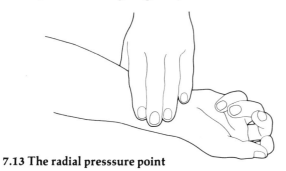

7.13 The radial presssure point

1   Sit quietly for a few moments and feel your radial pulse. Wait until you have definitely located it before you attempt a count.
2   Use a clock with a seconds hand to time the number of pulses for thirty seconds. Repeat this several times until a steady rate is obtained.
3   Record your pulse rate in beats per minute.
4   Obtain the results of the other members of your class and construct a bar chart. Compare this with the chart from Activity 7.3.
5   Run on the spot vigorously for one minute.
6   Take your pulse rate again.
7   Record your pulse rate after exercise in beats per minute.
8   Obtain the results of other members of your class and construct another bar chart.

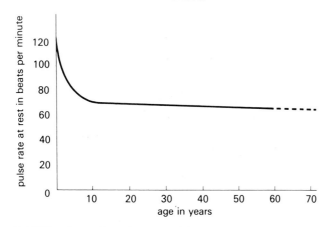

7.14 The change in pulse rate with age

▶ **Questions**

7.20   What is an average pulse rate at rest for someone of your age? See Fig 7.14.
7.21   What is the effect of exercise on the pulse rate? What is the reason for the difference?
7.22   Some members of a class show very little increase in their pulse rate after exercise. This is shown in the second bar chart. Is there anything special about this group of people?

▶ **Questions**

7.23   Describe what happens to the pulse rate at rest as a person gets older. See Fig 7.14.
7.24   What effect would you expect this change to have on a person?
7.25   Apart from age and exercise, can you think of any other factors which affect your pulse rate?

'Blood pressure' is frequently discussed these days. If we say a person has blood pressure, we mean he is suffering from high blood pressure. Blood pressure is simply a measure of the force of the blood against the wall of the vessel containing it. The pressure varies at different points in the circulation, but is usually measured in the upper arm. Fig 7.15 shows the instrument used to measure blood pressure called a sphygmomanometer.

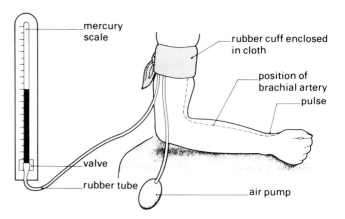

7.15 A sphygmomanometer

A rubber cuff is wrapped around the upper arm. The rubber cuff is blown up until the blood in the brachial (arm) artery has to force its way through it. This point can be detected by feeling the pulse or listening to it with a stethoscope. The pressure recorded by the sphygmomanometer must then be equal to the blood pressure. The maximum and minimum pressures are recorded.

7.16 Normal blood pressure in a 20-year-old

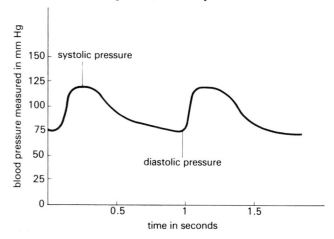

7.26 (a) In Fig 7.16 what do you think 'systolic' pressure means?

(b) What is 'diastolic' pressure?

7.27 What is the maximum and the minimum blood pressure of this person?

7.28 What factors in the circulatory system could make the blood pressure become abnormally high?

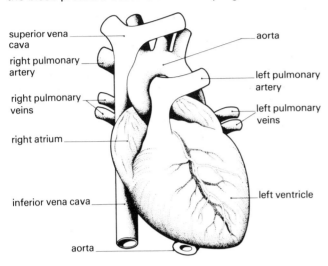

7.17 The main blood vessels near the heart

7.18 Main blood vessels in man

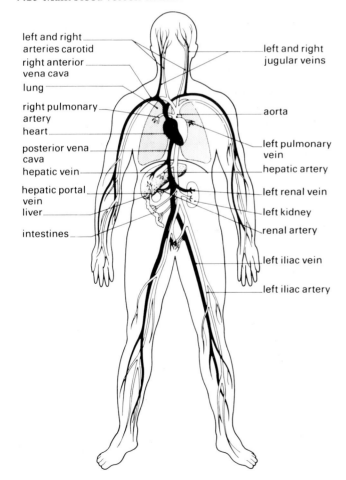

7.19 Dissection to show the main blood vessels in a rat

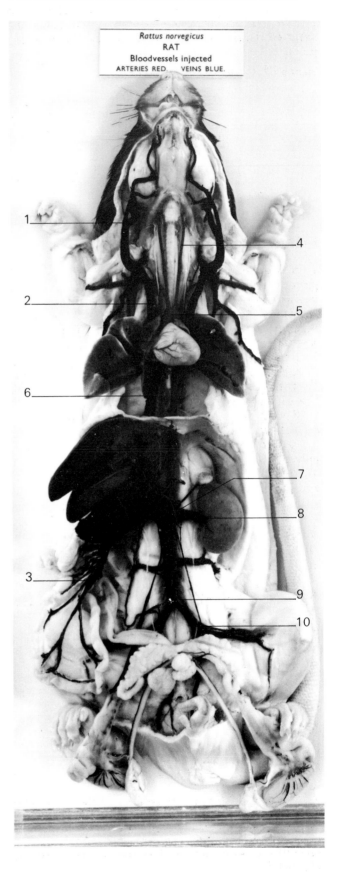

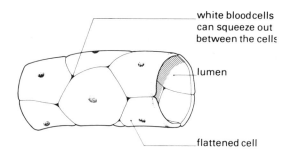

7.20 Part of a capillary vessel

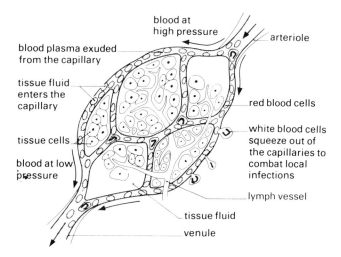

7.21 Exchange of substances in a capillary bed

Activity 7.5 Investigating capillary circulation in a tadpole's tail

1 Take a tadpole which has been slowed down by an anaesthetic.
2 Place the tadpole in water on a watchglass.
3 View the blood vessels, particularly of the tail, under a microscope.

▶ Questions

7.29 How does the diameter of the smallest blood vessels in the tadpole's tail compare with the veins you can see in your wrist?
7.30 Explain how the structure of the capillary shown in Fig 7.20 is well-suited to its role of exchanging materials between the blood and the cells.
7.31 List as many as you can of the substances which leave the blood and diffuse into the cells. Name some of those which leave the tissues and diffuse into the capillaries.
7.32 Not all of the substances leaving the cells go into the capillary. Where do some of them go?
7.33 There are many similarities between the blood vessel system of man and that of other mammals. Study Figs 7.18 and 7.19, then identify the numbered blood vessels in Fig 7.19 using Fig 7.18 as a reference.

▷ Homework

Compare the pulse rates of members of your family and devise an experiment to discover which member is the fittest without exhausting them.

4 The composition of blood

When a wound is bleeding, the blood appears as a red, tacky fluid. Viewed under a microscope, it is found to contain many cells, called **corpuscles**.

Activity 7.6   Making a blood smear

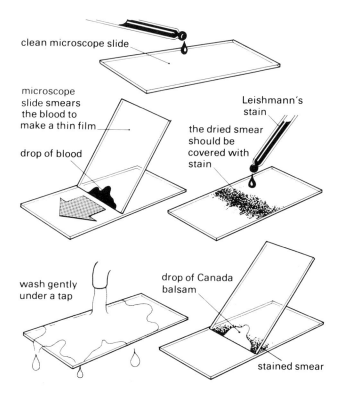

7.22 Making a blood smear

1 Prepare a clean microscope slide.
2 Allow a drop of blood from a freshly killed mammal to fall on a clean slide and smear the drop thinly across the slide with a coverslip.
3 Dry the blood smear, then add a few drops of Leishmann's stain to cover it.
4 Leave it for five minutes, then wash gently under a tap.
5 Add a drop of Canada balsam to keep the coverslip in position.
6 Lower a coverslip over the Canada balsam and examine the smear under a microscope.
7 Draw the cells as seen under the high power of the microscope.
8 Use a Hillier graticule to estimate the size of the pink, disc shaped cells and of the irregular, colourless cells.

▶ Questions

7.34 How many different types of cell can you see?
7.35 What are the structures in the irregular colourless cells which take up the blue Leishmann's stain?
7.36 What are the diameters of the two types of cell you measured in millimetres?

Red blood cells are different from any other cells in the body in several ways. Firstly red blood cells have no nuclei. Because of this they only live for about four months, after which time they are destroyed in the spleen. The biconcave disc shape of red blood cells is another unique feature. They are the only human cells which appear red. This is due to the pigment haemoglobin.

Red blood cells transport oxygen from the lungs to all the body tissues in the form of oxyhaemoglobin.

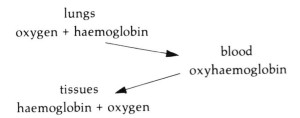

The red pigment, haemoglobin, has an affinity for oxygen where oxygen concentrations are high. In areas of low oxygen concentration, such as the tissues, the haemoglobin readily gives up this oxygen.

The biconcave shape of a red blood cell presents a very large surface area in relation to its volume. This allows rapid absorption of oxygen to occur in the lungs and rapid release of oxygen to occur in the tissues. Lack of a nucleus creates more space for haemoglobin and therefore better oxygen carrying capacity.

7.23 Scanning electronmicrograph of some red blood cells
Note that some of the older cells have lost their regular shape, and many cells have protein filaments on the surface.

7.37 List ways in which white blood cells differ from red.
7.38 What is the basic difference between a polymorph and a lymphocyte?

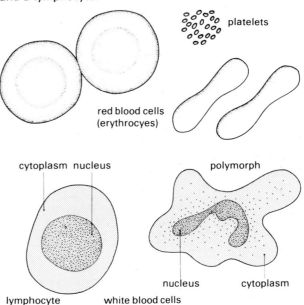

7.24 Main types of blood cell in human blood

Less than half of the blood is composed of cells. Fifty-five per cent consists of a straw-coloured liquid called **plasma**. Fig 7.25 summarises the composition of blood.

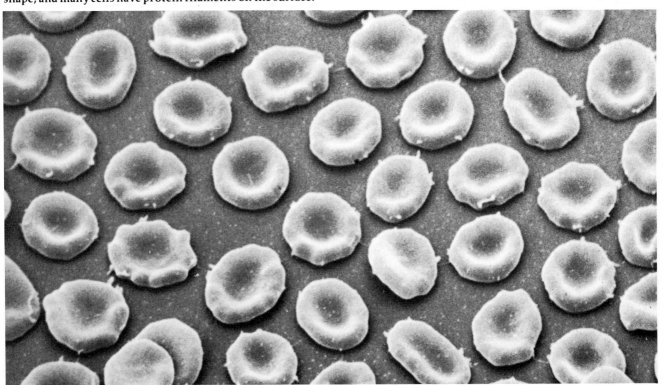

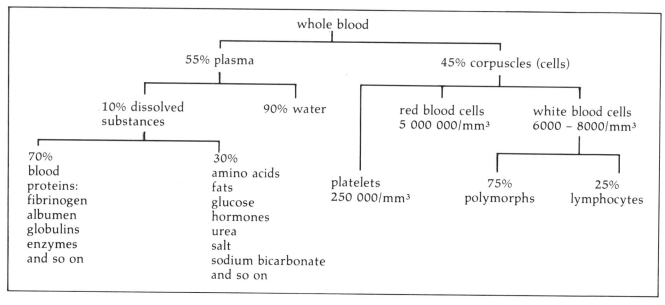

7.25 Composition of the blood

▶ **Questions**

7.39 Which blood cells are the most numerous?
7.40 Why does the number of white blood cells per cubic millimetre vary?
7.41 In what way do amino acids differ from blood proteins?

Platelets or thrombocytes are very small structures which were thought to be fragments of red blood cells. It is now believed that they represent detached parts of the lining cells of blood vessels. This theory is supported by the role of the platelets in the clotting of the blood. Blood clotting is brought about by the action of a substance called thrombin, and the blood protein fibrinogen. Thrombin is only produced in an active form on the release of an activator called thrombokinase. This activator is produced by the platelets and the walls of the blood vessels when they are damaged. See Fig 7.26. Note that calcium ions must also be present in the blood to assist in the final conversion of fibrinogen to fibrin.

▶ **Questions**

7.42 What effect does thrombin have on fibrinogen?
7.43 Why is it important that the blood is able to clot?
7.44 Why is thrombin normally in the inactive form, prothrombin?

White blood cells and gamma globulin are concerned with defence against foreign bodies, such as disease organisms. Foreign bodies, called **antigens**, stimulate the production of lymphocytes and antibodies which destroy them in a variety of ways. These will be discussed in Unit 14.

▶ **Question**

7.45 What would happen to a person who was unable to produce antibodies?

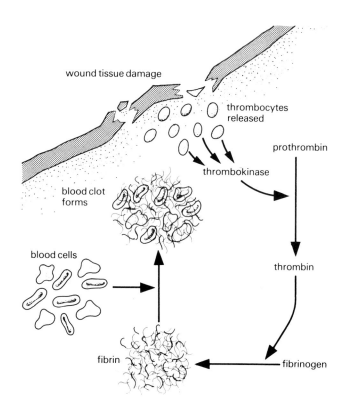

7.26 Mechanism of blood clotting

▶ **Question**

7.46 Study Table 7.1 and suggest what should go into the numbered spaces.

▷ **Research project**

Some individuals are found to have an excess of either red blood cells or white blood cells in their blood. Investigate the causes of these abnormal blood counts.

Table 7.1 Transport of substances by the blood

Substance transported	Origin	Destination	Medium of transport	Function in the body
Oxygen	Lungs	All tissues	Haemoglobin in red blood cells	Respiration
Carbon dioxide	All tissues	1	As sodium bicarbonate in the plasma	2
Amino acids	Ileum	Liver, then all tissues	3	4
Glucose	5	6	Plasma	7
Fats	Ileum and innominate vein	8	Plasma	Energy store, insulation, protection
Urea	Liver	9	Plasma	(Waste)
Hormones	Ductless glands	Distant tissues	10	11
Fibrinogen	Liver and blood	Wounded area	12	13
Antibodies	Lymph glands and bone marrow	Area of infection	14	15
Heat energy	Liver	All tissues	All parts of the blood	Temperature regulation

5 Blood groups

In the early days of blood transfusions, it was found that some recipients reacted against the donor's blood and agglutinated it. This caused a number of deaths, since the kidneys of the patient became blocked by the agglutinated blood.

Fig 7.27 shows two mixtures of blood. The mixture on the left is of two compatible types of blood, while that on the right is of two types of blood which are incompatible. We now know that compatibility depends on a person's blood group. There are many of these groups, but the most important are the ABO group and the Rhesus group. The problem is due to antigens present on some red blood cells, and to antibodies present in the plasma of some individuals.

The table summarises the antigens and antibodies present in different ABO blood groups. As a rule, a group contains the opposite antigen to its antibody (group A has A antigens and anti-B antibodies).

7.27 Non-agglutinated and agglutinated blood

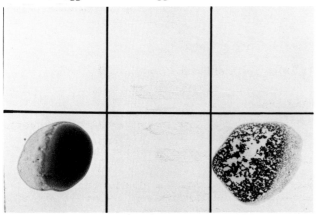

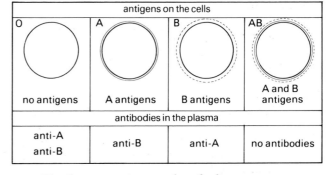

antigens on the cells			
O	A	B	AB
no antigens	A antigens	B antigens	A and B antigens
antibodies in the plasma			
anti-A anti-B	anti-B	anti-A	no antibodies

7.28 Blood group antigens and antibodies

7.47 Examine Fig 7.28. Explain why it would be dangerous for a person of blood group A to receive a blood transfusion of group B.

A Rhesus negative individual has anti-Rhesus antibodies in the plasma. A Rhesus positive person has antigens called Rhesus bodies on the red blood cells. About 85% of the population has Rhesus bodies. If a Rhesus negative woman delivers a Rhesus positive baby, she will be sensitised by Rhesus bodies which cross the placenta and enter her blood when the placenta separates from the uterine wall after delivery. In response, she will produce anti-Rhesus antibodies. These will cross the placenta of subsequent pregnancies and begin to destroy the red blood cells of the foetus. The baby will be born jaundiced and anaemic if this happens. It is unusual for this to occur in the first child, but the antibodies once formed remain in the mother's blood until subsequent pregnancies. Nowadays an injection is given to Rhesus negative expectant mothers. This contains a measured amount of Rhesus antibodies which prevent any Rhesus bodies from surviving to cross the placenta. Thus the mother's blood is not sensitised.

Table 7.2 ABO blood transfusions

Recipient's blood group	Donor's blood group
A	A, O
B	B, O
AB	A, B, AB, O
O	O

▶ Questions

7.48   One of these groups can be given to anyone, without coagulation occurring. It is called the universal donor. Another group can receive all the others without coagulation and is called the universal recipient. Identify these two groups.
7.49   Group O contains anti-A and anti-B antibodies in its plasma. Why does it not coagulate the recipient's blood?
7.50   Using Table 7.2 and Table 7.3, decide which are the most useful blood groups for transfusion purposes.

Table 7.3 Frequency of blood groups in the British population

Blood group	Percentage
O	46
A	42
B	9
AB	3
Rh positive	85
Rh negative	15

▷ Research project

Find references to the relative frequencies of blood groups in populations of other countries.

6 Lymph and the lymphatic system

In section 4, exchange of substances between the capillaries and the cells was illustrated. In addition to the ordinary capillaries, Fig 7.21 illustrates a tiny, branching **lymph capillary**. A proportion of the substances produced by the cells diffuses not into the blood capillary, but into the lymph capillary. Fig 7.29 illustrates what happens to these substances, contained in the tissue fluid, after they have entered the lymphatic capillary.

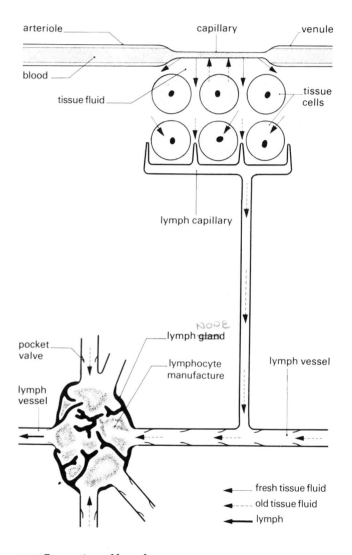

7.29 Formation of lymph

▶ Questions

7.51   Briefly describe the formation of lymph from tissue fluid.
7.52   Construct a table to summarise the differences between lymph and fresh tissue fluid.
7.53   Refer to Fig 7.29, to the table you constructed for 7.52, and Unit 5, section 4, and then list the functions of lymph in the body.
7.54   Where does the lymph enter the blood stream (see Fig 7.30)?

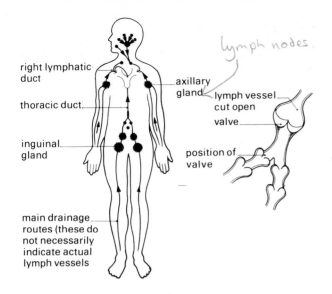

right lymphatic duct

thoracic duct

inguinal gland

axillary gland

lymph nodes.

lymph vessel cut open

valve

position of valve

main drainage routes (these do not necessarily indicate actual lymph vessels

7.30 The human lymph system

Circulation of the lymph in the lymphatic vessels is maintained by a series of large **pocket valves**. Pressure of contracting muscles squeezes the lymph vessels, and the valves allow the lymph to move in only one direction.

7 Distribution of the blood

The body's needs for food and oxygen vary considerably from one moment to the next, depending mainly on our activity. If you are running to catch a bus, your muscles require extra food and oxygen. If you have just eaten a big meal, your digestive system needs more blood for the uptake of the food. The volume of blood remains more or less constant, so when extra blood is needed in one place, it is at the expense of other areas. The blood has to be redistributed to where it is most needed. This is brought about by small arteries called **arterioles**, which constrict or dilate according to needs.

7.31 Arterioles react to a hot bath

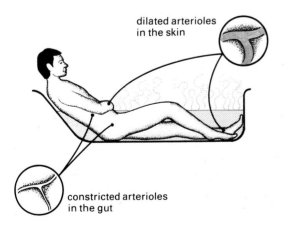

dilated arterioles in the skin

constricted arterioles in the gut

▶ **Questions**

7.55 Why are the skin arterioles of this bather dilated?
7.56 Why is it unwise to have a heavy meal just before a bath?

As well as volume changes occurring from one part of the circulation to another, there are many composition changes. You should be able to work these out for yourself by consulting Fig 7.3 and Table 7.1. Using the information from these sources, work out the answers to the following questions based on Fig 7.32, which is a summary scheme of the circulation of man.

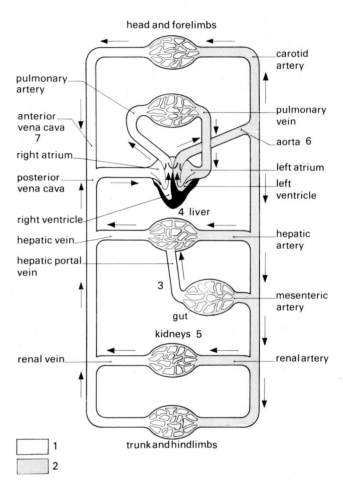

head and forelimbs

pulmonary artery

anterior vena cava 7

right atrium

posterior vena cava

right ventricle

hepatic vein

hepatic portal vein

renal vein

carotid artery

pulmonary vein

aorta 6

left atrium

left ventricle

4 liver

hepatic artery

3

mesenteric artery

gut

kidneys 5

renal artery

trunk and hindlimbs

1

2

7.32 Blood circulation in man

▶ **Questions**

7.57 1 and 2 represent a key for oxygenated or deoxygenated blood. Identify these correctly.
7.58 What is picked up by the blood at 3?
7.59 What is picked up by the blood at 4 and delivered at 5?
7.60 Describe the composition of the blood in terms of oxygen and food at 6 and 7.
7.61 Make a list of six major functions of the blood. Refer to Units 3, 5 and 11.

▷ **Homework**

List four examples of blood redistribution.

Answers and discussion

1 The blood circulatory system

7.1 The G cell in Fig 7.1(b) receives more of the substance than that in Fig 7.1(a). This is because diffusion is slow through a chain of cells, and the number of molecules reaching G in Fig 7.1(a) is very low. More rapid spreading of the substance by a transport channel distributes the molecules more uniformly over a large area. This is why a transport system is necessary to man.

7.2 Man has a relatively small surface area to volume ratio. He is therefore unable to gain sufficient oxygen, food and other requirements by simple diffusion through the body surface.

7.3 The vein still appears to be full of blood. There is very little change.

7.4 The vein empties of blood and more flows up to fill it. This indicates that the blood normally only flows in one direction, which is up the arm, towards the heart. Blood therefore does not ebb and flow.

7.5 Your trace should pass through the heart twice for each complete circuit in the body. It should follow a figure of eight pattern. This is called a double circulation because one side of the heart pumps blood to the lungs, while the other side pumps blood to the rest of the body. The heart has a double action, and pumps a double circulation – heart to lungs to heart is one circuit and heart to rest of body to heart is the other.

7.6 The double circulation system means that freshly oxygenated blood is returned to the heart from the lungs for pumping round the body. This helps to ensure that it reaches the tissues as quickly as possible. Also deoxygenated blood coming back from the tissues is not mixed in with the oxygenated blood in the heart, but is sent straight back to the lungs for re-oxygenation.

2 The heart

7.7 Inside the aorta there are pocket-like flaps. These are valves. The areas between the atria and ventricles have a different type of flap held in position by tough cords which attach them to the ventricle walls.

7.8 These valves stop blood from flowing backwards through the heart. They ensure that blood can only pass from the atria to the ventricles and the ventricles to the arteries.

7.9 (a) At the start of atrial systole, the atrium is full of blood. As it contracts, the cuspid valves are forced open and blood enters the ventricle, which is relaxed. Blood present in the aorta is prevented from re-entering the ventricle by the closure of the semi-lunar valve.
(b) At the start of ventricular systole, the ventricle is full of blood. The ventricle then contracts, forcing the blood past the semi-lunar valve in the aorta. The cuspid valve is forced to close by the upthrust of blood so that the relaxed atrium is sealed off. One heartbeat takes about $0 \cdot 8$ seconds: $0 \cdot 3$ seconds is systole (active contraction) and $0 \cdot 5$ seconds is diastole (rest).

7.10 The cuspid valves consist of flaps of tissue supported by tendons. When the blood is forced up from beneath them, they fill out like parachutes and block the entrance to the atria by floating on the blood. Note that the left valve has two flaps and is known as the bicuspid valve. Because it looks like a bishop's hat it is also called the mitral valve. The right valve has three flaps and is called the tricuspid valve. The semi-lunar valves are like pockets. When blood is forced through them from below, they are flattened against the wall of the aorta. When the blood falls back, it fills the pockets up. The three pockets together close the base of the aorta.

7.11 The sounds heard during heart beat are usually described as 'lub, dupp'. These are deep sounds which represent the closure of first, the cuspid valves (lub), and second, the semi-lunar valves (dupp).

7.12 In the electrocardiogram, P represents contraction of the atria and R represents contraction of the ventricles.

7.13 An artificial pacemaker works by sending out electrical impulses to stimulate the heart muscle. The output of the pacemaker will be controlled by the activities of the body, such as sleep, rest or exercise. The pacemaker is able to detect consequent changes in blood requirement.

7.14 Mixed oxygenated and deoxygenated blood in the left ventricle will result in blood lower in oxygen than normal being distributed to the body tissues. The individual will therefore have less oxygen for respiration, so will be lacking in energy.

3 The blood vessels

7.15 1 blood cells; 2 thin muscle layer; 3 thick muscle layer; 4 connective tissue.

7.16

Arteries	Veins
Thick muscle layer	Thin muscle layer
Elastic layer present	No elastic layer
Smaller lumen	Larger lumen

Because of their thick walls, arteries appear paler in dissection than veins. In veins the dark colour of the blood shows through the relatively thin walls.

7.17 Arteries require a thick muscle layer to withstand the pressure of blood against their walls. Blood is forced through the arteries by ventricular contraction. It pulsates through the arteries under high pressure. In veins the blood pressure is much lower since the blood has flowed slowly through the small capillaries before reaching the veins.

7.18 The elastic fibres in the artery wall give it the property of recoil. After a wave of blood stretches the artery wall, the elastic fibres bring it back into shape. This forces the blood further along the artery. Veins, in which blood flows smoothly, do not require this property.

7.19 Veins require pocket valves to aid the return of the blood to the heart, particularly from the legs where it is flowing against gravity. Contraction of muscles against the veins also helps to squeeze the blood back. The pumping action of the heart is very distant from the veins.

7.20 The average pulse rate of a fifteen year old is around 85 per minute.

7.21 Exercise increases the pulse rate. This is because more blood is needed by the muscles to provide oxygen and glucose for respiration and activity.

7.22 The class members whose pulse rates are little affected by exercise are probably fit or athletic individuals. Regular exercise makes the body more efficient and more able to function without drawing on a lot of extra food and oxygen.

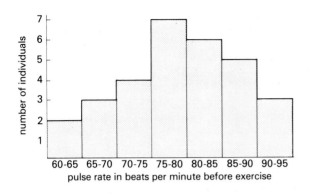

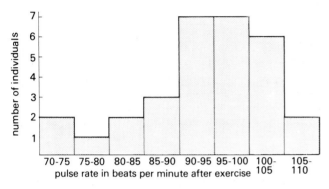

7.33 Pulse rates in a class of 15-year-olds

7.23 As a person gets older, the pulse rate decreases. A newborn baby has a pulse rate of 120 per minute, a 65-year-old one of only 65 per minute.

7.24 A slowing of the pulse rate often slows an individual down. Their cells will be receiving food and oxygen at a slower rate and respiration will consequently be slower.

7.25 Other factors which affect pulse rate include excitement, fear and anger. These all increase the rate. A high temperature (fever) has the same effect.

7.26 (a) Systolic pressure is the maximum pressure which occurs when the heart is contracting (systole).   (b) Diastolic pressure is the minimum pressure. This represents the resting phase of the heart (diastole).

7.27 The maximum (systolic) pressure of the person illustrated is 120 mm Hg, and the minimum (diastolic) pressure is 80 mm Hg.

Normal blood pressure is usually given as

$$\frac{100 + \text{your age (systolic)}}{70 \text{ to } 80 \text{ (diastolic)}} \text{ mm Hg.}$$

It is commonly written as a fraction. Your blood pressure is probably about 115/70 mm Hg.

7.28 Factors in the circulatory system causing high blood pressure include an extra large volume of blood in the circulation, resistance to flow encountered in the smaller arteries and hardened arteries. Blood pressure is proportional to the volume of blood and the peripheral resistance. Resistance to flow is normal in the capillaries, but in some diseases the smaller arteries become silted up and their diameter is decreased, thus increasing their resistance to blood flow. (See Unit 16.)

7.29 The diameter of our veins is many hundreds of times greater than that of a capillary. If you have a powerful

enough microscope, it is possible to see that the minute red blood cells(0.0072 mm in diameter) are sometimes forced to pass in single file through a capillary!

7.30 The wall of the capillary is only one cell thick, and these cells are pavement epithelium. There is very little resistance, therefore, to the diffusion of substances in and out of capillaries. White blood cells are able to squeeze out between the cells to help to combat disease in the tissues.

7.31 Substances leaving the blood include amino acids, fats, glucose, oxygen and white blood cells. Substances entering the blood include urea and carbon dioxide.

7.32 Some urea and carbon dioxide enter the lymphatic capillaries.

7.33 1 right jugular vein; 2 anterior vena cava; 3 hepatic portal vein; 4 left carotid artery; 5 aorta; 6 posterior vena cava; 7 left renal artery; 8 left renal vein; 9 left iliac artery; 10 left iliac vein.

4 The composition of blood

7.34 Three different types of cell should be visible; regular, pink disc shaped cells, larger irregular cells with a lobed nucleus and similar cells with an ovoid nucleus.

7.35 The structures which take up the Leishmann's stain are the nuclei.

7.36 Red cells are around 0.0072 mm in diameter and white cells (the larger, irregular cells) between 0.02 mm and 0.03 mm in diameter.

7.37 White blood cells differ from red blood cells in the following ways:

1 They possess a nucleus.
2 They are irregular in shape.
3 They are larger.
4 They have no haemoglobin.
5 A variety of types are produced.
6 They are fewer in number.

7.38 A polymorph has a lobed nucleus; a lymphocyte has an ovoid nucleus.

7.39 There are 5 000 000 red blood cells per mm³ of blood and only 6000 to 8000 white blood cells. Red cells are about 600 times more numerous.

7.40 The white blood cell count varies depending on the state of health of the individual. During an infection there may be as many as 60 000 cells per mm³.

7.41 Amino acids are the final products of protein digestion which are merely being transported in the plasma. The blood proteins are substances built up in the liver which have functions in the blood itself. Albumen gives the blood its tacky consistency. The function of the other proteins is discussed below.

7.42 Thrombin makes fibrinogen come out of solution and form fibres called fibrin. The fibrin entangles blood cells to make a clot or scab over a wound.

7.43 Blood must be able to clot, otherwise every time we cut ourselves we would lose a lot of blood. Some individuals are born with blood which will not clot. They are in danger of bleeding to death even if they only have a tooth extracted. See Unit 14 for more details. Sealing off a wound with a clot also prevents entry of disease organisms.

7.44 If thrombin circulated in the blood in an active form it would constantly convert fibrinogen into fibrin. The blood would clot in the blood vessels. Certain diseases result in the formation of clots in the absence of air. Coronary thrombosis is blockage of the coronary arteries, which supply the heart muscle with food and oxygen, by such a blood clot.

7.45 An individual who is unable to produce antibodies is likely to die from an infection of even a mild disease. Such diseases are mild for normal individuals because they have antibodies to deal with them.

7.46 1 lungs; 2 (waste); 3 plasma; 4 body building and repair; 5 ileum; 6 all tissues; 7 respiration; 8 skin and kidneys; 9 skin and kidneys, 10 plasma; 11 co-ordination of the body; 12 plasma; 13 blood clotting; 14 lymphocytes and plasma; 15 defence against infection.

5 Blood groups

7.47 Group B blood contains anti-A antibodies. These would attack all the recipients blood cells because these are group A, and carry A antigens. The A blood cells would be clumped together by the anti-A antibodies, causing agglutination and blocking of the blood vessels.

7.48 Group O is the universal donor. Group AB is the universal recipient.

7.49 The relatively small volume of plasma from a donor will not contain sufficient antibodies to destroy or coagulate many red blood cells of the recipient.

7.50 Group O is a very useful group for transfusions because it can be given to anyone. Rhesus negative blood is also very useful because if a Rhesus negative person is given Rhesus positive blood, they will coagulate it.

6 Lymph and the lymphatic system

7.51 Tissue fluid diffuses into a lymphatic capillary and from this is enters a larger lymphatic vessel which conveys it to a lymph gland. In the lymph gland, lymphocytes are made. These are added to the tissue fluid, which is now known as lymph.

7.52

Lymph	Fresh tissue fluid
Contains urea	No urea
Contains carbon dioxide	No carbon dioxide
Contains no oxygen	Contains oxygen
Contains very little food	Contains products of digestion
Contains lymphocytes	Contains no lymphocytes

7.53 1 Formation of lymphocytes, which produce antibodies.

2 Recirculation of urea and carbon dioxide for excretion.

3 Transport of fats from the ileum to the liver.

In addition, lymph glands help to localise infection. Antigens pass from the cells to the nearest lymph gland, which filters out the antigens with the help of the lymphocytes. Tonsils, adenoids, and the small glands around the ears and neck are examples of lymph glands.

7.54 Lymph from the legs, trunk and left arm enters the left innominate vein in the neck and lymph from the head and right arm enters the right innominate vein. The largest collecting vessel is called the thoracic duct.

7 Distribution of the blood

7.55 The water in the bath is hot, and it tends to overheat the body. Therefore it is necessary to lose excess heat from the body, and this is done by radiation from the dilated blood vessels, and by sweating which uses up body heat in evaporation.

7.56 It is unwise to have a heavy meal just before a bath because the gut arterioles will be dilating at a time when the skin arterioles need to dilate. Normally the digestive system arterioles are constricted so that more blood is available to flow to the skin during a hot bath.

7.57 1 deoxygenated; 2 oxygenated.

7.58 Glucose; amino acids, fats.

7.59 Urea.

7.60 6 high glucose and oxygen
7 low glucose and oxygen.

7.61 The major functions of the blood are as follows:

1 transport of oxygen from the lungs to the tissues,

2 transport of carbon dioxide from the tissues to the lungs,

3 transport of waste products from the tissues to the kidneys,

4 distribution of heat to all parts of the body,

5 distribution of hormones from their glands to all parts of the body,

6 transport of food digestion products from the gut to the liver,

7 supply of glucose and metabolic requirements to all tissues.

8 Excretion

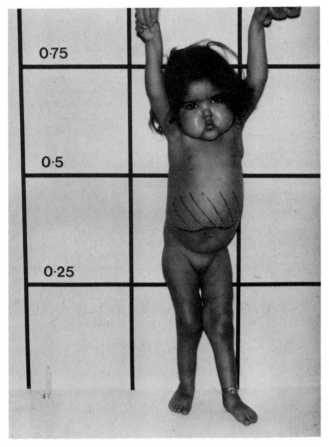

8.1 The 3 year old girl has a form of glycogen storage disease which has caused stunting of her growth and enlargement of her liver (marked).

1 Metabolic wastes

One result of almost every chemical reaction in the body is the formation of unwanted by-products. Some of these are relatively harmless, but a majority will damage the body if allowed to accumulate. These are **toxic** wastes. They are normally eliminated by the body. This elimination process is called excretion. Before excretion can occur, in some cases, the toxic waste has to be converted into a less toxic substance for transport to the excretory organ. In Unit 5 you learnt that excess amino acids are converted in the liver to carbohydrate, which is stored as glycogen, and ammonia, which is toxic. The ammonia is converted to the less harmful substance, **urea**, which is excreted through the kidneys.

$$2\,NH_3 \quad + \quad CO_2 \longrightarrow CO(NH_2)_2 \quad + \quad H_2O$$

ammonia   carbon   urea   water
         dioxide

Some people are born with an inability to break down all the excess amino acids they consume. In phenylketonuria, one amino acid, phenylalanine, accumulates in the blood and produces toxic effects. It eventually damages the brain cells and the individual becomes mentally retarded. They lack a crucial enzyme needed to break phenylalanine down into urea, and so some phenylalanine compounds are excreted in the urine.

▶ **Questions**

8.1 How might this condition be detected?
8.2 How can the disease be arrested to avoid mental changes?

Apart from urea, there are other metabolic wastes with which you should be familiar.

▶ **Questions**

8.3 What metabolic wastes are produced in respiration?
8.4 Which organs excrete these wastes?
8.5 Suggest some waste substances which are excreted in sweat.
8.6 Complete a table headed Waste Product and Organ Responsible, to summarise excretion.

2 The skin as an excretory organ

Activity 8.1 Observing the skin

1 Use a hand lens to observe the skin of your palms, the back of your hand, the inside of your arm and your partner's face.
2 Search particularly for the tiny pores through which sweat reaches the skin surface.

8.7 Which of the areas examined contains the most sweat pores per square centimetre?

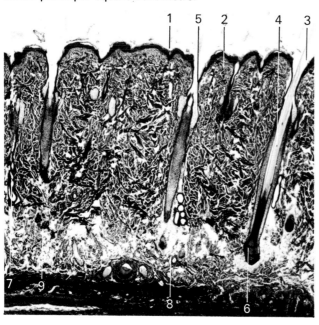

8.2 Photomicrograph of human skin

8.3 Vertical section through the skin

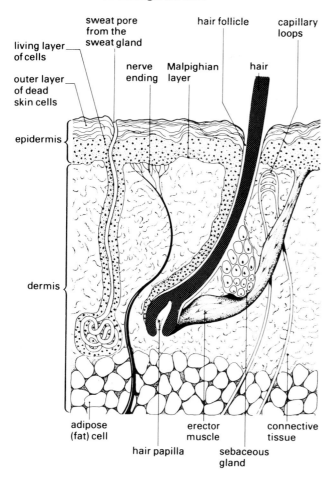

living layer of cells

outer layer of dead skin cells

epidermis

dermis

sweat pore from the sweat gland

nerve ending

Malpighian layer

hair follicle

capillary loops

hair

adipose (fat) cell

hair papilla

erector muscle

sebaceous gland

connective tissue

8.8 Using Fig 8.3 as a guide, identify the numbered parts of the skin in Fig 8.2.

8.9 The Malpighian layer is also called the germinative layer. It contains cells which are constantly dividing. Suggest the important function of this layer.

The dermis is made up of connective tissue, and contains a high proportion of matrix to cells. It forms an efficient packing layer.

Sweat is a watery liquid. Over 90% is actually water. About 1.2% is urea, and salt (sodium chloride) varies from about 1% to 2%. Excretion is a secondary role of the sweat glands. Their primary role lies in the regulation of the body temperature. This is discussed in Unit 11.

▶ **Question**

8.10 Suggest a reason for the rich blood supply of the sweat glands.

▷ **Research project**

Find out about the distribution of sweat glands throughout the body surface.

3 The urinary system

Some urea, salts and excess water, are excreted through the sweat glands as described in section 2. The urinary system, however, excretes a more substantial amount of all these wastes. The lungs also excrete a lot of water, as well as carbon dioxide. Refer to Unit 6 for information on the functioning of the lungs.

8.4 Dissection of the urinary system of a mammal

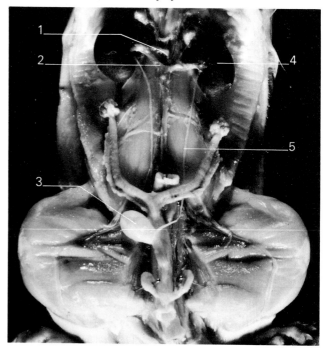

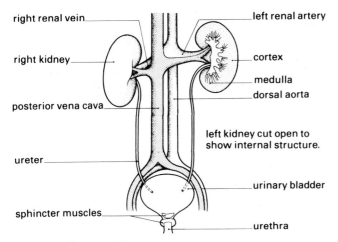

8.5 Ventral view of the urinary system

▶ Questions

8.11 Which organs have been removed in order to display the urinary system in Fig 8.4 (refer to Unit 2)?
8.12 Identify the parts in Fig 8.4 using the labelled diagram of the urinary system in Fig 8.5.
8.13 Which blood vessels take blood to the kidneys and which remove blood from them?

Activity 8.2 Investigating the structure of a sheep's kidney

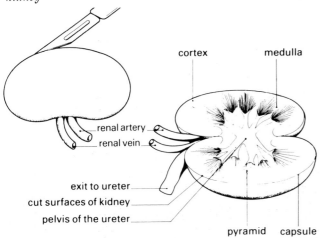

8.6 Dissection of a sheep's kidney

1 A sheep's kidney is basically similar in size and shape to that of man. Examine the external structure of the kidney carefully.
2 Using a scalpel or sharp knife, bisect the kidney as shown in Fig 8.6.
3 Using Fig 8.6 as a reference for labelling, draw one half of the dissected kidney.

▶ Questions

8.14 Describe the external structure of the kidney.
8.15 Are the cut surfaces uniform, or can you identify different regions?
8.16 Describe the connection between the ureter and the kidney.
8.17 Using Fig 8.6 as a guide, identify the numbered parts in Fig 8.7.

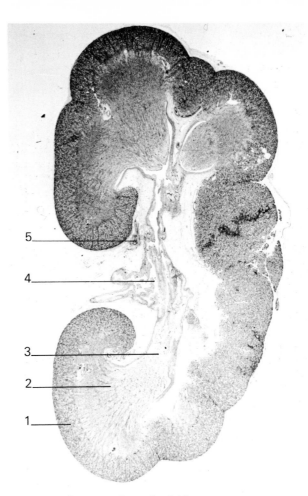

8.7 Vertical section through a kidney

The outer, dark red area of the kidney has a granular appearance. This is due to the presence of minute knots of capillaries called **glomeruli**. This region is called the **cortex**. The inner **medulla** region is pink and smooth, being mainly composed of the straight parts of about 1 000 000 minute tubules called renal tubules or **nephrons**. Each nephron begins as a wine glass shaped cup called the Bowman's capsule (see Fig 8.8).

8.8 A Bowman's capsule

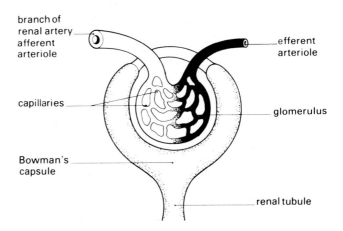

99

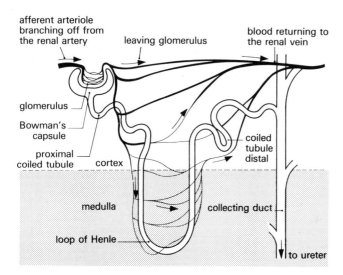

8.9 A nephron in the kidney

► **Questions**

8.18 In which part of the kidney are the Bowman's capsules?

8.19 Describe the course of a nephron from the Bowman's capsule to the collecting duct.

8.20 Where do the collecting ducts ultimately lead?

4 Filtration in the nephron

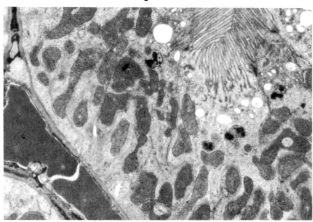

8.10 Electron micrograph of a proximal tubule cell

The structure of the nephrons is well-suited to their function of filtering waste substances from the blood. The smaller diameter of the efferent arteriole offers resistance to the flow of blood from the glomerulus. This raises the blood pressure in the glomerulus, which aids filtration of substances into the Bowman's capsule.

The proximal tubule cells possess numerous microvilli which vastly increase their internal surface area. This suggests that they are involved in the absorption of substances from the inside of the proximal tubule. The large number of mitochondria indicate that the cells have a high energy demand. They probably actively absorb substances from inside the nephron.

Activity 8.3 Finding out what the kidney filters from the blood

1 Take three test tubes and label them A, B and C. In A place 2 cm³ of plasma (from centrifuged blood), in B place 2 cm³ of urine and in C place 2 cm³ of distilled water.
2 Add 1 cm³ of urease to each tube and place stoppers in the tubes.
3 Place a piece of moist red litmus paper in each tube between the stopper and the glass. Do not allow the litmus paper to touch the liquid.
4 Incubate the tubes at 37 °C for one hour.
5 Note the colour of the litmus paper.
6 Test samples of A, B and C with Clinistix and Albustix. Clinistix turns yellow if glucose is present in solution, and Albustix turns red if protein is present. If it is difficult to obtain Clinistix or Albustix, the Benedict's and Biuret tests for glucose and protein respectively may be used instead.

► **Questions**

8.21 Construct a table and record the results of the three tests on A, B and C.
8.22 Suggest the substance which changes red litmus paper to blue. Why is it necessary to incubate the tubes at 37°C?
8.23 Name the substances found in A, B and C. What is the purpose of C?

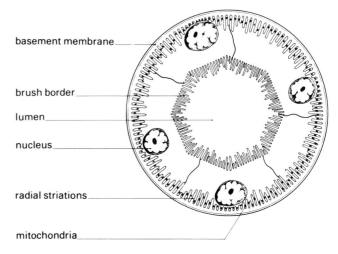

8.11 Transverse section of a proximal tubule

Table 8.1 Concentration of substances in plasma, filtrate and urine

Substance	% in plasma	% in filtrate in Bowman's capsule	% in urine
Water	90–93	99–100	97.5
Protein	7.0	0	0
Glucose	0.1	0.1	0
Salts	0.35	0.35	0.5
Urea	0.03	0.03	2.0

8.24 From Table 8.1, say what substance present in plasma is not filtered into the Bowman's capsule. Suggest a reason.

8.25 What are the basic differences between glomerular filtrate and urine?

8.26 What has happened to the glucose?

In the glomerulus, plasma, under pressure, is forced out through the selectively permeable capillary walls into the Bowman's capsule. Larger molecules, such as albumen and globulin, will not pass through the capillary wall. This process is called ultra-filtration. The filtrate in the Bowman's capsule contains substances useful to the body, such as glucose. The microvilli of the brush border of the proximal tubule cells re-absorb useful substances. This is called **selective re-absorption**.

The filtrate entering the loop of Henle is further adjusted depending on the water and salt requirements of the body. If water is in short supply, a lot of it is reabsorbed through the loop of Henle into the capillaries of the renal vein. Sodium ions are actively taken up in the loop of Henle to maintain the osmotic level of the blood. The regulation of this mechanism is discussed in Unit 11. The fluid entering the collecting duct is now a more concentrated solution, containing a higher percentage of urea than the glomerular filtrate. It is called **urine**. It passes into the collecting duct for transport to the pelvis of the ureter. From there it passes through the ureter to the bladder where it is stored until it is passed out.

Blood leaving the kidney in the renal vein is now purified. It is without urea and excess salts. It also contains the correct proportions of water and salt to maintain the correct osmotic level of the blood.

8.27 The composition of the urine depends on a number of factors. Suggest what would be the effect on the urine of the following situations.
   (a) drinking a lot of water in a short period of time
   (b) eating a very salty meal
   (c) eating a high protein diet
   (d) living in a hot desert

A number of people suffer from kidney disease which can lead to **kidney failure**. Their kidneys are no longer able to filter the wastes and excesses. Toxins accumulate in the blood, which if not removed, will result in death. In recent years an artificial kidney in the form of a bulky machine has been developed. Fig 8.12 illustrates the principle on which the artificial kidney works. It is called dialysis.

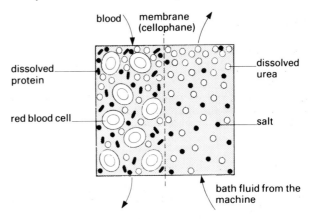

8.12 Dialysis

8.13 An artificial kidney in use

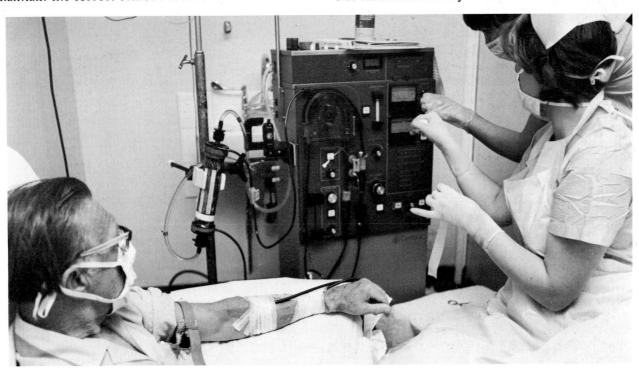

8.28 What substances are allowed through the membrane (usually cellophane) into the bath fluid of the machine?

8.29 What sort of membrane must cellophane be?

8.30 In order to work without damaging the patient in any way, what must the bath fluid contain?

8.31 Describe, very simply, how you think the machine in Fig 8.13 works.

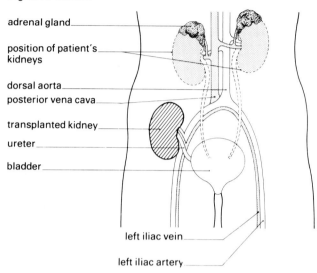

8.14 A transplanted kidney

Fig 8.14 is a simplified diagram of a kidney transplant. The diseased kidneys of the patient were removed and the transplanted kidney is placed lower in the abdomen.

▶ **Question**

8.32 Which blood vessel supplies blood to the transplanted kidney and which blood vessel returns the purified blood into the circulation?

▷ **Homework**

Write a brief essay on the way in which the kidneys remove waste products from the blood.

5 Micturition

Micturition is the act of passing urine. A normal person passes about three pints (two litres) of urine per day.

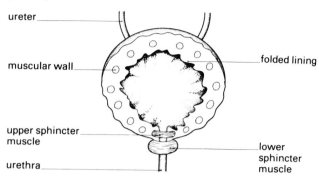

8.15 Section through a bladder

▶ **Questions**

8.33 What is the function of the bladder?

8.34 In what ways is the wall of the bladder well-suited to its function in the body?

8.35 What is the function of the sphincter muscles?

Answers and discussion

1 Metabolic wastes

8.1 It is detected by a urine test. Some phenylalanine is converted to phenylketones which are excreted in the urine.

8.2 The disease can be arrested by giving the person a synthetic diet containing measured amounts of phenylalanine. This avoids an excess of the amino acid entering the body.

8.3 Carbon dioxide and water are the waste products of respiration.

8.4 These substances are excreted by the lungs in expiration.

8.5 When sweating is rapid, salts are sometimes left on the body surface. Sweat contains unwanted salts, traces of urea and excess water.

8.6

Waste products	Excretory organs responsible
Urea	Kidneys, skin
Carbon dioxide	Lungs
Water	Lungs, kidneys, skin
Salts	Kidneys, skin

Note that faeces are not excretory products. They are not formed by metabolism in the body.

2 The skin as an excretory organ

8.7 The face and the palm of the hand normally have more sweat pores per square centimetre than the back of the hand or the inside of the arm.

8.8 1 epidermis; 2 dermis; 3 hair follicle; 4 hair; 5 sebaceous gland; 6 hair bulb; 7 sweat gland; 8 arteriole; 9 adipose (fat) tissue.

8.9 The Malpighian layer is an actively dividing layer which constantly produces new epidermal cells. As the cells get near the surface, they become flattened and hardened from wear and tear and actually die. They are then replaced by new cells growing up from below. All the epidermis you have today will have been replaced in six months time!

8.10 The sweat glands require a rich blood supply since sweat is formed from substances extracted from the blood. The more dilated the arterioles, the more blood there is available for sweat production.

3 The urinary system

8.11 The digestive system has been removed in order to show the urinary system.

8.12 1 right renal artery; 2 right renal rein; 3 urinary bladder; 4 left kidney; 5 left ureter.

8.13 The renal artery brings blood to the kidney and the renal vein removes it.

8.14 The kidney is a compact, dark red, bean-shaped organ about 7 cm long and 5 cm wide at its widest point. Arising from an indentation on one side of the kidney are the pale remains of the ureter, and the main blood vessels (renal artery and vein).

8.15 Two distinct regions are visible on the cut surfaces of the kidney. The outer region is dark and granular and the inner region is pink and smooth.

8.16 The ureter expands in the centre of the kidney to form the pelvis which has connecting ducts linking it with structures inside the kidney (see later text in section 3).

8.17 1 cortex; 2 medulla; 3 pyramid; 4 pelvis of the ureter; 5 renal blood vessel.

8.18 The Bowman's capsules are in the cortex of the kidney.

8.19 The Bowman's capsule leads into a twisting tubule which later straightens out and descends into the medulla. A parallel straight tubule loops back upwards and the nephron returns into the cortex where it coils again before entering a collecting duct.

8.20 The collecting ducts descend into the centre of the kidney where they link up with the pelvis of the ureter.

4 Filtration in the nephron

8.21

Test	A	B	C
Litmus	Turns blue	Turns blue	No change
Clinistix	Turns yellow	No change	No change
Albustix	Turns red	No change	No change

8.22 The alkaline substance in A and B is probably urea or ammonia. The tubes are incubated at 37 °C to allow the enzyme urease to act. Urease breaks urea down to ammonia. In water, ammonia forms ammonium hydroxide which is an alkali. This turns the red litmus paper blue.

8.23 A contains urea, glucose and protein, B urea only and C none of these. C, distilled water, is a control to emphasise that water alone would not contain these substances. Urine does not normally contain glucose or protein. If either of these are present, an abnormality is indicated which should be checked.

8.24 Protein is not filtered into the Bowman's capsule. Protein molecules are too large to pass through the selectively permeable capillary and capsule walls.

8.25 Glomerular filtrate contains glucose; urine does not. There is a higher percentage of salts and urea in urine. There is usually less sodium in urine than in glomerular filtrate, since this element is pumped back into the blood in the region of the loop of Henle.

8.26 The glucose present in glomerular filtrate is reabsorbed into the blood through the cells of the promixal tubule.

8.27 (a) The effect of drinking a lot of liquid will be to make the blood and body fluids more dilute than usual. This excess liquid will be removed by the kidneys which will form large amounts of dilute urine.
(b) Excess salt taken into the body must be excreted. This has to be done in solution, so the kidneys will make an extra amount of urine to take the salt out. This can result in a shortage of water inside the body, and then the thirst response is stimulated. This is why a salty meal often makes you feel thirsty.

(c) A high protein diet will lead to high amino acid levels; these are then converted eventually to urea which is excreted by the kidneys. The urine in this case will have a high urea concentration.

(d) Living in a hot desert will increase water loss by sweating. The kidneys will therefore excrete less water themselves, and what urine is formed will be highly concentrated and with the minimum amount of water.

8.28 Urea and salts are allowed through the membrane.

8.29 The membrane must be selectively permeable.

8.30 The bath fluid must contain the correct proportions of water and salts normally found in the plasma so that the balance can be maintained.

8.31 Blood is withdrawn from an artery (upper tube) and enters the top of the artificial kidney. A continuous supply of fresh bath fluid enters the machine (lower left), passes over the dialysis membranes and leaves (upper right) to be discarded. Purified blood leaves the bottom of the artificial kidney and is returned to an arm vein (lower tube).

8.32 Blood is supplied to the transplanted kidney from the iliac artery. Purified blood re-enters the circulation in the iliac vein.

5 Micturition

8.33 The function of the bladder is to store urine so that it can be discharged at intervals. It can hold about one pint (0.6 litre), but is usually emptied when half full.

8.34 The bladder wall has a folded lining which allows it to stretch to accommodate urine. The muscles in the wall of the bladder relax as it fills and contract as it is emptied.

8.35 The sphincter muscles contract and keep the exit to the bladder closed. When a certain pressure of urine on the wall of the bladder is transmitted to the brain, the sphincter muscles are instructed to relax, releasing the urine. This is initially a reflex action, but with learning it becomes a voluntary, controlled, action.

diffuses across each synapse which sets up depolarisation in the next neuron. In most cases, the chemical involved is a neuro-transmitter called **acetylcholine**. This substance is also released at the motor end plates to stimulate effectors. In some cases (see section 5), the transmitting substance is adrenalin. Chemical transmission is slower than electrical transmission. The more synapses involved in an action, therefore, the slower it is.

▷ **Research project**

Some lethal nerve poisons occur naturally in plants and animals. For example, some snakes produce a poison venom, and the South American Indians use a plant preparation for their poison-tipped arrows. Find out as much as you can about how these nerve poisons work.

3 Actions of the nervous system

Most actions controlled by the nervous system are either reflex actions or voluntary actions.

Reflex actions

▶ **Question**

9.13 Explain what happens if you touch a sizzling hot plate with your hand.

Fig 9.13 is an example of a reflex action. Arrows indicate the path of the reflex arc involved. You should be familiar with the various components. Study the figure carefully, then answer questions 9.14 and 9.15.

9.13 Nerve pathway used in reacting to a hot plate

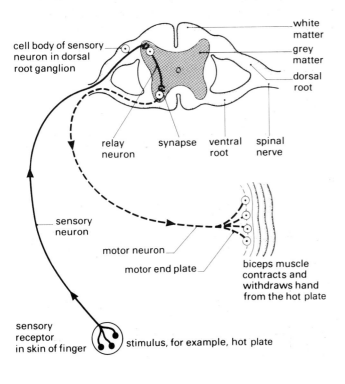

▶ Questions

9.14 How many neurons are involved in this reflex arc?
9.15 What is the function of the relay neuron?

Activity 9.1   What happens when the knee is tapped

1   Sit with one leg crossed over the other.
2   Get your partner to tap you sharply just below the knee with a rod. Do not watch him!

▶ **Question**

9.16 What happens to your leg? Did you think about it?

This activity demonstrates a simple reflex action called the knee jerk reflex.

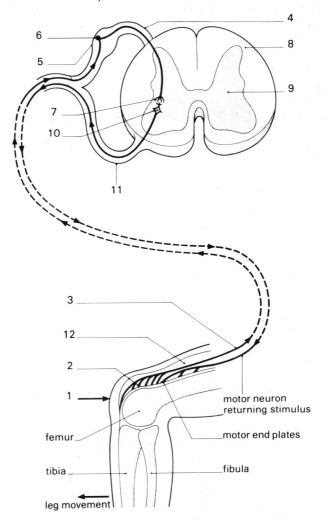

9.14 Nerve pathway for knee jerk reflex

▶ **Questions**

9.17 Identify the numbered parts in the knee jerk reflex shown in Fig 9.14.
9.18 What is missing in the reflex arc in Fig 9.14 which is present in Fig 9.13?
9.19 Which of these two reflex actions would you expect to be the faster and why?
9.20 Can you now define a reflex action?

Table 9.1 Some reflex actions

Reflex	Stimulus	Receptor	Effector	Response
1 Blinking				
2	Sharp tap on patella tendon			
3 Secretion of saliva	Food			
4 Withdrawal of hand from hot plate				
5 Coughing	Foreign body in trachea	Touch receptors trachea	Diaphragm and chest muscles	Ejects foreign body
6	Foreign body in nasal passages			
7				
8				

▶ **Question**

9.21 Table 9.1 summarises what happens in the coughing reflex. Five other reflex actions are represented by incomplete information. Copy out Table 9.1 and work out the necessary information to complete the summaries of reflexes 1, 2, 3, 4 and 6. Think of two more examples of reflex actions and write them in for 7 and 8.

Reflex actions, as well as being involuntary, are inborn, instinctive actions. They use regular pathways, but they can be slightly altered with experience. A Russian scientist, Pavlov, demonstrated this using dogs. Each time the dogs were presented with food, saliva appeared in the mouth. Pavlov then rang a bell every time food was presented. Eventually he only had to ring a bell for saliva to be produced. The dogs had associated the stimulus of the bell ringing with the stimulus of food, and by a conditioned reflex salivated at the bell stimulus.

▶ **Questions**

9.22 Suggest an example of a conditioned reflex in your behaviour.
9.23 In what way could conditioned reflexes be important to the young?

Voluntary actions

▶ **Question**

9.24 In what respects is the response shown in Fig 9.15 different from a reflex action? See Fig 9.13 and 9.14.

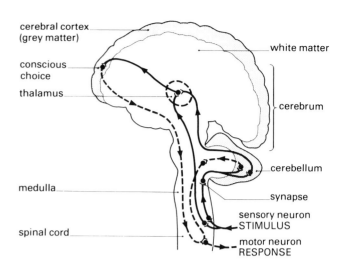

9.15 Nerve pathway for a simple voluntary action such as sitting down

In voluntary actions the cerebral cortex actually interprets what response is required. The sensory and motor areas of the cerebrum have been most closely mapped (see Fig 9.3). The sensory and motor areas for each part of the body are adjacent to each other. This helps to speed up reactions.

Visual stimuli are perceived in the occipital lobe. This is one of the higher behaviour centres. Hearing, speech, taste etc. are all dealt with in specific areas. The association zone associates stimuli, producing memory and making reasoning possible. The intelligence of an individual largely depends on this area, situated in the frontal lobes of the cerebrum.

▶ **Question**

9.25 Construct a table summarising the differences between a reflex action and a voluntary action.

▷ **Homework**

Analyse all your actions during half an hour and list the reflexes, conditioned reflexes and voluntary actions.

4 The autonomic nervous system

Although you do not have to think about a reflex action, you are usually aware that it has happened. You know your hand has withdrawn from a hot plate, or that your mouth is watering at the sight of tempting food.

Totally unconscious actions, such as breathing or the heart beating, are controlled by an additional system of neurons which comprise the autonomic nervous system (see Fig 19.16). Two sets of neurons make up the system, known as the **sympathetic** and the **parasympathetic** components.

The parasympathetic neurons are found in the medulla oblongata of the brain. The axons of these neurons run along the vagus nerve. The sympathetic neurons originate in separate ganglia which are connected by branches to the ventral roots of the spinal nerves. Study Fig 9.16 carefully. It gives

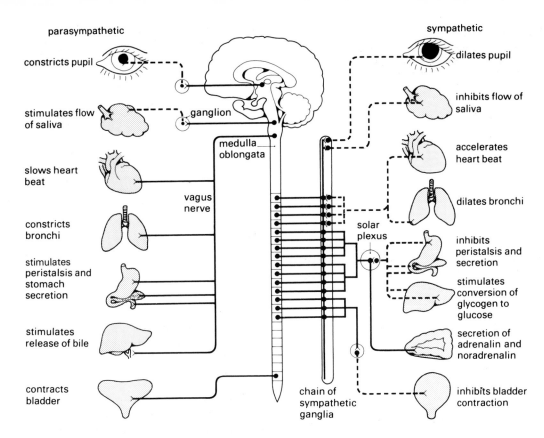

9.16 The autonomic nervous system

information about the way the autonomic nervous system works.

Generally, the sympathetic neuron brings about the opposite effect to the parasympathetic neuron. The sympathetic neuron accelerates activity, such as the heartbeat rate, while the parasympathetic neuron slows it down. The different responses of an organ are due to the effect of different chemicals being released by the two types of neuron. The sympathetic neurons release adrenalin, the parasympathetic neurons release acetylcholine.

▶ Questions

9.26 Suggest examples of actions which are going on in the body of which you are totally unaware.
9.27 Construct a table to summarise the action of the sympathetic neurons and the parasympathetic neurons on the following organs: salivary glands; heart; bronchi; gut; pupil; bladder.
9.28 Identify the numbered parts and functions involved in regulating peristalsis shown in Fig 9.17.

▷ Homework

Write a brief essay explaining why we need an autonomic system, and discuss what might happen if we did not have one.

5 The endocrine system

Not all co-ordination is by the nervous system. Many of our body responses are stimulated by chemical substances.

9.17 Parasympathetic and sympathetic reflexes controlling the rate of peristalsis in the intestine

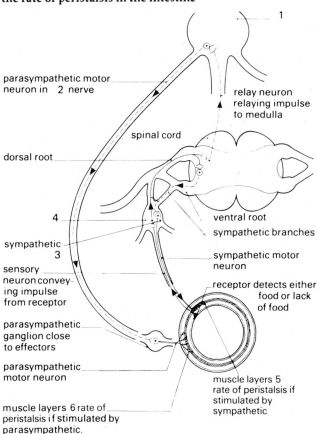

▶ Question

9.29 Name a chemical substance in the small intestine which stimulates the production of intestinal juice. (See Unit 5.)

These substances are known as chemical messengers or **hormones**. Their origin and composition was little known until around 1922, when Dr Frederick Banting succeeded in isolating the hormone, **insulin**. Earlier, it had been noticed that dogs in which the pancreas was removed, excreted large amounts of glucose in their urine. This is a sympton of sugar diabetes. Dr Banting suggested that there might be a substance in the pancreas which is necessary to regulate the concentration of glucose in the blood. The pancreas produced many substances, so the task of isolating just one substance was very difficult. Then Dr Banting discovered that if the pancreatic duct was tied off, glucose did not appear in the urine and the dog's sugar metabolism was not disturbed.

Dr Banting deduced that there must be a glucose-regulating substance present in the pancreas which does not require the pancreatic duct for distribution. It is distributed in some other way. The pancreatic juice which travels down the pancreatic duct contains digestive enzymes, not hormones.

Using a microscope, he identified some patches of cells in the pancreas which did not lead into the pancreatic duct. He suggested that these cells were producing the glucose-regulating substance. To prove this, he removed the pancreas from another dog, then injected the dog with an extract of the isolated patches of cells. Glucose did not appear in the dog's urine.

▶ Question

9.30 How must the glucose-regulating substance be transported in the body?

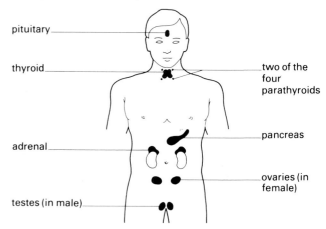

9.18 Glands of the endocrine system

Table 9.2 A summary of the functions of the main endocrine glands   * See Unit 12.

Gland	Secretions	Effects in the body
Pituitary	Thyrotrophin	Controls the output of thyroxin
	Gonadotrophins	Control the output of sex hormones
	Anti-diuretic hormone	Controls water-balance in kidneys
	Phyone	Controls bone growth
Thyroid	Thyroxin *Iodine*	Controls basal metabolic rate and mental and physical growth
Parathyroids	Parathormone	Controls calcium uptake
Pancreas (Islets of Langerhans)	Insulin *Glycogen*	Regulates blood sugar
Adrenal glands	Adrenalin – 'fight, fright and flight' hormone	Raises blood sugar Increases muscle tone Increases rate of heartbeat Increases rate of breathing – equips for emergencies
	Cortisone	Releases glucose from storage under stress Controls salt balance
Intestinal wall	Secretin and gastrin	Control secretion of intestinal juices
Ovaries	Oestrogen	Controls ovulation and secondary sexual characteristics*
Testes	Testosterone	Controls sperm production and secondary sexual characteristics*

He later isolated the active glucose-regulating substance from the cells, which he called insulin. Like all hormones, insulin is produced by cells in a gland which are not connected to a duct. The secretion passes straight into the blood, to be transported all over the body. The glands producing hormones are called ductless or endocrine glands. Glands with ducts are called exocrine glands.

9.19 The pituitary body

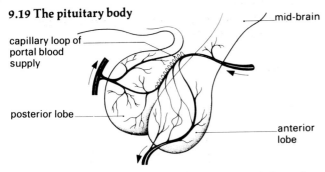

The pituitary gland controls the output of the other endocrine glands by a negative feedback system.

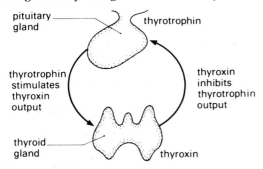

9.20 Pituitary-thyroid cycle

▶ **Questions**

9.31 Explain what happens when the amount of thyroxin secreted by the thyroid reaches the normal level in the blood.

9.32 Copy Table 9.3 and fill in the gaps to compare the mode of action of the endocrine and nervous systems.

Table 9.3

Component	Nervous system	Endocrine system
Stimulus		
Messages	Electrical impulse	
Mode of transport		
Effectors		
Speed of reaction		Relatively slow
Receptors		

▷ **Research project**

Sometimes hormone levels are abnormal. This can lead to people becoming giants or dwarfs. Find out as much as you can about acromegaly and cretinism.

Answers and discussion

1 The brain and spinal cord

9.1 The tissue of the brain and spinal cord is very delicate, so it has to be protected by a covering of bone.

9.2 1 cerebral hemisphere; 2 corpus callosum; 3 midbrain; 4 cerebellum; 5 pons; 6 medulla oblongata; 7 pituitary body.

9.3 The cerebral hemispheres are held together by bands of fibres running across the brain, called the corpus callosum.

9.4 The two halves of the cerebellum are joined by a bridge of fibres called the pons.

9.5 The pituitary body is attached to the midbrain area known as the hypothalamus.

9.6 Cell bodies are concentrated in the grey matter in the centre of the spinal cord.

9.7 Distribution of white and grey matter is reversed in the spinal cord when compared with the brain. The main function of the spinal cord is in the transport of messages to and from the brain. Only simple actions (see section 3) are actually initiated in the spinal cord.

9.8 1 grey matter; 2 white matter; 3 central canal.

9.9 Cerebrospinal fluid is found in both the brain (hence 'cerebro') and the spinal cord. It occurs in the spaces (ventricles) in the brain which are continuous with the central canal of the spinal cord.

2 The nerves and nerve cells

9.10 Each fibre within a bundle is an integral part of a nerve cell, either an axon or a dendron.

9.11 1 cell body; 2 nucleus; 3 dendron; 4 axon.

9.12 1 myelin sheath; 2 axon; 3 Schwann cell; 4 Schwann cell nucleus.

3 Actions of the nervous system

9.13 If you touch a sizzling hot plate, you withdraw your hand immediately. This is a reflex reaction.

9.14 Three neurons are involved in this reflex, a sensory neuron, a relay neuron, and a motor neuron.

9.15 The relay neuron switches the impulse from the sensory neuron to the appropriate motor neuron. It initiates the reaction to the sensory impulse.

9.16 The lower leg jerks up sharply. This happens automatically, without thought.

9.17 1 stimulus (tap); 2 (stretch) receptor; 3 sensory neuron; 4 dorsal root; 5 dorsal root ganglion; 6 cell body; 7 synapse; 8 white matter; 9 grey matter; 10 motor neuron; 11 ventral root; 12 effector muscle (quadriceps femoris) contracting.

9.18 There is no relay neuron in the knee jerk reflex.

9.19 The knee jerk reflex should be faster because it only involves two neurons. There is one less synapse to cross.

9.20 A reflex action is an immediate action which does not involve conscious thought. It is called involuntary because we do not have to think about it.

Reflex	Stimulus	Receptor	Effector	Response
1 Blinking	Bright light or foreign body	Retina of eye or touch receptor on eye	Eyelid muscles	Eyelid closes
2 Knee jerk	Sharp tap on patella tendon	Stretch receptor in skin	Quadriceps femoris (thigh muscle)	Lower leg jerks upwards
3 Secretion of saliva	Food	Taste buds	Salivary gland	Production of saliva
4 Withdrawing of hand from hot plate	Hot plate	Touch receptor in skin	Biceps in arm	Withdraws arm and hand
6 Sneezing	Foreign body in in nasal passage	Touch receptor in nose	Respiratory muscles	Foreign body ejected

9.22 When the bell goes, signalling the end of the last lesson before school lunch, saliva is (sometimes!) produced.

9.23 Conditioned reflexes are important in learning. A baby comes to associate the use of a potty with the stimulus of a desire to urinate. Skills such as driving are learned through conditioned reflexes.

9.24 The voluntary action illustrated involves the brain. At least seven neurons are involved, so the action will be slower than a reflex action. Voluntary actions also involve choice. A decision is made in the cerebral cortex whether or not to carry out a particular action. This can cause further delay in response.

9.25

Reflex action	Voluntary action
Not under the control of the will: involuntary. The brain is not involved.	Under the control of the will involving several parts of the brain.
Immediate: involving a minimum of two neurons	Delayed involving a large number of neurons. Choice also involved.
Simple self-preservation actions, instinctive	More complex actions, they are learned and dependent on memory and reasoning

4 The autonomic nervous system

9.26 Pupil dilation; peristalsis; heartbeat; posture maintenance.

9.27

Organ	Effect of sympathetic	Effect of parasympathetic
Salivary glands	Inhibits flow of saliva	Stimulates flow of of saliva
Heart Bronchi	Accelerates heartbeat Dilates bronchi	Slows down heartbeat Constricts bronchi
Gut	Inhibits peristalsis and secretion	Stimulates peristalsis and secretion
Eye Bladder	Dilates pupil Inhibits bladder contraction	Constricts pupil Contracts bladder

9.28 1 the medulla oblongata, the portion of the brain stem from which the vagus nerve arises; 2 the vagus; 3 ganglion; 4 neuron cell body; 5 decrease; 6 increase.

5 The endocrine system

9.29 Secretin is secreted in the wall of the duodenum, and stimulates the production of intestinal juice.

9.30 The glucose-regulating substance must reach the target organs (liver and skeletal muscle) in the blood.

9.31 When the level of thyroxin in the blood is correct, the pituitary is able to detect the fact as blood flows over it. In response, the pituitary stops secreting thyrotrophin. When the level of thyroxin falls below the required level, thyrotrophin will again be secreted to stimulate the thyroid gland to produce thyroxin.

9.32

	Nervous system	Endocrine system
Stimulus	Light, sound and other external sources	Internal, factors such as glucose levels with the exception of adrenalin which reacts to input from the brain
Messages	Electrical impulse	Complex chemical
Mode of transport	Neurons	Blood
Effectors	Muscles and glands	Whole body, organ or organ systems
Speed of reaction	Rapid reactions	Relatively slow
Receptors	Sense organs and brain	Sensors throughout the body

10 The senses

▶ **Questions**

10.1 What are the six senses?
10.2 Indicate in a table which parts of the body are the special receptors or sense organs for each sense.

1 Skin, tongue and nose

Skin receptors

Activity 10.1 Finding out which part of the body has the most touch receptors

1 Mount two pins about one centimetre apart in a piece of card.
2 Get your partner to close her eyes. Touch her skin either with one pin or the two pins simultaneously, first at the finger tips, then the palm of the hand, the back of the hand, the back of the neck etc. Avoid sharp contact with the pins.
3 Record what your partner says about whether you are using one pin or two in each case.

▶ **Questions**

10.3 What can you deduce if in one case your partner says that you only used one pin when you were actually using two?
10.4 How can you modify the experiment to distinguish between the more sensitive areas?
10.5 Which of the areas tested had the highest percentage of receptors per given area?
10.6 What general conclusion can you make from Activity 10.1?

Activity 10.2 Can the hands distinguish between hot and cold stimuli?

1 Set up three jars and fill jar A with cold water (10 – 15 °C), jar B with warm water (around 25 °C and jar C with hot water (40 – 45 °C).
2 Place the first finger of the left hand in the cold water in A and the first finger of the right hand in the hot water in C. Leave both fingers immersed for about thirty seconds.
3 Remove your fingers from both hot and cold water and dip them together into the warm water in jar B.
4 Describe what you feel.

▶ **Questions**

10.7 What can you conclude from this experiment?
10.8 How does the skin distinguish between a light touch, such as a cat's whisker, and a heavy touch, such as someone prodding the skin?
10.9 Why do we need pain receptors?
10.10 Using information from Fig 10.1, match the numbered receptors with the lettered stimuli in Fig 10.2.

10.1 Skin section to show skin receptors. There are five different types of receptor.

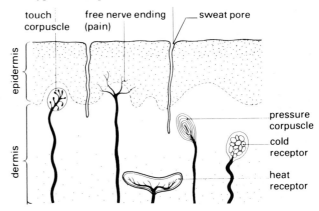

10.2 Receptors and stimuli

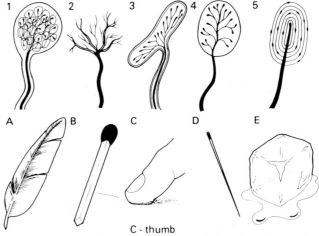

A - feather   B - match   C - thumb pressing down   D - needle   E - ice cube

Tongue

Tasting is one of the pleasures of life. Embedded in grooves in the tongue are groups of sensory cells called **taste buds**. Each taste bud is only able to detect one particular taste. Food contains one or more of the following detectable tastes: sweet, salty, bitter and sour.

Activity 10.3   Finding out which areas of the tongue detect the four tastes

1 Prepare four solutions as follows: A sucrose solution (sweet); B sodium chloride solution (salty); C citric acid solution (sour); D quinine solution (bitter).
2 Obtain a glass rod for each solution.
3 Get your partner to put his tongue out and place a drop of the first solution (A) on the back, front, sides and middle of the tongue. Your partner must not be told which solution you are applying.
4 Your partner identifies the taste if he can.
5 Make a mark on an outline map of the tongue for every positive result.
6 Repeat with the other three solutions. Use different marks on the outline map for each solution.

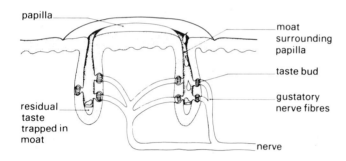

10.3 (a) Position of taste buds in the tongue

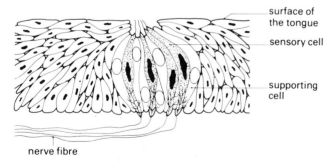

10.3 (b) Structure of taste buds

▶ Questions

10.11 How is tasting important apart from giving pleasure?
10.12 In which areas of the tongue are sweet, salty, bitter and sour detected? Draw an outline of the tongue and mark the areas involved.
10.13 Study Fig 10.3 and suggest why we continue to taste certain substances after we have swallowed them.
10.14 How are we able to taste flavours in food apart from salty, sweet, bitter and sour?

Nose

The sense of smell is believed to depend on the chemical composition of the object smelled. The smell receptors or **olfactory cells** are therefore chemical receptors or chemoreceptors. Fig 10.4 illustrates the smell receptors in the nasal epithelium. The nerve fibres conduct impulses to the olfactory lobes situated in the cerebrum.

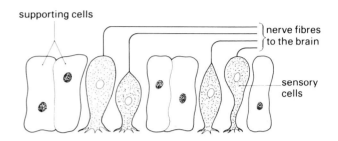

10.4 Smell receptors in nasal epithelium

▶ Question

10.15 Many animals have a more highly developed sense of smell than humans. How does a sense of smell help them and us?

▷ Homework

Imagine that you have lost your sense of smell and describe the ways in which it would affect you.

2 The eye

The eyes are delicate organs protected in deep, bony sockets called **orbits**. Their structure is best seen by examination and dissection of a sheep's eye.

Activity 10.4   Investigating the structure of a sheep's eye

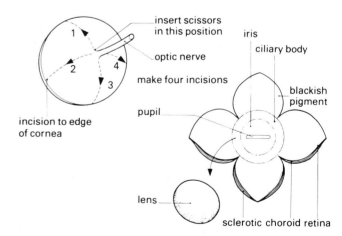

10.5 Dissection of a sheep's eye

1 Remove extra fat from around the base of the white stalk (the optic nerve) opposite the front of the eye.

116

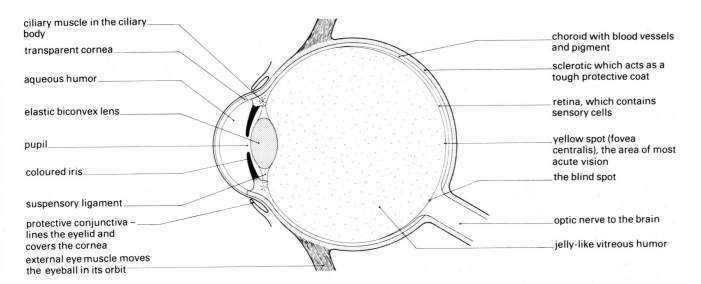

ciliary muscle in the ciliary body

transparent cornea

aqueous humor

elastic biconvex lens

pupil

coloured iris

suspensory ligament

protective conjunctiva – lines the eyelid and covers the cornea

external eye muscle moves the eyeball in its orbit

choroid with blood vessels and pigment

sclerotic which acts as a tough protective coat

retina, which contains sensory cells

yellow spot (fovea centralis), the area of most acute vision

the blind spot

optic nerve to the brain

jelly-like vitreous humor

10.6 Section through a human eye

2 Make a labelled drawing of the external features of the eye.
3 Hold the optic nerve with strong forceps and thrust the point of a pair of sharp scissors into the outer covering of the eye, close to the base of the optic nerve.
4 Make four incisions at right angles to each other from the base of the optic nerve to the cornea as shown in Fig 10.5. Keep the scissors upwards as you cut to avoid damaging the internal structures.
5 Make a drawing of the displayed structures. Identify the layers of the eye from Fig 10.5.

The **sclerotic** is a very tough outer layer which protects the delicate structures inside the eye. It also provides a tough base for the attachment of the external eye muscles which move the eyeball in its socket. The **choroid** contains blood vessels which nourish all the cells in the eye.

The eyeball is filled with humors which help to keep it in shape. In front of the lens is the watery **aqueous humor**, while behind the lens the more jelly-like **vitreous humor**. The **cornea** is transparent to allow light to enter the eye, and its curvature assists in the focusing of the light rays into the pupil and onto the retina.

▶ **Question**

10.16 Suggest the function of the iris, the coloured part of the eye.

Activity 10.5 Investigating the function of the lens

1 Fill a 500 cm³ round-bottomed flask with water. This represents the lens.
2 Fix a sheet of white paper on a piece of hardboard and stand it upright on the bench. This represents the retina.
3 Place the filled flask between the paper and the window about 25 cm from the window. Move the flask away from the paper, observing the paper.

▶ **Questions**

10.17 What do you see on the paper?
10.18 Remove the lens from the dissected eye and view print through it. Why does the eye need a lens?
10.19 From the position of the retina, and its structure as illustrated in Fig 10.7, what conclusion can you reach concerning its function in the eye?

10.7 Detail of the retina and outer layers of the eye

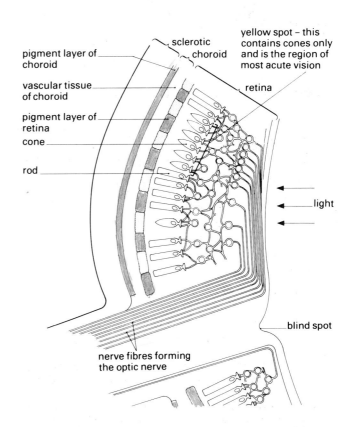

pigment layer of choroid

vascular tissue of choroid

pigment layer of retina

cone

rod

sclerotic

choroid

yellow spot – this contains cones only and is the region of most acute vision

retina

light

blind spot

nerve fibres forming the optic nerve

The two types of receptors, rods and cones, are easily identified by their shape. They react to different stimuli. **Cones** are concerned with detailed colour vision, while **rods** are concerned with tones from black through grey to white. Rods operate primarily in low light intensity. You may notice that colours appear to fade at twilight; this is because the cones which give us colour vision require fairly bright light, so it is the rods which are mainly used at twilight.

Activity 10.6 Investigating the distribution of rods and cones in the retina

1 Select a partner, then sit on a chair looking at a point on the blackboard straight in front of you.
2 Ask your partner to stand behind the chair. Cover your left eye and extend your arm out sideways. Ask him to place a piece of chalk of a colour unknown to you in your right hand. Move the chalk forward until it just enters your field of vision.
3 Stop as soon as the chalk is visible. Keep looking directly ahead.
4 Identify the colour of the chalk.
5 Move the chalk further forward.
6 Identify the colour again.

▶ **Question**

10.20 What does this experiment illustrate about the distribution of the rods and cones?

The area of the retina directly opposite to the pupil contains cones only. This is the area of most acute vision. It is called the **fovea** or **yellow spot**.

Activity 10.7 Finding out if there is an area of the retina without rods or cones

10.8

1 Hold this book upright, about 45 cm from your eyes.
2 Close the left eye and concentrate on the cross with the right eye.
3 Slowly bring the book closer to the face.

▶ **Question**

10.21 What happens to the dot during this time? Suggest an explanation.

The rods and cones form synapses with sensory neurons which unite to form the optic nerve. Where the optic nerve leaves the eyeball, a patch of sensory neurons take the place of rods and cones on the retina (see Fig 10.7). This is called the **blind spot**.

Activity 10.8   How the image is received by the retina

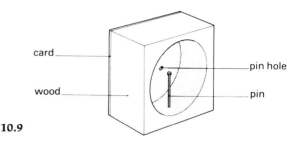

10.9

1 Hold the apparatus illustrated in Fig 10.9 with the card close to the eye.
2 Look through the pinhole and record what you see.
3 Reverse the apparatus, bringing the pin closer to the eye. Move the apparatus until the pinhead can be seen against the outline of the pinhole.

▶ **Question**

10.22 State what you see and suggest an explanation.

From Fig 10.7 it can be seen that the rods and cones are upside-down with respect to the direction of incoming light. This, together with the action of the lens, results in the reception of an inverted image by the retina, which is later interpreted the right way up in the occipital lobe of the cerebrum (see Unit 9). The conversion of light stimuli to electrical nerve impulses occurs when the visual pigments in the retina are bleached by the light.

10.10 (a) Image of a cube seen by the left eye
(b) Image of a cube seen by the right eye.

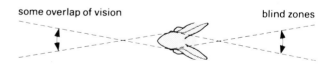

10.10 (c) Visual fields in binocular vision of a hare

10.10 (d) Binocular vision in man

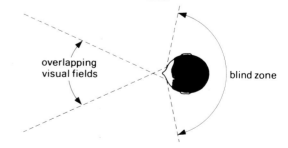

118

Stereoscopic vision

Why do we need two eyes, both directed forwards? As seen in Fig 10.10(c), animals with eyes on either side of their heads have a wider range of vision.

Activity 10.9 *The effect of binocular vision on depth perception*

1 Stretch out both arms horizontally at an angle from the midline in front of your body and point two pencil points towards each other.
2 Bring the pencils together to touch directly in front of you.
3 Repeat the operation closing one eye.

▶ **Question**

10.23 What do you infer from this experiment?

Accommodation

How is the eye able to view near and distant objects with equal clarity? Activity 10.10 will help to explain.

Activity 10.10 *Investigating lenses*

10.11

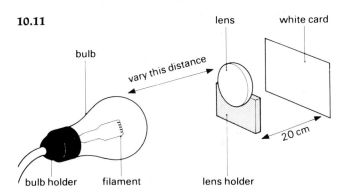

1 Set up the apparatus as shown in Fig 10.11.
2 Shine the light through the lens onto the card and move the light until you get a clear image of the bulb filament on the card.
3 Draw the shape of the lens and record the distance between the light and the lens.
4 Repeat steps 2 and 3 using other lenses of different shapes.

▶ **Question**

10.24 What is the relationship between the shape of the lens and the distance between the bulb and the lens which gives the clearest image?

The eye is able to view near and distant objects due to the elasticity of the lens. As the shape of the lens is changed, so is its focusing powers and we are able to view objects at varying distances as in Activity 10.10. Fig 10.12 illustrates the structures involved in altering the shape of the lens. In the choroid, close to the lens, is a circular band of muscles, the ciliary muscles. The lens is suspended from these muscles by a sheet of ligament, called the suspensory ligament. Study Fig 10.12 carefully, then answer the following questions.

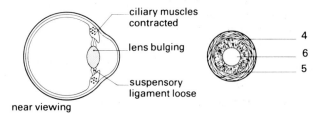

10.12 (a) Eye viewing near object

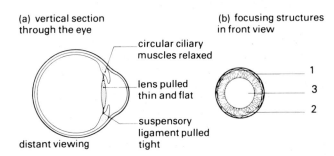

10.12 (b) Eye viewing distant object

▶ **Questions**

10.25 When the ciliary muscles contract, what effect does this have on the shape of the lens? Which objects are in focus when the muscles are contracting?
10.26 Describe the effect of relaxation of the ciliary muscles on lens shape and focusing ability.
10.27 Identify the numbered parts in Fig 10.12 and their condition.
10.28 Observe pupil size when a partner has been reading, then when the partner has been looking at the blackboard. What difference do you notice?
10.29 Which iris muscles cause pupil constriction when they contract? Which muscles contract to bring about dilation?

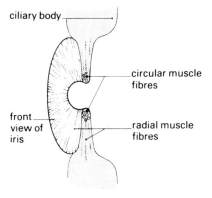

10.13 Muscles of the iris

Eye defects

The two most common eye defects are due to focusing problems. They are long-sight (hypermetropia) and short-sight (myopia). As people become older the elasticity of the lens becomes reduced. This causes presbyopia or old sight, where neither near nor distant objects can be clearly focused. This may be corrected by bifocal lenses which are biconcave in the top half and biconvex in the lower half.

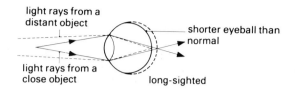

10.14 (a) Long-sighted eye

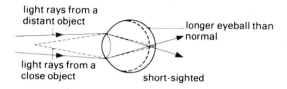

10.14 (b) Short-sighted eye

▶ **Questions**

10.30 In what respect do these eyeballs differ from a normal eyeball?
10.31 Why is a blurred image received from a close object in (a) and from a distant object in (b)?
10.32 What sort of lenses could be used to correct these defects?

▷ **Homework**

Carry out an eye test at home to discover which member of your family has the best focusing power.

3 The ear

The receptive parts of the ear lie embedded deep in the temporal bone of the skull. Receptors for both hearing and balance stimuli are located in the complex coils of the fluid filled inner ear. The ear is divided into the outer, middle and inner ear. The outer ear includes the

flexible **pinna** which leads into a short canal, the **meatus**. At the base of the meatus is a taut membrane, the **tympanum** or eardrum. Behind the eardrum is the air filled middle ear chamber, containing three tiny bones called the **auditory ossicles**. The innermost ossicle is attached to a small membrane called the **fenestra ovalis** or oval window. Behind the oval window is the coiled, fluid filled inner ear. Floating in the fluid, the **perilymph**, is a complicated membranous structure (see Fig 10.15), the top part of which contains sensory cells perceiving balance stimuli, the lower part containing sensory cells perceiving sound stimuli. The semi-circular canals, ampullae and utriculus are concerned with balance perception. The cochlea is concerned with sound perception.

▶ **Question**

10.33 The eustachian tube is collapsible. Suggest the role of this tube.

Hearing

Activity 10.11   Finding out how sound is located

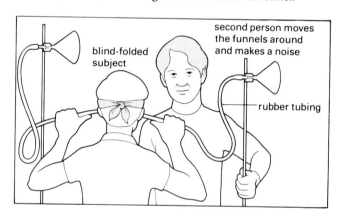

10.16

10.15 Section through a human ear

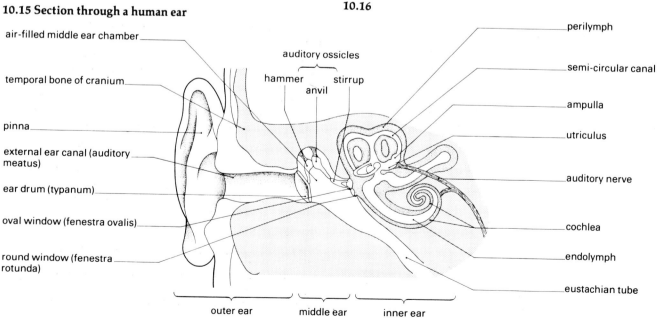

1 Rinse the tubes in a mild disinfectant, then hold the tubes in your ears. Only sound entering the funnels will enter your ears.

2 While you are blindfolded, your partner should move the funnels in various directions. Each time the funnels are moved, your partner should ring a bell.

3 State the location of the sound each time the bell is rung.

▶ **Question**

10.34 How accurate were you in your detection of sound direction? What can you conclude from this experiment?

Sound waves are collected by the pinna and directed to the eardrum, which vibrates. Vibration of the tympanum causes the auditory ossicles to vibrate. Vibrations of the ossicles are transferred to the oval window. The surface area of the tympanum is twenty times that of the oval window, so vibrations are magnified about twenty times at the oval window. Waves are set up in the perilymph by the inpushing of the fenestra ovalis. These waves surge against the cochlea, stimulating sensory cells found along the length of that organ. Impulses are set up in sensory neurons which form part of the auditory nerve. In the temporal region of the brain these impulses are interpreted as sound.

The cochlea is able to detect different frequencies of sound. High frequencies are interpreted by the brain as sounds high in pitch, low frequencies as low pitch. The range of frequencies detected by man is considerably more restricted than that of certain animals. Dogs can hear sounds above 40 000 hertz (cycles per second), and bats above 100 000 hertz. Man's upper limit of frequency perception varies with age, as shown in Fig 10.17. Man has difficulty in hearing frequencies below 100 hertz.

10.17 Frequency perception related to age

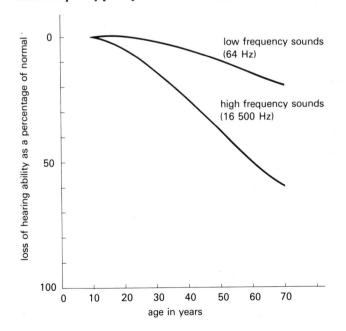

▶ **Questions**

10.35 What is the percentage loss of hearing ability of upper frequency sounds by a person of your age?

10.36 What is the percentage loss of hearing ability of lower frequency sounds by a 65 year old?

10.37 What is the percentage loss in ability to hear high sounds for every ten years of life after maturity?

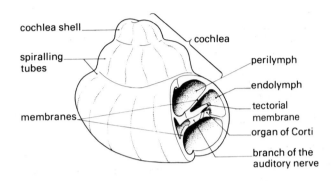

10.18 Model of the cochlea showing the cells comprising the organ of corti

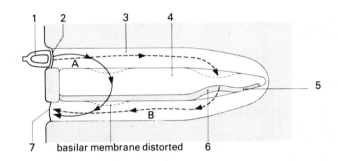

10.19 Sectional view of the cochlea straightened out

The 30 000 sensory cells which make up the organ of Corti stretch along the twisted length of the cochlea and arise from a basilar membrane. Their free ends bear stiff sensory hairs which are in close contact with a gelatinous strip called the tectorial membrane. Vibrations in the perilymph push up against the basilar membrane, bending the hairs of the sensory cells into the tectorial membrane. This stimulates the sensory cells, which set up a nerve impulse. High frequency sound waves surge against the basilar membrane at the base of the cochlea, low frequency sound waves stimulate the sensory cells at the tip of the cochlea. The hairs detect pitch accordingly.

▶ **Questions**

10.38 Identify the structures numbered on Fig 10.19.

10.39 Indicate which arrows in Fig 10.19 represent low frequency sound waves and which represent high frequency sound waves.

10.40 Suggest the function of the round window.

Balance

Activity 10.12   The semi-circular canals

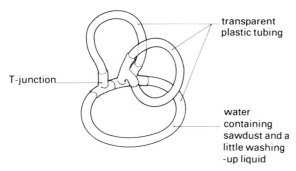

10.20 Model of the semi-circular canals

1   Assemble the model shown in Fig 10.20 in a shallow dish of water.
2   Add fine sawdust to the water to make movement easier to see, and washing-up liquid to reduce surface tension.
3   Fill each tube separately, then join to the neighbouring one.
4   Keep all three tubes horizontal under the surface while filling. Adjust the canals to their final position in three planes at right angles to each other.
5   Rotate the model in the plane of any one of the canals.

▶ **Question**

10.41   Describe what happens as you rotate the model. How can this be related to balance perception?

The utriculus, from which the ampullae arise, is also lined with sensory cells having hairs embedded in gelatinous plates. Contained in some of the gelatinous plates are fine chalky granules called **calcoliths**.

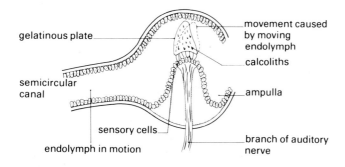

10.21 Section through an ampulla and semi-circular canal

▶ **Questions**

10.42   Using information from Activity 10.12 and Fig 10.21, suggest how the balance organs are able to detect changes in our body position and relay the information to the brain.
10.43   Why do we feel giddy after spinning around for some time?

▷ **Research project**

There are several different causes of deafness. Find out as much as you can about the common causes, and explain how they may be overcome.

122

Answers and discussion

10.1 The six senses are sight, hearing, smell, taste, touch and balance.

10.2 *Sense*	*Sense organ*
Sight	Eyes
Hearing	Ears
Smell	Nose
Taste	Tongue
Touch	Skin
Balance	Inner ears

1 Skin, tongue and nose

10.3 The number of touch receptors in that area of your partner's skin is few.

10.4 Put the pins more closely together on the card to detect the most sensitive areas.

10.5 The fingertips probably had the highest percentage of receptors per unit area of the regions tested.

10.6 The most numerous touch receptors are in the fingertips, then the palm of the hand, then the back of the neck and, finally, the back of the hand. There is a variation in sensitivity to touch in different parts of the body.

10.7 The fingers are able to detect changes in temperature rather than absolute heat and absolute cold.

10.8 There are separate receptors for light touch (such as a cat's whisker) and pressure (such as that applied by a finger).

10.9 Pain is an indication that something is wrong. It is important that we are able to detect injuries and to treat them.

10.10 1 E; 2 D; 3 B; 4 A; 5 C

10.11 It is important that we are able to taste in order to detect any possible toxic food. Bitterness is often a sign of potential poison.

10.12

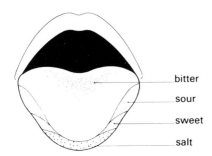

bitter
sour
sweet
salt

10.22 Taste areas of the tongue

10.13 We experience an aftertaste of substances which are trapped in the base of the pits containing the taste buds.

10.14 Subtle, interesting qualities of food are detected by smell receptors in the nose. Most of what we 'taste' is actually smelled in our head. This explains why it is difficult to taste food when we have a cold.

10.15 Unpleasant smells are often a warning of danger to animals, and to us. Many poisonous gases have an obnoxious smell, for example ammonia and sulphur dioxide.

2 The eye

10.16 The iris regulates the size of the pupil. If the light is too bright, the iris constricts the pupil. This is further explained under Accommodation.

10.17 At one point, an image of the window and the outside scene appears on the white paper screen. The image is inverted. The water-filled flask acts as a convex lens and light from the outside is refracted (bent), forming an image on the screen of white paper.

10.18 Without a lens, images of objects viewed would not be focused on the retina, so would not be clearly seen.

10.19 The retina is the sensitive layer of the eye. It contains the sensory cells which are stimulated by light. It is equivalent to the film in a camera. Images of objects viewed are formed on it.

10.20 When the chalk first enters the visual field, it appears dark grey. Nearer the centre of the visual field, if it is red chalk, it appears red. This shows that there are more cones concentrated in a spot directly opposite the pupil than in the periphery of the retina.

10.21 When the book is about 20 cm from the eye, the dot disappears, then reappears as the book is brought even closer. There must be an area on the retina which is not sensitive to light or darkness.

10.22 An enlarged shadow of an upside down pinhead is seen. The shadow cast on the retina was actually the right way up, but the brain 'corrected' it as in normal viewing. The images received by the retina are inverted.

10.23 Two eyes with overlapping visual fields are necessary to perceive depth with any accuracy. Binocular vision is stereoscopic, monocular vision is not. Man is also able to interpret what he sees. For example if he sees a house obscuring a part of another house he knows it must be in front of the other one and therefore nearer.

10.24 The more biconvex the lens, the shorter the distance between the lens and the bulb required to give a clear image.

10.25 Contraction of the ciliary muscles reduces the circumference of the ciliary body. Tension on the suspensory ligament is slackened, so the lens bulges and becomes more convex. This allows near objects to be focused.

10.26 Relaxation of the ciliary muscles increases the circumference of the ciliary body. This pulls the suspensory ligament taut and flattens the lens. This allows distant objects to be focused.

10.27 1 ciliary muscles relaxed; 2 suspensory ligament taut; 3 lens thin and flat; 4 ciliary muscles contracted; 5 suspensory ligament slack; 6 lens bulging.

10.28 When reading, the pupils are constricted. When viewing a blackboard, the pupils are dilated. A lot of light falls onto the retina from a close page of a book, so this is cut down. Too much light can damage the delicate retina. In order to obtain sufficient light from a distant object to view it clearly, the pupil opens wide.

10.29 Circular muscles of the iris constrict the pupil size when they contract. Dilation of the pupil is brought about by contraction of the radial muscles.

10.30 The long-sighted eye has a shorter distance between the lens and the retina than a normal eye. The short-sighted eye has a greater distance between the lens and the retina than a normal eye.

10.31 In (a) a blurred image is perceived from a close object because the lens is unable to converge the diverging light rays soon enough to focus them on the retina. The light rays converge at a point behind the retina. There is no difficulty in viewing distant objects which have parallel light rays.

In (b) a blurred image is received from a distant object. The parallel rays converge at a point in front of the retina. Close objects with diverging rays are viewed clearly.

10.32 Long-sight is corrected by a converging lens (biconvex) placed in front of the eye. Short-sight is corrected by a diverging lens (biconcave). See Fig 10.23.

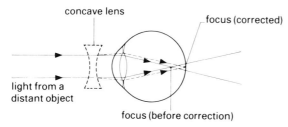

10.23 (a) Corrected short sight

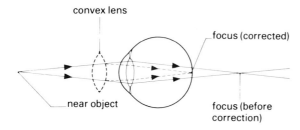

10.23 (b) Corrected long sight

3 The ear

10.33 If air pressure in the middle ear chamber is above that in the meatus, it could burst the eardrum. To prevent this, the eustachian tube can open to release air into the throat. You may have noticed your ears 'popping' in an aeroplane, or going up a tall building in a lift.

10.34 Many mistakes will be made in this experiment. If the funnels are crossed over, when sounds are coming from the right, you will think they are coming from the left. This shows that the funnels collect the sound. The pinnae act in the same way, and since they are not transferable from left to right, they must help in locating the direction of sound.

10.35 There is about a 3% loss in hearing ability of upper frequency sounds by a 15 year old.

10.36 There is about a 60% loss in hearing ability of higher frequency sounds by a 65 year old.

10.37 Loss of high frequency hearing ability amounts to about 13% every ten years.

10.38 1 stirrup; 2 oval window; 3 perilymph; 4 endolymph; 5 basilar membrane; 6 organ of Corti; 7 round window.

10.39 A arrows, high frequencies; B arrows, low frequencies.

10.40 When the oval window is pushed into the inner ear by vibration of the auditory ossicles, pressure does not build up in the perilymph because the round window is pushed out.

10.41 The fluid in the rotated canal moves round due to inertia. The fluid in the other canals is carried with the model in the direction of rotation. In the semi-circular canals, movement of the head as we change our position causes movements in the endolymph.

10.42 As the endolymph moves in the canals, the ampullae, and the utriculus, it pushes against the gelatinous plates. This causes the hairs of the sensory cells to bend, triggering off an impulse in those particular cells. The impulse passes along a sensory neuron in the auditory nerve to the balance centre of the cerebrum, which interprets the body's position. With every movement, different cells will be stimulated. The calcoliths in the gelatinous plates of the utriculus make these plates more dense and more effective in stimulating the sensory hairs.

10.43 Giddiness is caused by continuing surging of the endolymph stimulating a number of sensory cells after movement of the body has ceased.

11 Homeostasis

1 Defining homeostasis

To ensure that the body is able to work efficiently, certain factors must be kept more or less constant. Some of these factors are illustrated below.

11.1 On a sunny beach

11.2 Out in the cold

11.3 Body temperatures of a man and a frog

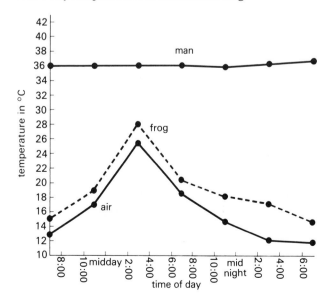

▶ Questions

11.1 Suggest a reason why the blood of the girl in Fig 11.1 does not overheat when she is exposed to the hot sun. Why does the blood of the girl in Fig 11.2 not freeze?

11.2 In Fig 11.3, how does the temperature of the frog compare with the air temperature over a period of twenty-four hours?

11.3 How does the temperature of the man compare with the air temperature over a period of twenty-four hours?

11.4 What is the temperature range of (a) the frog and (b) the man over twenty-four hours?

A constant body temperature makes it possible for man to be active all the time, regardless of the external temperature. On the other hand, many animals are not able to maintain a constant body temperature, and they become less active during the colder parts of the day, and, in some cases, they become completely inactive during the winter months when they hibernate. When the body temperature falls, as in the frog in Fig 11.3, enzymes become less active, and many body processes cannot take place.

Fig 11.4 shows the results of an investigation into the levels of glucose in the blood of a fifth form pupil, and the levels of glucose in his small intestine over a twenty-four hour period.

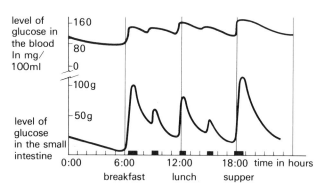

11.4 Blood glucose levels and small intestine glucose levels over 24 hours

▶ **Questions**

11.5 What is the range of blood glucose levels over a period of twenty-four hours shown in Fig 11.4?
11.6 What is the range of glucose levels in the small intestine over the same period of twenty-four hours?
11.7 Which glucose level fluctuates least?
11.8 What happens to the blood glucose level at 08.00? Can you explain this?

11.5 Input and output of water over 24 hours

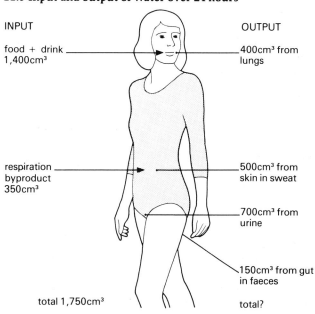

11.9 What has happened to the blood glucose level by 12.00?
11.10 At 20:00 the level of glucose in the small intestine is still relatively high, but the blood glucose level is already decreasing. Can you suggest what is happening to the glucose in the blood.
11.11 What is the total output of water shown in Fig 11.5?
11.12 What can you say about the total water content of the girl in Fig 11.5?
11.13 How will water balance be achieved if the amount of sweat produced goes up to 1000 cm³ per twenty-four hours?

Many other substances in the blood are maintained at their correct levels. For example it is very important to control the levels of specific hormones such as thyroxin and oestrogen.

▶ **Questions**

11.14 What system in the body plays an important part in maintaining the necessary balance in all the examples quoted here?
11.15 Suggest some of the consequences which might result from a disturbance of steady states of (a) temperature, (b) blood glucose levels or (c) water levels.

To summarise, homeostasis is the system of maintaining an internal steady state of the levels of temperature and all important substances.

▷ **Homework**

Write a list of animals other than man which are capable of maintaining a constant body temperature.

2 Temperature regulation

Activity 11.1   Finding out how hot your body is

1   Use a clinical thermometer. Sterilise it in antiseptic and then wash it in clean water.
2   Hold the bulb under the tongue with only the top few millimetres of mercury showing.
3   Wait for about two minutes until the mercury has stopped rising before taking a reading.
4   Record your temperature in your notebook, and on the blackboard.
5   Construct a bar graph of the class results, plotting temperature on the horizontal axis.

▶ **Questions**

11.16 What is the modal (most frequent) temperature? How does it compare with Fig 11.3?
11.17 Would you expect to obtain the same results if you repeated the experiment on a hotter or colder day?

Activity 11.2   Finding out how uniform the body temperature is

1   Take the temperature of the different parts of the body shown in Fig 11.6, by placing the bulb against the skin, and covering the bulb with cotton wool.

126

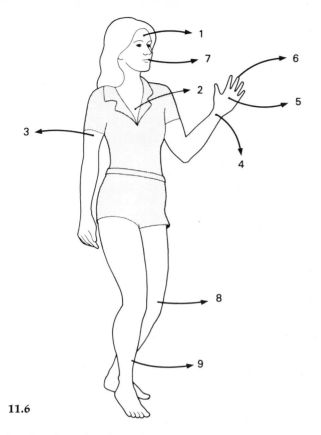

11.6

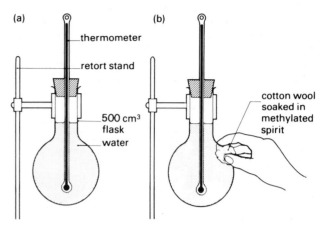

11.7

2   Sterilise the thermometer after use.
3   Record the temperatures on a simple human figure outline.
4   Additionally, try taking your temperature at different times of the day, starting early in the morning and finishing late in the evening.
5   Plot the results of step 4 on a graph, with time on the horizontal axis.

▶ Questions

11.18   How does the temperature vary in different parts of the body?
11.19   How does the temperature vary at different times of the day?

The areas you have been testing constitute primarily the skin temperature, or peripheral temperature as it is sometimes known. Skin temperature is variable, as shown in Activity 11.2, but core temperature (deep in the body) varies very little. Taking the temperature under the tongue is as close as we can get to core temperature.

Ways in which heat is lost

We feel hot in hot weather and cold in winter conditions, so it is obvious that we do not maintain a totally constant temperature. It is variations in skin temperature which are detected. Core temperature is rarely affected by climatic conditions because of the mechanisms used by the body to correct the temperature level in response to the skin receptors. If we are in danger of overheating, like the girl in Fig 11.1, there are a number of ways in which the body actively loses heat.

1   Boil 500 cm³ of water and pour it into a round bottomed flask supported by a clamp as in Fig 11.7. Turn off the bunsen.
2   Fit a rubber bung containing a thermometer. The bulb of the thermometer should be in the centre of the flask.
3   Record the temperature of the water immediately after fitting the bung.
4   Repeat temperature readings at one minute intervals for ten minutes. Record each time and temperature in a table.
5   For five minutes, wipe the surface of the flask with methylated spirit as in Fig 11.7. Take temperature readings and record as in step 4.
6   Stop wiping with meths and repeat step 4.
7   Make a note of the room temperature.

▶ Question

11.20   Use your results to plot a graph, with time on the horizontal axis. Calculate the three rates of temperature fall for steps 4, 5 and 6.

Ethanol (methylated spirit) has a lower boiling point than water (80 °C), which means that ethanol at room temperature is closer to its boiling point and therefore evaporates more rapidly. This is what happened in step 5.

Fig 11.8 illustrates variations in skin temperature when a person wandered in and out of a warm overheated room on a cold day. It also shows a relationship between this temperature variation and the rate of sweating by the subject.

▶ Questions

11.21   (a) What effect does rising skin temperature have on the volume of sweat produced?
(b) What effect does moving out into the cold have on the volume of sweat produced? Can you explain why?

11.22   Remembering Activity 11.3, suggest how sweating keeps the skin cool.

127

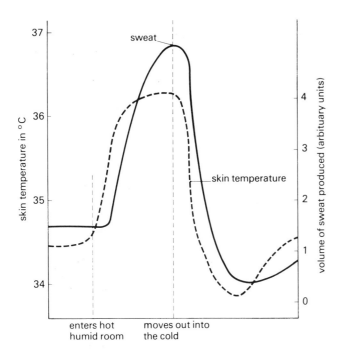

11.8 Skin temperature and sweating rates

▶ **Question**

11.23 Apart from sweating, what other changes are visible on the skin surface when you are hot?

Fig 11.9 shows why you flush when you are too hot. The arterioles in the skin dilate, allowing more blood into the surface capillaries. Blood contains heat produced by body activities. This heat radiates from the body surface. You can feel this if you touch your skin when you are flushed.

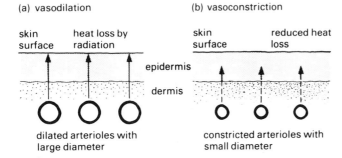

11.9 Vasodilation and vasoconstriction in skin arterioles

▶ **Questions**

11.24 Dilation of these arterioles will also bring more blood to the sweat glands. What effect will this have on the rate of sweating?

11.25 Under what circumstances would you expect the skin arterioles to constrict and reduce the amount of blood in the surface capillaries?

Loss of heat by **evaporation** and **radiation** are only two of the methods of temperature control involved. As heat leaves the body surface, air currents move the warmed air close to the skin away from the body by **convection**. Heat loss by convection may be reduced in several ways.

Activity 11.4   Finding out how heat flow by convection from a surface can be reduced

1 Set up two round bottomed flasks like the one in Fig 11.7(a). The second flask is covered with insulating material such as cotton wool, but in all other respects is identical to flask A. (Refer to Activity 11.3.)
2 Record the initial temperature of the water in both flasks.
3 Take temperature readings from both flasks at one minute intervals for twenty minutes. Record time and temperature in each case in a table.
4 Make a note of the room temperature.

▶ **Questions**

11.26 Construct a combined graph for the two flasks, with time on the horizontal axis.
11.27 Calculate the rate of temperature fall for the water in both flasks.
11.28 What can you conclude from the graphs and calculations?

There are two ways in which the body provides **insulation** against heat loss. (a) A layer of fat cells in the dermis forms a barrier to heat loss by convection. In winter you are often fatter than in summer. We eat foods of a higher joule value in winter than in summer, and have greater appetites. This results in extra fat being stored in the skin. (b) Hairs distributed throughout the skin surface trap a layer of warm air as it rises from the skin, cutting down convection currents. Hairs normally rest at an acute angle to the skin surface, that is they are flattened. In response to cold, the erector muscle attached to the hair follicle contracts, pulling the hair up straight at right angles to the skin surface. When all the hairs are erect, a deeper layer of warm air is trapped close to the surface, keeping heat loss by convection to a minimum. This is a significant help in most mammals, but is less so in man where body hair is usually sparse. The body still tries to utilise the hairs – hence the 'goose pimples' seen in cold weather. Each bump represents an erected hair.

11.10 The skin showing methods of heat insulation

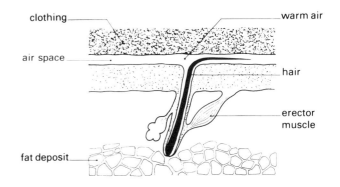

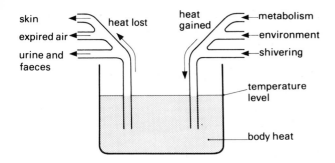

11.11 Temperature balance

▶ Questions

11.29 How can man obtain an additional source of insulation and why does he need it?

11.30 Fig 11.11 shows how the body maintains a normal temperature level. How else does the body lose heat apart from through the skin surface?

11.31 List the ways in which we gain heat. In what ways do we gain heat from the environment? How does shivering enable us to gain heat?

In order to keep the balance level, there must be some sort of control to regulate heat production and heat loss. The control is the heat centre found in the hypothalamus of the midbrain (see Unit 9). As blood flows over the heat centre it detects the temperature

11.12 Temperature regulation by the hypothalamus

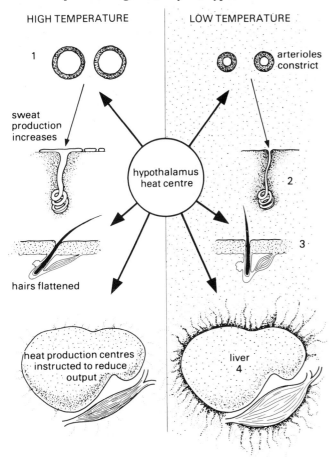

of the blood. If the temperature is too high, impulses are sent via the autonomic nervous system to increase skin arteriole dilation and the rate of heat loss is accelerated. If the temperature is too low, the heat centre relays impulses to the skin causing constriction of arterioles and consequent reduced heat loss. To some extent the hypothalamus can also regulate heat production.

▶ Question

11.32 Identify what is happening in the parts of Fig 11.12 which are numbered.

In some situations the heat centre fails to work properly. As people age, the heat control mechanism becomes less efficient. Very old people frequently suffer in cold weather because they are unable to conserve their body heat. The core temperature falls dangerously low and some elderly people die as a result. The condition is called hypothermia. (See Unit 18). The body becomes overheated when we have a fever. This is because the micro-organisms causing the infection interfere with the functioning of the temperature centre, which no longer recognises temperature changes in the blood. Death will result if the temperature rises much beyond 40 °C. This is called hyperthermia.

Body shape and heat loss

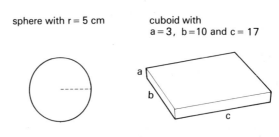

sphere with r = 5 cm   cuboid with
                            a = 3, b = 10 and c = 17

11.13 (a) A sphere   **11.13 (b) A cuboid**

11.14 (a) A typical eskimo family

Table 11.1 Measurements of an eskimo and a Sudan negro

Measurement	Eskimo	Negro
Height	150 cm	190 cm
Volume	0.09 m³	0.07 m³
Surface area	1.8m²	2.1m²

11.14(b) Sudan negro girls

Table 11.2 Measurements of an adult and a newborn baby

Measurement	Adult	Newborn baby
Height	165 cm	60 cm
Volume	0.07 m³	0.003 m³
Surface area	1.8 m²	0.8 m²

► **Questions**

11.33 Work out the surface area to volume ratio for each of the shapes shown in Fig 11.13. Refer to Unit 6 section 3 to see how to do this.
11.34 Which of the shapes in Fig 11.13 corresponds more closely to the negro and which to the eskimo?
11.35 From Table 11.1 calculate the surface area to volume ratio for the eskimo and the negro.
11.36 Which body shape do you think is more suitable for living in a hot climate? Explain your answer.
11.37 Explain why it is necessary to wrap a newborn baby in a blanket in a room where adults do not feel particularly cold (see Table 11.2).

▷ **Research project**

Why do you think hypothermia is becoming increasingly common amongst the elderly? Find out how you would diagnose and treat it yourself.

3 Water and salt balance

To function properly the body must contain the right balance of water and salts.

► **Question**

11.38 Which part of the body is primarily responsible for regulating water loss? (Refer to Unit 8).

Absorption of water occurs in the kidney tubules. The amount reabsorbed into the blood depends on the permeability of the tubules, which is in turn affected by the pituitary gland. Fig 11.15 illustrates the effect of ADH (anti-diuretic hormone) levels in the blood on the amount of water absorbed in the kidney tubules. ADH is produced in the pituitary gland. The pituitary detects the water level in the blood as it flows through the pituitary and it secretes an appropriate quantity of ADH.

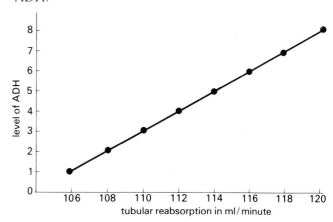

hypothetical — units of ADH arbitrary

11.15 ADH levels and tubular reabsorption of water

► **Questions**

11.39 Using the graph, suggest how ADH affects the kidney tubules, and explain the function of ADH in the body.
11.40 Some people have a deficiency of ADH and suffer

from a disease called diabetes insipidus. Suggest what symptoms they would show.

11.41 Under what circumstances would you expect the highest levels of ADH to be produced?

11.42 Refer to Fig 11.16 and explain why ADH levels may be relatively low on a cold day.

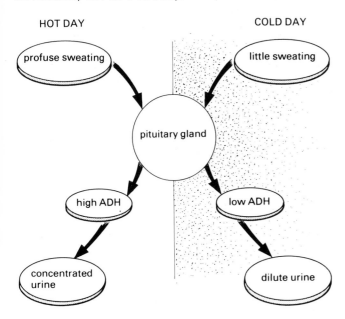

11.16 Water balance on hot and cold days

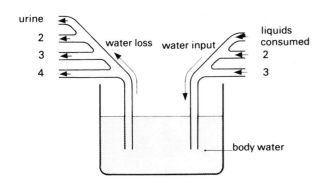

11.17 Water balance

▶ **Questions**

11.43 What are the two other sources of water and the three other methods of losing water not listed in Fig 11.17?

11.44 What happens to the body if more water is taken in than is passed out?

11.45 What happens to the body if more water is lost than is taken in?

As the water balance tips towards excess loss, the sensation of thirst is produced, causing us to restore the balance by drinking liquid.

Body fluids contain a critical amount of salt. Salt is necessary to maintain the correct osmotic level of all the cells. Water is only drawn into a cell if the concentration of the cytoplasm is greater than that of the surrounding tissue fluid. Salt balance is therefore very important to the body.

▶ **Questions**

11.46 Which organs of the body are responsible for loss of salt?

11.47 Which of these areas is able to reabsorb salt and regulate the amount the body loses?

Uptake of sodium ions still needed by the body occurs in the loop of Henle (see Unit 8) in the nephrons of the kidney. The amount reabsorbed is controlled by the hormone **aldosterone**. Aldosterone, a form of cortisone, is produced in an endocrine gland close to the kidney called the adrenal cortex. The adrenal cortex is under the control of the pituitary gland. The pituitary detects salt levels in the blood and stimulates the adrenal cortex to produce the necessary amount of aldosterone.

▷ **Research project**

Find the longest time for which a man has survived without (a) water and (b) food. Why is it only possible to survive for a much shorter time without water?

4 Blood glucose regulation

The level of glucose in the blood needs to be maintained at around 100 mg/100 ml. It can fall as low as 60 mg/100 ml, but below that level there could be glucose shortage for vital organs such as the brain. Refer to Fig 11.4 (upper portion). In order to maintain glucose levels at around 100 mg/100 ml of blood, the glucose taken in at meals must be stored and then released gradually during the fasting periods. A high proportion of the glucose consumed is converted to glycogen, an insoluble carbohydrate, in the liver. In this form, carbohydrate can be stored until it is needed for body activities.

Diabetes mellitus

▶ **Question**

11.48 Which hormone is necessary to enable the liver to take up glucose for storage? (Refer to Unit 9.)

11.18 Glucose levels in the urine of a diabetes mellitus sufferer

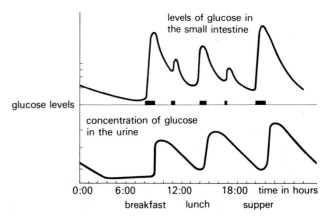

131

Fig 11.18 shows how the level of glucose in the urine of a subject fluctuated over a period of twenty-four hours. The subject consumed glucose tablets during this period and was suffering from an insulin insufficiency disease called diabetes mellitus.

▶ **Questions**

11.49 Why does the amount of glucose in the urine fluctuate?
11.50 Glucose does not usually appear in the urine of a healthy person. Suggest why it appears in that of the subject of this graph.

Individuals such as the subject of Fig 11.18 possess a defective pancreas which does not produce insulin. Their liver and respiring cells are unable to take up glucose from the blood, so it remains in the blood after a meal and is excreted in their urine. Soon after the meal, all the glucose will have been lost and a common result is a coma (unconsciousness) as the brain cells are starved of glucose. (See Unit 15.) Other hormones are now known to be involved in glucose uptake and storage, but since they are also sited in the pancreas, this does not help the diabetic.

▶ **Question**

11.51 What substance initiates the release of glucose from stored glycogen into the blood? (Refer to Unit 9.)

▷ **Research project**

Investigate the diet recommended for a diabetic person.

5 Regulation of breathing and heartbeat rates

The maintenance of a steady internal state requires a transport system which can be regulated to restore balance after strenuous activity and a respiratory system which can be adjusted to keep the body functioning normally while undergoing different activities.

Carbon dioxide is transported in the blood plasma in the form of either sodium bicarbonate ($NaHCO_3$) or carbonic acid (H_2CO_3). Both of these compounds are usually mostly dissociated in the blood, giving sodium, hydrogen and bicarbonate ions. These bicarbonates are produced from carbon dioxide formed in respiring cells and released into the blood. If the rate of cell respiration rises, then so does the concentration of bicarbonates in the plasma.

▶ **Question**

11.52 Suggest what happens to the breathing rate as the level of bicarbonate ions in the blood rises.

The level of bicarbonates in the blood is detected by the **respiratory centre** which is situated in the medulla oblongata. If cell respiration is high, a lot of carbon dioxide is formed and the medulla sends impulses along the vagus nerve stimulating the respiratory muscles to contract more quickly to expel the carbon dioxide more rapidly. Low cell respiration will produce much less carbon dioxide, so the medulla instructs the respiratory muscles to contract more slowly.

To a lesser extent, oxygen content is also detected by the respiratory centre. A shortage of oxygen will ensure that the medulla stimulates the respiratory muscles to obtain more oxygen.

11.53 (a) Under what circumstances would cell respiration be high?
(b) When would cell respiration be low?

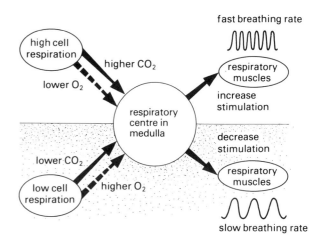

11.20 Control of respiration

In addition to the respiratory centre, there is a **cardiac centre** in the medulla. This operates in a similar way to the respiratory centre, but it is also affected by pressure receptors in the big arteries. The cardiac centre controls heartbeat by sending impulses to the pacemaker, the sino-auricular node, a patch of neurons in the right ventricle (see Unit 7). The cardiac centre sends its impulses via the vagus nerve and the sympathetic system system. Stimulation of the vagus slows down the heartbeat rate, while stimulation from the sympathetic stimulates the heart and accelerates the rate.

▷ **Homework**

List five activities which will test the homeostatic mechanisms involved in breathing and heartbeat rates.

6 Role of the liver in homeostasis

▶ **Questions**

11.54 From Unit 5 and section 3 of the unit, list the ways in which the liver helps to maintain a constant composition for the blood.
11.55 In what other way does the liver help to maintain a steady state?
11.56 Identify numbered items in Fig 11.21.

▷ **Research project**

List some of the effects on the body of a diseased liver.

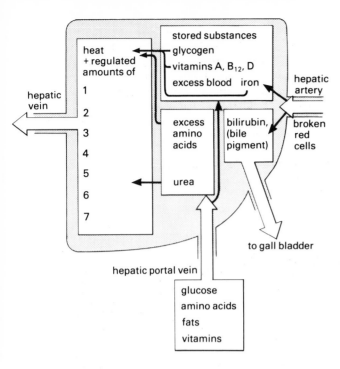

11.21 Homeostatic functions of the liver

Answers and discussion

1 Defining homeostasis

11.1 The girl in Fig 11.1 must be able to lose heat to stop her blood from overheating. The girl in Fig 11.2 must be able to conserve heat to prevent her blood from freezing.

11.2 The temperature of the frog closely follows that of the air.

11.3 The temperature of the man is unaffected by that of the air.

11.4 (a) The temperature range of the frog is between 15 °C and 28 °C.
(b) The temperature range of the man is very small – it hovers around 36 °C.

11.5 Glucose levels in the blood range from 80 mg/100 ml – 160 mg/100 ml in twenty-four hours.

11.6 Glucose levels in the small intestine range from 0 g to 100 g.

11.7 The level of glucose in the blood fluctuates much less than the level in the small intestine.

11.8 At 08:00 the blood glucose level rises because the products of digestion of the pupil's breakfast are beginning to enter the blood.

11.9 By 12:00 the blood glucose level has gone down again to about 100 mg/100 ml.

11.10 Although the glucose level in the intestine is still high and glucose is probably still entering the blood from the intestine, the level in the blood is going down. Glucose is being taken out of the blood by the liver and stored as glycogen. It will be released from here as it is needed.

11.11 Total water output is 1750 cm³.

11.12 The total amount of water input in the girl in Fig 11.5 remains the same over twenty-four hours, despite a large input and output. Her water content is balanced.

11.13 If 1000 cm³ of sweat is produced instead of 500 cm³, in order to achieve balance less urine will be produced and possibly more water will be consumed.

11.14 The blood system plays an important part in maintaining a steady state. It distributes heat to maintain a constant body temperature, as well as circulating hormones, glucose, carbon dioxide and oxygen.

11.15 (a) A steep rise in temperature could result in heat stroke and death. Enzymes are destroyed at high temperatures. Low temperatures such as those caused by excessive exposure to Arctic conditions produce what is called exposure, an impairment of function of all the main body systems.
(b) If blood glucose is not withdrawn into the liver and the body cells, the amount in the blood rises and much of it is wasted by excretion in the urine. Too low blood glucose levels can cause shock and brain damage.
(c) Excess water loss will produce dehydration and death, and excess water intake without a balanced loss will result in fluid retention and swelling (oedema).

2 Temperature regulation

11.16 The most frequent temperature is around 37 °C which is the same as that of the man recorded in Fig 11.3.

133

11.17 On hotter or colder days the temperature should not vary by more than 1 °C.

11.18 The temperature varies between 29.5 °C and 36.5 °C as shown in Fig 11.22.

11.19 The temperature is low first thing in the morning (36 °C), higher by mid morning (36.5 °C), lower in mid afternoon (36 °C) and highest in the evening (37 °C). The temperature is still relatively constant, varying only by 1 °C at extremes.

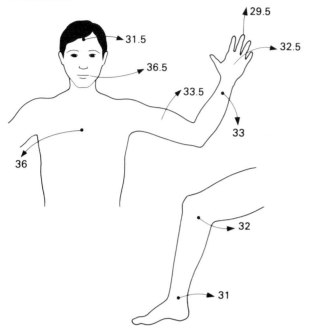

11.22 Temperature variations over the body

11.20 Results for Activity 11.3

Time (min)	Fall in temperature in first 10 min (°C)	Fall in temperature with meths	Fall in temperature in second 10 min (°C)
1	95.0	82.0	74.0
2	92.5	80.0	73.5
3	90.4	79.0	72.0
4	90.0	76.0	70.5
5	89.5	75.0	68.0
6	88.0		66.0
7	87.0		65.0
8	86.5		64.0
9	85.0		63.0
10	84.0		62.0

Room temperature = 21 °C
The following rates of fall were calculated at a room temperature of 21 °C:
Step 4: 1.1 °C/min
Step 5: 1.4 °C/min
Step 6: 1.2 °C/min   See Fig 11.23

11.21 (a) Rising skin temperature causes an increase in sweat production, which helps to reduce the skin temperature rise.
(b) Moving into the cold causes the skin to cool, and this causes reduction in the volume of sweat produced. The skin cools very quickly because it is covered in evaporating sweat.

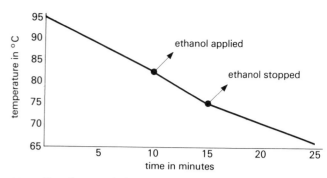

11.23 Results graph for Activity 11.3

11.22 Sweat is over 90% water. As it is secreted onto the skin through the sweat pores, it draws heat from the body in order to evaporate. This cools the skin surface and eventually lowers the body temperature.

11.23 When we get too hot, our skin appears flushed.

11.24 As the skin arterioles dilate, more blood is brought to the sweat glands which consequently extract more water and dissolved substances in a given amount of time. Vasodilation therefore increases the rate of sweating.

11.25 If the atmospheric temperature is low, heat loss from the skin surface must be reduced. Constriction of the skin arterioles reduces the flow of blood to the skin surface. Less heat is therefore lost by either radiation from the arterioles or evaporation of sweat.

11.26 Results for Activity 11.4 See Fig 11.24.

Time (min)	Flask A (°C)	Flask B (°C)
1	95.0	95.0
2	92.5	95.0
3	90.4	91.0
4	90.0	89.5
5	89.5	89.0
6	88.0	88.5
7	87.0	88.0
8	86.5	87.5
9	85.0	87.0
10	84.0	86.5
11	81.0	86.0
12	79.5	85.5
13	78.0	85.0
14	76.5	84.5
15	75.5	84.0
16	73.0	83.5
17	70.0	83.0
18	69.5	82.5
19	69.0	82.0
20	68.0	81.0

11.27 The following rates of fall were calculated at room temperature of 21 °C:
Flask A, 1.35 °C/min; Flask B, 0.70 °C/min.

11.28 The rate of temperature fall was reduced in Flask B by the insulating material.

11.29 Man uses clothing to trap warm air close to his skin and cut down convection. In most parts of the world he must do this in order to keep warm since his body hairs are minimal and ineffective.

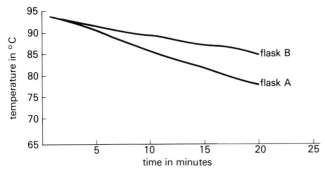

11.24 Results graph for Activity 11.4

11.30 Heat is also lost from the body in expired air, urine and faeces.

11.31 Heat is gained for the body by metabolism. This includes respiration, which is particularly high in the liver where many metabolic processes are proceeding. Environmental heat comes from the sun and from hot food. Heat may be gained by conduction if you sit on a radiator!

Shivering is involuntary, fast contraction of the skeletal muscles. It is a way of inducing the body to produce heat. It serves the same purpose as exercise. By curling up in a cold bed we reduce our surface area in relation to our volume and so conserve more heat.

11.32 1 arterioles dilated; 2 sweat production decreased; 3 hairs erect; 4 heat production centres stimulated

11.33 The surface area of the sphere is $4\pi r^2 = 310 \text{cm}^2$
The volume of the sphere is $^4/_3\pi r^3 = 517 \text{cm}^3$ (taking $\pi = 3.1$)
The surface area to volume ratio of the sphere is $310:517$
$= 1:1.7$
The surface area of the cuboid is $2(ab + bc + ac) = 502 \text{ cm}^2$
The volume of the cuboid is $abc = 510 \text{ cm}^3$
The surface area to volume ratio of the cuboid is $502:510$
$= 1:1.01$

11.34 The sphere is more like the eskimo, and the cuboid is more the shape of the negro.

11.35 The surface area to volume ratio of the eskimo is 20:1. The surface area to volume ratio of the negro is 30:1.

11.36 The negro, in a hot climate, needs to lose heat. His large surface area to volume ratio enables him to do this. The eskimo, in arctic conditions, needs to conserve heat. His smaller surface area to volume ratio helps him to do this.

11.37 A small baby has a very large surface area to volume ratio and will lose heat very rapidly in a cold room. A blanket will insulate the baby. Some newborn babies have died from hypothermia.

3 Water and salt balance

11.38 The urinary system is primarily responsible for regulating water loss.

11.39 As the level of ADH rises, tubular absorption increases. This suggests that ADH makes the kidney tubules more permeable to water. The function of ADH in the body is to reduce water loss when necessary.

11.40 Someone suffering from diabetes insipidus would not be able to take up water from the kidney tubules and they would produce a large amount of very dilute urine. They would feel constantly thirsty and drink all the time.

11.41 If the body is losing a lot of water through sweat, more ADH will be produced to reduce water loss in urine. In hot weather less urine is produced than on cold days. Also, if a person is unable to get a drink over a long period, high ADH levels will conserve as much water as possible and the volume of urine will be reduced.

11.42 On a cold day very little water is being lost from the skin. Insensible (invisible) perspiration only amounts to about a litre on cold days. The kidneys will need to lose more water to maintain water balance, so less ADH is secreted.

11.43 The two other sources of water are: 2 moisture in food; 3 metabolic water (from respiration and other body processes). Three other sources of water loss are: 2 sweating; 3 expired air; 4 faeces.

11.44 If the body gains more water than it loses, it swells up. This is called oedema.

11.45 If the body loses more water than it gains, dehydration results. If not rectified, dehydration can eventually cause death.

11.46 Salt is lost by the body through the skin in sweat, and the kidneys in urine.

11.47 The kidneys are able to actively regulate the amount of salt lost.

4 Blood glucose regulation

11.48 The hormone insulin is necessary for the uptake of glucose from the blood. (See Unit 9.)

11.49 Glucose in the urine fluctuates with intake of glucose by the subject, suggesting that the glucose is immediately excreted by the kidneys.

11.50 The subject of the graph is suffering from a deficiency of insulin. Without insulin, the glucose will not be taken up by the liver or respiring cells and the excess glucose remaining in the blood is excreted by the kidneys.

11.51 Adrenalin, the hormone produced by the adrenal medulla, initiates the release of glucose from stored glycogen into the blood.

5 Regulation of breathing and heartbeat rates

11.52 As the level of bicarbonates in the blood rises, so does the breathing rate.

11.53 (a) Cell respiration will be fast during strenuous activity such as running or swimming, during excitement or fear, and during some types of fever.
(b) Cell respiration will be slow during sleep or rest or during sedentary work.

6 Role of the liver in homeostasis

11.54 The liver helps to maintain a constant composition in the blood by:
(a) storing excess glucose as glycogen;
(b) deaminating excess amino acids to form urea for excretion;
(c) desaturating fats;
(d) storing vitamins B_{12}, A and D if in excess;
(e) storing excess blood in the sinuses;
(f) removing pigments from broken down red blood cells to form bile;
(g) storing excess iron from broken down red blood cells;
(h) manufacturing clotting substances (prothrombin and fibrinogen – see Unit 7).
All these substances are released into the blood as the need arises.

11.55 All the chemical processes going on in the liver produce the bulk of the heat necessary to maintain a constant body temperature above that of the environment.

11.56 1 glucose; 2 amino acids; 3 desaturated fats; 4 urea; 5 vitamins; 6 iron; 7 blood.

12 Reproduction

1 Reproductive organs

In addition to the obvious external differences between males and females, there are internal differences in the structure of the reproductive organs. Male and female reproductive systems are similar in basic design: both consist of a pair of organs which produce specialised reproductive cells, called gametes, and both systems include tubes to convey the gametes to the place where fertilisation occurs.

Male reproductive system

The testes are the paired organs which produce the male gametes, called spermatozoa. They lie outside the body cavity in a sac called the scrotum. The sperm ducts which convey the spermatozoa towards the outside are called the vasa deferentia (singular: vas deferens). These tubes twist round and unite just behind the base of the bladder, discharging their contents into the urethra (see Unit 8). A pair of sacs lead off from the sperm ducts prior to their union. These are the seminal vesicles and store the sperm as it is passed along the sperm ducts. An accessory gland in this region, the prostate gland, produces a viscous fluid in which the sperms are transfered to the female. The fluid containing sperms is called semen. It is transfered to the female through a distensible organ called the penis.

12.1 Male reproductive organs

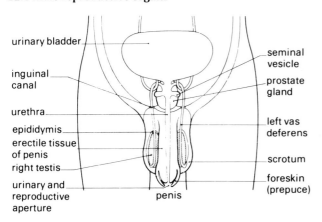

urinary bladder
inguinal canal
urethra
epididymis
erectile tissue of penis
right testis
urinary and reproductive aperture
penis
seminal vesicle
prostate gland
left vas deferens
scrotum
foreskin (prepuce)

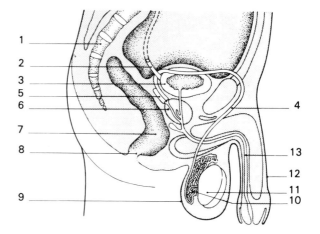

12.2 Lateral view of male reproductive organs

▶ Questions

12.1 Using Fig 12.1 and information from Units 2 and 8, identify the parts numbered in Fig 12.2.

12.2 Which part of the system displayed in Fig 12.2 is shared by both the urinary and reproductive components?

12.3 Vertical section through a human testis.

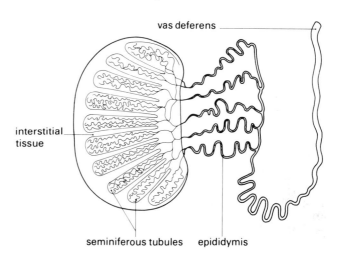

vas deferens
interstitial tissue
seminiferous tubules
epididymis

A human testis, as shown in Fig 12.3, is formed of a large number of tubules which eventually join to form the twisted beginning of the vas deferens, called the epididymis. Spermatozoa are produced from dividing cells lining each tubule. Between these seminiferous tubules, packing tissue, called interstitial tissue, produces the male hormone, testosterone. (See Unit 9.) Fig 12.4 shows stages in the production of spermatozoa. Sertoli cells (or nurse cells) are thought to help in the nourishment of the developing spermatozoa.

▶ **Question**

12.3 Study Figs 12.4 and 12.5 carefully, then identify the numbered parts in Fig 12.5.

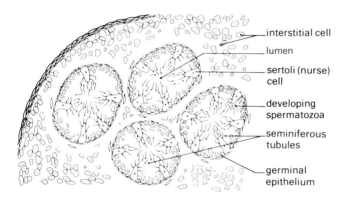

12.4 Transverse section of seminiferous tubules

12.5 Photomicrograph of seminiferous tubules

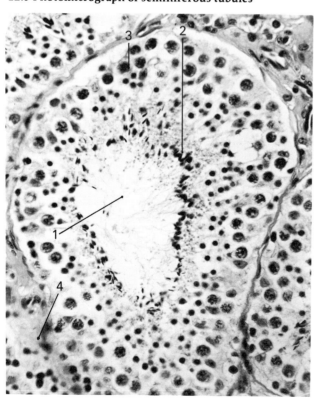

Female reproductive system

The ovaries, which produce the female gametes or ova (singular: ovum) are smaller than the testes, and lie in the abdominal cavity. The egg tubes (called oviducts or fallopian tubes) are not directly connected to the ovaries, but form a pair of funnels closely applied to the ovary surfaces (see Fig 12.6). In the centre, the fallopian tubes open into a muscular sac which is about 6 cm in depth and 4 cm wide at its widest point. This is the womb or uterus. Posteriorly, the uterus narrows to form the cervix or neck, which leads into a muscular tube, the birth canal or vagina.

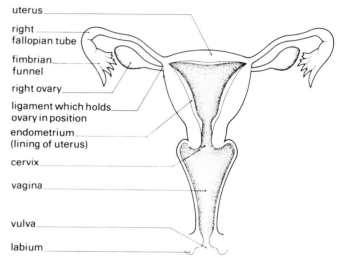

12.6 Female reproductive organs

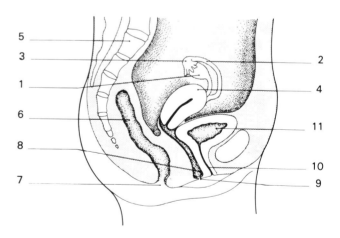

12.7 Lateral view of female reproductive organs

▶ **Questions**

12.4 What does the birth canal (vagina) open into?
12.5 Describe the position of this exit in relation to the urethra and the anus.
12.6 Identify the parts numbered in Fig 12.7. Units 2 and 8 should help you.
12.7 Which parts of the system displayed in Fig 12.7 are shared by both the urinary and reproductive components?

Until puberty (the beginning of sexual maturity), the opening of the birth canal is protected by a part of its wall which forms a membrane, the hymen. This is penetrated during the first sexual intercourse, and may even have been previously widened during non-sexual athletic activities. The openings of both the vagina and urethra are within the slit-like vulva, which is protected by soft folds of flesh called the labia.

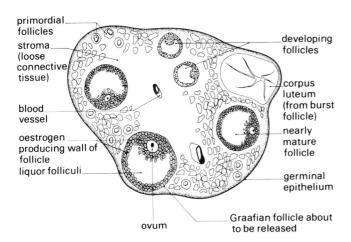

primordial follicles
stroma (loose connective tissue)
blood vessel
oestrogen producing wall of follicle
liquor folliculi
ovum

developing follicles
corpus luteum (from burst follicle)
nearly mature follicle
germinal epithelium
Graafian follicle about to be released

12.8 Section through a human ovary

A human ovary, as shown in Fig 12.8, differs basically in structure from a testis, since it is not formed of a mass of tubes. The bulk of the structure is a loose connective tissue or stroma, and the surface consists of dividing cells or germinal epithelium. These cells divide and mature to form fully developed ova. From puberty until about the age of fifty, a fully developed ovum breaks out of the surface of the ovary about every month. The surface of a mature ovary has scars where ova have been released, and grooves where cell division is active. An ovum is surrounded by nutrient follicle cells as it matures. These cells produce a liquid, called liquor folliculi to nourish the ovum. They also produce the female hormone, oestrogen. A mature follicle, about to burst, is called a Graafian follicle.

12.9 Photomicrograph of a section through an ovary

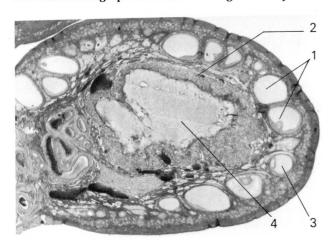

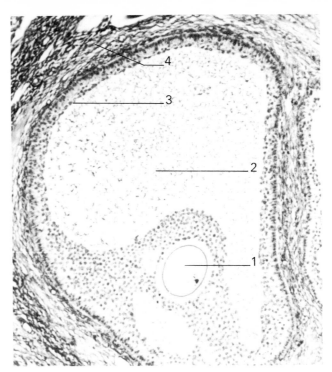

12.10 Photomicrograph of a Graafian follicle

▶ **Questions**

12.8 Using Fig 12.8, identify the numbered parts in Fig 12.9.
12.9 Using Fig 12.8, identify the numbered parts in Fig 12.10.
12.10 Refer to Fig 12.8 and suggest what is left in the ovary when the mature ovum is released from the Graafian follicle into the fimbrian funnel.

A second female hormone, progesterone, is produced from the remaining follicle cells, which develop to form a structure called the yellow body or corpus luteum. The role of the ovarian hormones will be discussed below.

▷ **Homework**

From the diagrams in this section and those in Unit 8, attempt to draw a ventral view of the urinogenital system of a human female. Label your drawing.

2 Secondary sexual characteristics

The primary sexual characteristics of a male or a female are their reproductive organs. Other sexual characteristics are also present, partly as an aid to fertilisation of the ovum by a sperm to produce a zygote which will grow into a new individual, and partly as an aid to the nourishment of the newly born baby. Such characteristics are called secondary sexual characteristics, and their development is the outward sign of puberty or the onset of sexual maturity. Fig 12.11 shows three stages in the development of some of the male secondary sexual characteristics, from the ages of ten and sixteen to adulthood. In addition to these physical changes, another sign that puberty has arrived is the production of semen. Spontaneous ejaculation of this sticky, creamy fluid from an erect penis, may occur at night.

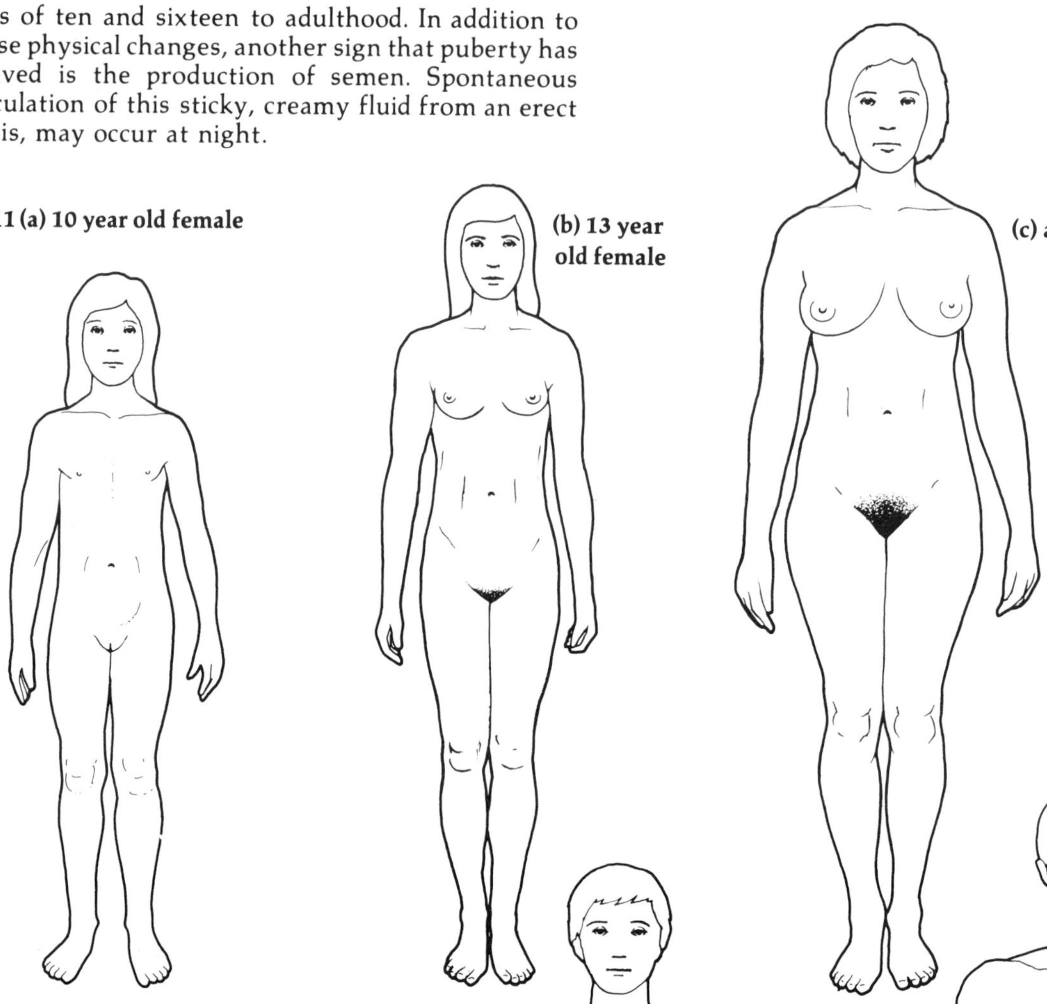

12.11 (a) 10 year old female

(b) 13 year old female

(c) adult female

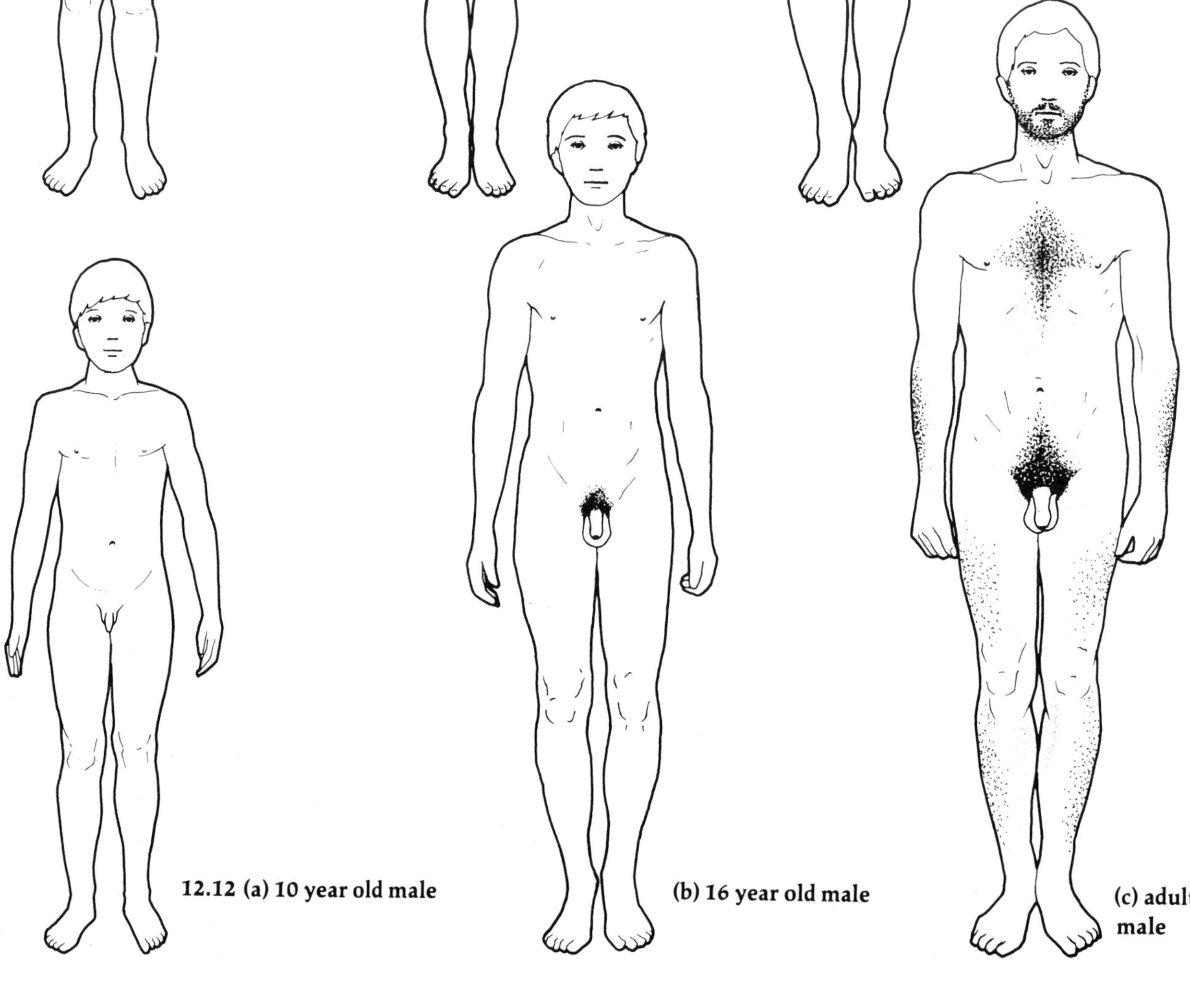

12.12 (a) 10 year old male

(b) 16 year old male

(c) adult male

12.11 List the differences you can see in Fig 12.11 between (a) and (b), then (b) and (c).

12.12 What other physical change occurs from the age of sixteen to adulthood?

12.13 List the differences you can see in Fig 12.12 between (a) and (b), then (b) and (c)

Another indication of puberty in a female is menstruation. The onset of puberty in both males and females is entirely under the control of hormones. Fig 12.13 shows the control of the production of oestrogen and progesterone in the female. In the male there is a similar control by the pituitary of the male hormone testosterone.

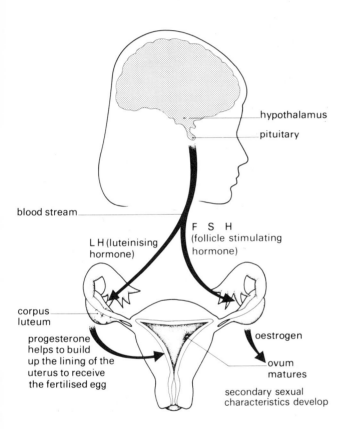

12.13 Pituitary control of oestrogen and progesterone

▶ **Questions**

12.14 Refer to Unit 9, and then explain why all the characteristics of puberty will only develop if the pituitary gland is producing FSH (follicle stimulating hormone).

12.15 Which pituitary hormone stimulates the development of the corpus luteum (yellow body)? What does the hormone progesterone, produced by the yellow body, affect?

From the age of about eleven years, sufficient FSH is produced in the female by the pituitary gland to stimulate the undeveloped follicles in the ovaries to begin development. Only one follicle is stimulated at a

time. As the follicle cells mature, they produce oestrogen, which stimulates the growth of the enclosed ovum, and initiates the development of the secondary sexual characteristics. Oestrogen also begins the preparation of the lining of the uterus to receive a fertilised egg. Glandular tissue and blood sinuses form a soft, nutritive cushion in readiness. An ovum reaches maturity about once every twenty-eight days, when it bursts from the follicle and is caught in the fimbrian funnel. This is called ovulation. The minute ovum is wafted down the fallopian tube by the lining of cilia (see Unit 2). Most ova are not fertilised, and after a number of days the prepared lining of the uterus, the endometrium, and the unfertilised ovum are discharged from the womb during menstruation. The menstrual flow is largely blood and mucus, and usually lasts for about five days. Following menstruation, the wall of the uterus is repaired under the influence of oestrogen.

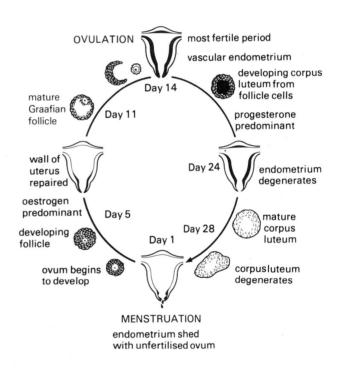

12.14 The menstrual cycle

▶ **Questions**

12.16 How many days after menstruation does ovulation occur?

12.17 When would fertilisation of the ovum (conception) be most likely?

12.18 What is the role of progesterone in this cycle?

12.19 Fig 12.15 shows a woman's temperature variation during a menstrual cycle, together with the condition of the endometrium (uterine lining). What event coincides with the lowest temperature in the cycle? See Fig 12.14.

12.20 How may temperature be used as a guide to the best time for conception to occur?

12.21 At what stage in the cycle is the endometrium in optimum condition for receiving a fertilised egg?

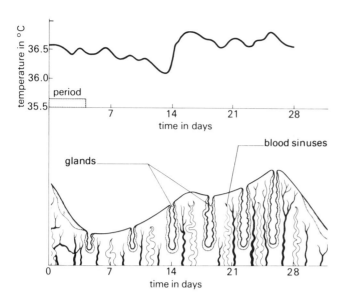

12.15 Temperature and endometrial changes in the menstrual cycle

▷ **Homework**

Explain how a malfunctioning pituitary gland could cause infertility.

12.16 Gametogenesis

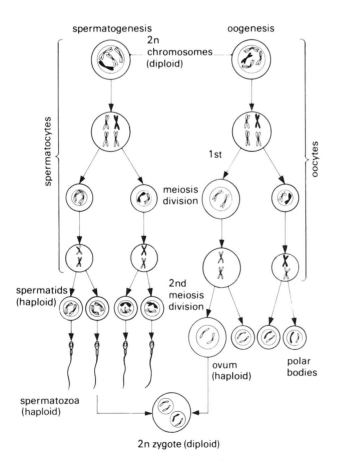

3 Gamete formation and fertilisation

Sexual reproduction in mammals is brought about by the fusion of specialised male and female cells (gametes) to form a zygote. The zygote then grows to form a new individual, which has characteristics of both parents. Both ova and sperms are produced by a series of cell divisions of germinal epithelium. The seminiferous tubules are lined with such epithelium and the ovary is covered with it (see section 1).

▶ **Question**

12.22   Refer to the description of mitosis in Unit 2. How many chromosomes would you expect each gamete to possess if all cell division is by mitosis? What would be the resulting chromosome number in the zygote?

Fig 12.16 shows the cell divisions which occur in the germinal epithelium of both male (♂) and female (♀) as gametes are produced. The process is called gametogenesis. Spermatogenesis is sperm production and oogenesis is ovum production. Only four chromosomes are shown instead of forty-six to make the process clearer.

▶ **Questions**

12.23   What happens to the number of chromosomes in the spermatocytes and oocytes during cell division?
12.24   What is the name of the division process which brings this about?
12.25   How does the chromosome number of the zygote compare with the original spermatocytes and oocytes?

The usual chromosome number in a human cell, twenty-three pairs, is called the diploid number. When gametes are produced, they only possess twenty-three chromosomes. This is known as the haploid number. The diploid number is restored in the zygote.

12.17 A spermatozoon

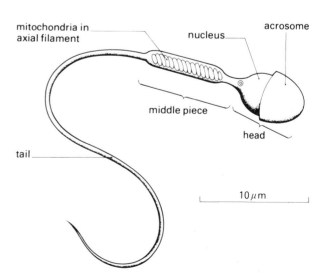

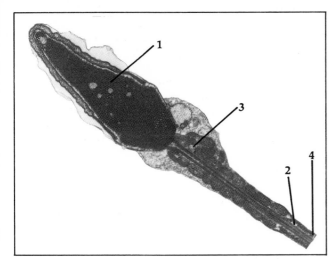

12.18 Electron micrograph of a spermatozoon

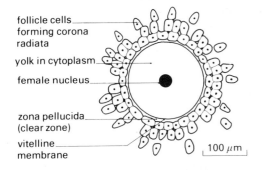

follicle cells
forming corona
radiata

yolk in cytoplasm

female nucleus

zona pellucida
(clear zone)

vitelline
membrane

100 μm

12.19 An ovum

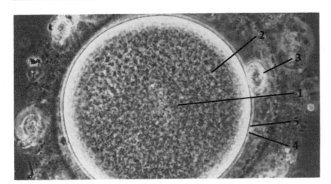

12.20 Photomicrograph of an ovum

▶ **Questions**

12.26 Calculate the length of a spermatozoon from the scale given in Fig 12.17.

12.27 A mature spermatozoon consists of a middle piece, and a tail which is capable of active movement. Suggest the role of the tail.

12.28 Identify the parts numbered in Fig 12.18, using Fig 12.17.

12.29 Why are a large number of mitochondria present in the middle piece?

12.30 Calculate the diameter of an ovum from the scale in Fig 12.19.

12.31 Identify the numbered parts in Fig 12.20, using Fig 12.19.

12.32 Describe the differences between the ovum and sperm and suggest reasons for these differences.

In order that fertilisation of an ovum can occur, spermatozoa have to be transfered from the male into the body of the female. In humans this can take place at any time of the year. It is dependent on the arousal of the male by the female. When a male is excited by a female, blood sinuses in the penis become distended with blood and the normally flaccid organ becomes erect and hard. In this condition the penis is able to penetrate the vagina of the female. If the female is receptive, mucus is produced by the vagina to help penetration. After a series of rhythmical muscular spasms, semen is released (ejaculated) from the penis into the top of the vagina. The penis becomes flaccid again and is withdrawn.

Semen contains many millions of spermatozoa per cm^3. Since several cm^3 are deposited in the vagina, a very large number of spermatozoa begin to swim in the moist lining of the uterus and up the fallopian tubes in search of an ovum. Fig 12.21 illustrates what happens when an ovum is encountered high up in a fallopian tube.

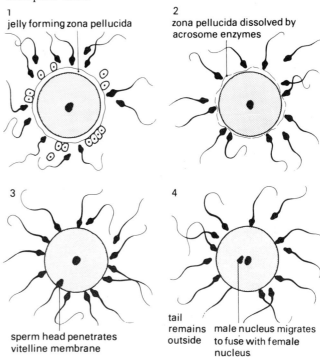

1
jelly forming zona pellucida

2
zona pellucida dissolved by acrosome enzymes

3
sperm head penetrates vitelline membrane

4
tail remains outside

male nucleus migrates to fuse with female nucleus

12.21 Stages in fertilisation

12.22 Fertilisation of a human ovum

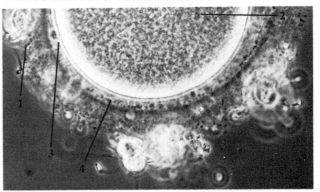

12.33 Using Fig 12.21 describe the process of fertilisation.
12.34 Identify the parts numbered in Fig 12.22, using Fig 12.21.
12.35 Suggest the role of the thick membrane which is formed around the ovum following fertilisation.

▷ **Homework**

Suggest what would happen if formation of the gametes involved mitosis only.

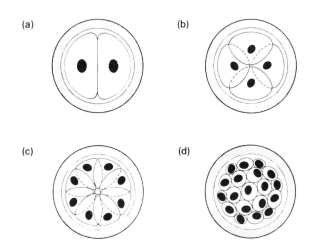

12.23 Cleavage - the early stages after fertilisation

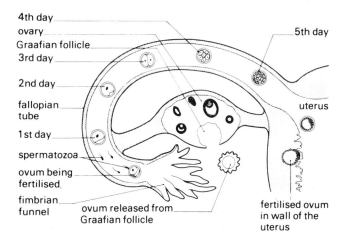

12.24 Progress of a zygote after fertilisation

4 After fertilisation

The early stages after fertilisation, shown in Fig 12.23 are as follows. (a) The fertilised zygote cleaves into two. (b) A division at right angles to the first produces four cells. (c) The cells produced in (b) divide into two, producing eight cells. (d) A hollow ball of cells is produced by further divisions. This hollow ball is called a **blastula**.

► **Question**

12.36 How many days after fertilisation does implantation in the wall of the uterus occur in the example in Fig 12.24?

The hollow ball of cells which is produced about three days after fertilisation, becomes organised into two components, one of which develops into the embryo, the other producing the embryonic membranes. Most important of these foetal membranes later in development are the chorion which develops into the placenta, and the amnion.

The amnion, or water bag, produces and retains the amniotic fluid. This is a watery fluid which cushions the embryo from shocks applied to the mother (for example, she could fall down the stairs). As the foetus enlarges and is cramped in a small space, fluid between the developing parts helps to prevent them from joining together.

12.25 A human foetus in the uterus is protected by the ammniotic fluid inside the ammnion.

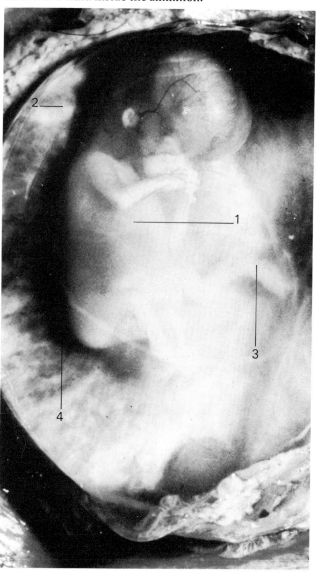

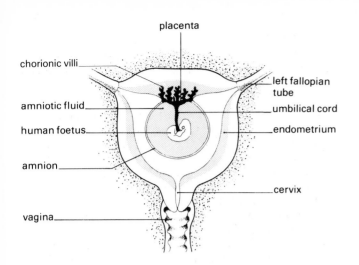

12.26 Section through a uterus and foetus

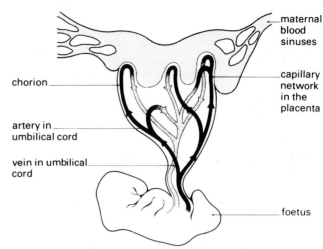

12.28 Structure of the placenta

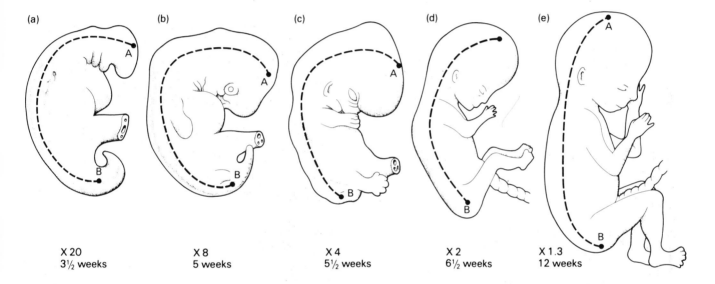

(a) X 20 3½ weeks

(b) X 8 5 weeks

(c) X 4 5½ weeks

(d) X 2 6½ weeks

(e) X 1.3 12 weeks

12.27 A developing foetus

▶ Questions

12.37 Identify the structures numbered in Fig 12.25, using Fig 12.26.

12.38 Work out the actual length of each of these foetuses in Fig 12.27 in mm from the scales given, measuring in each case from A to B.

12.39 At what stage in the series would you place the foetus illustrated in Fig 12.25?

The placenta is formed from both maternal and foetal tissue. The endometrium develops to form more glandular tissue and blood sinuses. The chorion produces villi which contain foetal capillaries and which dip into the maternal blood spaces. In this way the blood of the mother and the foetus are brought very close together without any mixing of the blood.

▶ Questions

12.40 Suggest what substances pass from the maternal vessels into the foetal capillaries.

12.41 Suggest any reasons you can think of that make it important to prevent the mixing of maternal and foetal blood.

12.42 How are these substances from the maternal vessels then transported to the foetus?

12.43 What substances pass from the foetal capillaries into the maternal vessels?

12.44 How are these substances from the foetus transported to the placenta?

12.45 By what process do substances exchange between maternal and foetal parts of the placenta?

▷ Homework

Write a brief essay explaining why it is important for a pregnant woman to take care in what she eats and drinks.

5 Pregnancy

Following fertilisation, the hormone balance of the pregnant woman is altered. The yellow body does not degenerate as happens in the normal menstrual cycle. Rather, it grows and produces more progesterone. LH is the predominant pituitary hormone, and the hormone also stimulates the placenta to produce its own progesterone. Progesterone is essential for the continued development of the placenta, and low progesterone levels are one cause of early miscarriage, or spontaneous abortion. Progesterone also inhibits ovulation, and the menstrual cycle stops during pregnancy.

► **Question**

12.46 Why is it important that the menstrual cycle should stop during pregnancy?

As well as changes in her body, the pregnant woman may find that her general attitude is altered by hormonal changes. In a sense she is becoming 'conditioned' to the role of motherhood. It is essential that the mother-to-be takes extra care of herself during pregnancy, both for herself and for the developing baby. Ante-natal (or pre-natal) clinics are to help the pregnant woman to take care of herself and prepare herself for parenthood.

Pre-natal tests

Throughout pregnancy, checks are made on the pregnant woman to make sure that she and her baby are progressing normally. Among these are weight tests, uterus size, blood pressure, blood tests, urine tests and amniocentesis.

Every time the pregnant mother visits the ante-natal clinic she will be weighed. She will be expected to show a weight gain of about a half a kilogram a week in the latter half of pregnancy, but excessive weight gain is a problem. This is because excessive weight gain may indicate the retention of abnormal amounts of fluid by the mother. This is called oedema and may lead to high blood pressure and kidney problems, and in severe cases to a disease called eclampsia when the high blood pressure causes convulsions, and the kidneys allow abnormal amounts of protein to be excreted in the urine.

The normal weight of a foetus at birth is 3.5 kg, but the mother may be as much as 12.5 kg heavier than her normal weight because of increased fluid content and fat and protein storage.

► **Question**

12.47 What is the test shown in Fig 12.29 and why is it of particular importance during pregnancy?

Blood samples will be taken from a vein in the arm during the course of pregnancy. The routine test applied to this blood is a haemoglobin count. The first blood sample is used to determine the blood group of the pregnant woman.

► **Questions**

12.48 What is the purpose of a haemoglobin count and why is it so essential during pregnancy?
12.49 Why must the blood group of the mother be known? (Refer to Unit 7.)

Urine samples are checked during pregnancy. The basic tests are for the presence of blood sugar and albumen in the urine.

► **Questions**

12.50 How is albumen detected in a urine sample? (See Unit 8.)
12.51 What does the presence of glucose in urine signify?
12.52 What must have happened to the kidneys for albumen to appear in the urine?

If complications are anticipated in pregnancy, it may be necessary to do additional tests. Ultra sound may be used to locate the positions of the placenta, amnion and foetus. Sometimes a small amount of amniotic fluid may be withdrawn which will contain some of the skin cells of the foetus. These cells can be tested for abnormalities. This process is called amniocentesis.

► **Question**

12.53 Suggest some circumstances under which it could be decided to carry out amniocentesis.

Other aspects of care during pregnancy are discussed in other units. The importance of diet is stressed in Unit 4 and of care of the teeth in Unit 15.

Problems in pregnancy

In a few instances, despite observing all possible care during pregnancy, a woman may give birth to a deformed baby. One cause is that the mother could have been contact with German measles, rubella, during the first three months of pregnancy. The rubella virus can cross the placenta and cause congenital heart disease, blindness, deafness and other deformities.

► **Question**

12.54 How could this cause be avoided these days?

If possible it is best to avoid the use of drugs during pregnancy, and to rely on correct diet, adequate rest and a reasonable amount of exercise to ensure healthy development. A few years ago, the drug thalidomide was prescribed to mothers to help overcome nausea during the first three months of pregnancy. It diffused across the placenta and inhibited the development of the limb buds of the foetuses, and many babies were born with deformed limbs.

▷ **Research project**

Find out what happens at ante-natal classes for mothers and their husbands, and explain why these classes are helpful to the parents.

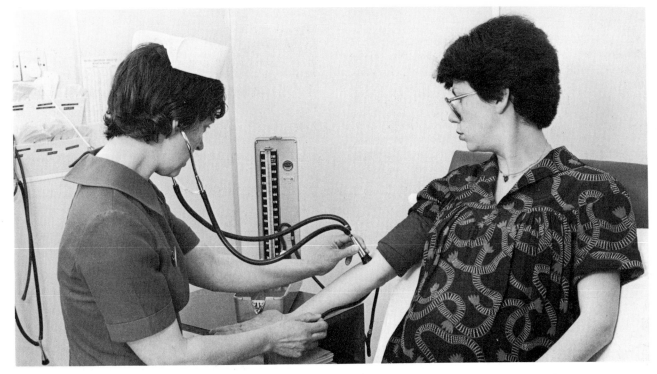

12.29 An ante-natal test being applied to an expectant mother

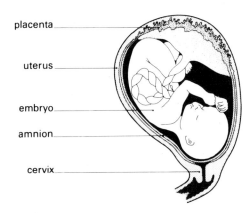

placenta

uterus

embryo

amnion

cervix

12.30 A full-term foetus ready for birth

6 Birth and aftercare

During the 242 days, thirty-six weeks or nine months spent on average in the uterus, the foetus changes from a ball of cells to a fully formed baby. At twelve weeks all the basic structures are present, though the skeleton is only laid down as cartilage. At sixteen weeks, calcification of the cartilage begins and bone is formed. From this time the foetus increases in size, and at around twenty weeks, active limb movements begin and are seen and felt by the mother. Movements slow down at around thirty-six weeks, when the head of the foetus becomes engaged, just above the cervix, in a position lined up for birth. Fig 12.30 shows a full-term (fully developed) foetus presented in the birth position. Some foetuses do not present themselves in the correct position and may have to be turned. In extreme cases they cannot be turned and are born feet first. This is called a breach birth.

12.31 X-ray photograph of foetus with its head engaged ready for birth

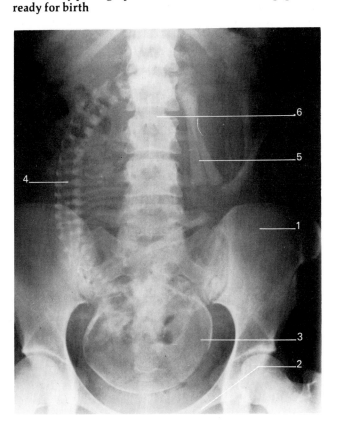

12.55 Why should a breach birth be a problem?
12.56 Identify the parts numbered on the X-ray photograph in Fig 12.31.

The process of birth (parturition) begins when the level of oxytocin (posterior pituitary hormone) in the blood is sufficient to stimulate contraction of the uterine muscles. First signs that birth is imminent vary from a show of blood as the mucus plug closing the cervix is released, a trickle or shower of amniotic fluid (water), to period-like pains as the uterine muscles begin the rhythmic contractions necessary to expel the baby. Time taken for a birth varies from about an hour for an exceptionally quick one to three days for a very slow one. First births are usually longer than subsequent ones.

Two stages of labour characterise birth. The first stage, illustrated in Fig 12.32, involves the dilation of the cervix of the uterus. The mother is advised to take short, shallow breaths towards the end of this stage.

The second stage in labour, shown in Fig 12.33 is the hard work from which labour gets its name. The widest part of the baby, its head, has to be forced through the cervix and vagina. Here the mother

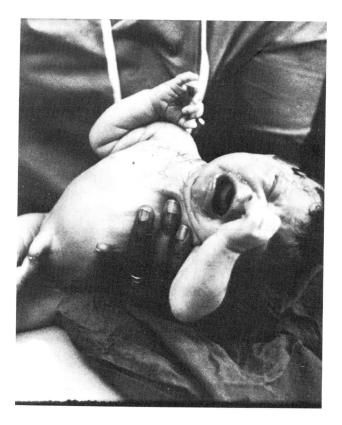

12.34 A newborn baby

inhales deeply between each contraction of the uterine muscles and pushes hard as the contraction comes, exhaling deeply at the same time. The forcing action necessary is similar to that required for extreme constipation.

▶ **Questions**

12.57 Why must the cervix dilate?
12.58 What has happened to the shape of the baby's head in Fig 12.33? How has this occured?
12.59 How can you tell that the baby in Fig 12.34 is in good health?

The baby changes to air breathing from the moment of birth. Until that moment its lungs have not functioned. This necessitates changes in the circulation, because the placental supply of oxygen is cut off, and the lungs start to function. To accommodate the change to air-breathing, the ductus arteriosus, the foetal vessel connecting the pulmonary artery to the aorta, must close and the blood must overcome any resistance to flow in the pulmonary artery and open up the circulation to the lungs. The foramen ovale (hole between the right and left atria in the heart) must close, allowing total separation of deoxygenated and oxygenated blood in the heart. The remains of the umbilical arteries and vein must be closed.

▶ **Question**

12.60 What happens to the umbilical cord which was still attached in Fig 12.34?

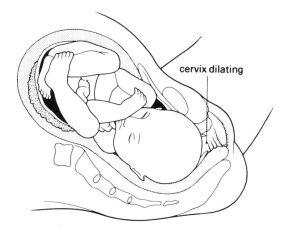

12.32 First stage of labour

12.33 Second stage of labour

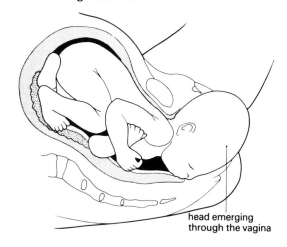

Table 12.1 Comparison of human and cow milk (per 100 cm³ milk)

	Protein	Lactose	Fat	Vit A	Vit B₁	Vit B₂	Vit C	Vit D	Calcium
Human	1.9 g	7.0 g	3.8 g	176 iu	0.2 mg	0.4 mg	4.3 mg	0.4 iu	33 mg
Cow	6.5 g	4.8 g	3.7 g	113 iu	0.4 mg	0.15 mg	1.6 mg	2.36 iu	125 mg

Soon after birth, the uterus begins to contract again. This is to expel the placenta and attached umbilical cord. The placenta, with blood sinuses inflated after expulsion, looks like a purple balloon, and usually weighs about 1.5 – 2.0 kg. It is called the afterbirth.

Within twenty-four hours of birth, prolactin, a pituitary hormone, initiates the production of milk in the mammary glands. This is called lactation. The forerunner of milk is a yellowish substance called colostrum. A newly born baby suckling colostrum obtains a very high proportion of protein, vitamins, mineral ions and antibodies.

▶ **Questions**

12.61   List the apparent nutritional advantages of cow's milk over human milk. See Table 12.1.
12.62   List the apparent nutritional advantages of human milk over cow's milk. See Table 12.1.
12.63   Suggest reasons why it is preferable for a baby to receive human milk.

▷ **Homework**

Study the contents listed on a tin of dried milk prepared for babies. Compare this list with Table 12.1.

7 Which sex and how many?

It will soon be possible for a woman to find out the sex of her unborn child early in pregnancy. Amniocentesis is occasionally used in the United States of America for just this purpose. The sex of a foetus depends on its chromosomes. Males and females possess twenty-three pairs of chromosomes each, twenty-two of which are identical in both sexes. The twenty-third pair of chromosomes are different in males and females. Fig 14.12 on page 176 illustrates the difference between male and female sex chromosomes.

12.35 Determination of sex of offspring

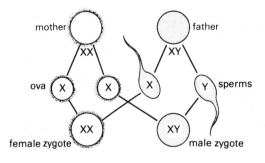

▶ **Question**

12.64   What are the chances of a male or a female being formed on fertilisation? What is the precise determining factor?

Multiple births

Most births yield a single baby, but twins, triplets, quadruplets, and in these days of fertility drugs, even octuplets are also born occasionally. Twins are by far the most common of the multiple births.

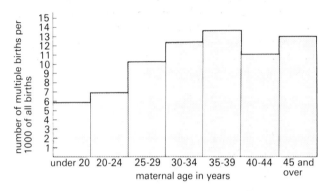

12.36   Incidence of twins born to mothers of increasing age

▶ **Questions**

12.65   How can a potential multiple birth be verified early in pregnancy?
12.66   Which type of twins, identical or non-identical, would you guess are the more common?
12.67   At what age does a woman become most likely to have a set of twins?
12.68   How many ova and sperm are involved in the conception of the twins in Fig 12.37?

12.37 Twin formation I

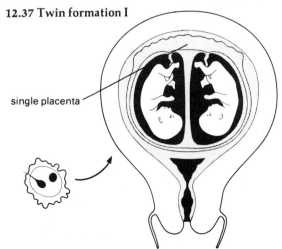

single placenta

12.69 Early on the zygote split into two portions, which have developed separately. Will the twins look identical or not?

12.70 How many ova and sperm are involved in the conception of the twins in Fig 12.38?

12.71 Will these twins be identical or not? Will they differ from ordinary brothers and sisters?

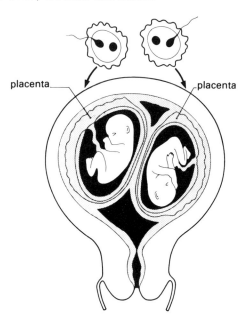

placenta   placenta

12.38 Twin formation II

Fertility drugs

Many women who, in the past, would have remained childless are now helped by fertility drugs. These drugs are based on the gonadotrophins (FSH and LH).

▶ Questions

12.72 What effect will the administration of a dose of FSH have on an infertile woman? Refer to Fig 12.13.

12.73 What effect may too high a dose of FSH possibly have on an infertile woman?

12.74 Would you expect multiple births in these cases to produce identical or non-identical offspring?

▷ Research project

Find the frequency of identical twins, non-identical twins, triplets and quadruplets in the British population.

Answers and discussion

1 Reproductive organs

12.1 1 vertebral column; 2 ureter; 3 urinary bladder; 4 vas deferens; 5 seminal vesicle; 6 prostate gland; 7 rectum; 8 anus; 9 scrotum; 10 epididymis; 11 testis; 12 penis; 13 urethra.

12.2 The urethra is a shared passage for both urine and semen (fluid containing sperm). When semen is released, a sphincter muscle prevents urine from passing at the same time.

12.3 1 lumen of tubule; 2 developing spermatozoa; 3 germinal epithelium; 4 interstitial tissue.

12.4 The birth canal opens into the vulva.

12.5 The opening/exit of the vagina lies between the urethra which is towards the front of the body, and the anus which is towards the back of the body.

12.6 1 ovary; 2 fallopian tube; 3 fimbrian funnel; 4 uterus; 5 vertebral column; 6 rectum; 7 anus; 8 vagina; 9 vulva; 10 urethra; 11 urinary bladder.

12.7 None of the parts of the urinary and genital (reproductive) systems are really shared in the female. The urethra opens into the vulva as does the vagina, but urine and reproductive products are conveyed independently to this region.

12.8 1 developing follicles; 2 stroma; 3 Graafian follicle; 4 corpus luteum (yellow body).

12.9 1 ovum; 2 liquor folliculi; 3 follicle cells; 4 stroma.

12.10 When the ovum bursts out of the Graafian follicle, the remaining follicle cells continue to develop and form a yellow body or corpus luteum.

2 Secondary sexual characteristics

12.11 1 (b) has a larger penis and scrotum in proportion to general body size than (a).
2 (b) has hair growing in the groin.
3 (b)'s shoulders are wider in relation to trunk size than those of (a).
4 The penis and scrotum in (c) are darker in colour than (b). They have a richer blood supply.
5 (c) has hair on his chest, trunk and face as well as his groin.
6 Muscular development in (c) is greater than in (b).

12.12 Between the ages of sixteen and eighteen in males, the voice deepens.

12.13 1 (a) has very little development of the breasts, but in (b) breast development has begun.
2 (b) has wider hips than (a).
3 (b) has developed pubic hair.
4 (c) has fully developed breasts which will be capable of producing milk for a baby.
5 (c) has hips which are wide enough for childbirth.
6 (c) has a more rounded body than (b), with more fat deposits under the skin (see her upper arm).

12.14 The pituitary is the master endocrine gland which stimulates other ductless glands such as the ovaries and testes to produce their hormones. Unless the follicles are stimulated to produce oestrogen, no ova will develop to maturity, there will be no ovulation, and no secondary sexual characteristics will appear.

12.15 LH (luteinising hormone) stimulates the production of the yellow bodies. Progesterone, produced by the yellow body, helps to develop the lining of the uterus for receiving the fertilised egg. It is most important during pregnancy (see section 5).

12.16 Ovulation occurs fourteen days after menstruation.

12.17 Just after ovulation is the best time for conception – fifteen to seventeen days after menstruation. The ovum remains in the fallopian tube and uterus for three to five days after ovulation. A sperm may live for up to seventy-two hours in the uterus.

12.18 Progesterone continues build-up of the endometrium, either for a few days if there is no fertilisation, or over a long period (pregnancy) if fertilisation occurs.

12.19 Temperature is at its lowest in the menstrual cycle at ovulation.

12.20 Conception is most likely when the temperature is high following a very low temperature – at day 16 on the graph. Women with fertility problems keep a chart of their temperature and arrange to have intercourse accordingly.

12.21 The endometrium is well-developed for receiving a fertilised egg at day 21, four to six days after likely fertilisation. Implantation of a fertilised egg usually occurs on about the fifth to seventh day after fertilisation.

3 Gamete formation and fertilisation

12.22 Each gamete will possess twenty-three pairs of chromosomes if mitosis is the process of cell division involved. The zygote would therefore possess forty-six pairs of chromosomes (ninety-two chromosomes), which is twice the normal number.

12.23 During division of the spermatocytes and oocytes, the chromosome number is halved.

12.24 Halving of the chromosome number is brought about by meiosis, or reduction division.

12.25 The chromosome number of the zygote is the same as that of the original spermatocytes and oocytes. The process of meiosis will be outlined in Unit 14.

12.26 A mature spermatozoon is about $60\,\mu$m or 0.006 mm in length.

12.27 The tail of the spermatozoon enables it to swim from the vagina up to the fallopian tubes to fertilise an ovum. The prostate fluid contains a substance which increases the motility of the tails.

12.28 1 male nucleus in head; 2 axial filament of middle piece; 3 mitochondria; 4 tail.

12.29 The large number of mitochondria are concerned with energy production which is necessary to keep the tail constantly moving.

12.30 The diameter of an ovum is about $170\,\mu$m or 0.017 mm.

12.31 1 female nucleus; 2 yolk-laden cytoplasm; 3 follicle cells; 4 vitelline membrane; 5 zona pellucida (clear zone).

12.32 The ovum is much larger than the sperm, containing a large proportion of cytoplasm which is laden with yolk. The yolk nourishes the zygote until it becomes implanted in the uterus wall. The ovum does not require a tail, since the sperm seeks it out.

12.33 (a) The sperms are attracted to the ovum and cluster around it.
(b) The zona pellucida (jelly) is dissolved by enzymes produced by the acrosomes of the sperms.
(c) A sperm head penetrates the vitelline membrane.
(d) The tail of the sperm remains outside the ovum and the male nucleus migrates through the cytoplasm to fuse with the female nucleus to form the fertilised egg or zygote.

12.34 1 unsuccessful sperm; 2 female nucleus; 3 male nucleus; 4 fertilisation membrane.

12.35 The thick fertilisation membrane prevents the entry of other sperms and protects the zygote during subsequent cell division.

4 After fertilisation

12.36 Implantation occurs on the seventh day after fertilisation in this example.

12.37 1 foetus; 2 amnion; 3 umbilical cord; 4 amniotic fluid.

12.38 (i) 3 mm (ii) 10 mm (iii) 18 mm (iv) 25 mm (v) 70 mm.

12.39 The foetus in Fig 12.25 comes between (d) and (e). It is probably eight or nine weeks old.

12.40 Mixing of foetal and maternal blood could burst the blood vessels of the foetus. Since the blood is under quite high pressure in the maternal circulation, the very small blood vessels of the foetus could not withstand it. Also natural and foetal blood groups may not be compatible (see Unit 7). A barrier is also necessary between foetal and maternal blood streams to prevent any damaging substances in the maternal blood stream from crossing into the foetal circulation. Some harmful foreign bodies do cross the placenta sometimes. (See section 5.)

12.41 Essential substances passing from the maternal to the foetal circulation include oxygen, amino acids, fats, glucose and other nutrients (vitamins and minerals are especially important) and antibodies. These provide energy, material for growth and protection against disease. The antibodies stay in the newborn baby's blood for up to a year, giving protection during a vital period.

12.42 These substances are transported to the foetus along the umbilical vein in the umbilical cord.

12.43 Waste substances such as carbon dioxide and urea pass to the placenta from the foetus.

12.44 These substances are transported to the maternal blood sinuses by the umbilical artery in the umbilical cord.

12.45 Diffusion is the process by which substances are exchanged in the placenta. Oxygen and food substances diffuse from a high concentration in the maternal blood sinuses to a low concentration in the foetal capillaries, and carbon dioxide and urea pass from a high concentration in the foetal capillaries to a lower concentration in the maternal blood sinuses.

5 Pregnancy

12.46 If the menstrual cycle failed to stop during pregnancy, the placenta would be at risk of being shed every month.

12.47 Blood pressure is being tested in Fig 12.29, using a sphygmomanometer. Increased blood pressure during pregnancy indicates an extra burden on the heart and tendency to eclampsia. Thrombosis is twenty times more likely to occur in a pregnant woman than in a non-pregnant woman of the same age and general health. A blood pressure over 140/90 is considered too high during pregnancy. Rest and a corrective diet will be prescribed to bring the blood pressure down.

12.48 A haemoglobin count gives an estimate of the oxygen-carrying power of the blood. A low haemoglobin count signifies anaemia. An anaemic person is lacking in energy, and this is dangerous for a pregnant woman. The foetus is dependent on sufficient oxygen for its development from her blood. It is recommended that an expectant mother takes in at least 1.6 g of dietary iron per day during the last three months of pregnancy. Some doctors prescribe iron tablets, but pilchards, sardines, liver and green vegetables will supply more than enough iron.

12.49 The blood group of the mother must be known at the outset so that if she is Rhesus negative the necessary action can be taken. Also, should she require a transfusion after the birth of the baby, she must receive compatible blood.

12.50 Albumen is detected in urine either by using Albustix or applying the Biuret test.

12.51 Glucose in the urine indicates the possibility of sugar diabetes (diabetes mellitus). Temporary diabetes is a feature of pregnancy. It must be controlled to prevent complications such as coma.

12.52 The appearance of albumen in the urine suggests kidney malfunction. The Bowman's capsules are allowing larger molecules to pass into the nephron.

12.53 Amniocentesis could be carried out where chromosomal defects of the baby were suspected. Mongolism (see Unit 14) can be detected using this method. The skin cells are used to make karyotypes. The amniotic fluid may also be analysed to give an idea of foetal maturity and to detect metabolic disorders. Spina bifida foetuses can be detected from the high level of alpha beta protein in the amniotic fluid. These disorders can be detected early in pregnancy.

12.54 Foetal damage by rubella can now be averted by use of the rubella vaccine. Vaccine containing weakened rubella virus is given to girls between the ages of eleven and fourteen years so that they will build up antibodies to prevent a later infection by Rubella.

6 Birth and aftercare

12.55 A breach birth could be difficult because the umbilical cord could wrap around the neck of the foetus and cause strangulation. It is also a more difficult delivery for the mother.

12.56 1 ilium; 2 pubis; 3 head of a foetus; 4 vertebral column of foetus; 5 hind limbs of foetus; 6 vertebral column of mother.

12.57 The cervix must dilate to allow the exit of the large head of the foetus.

12.58 The baby's head has become elongated to enable it to get through the birth canal. The skull bones are not totally joined at birth, so some displacement is possible.

12.59 The baby in Fig 12.34 is crying lustily, so it has obviously a good pair of lungs enabling it to breathe air.

12.60 After birth, the umbilical cord is clipped a few centimetres from the abdomen. This cuts off the flow of the umbilical blood vessels and separates the baby from the remainder of the cord. A dressing is applied to the stump of the umbilical cord. The stump drops off after a few days, leaving the navel as a permanent reminder of the foetal connection.

12.61 Cow milk has more: 1 protein; 2 vitamin B_1; 3 vitamin D; 4 calcium.

12.62 Human milk contains more: 1 lactose; 2 vitamin A; 3 vitamin B_2; 4 vitamin C.

12.63 From these lists above it is difficult to choose one milk in preference to the other. Protein, high in cow's milk, is important for growth, and calcium and vitamin D are vital for good bones and teeth. Human milk has a higher energy source in more lactose, and vitamin A and C protect well against infection.

However human milk is preferable to cow's milk. The fat it contains is more easily digestible by the infant and the high lactose is said to help absorption of amino acids and certain minerals. Human milk also contains antibodies which will give additional protection to the baby. The diet of the mother is important, and if her diet is balanced, the milk will be ideal. Breast feeding is considered to be superior to the use of a bottle and substitute milk because of the close relationship which develops between mother and child. It is also more hygienic than bottle feeding.

7 Which sex and how many?

12.64 The chances of an offspring being male or female are 50:50. The determining factor is whether the sperm which penetrates the ovum carries an X or a Y chromosome.

12.65 Use of ultrasound to produce a sonogram will confirm multiple births early in pregnancy.

12.66 Non-identical (fraternal) twins are far more common than identical.

12.67 A woman is most likely to have twins around the age of 35–39 years.

12.68 A single ovum and sperm are involved in conception.

12.69 These twins will be identical in every way. They are two halves of the same egg (monozygotic). They are certain to be the same sex.

12.70 Two ova and sperm are involved in the conception of these twins.

12.71 The twins will not look alike. They are totally separate individuals formed from two zygotes (dizygotic). They may be different sexes. They are only different from other brothers and sisters in that they happened to be conceived at about the same time.

12.72 FSH will stimulate follicle development, oestrogen production and ovulation in an infertile woman.

12.73 An overdose of FSH will result in multi-ovulation which is the cause of a lot of the multiple births which occur to women on fertility drugs.

12.74 This type of multiple birth will always produce non-identical offspring, since many ova will have been fertilised at the same time.

13 Growth

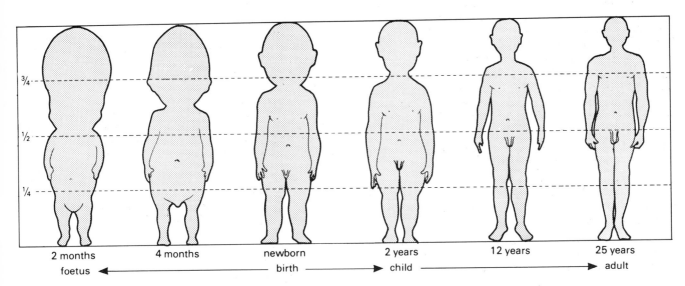

13.1 Proportions of the body in a foetus prior to birth and an individual after birth

1 Early growth and development

As was explained in Unit 1 all living things are able to grow at some stage in their lives. Growth is the production of more protoplasm and more cells, leading to an increase in mass, in size and in complexity. Increasing complexity is usually called development.

New cells are constantly being produced in humans from the time of conception. The rate at which new cells are formed is not the same everywhere in the developing embryo. Some parts of the body develop more rapidly than others, and this process continues even after birth.

▶ **Questions**

13.1 What is the predominant part of the body in a two month foetus? Suggest a reason for this.
13.2 Summarise the changes in the proportion of the head to the body after birth.
13.3 Which part of the body increases most in proportion after birth? What is the significance of this increase?
13.4 At what stage in Fig 13.1 do the reproductive organs appear? When do they begin to increase in proportion?

As well as proportions of different parts of the body changing during growth, proportions of individual structures also change. This is all part of development.

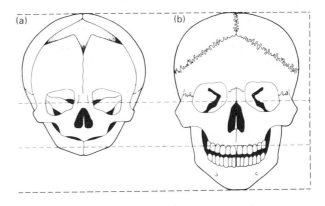

13.2 Skull proportions of a newborn baby and an adult

▶ **Question**

13.5 List the differences apparent in skulls (a) and (b) in Fig 13.2.

The proportionally larger cranium of the newborn baby houses a proportionally larger brain. The cranial bones are not fused, since some further growth of the bones is necessary before fusion occurs at about eighteen months of age. The toothlessness of the newborn baby does not matter as it feeds exclusively on a milk diet for the first few months, and it does not need teeth to deal with solid foods.

153

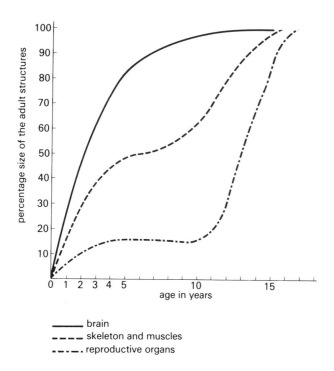

13.3 The different rates of growth of the brain, the skeleton and muscles, and the reproductive organs of a boy

▶ **Questions**

13.6 Study the graphs in Fig 13.3 and estimate what percentage of the total size is (a) the brain, (b) the skeleton, (c) the reproductive organs, of a five-year-old.

13.7 How well developed are the muscles of a one-year-old? What effect will this have on the baby?

13.8 What is the advantage of the relatively late development of the reproductive organs?

During the first months of life, the activities of human babies are very restricted by the comparatively slow development of the muscular and skeletal system in relation to the nervous system. Newborn calves and many other mammals are able to walk within minutes of birth, while only a minority of human infants are able to walk within a year. The drawings in Fig 13.4 illustrate increasing co-ordination of the developing muscle system over a period of thirteen months.

▶ **Questions**

13.9 Describe the ways in which the baby's muscular control has improved over the eight months shown in Fig 13.4(a).

13.10 How has the baby in Fig 13.4(b) developed over seven months? Explain what skills it has acquired, and what muscles and senses are necessary for these skills.

13.11 The importance of the precision grip was stressed in Unit 1. How long does it take the baby in Fig 13.4(c) to develop this grip properly?

13.12 Suggest two other skills which depend on good muscular co-ordination that most babies develop during their first year.

13.13 At what age do you suppose that a baby will really begin to explore his surroundings?

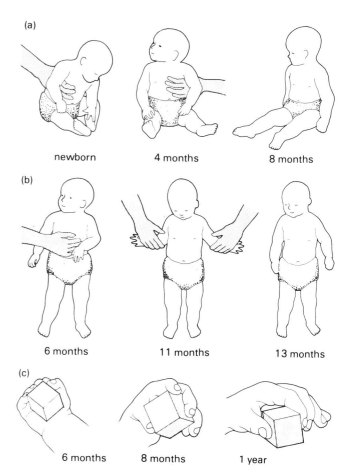

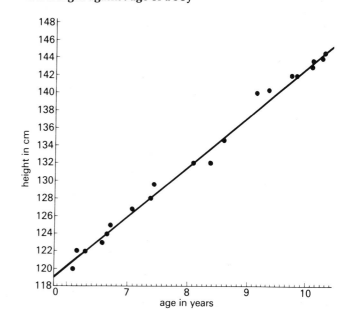

13.4 Stages in the development of a baby

Increase in height and weight

The simplest way to estimate growth of an individual is by measurement of height and weight. Fig 13.5 illustrates the increase in height of a boy from the age of six to just over ten years old. Study the graph.

13.5 Height against age of a boy

154

13.14 (a) How tall is the boy at seven years old?
(b) How tall is the boy at ten years old?
(c) How would you describe the pattern of growth in height between the ages of five and ten?

This graph only gives a limited picture of growth. How does height increase between the ages of ten and maturity? Does height gain differ in boys and girls?

Table 13.1 Average heights of boys and girls at yearly intervals

Age	Boys' height (cm)	Girls' height (cm)
Birth	50.6	50.2
1 year	75.2	74.2
2 years	92.2	86.6
3 years	98.2	95.7
4 years	103.4	103.2
5 years	110.0	109.4
6 years	117.5	115.9
7 years	125.1	122.3
8 years	130.0	128.0
9 years	135.5	132.9
10 years	140.3	138.6
11 years	144.2	144.7
12 years	149.6	151.9
13 years	155.0	157.1
14 years	162.7	159.6
15 years	167.8	161.1
16 years	171.6	162.2
17 years	173.7	162.5
18 years	174.5	162.5

▶ Questions

13.15 Using data from Table 13.1, construct graphs to show and compare height increase in girls and boys. Plot age on the horizontal axis.
13.16 How does the growth rate before the age of six years compare with growth between six and ten years in both sexes?
13.17 How does the rate of growth alter after ten years in (a) girls and (b) boys ?
13.18 What is the difference in average height between an eighteen year old boy and an eighteen year old girl?
13.19 Fig 13.6 shows the weight increase of the same boy as in Fig 13.5. (a) How heavy was the boy when seven years old?
(b) How heavy was the boy when nine years old?
(c) How heavy was the boy when ten years old?
(d) How would you describe weight increase between the ages of six and ten?
13.20 Using data from Table 13.2, construct graphs to show and compare weight increases in boys and girls. Plot age on the horizontal axis.
13.21 How does weight increase before the age of two compare with weight increase after two years?
13.22 How does weight increase differ in boys and girls between the ages of ten and fourteen years?
13.23 What is the difference in average weight between boys and girls at the age of eighteen?

Table 13.2 Average weight in kilograms of boys and girls in yearly intervals

Age	Boys' weight (kg)	Girls' weight (kg)
Birth	3.4	3.36
1 year	10.07	9.75
2 years	12.56	12.29
3 years	14.61	14.42
4 years	16.51	16.42
5 years	18.89	18.58
6 years	21.9	21.09
7 years	24.54	23.68
8 years	27.26	26.35
9 years	29.94	28.94
10 years	32.61	31.89
11 years	35.2	35.74
12 years	38.28	39.74
13 years	42.18	44.95
14 years	48.81	49.17
15 years	54.48	51.48
16 years	58.3	53.07
17 years	61.78	54.02
18 years	63.05	54.39

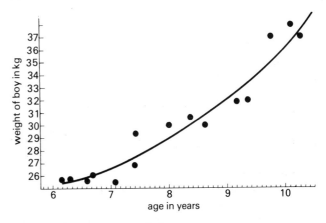

13.6 Weight against age of a boy

13.7 Heights of a group of 14 year old boys

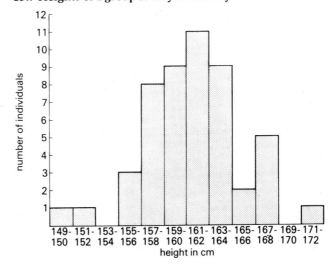

155

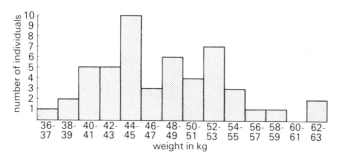

13.8 Weights of a group of 14 year old boys

▶ **Questions**

13.24 (a) What is the commonest (modal) height of the group of boys in Fig 13.7?
(b) What percentage of the group are this height?
(c) What percentage of the group are between 157 and 164 cm?
(d) What is the range of heights in this group?
13.25 (a) What is the commonest weight of the group of boys in Fig 13.8?
(b) What percentage of the group are this weight?
(c) What percentage of the group are between 41 and 53 kg?
(d) What is the range of weights in this group?
13.26 Consider all the data concerning height and weight in this section and state whether height or weight should be used as the main indicator of growth. Explain your choice.

Increase in height is an indication of the growth of the skeleton. Growth is frequently expressed as skeletal age, and height is one expression of this age. Weight is a much more variable factor than height. It is more dependent on diet and less on inherited genes (see Unit 14). Bone growth is dependent on the production of an anterior pituitary hormone called phyone. Individuals with an excess of phyone may grow exceptionally tall (up to 8 feet). This condition is called giantism. Individuals who have a deficiency of phyone may be exceptionally short (about 3 feet). This condition is called dwarfism. See Unit 9. Other hormones involved are thyroxin, which controls basal metabolic rate, and the sex hormones (see section 4).

▷ **Research project**

Being especially tall has some advantages and some disadvantages and so does being short. Write an essay discussing these advantages and disadvantages and find out about some especially tall or short people in history such as Goliath, Napoleon or Toulouse Lautrec.

2 Eruption of the teeth

Teeth are formed from a mass of thickened epithelial tissue growing close to the jawbone in the gum (see Fig 13.9). This tissue forms a tooth bud, the outer part of which, the enamel organ, produces the enamel by depositing calcium phosphate in its elongated cells. The inner part, the dental papilla, produces the dentine. Dentine is produced by cells called odonto-blasts, which lay down calcium salts in strands,

leaving living tissue between. While the milk (deciduous) teeth are being formed, the permanent teeth are already visible as rudiments (see Fig 13.9).

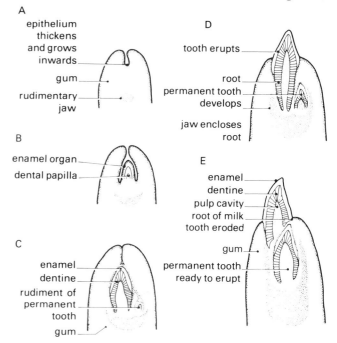

13.9 Formation of deciduous and permanent teeth

Table 13.3 Eruption of deciduous teeth

Teeth	Time of eruption
Central incisors	6 – 8 months
Lateral incisors	10 months
First molars	12 months
Canines	18 months
Second molars	24 months

13.10 Vertical section through a mature canine tooth

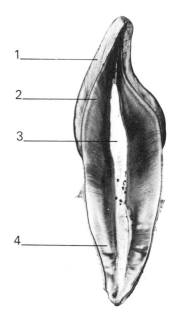

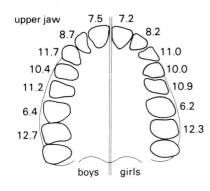

upper jaw

7.5 | 7.2
8.7 | 8.2
11.7 | 11.0
10.4 | 10.0
11.2 | 10.9
6.4 | 6.2
12.7 | 12.3

boys | girls

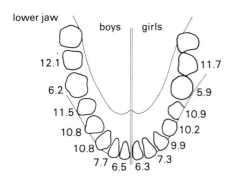

lower jaw

boys | girls

12.1 | 11.7
6.2 | 5.9
11.5 | 10.9
10.8 | 10.2
10.8 | 9.9
7.7 6.5 | 6.3 7.3

13.11 Age of eruption of permanent teeth in years and months

▶ Questions

13.27 What causes the loss of a deciduous tooth?
13.28 Why do teeth begin to erupt some time after birth?
13.29 Suggest a reason for the long period involved for the development of all the teeth.
13.30 Using Fig 13.9, as a guide, identify the numbered parts in Fig 13.10.
13.31 Using Fig 13.11, construct a table similar to Table 13.3 for the permanent teeth in both upper and lower jaws. Only construct a table for your own sex.

In girls all the teeth erupt two or three months earlier than the equivalent teeth in boys. The order of eruption of the lower canines and of the first lower premolars is different in males and females. No time is indicated for the third molars in Fig 13.11 – the 'wisdom' teeth. These are often very late erupting and sometimes do not erupt at all.

▷ Survey work

Carry out a survey on the number and type of teeth present in the jaws of two of your brothers or sisters or neighbours' children. Record the age of the two children in years and months.

3 Bone growth and development

Unit 3 outlined the basic material from which the skeleton is constructed.

▶ Questions

13.32 What is the name of the tissue from which most bone develops?
13.33 Describe the difference between the bone ends at A and B in Fig 13.12 (a) and (b).
13.34 Describe the differences between the bone shafts at C and D in Fig 13.12 (a) and (b).

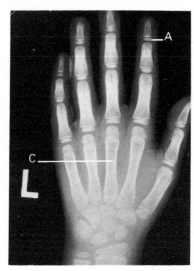

13.12 (a) X-ray photograph of the hand of a 6 year old

13.12 (b) X-ray photograph of the hand of a 25 year old

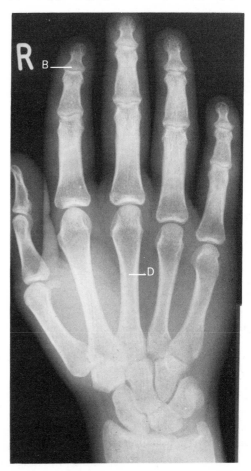

The structures arrowed in Fig 13.13 (c) and (d) are plates of cartilage called epiphyseal plates. They continue to grow and produce more cartilage which then gradually becomes ossified at the bone shaft side of the plates, resulting in an increase in length of the bone.

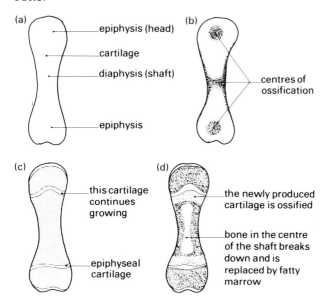

13.13 Stages in the ossification of a long bone

The process of cartilage being transformed into bone is called ossification. The cartilage-producing cells, the chondroblasts, start to divide and grow in layers, while at the same time, calcium phosphate is deposited in the gel matrix. Some of the calcified matrix then becomes eroded and cells called osteoblasts invade the spaces, laying down bone on the remains of the calcified matrix (see Unit 2). Blood is brought to the osteoblasts in capillaries which also invade the eroded spaces.

▶ **Questions**

13.35 Where are the three main centres of ossification in a long bone?
13.36 What is the name of the continually growing areas of cartilage at either end of the bone shaft?
13.37 How does growth in length of a long bone occur?

Growth in the girth of the bone occurs continuously as osteoblasts in the membrane of cartilage around the bone, the periosteum, ossify and lay down calcium salts as they divide.

▶ **Question**

13.38 How do the footprints in Fig 13.14 differ? How do the feet which made these prints differ?

Because the foot bones are still growing, selection of footwear for children must ensure that there is sufficient room for growth. Shoes which are too small will stunt the growth of the bones and cause deformities.

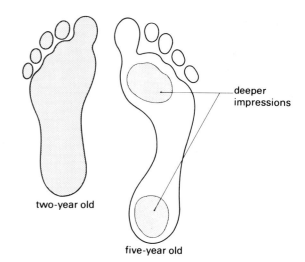

13.14 Footprint of 2-year-old and a 5-year-old

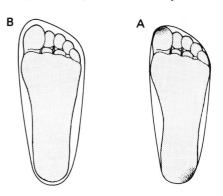

13.15 Correct and incorrect shoe fittings

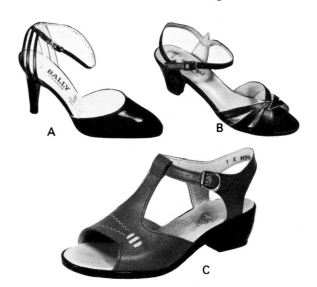

13.16 Some footwear for children

▶ **Questions**

13.39 Fig 13.15 shows correct and incorrect shoe fittings for a child. Say which one is correct and why.
13.40 Which of the shoes in Fig 13.16 would you consider to be the most comfortable and most beneficial to the development of the foot?

Excessively high-heeled shoes can also cause damage to the feet in addition to stunting the growth of the bones. For example callouses, bunions and misalignment of the bones may be caused.

▷ **Homework**

Some special types of footwear have been developed for sport and recreation, such as football boots and walking shoes. Choose four special types and explain why each has been designed as it has.

4 Growth at adolescence

In Unit 12 the appearance of secondary sexual characteristics at adolescence was discussed.

▶ **Questions**

13.41 What controls the development of secondary sexual characteristics? (Refer to Unit 12)
13.42 What growth changes, if any, occur at the same time?
13.43 Construct a graph to illustrtate height gain in both boys and girls using Table 13.4. Plot age on the horizontal axis. When you have completed the graph, study it carefully, then answer the following questions.
13.44 At what age is there a sudden, significant increase in height gain in girls?
13.45 At what age is there a sudden, significant increase in height gain in boys?
13.46 How do the times of the height spurts compare with the times of appearance of secondary sexual characteristics? What can you conclude?

Fig 13.17 demonstrates areas which may be measured to investigate differences in form apparent in the sexes at adolescence. These differences are called sexual dimorphism.

Activity 13.1 Investigating sexual dimorphism.

1 Measure the shoulders and hips of your partner.
2 Record the measurements in centimetres on a

Table 13.4 Height gain in centimetres per year

| | Height gain | |
Age	Boys	Girls
1	25	24
2	17	13
3	6	9
4	6	7
5	7	6
6	7	6
7	6	5.5
8	6	5
9	5	5
10	5	6
11	4.5	7
12	4.5	9
13	6	6
14	10.5	3
15	9	1
16	3	0
17	1	0
18	0	0

table drawn on the blackboard with the following headings:

Boys		Girls	
Shoulders	Hips	Shoulders	Hips

3 Work out the average measurements of shoulders and hips for boys and girls.
4 Work out the shoulder:hip ratio for males and females.
5 Refer to Fig 13.17 and devise other measurement comparisons to demonstrate sexual dimorphism.

▶ **Question**

13.47 What is the shoulder:hip ratio in males and females?

13.17 Male and female measurements

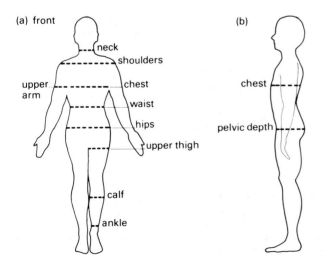

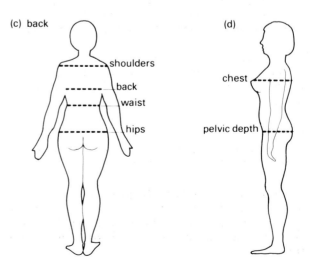

Sexual dimorphism is one aspect of secondary sexual characteristics. It is controlled by the pituitary gland, which in turn stimulates the sex hormones. Testosterone in the male increases muscle development which broadens the shoulders and oestrogen in the female causes the hips to widen as the pelvis broadens to accommodate childbirth. Gain in height and weight at adolescence is also controlled by the secretion of testosterone and oestrogen. The sex hormones stimulate bone growth at puberty.

▷ Homework

Throughout history changing fashion and clothing styles have emphasised different aspects of secondary sexual characteristics. For example the Elizabethans exaggerated the slimness of the female waist, but minimised the bust. Write about other examples of the ways in which sexual dimorphism is emphasised by clothing.

5 Senescence – ageing

13.18 An elderly lady

▶ Question

13.48 List the features in Fig 13.18 which indicate that this person is aged.

The process of ageing begins from about the age of twenty years. The body cells very gradually become less efficient, eventually producing symptoms of senescence. Skin changes occur and the skin loses its elasticity and wrinkles instead of staying firm. This is due to a reduction of elastin fibres in the skin. The nervous system becomes less efficient. Old people tend to have poorer hearing. The lens of the eye becomes less elastic and focusing is impaired. Many old people are confused because their short-term memory no longer operates. Growth of the hair declines, frequently leading to baldness. Very old women often have very thin hair. Hair pigment is no longer produced and the hair grows white. The muscles begin to waste away with age causing poor co-ordination for walking and other movements, and the bones become brittle. Brittle bones will not mend easily and old people may die from shock if their bones are badly broken.

Internal organs similarly become less efficient. The circulatory system is affected by atherosclerosis, which is the building up of deposits on the lining of the arteries reducing their diameter. This silting up of the arteries causes increased blood pressure and is the most common cause of coronary thrombosis. A less efficient circulation means impaired distribution of heat, and many old people are very sensitive to cold since they cannot maintain a constant body temperature. Hypothermia, where the core temperature falls below the critical level for body functioning, is a common cause of death in old people.

▶ Question

13.49 How can individuals and the community help the aged to cope with their problems?

Why do we age?

There are many theories of ageing, several of which may account for part of the cause of the inevitable decay of the body. One probable cause is faulty replication. In Unit 2 the building up of protein by DNA was briefly discussed. It is suggested that with age the DNA code breaks down and the wrong proteins are built up (replicated). Another theory is that the antigen–antibody reaction (see Unit 7) becomes less accurate and the antibodies begin attacking the body's own proteins. Arthritis is an example of a self-destructive disease, and since arthritis is mainly associated with age, it tends to support this theory.

The brains of rats which exhibit all the features of senescence have been shown to contain a high proportion of a pigment called lipofuschin. Post-mortems of very confused human subjects have shown a similar pigment. It is possible that lipofuschin blocks nervous or chemical transmissions in the brain, destroying, among other things, the short-term memory. This third theory is supported by the use of an anti-lipofuschin drug which is claimed to improve the short-term memory of some confused old people.

Finally, many people go through a change of life in their fifties when the levels of sex hormones produced decrease and the ovaries or testes no longer produce gametes. This **menopause** is usually more apparent in females than in males. In some individuals, cessation of oestrogen production results in the appearance of symptoms of ageing: loss of skin bloom, wrinkling, thinning of scalp hair, increase in facial hair, thinning of bones of the vertebral column. The abrupt appearance of these symptoms can cause extreme distress and hormone replacement therapy (HRT) is applied in some cases.

13.19 Compare the ages of this lady with the lady in Fig 13.18. Who do you think looks older?

▷ **Homework**

Write a brief essay discussing the advantages and disadvantages of hormone replacement therapy.

6 Growth of populations

The average life span of a human being is quoted in the Bible as 'three score years and ten'.

▶ **Questions**

13.50 Was the Bible quotation closer to the average life span in 1840, 1900 or 1960? See Fig 13.20.
13.51 Suggest reasons for the increased life spans in the 20th century.
13.52 From Fig 13.21 what is the average life span in (a) Sweden, (b) Argentina, (c) India?
13.53 Suggest reasons for the lower average life spans found in Argentina and India.

13.20 Average life spans in the UK at different times

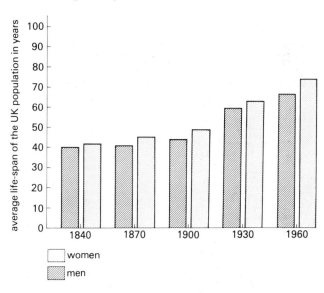

13.21 Average life-span in Sweden, Argentina and India in 1979

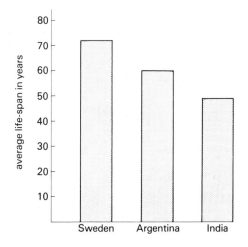

161

In less developed countries, life expectancy is still only around 40–50 years. In South America some people living in barren regions of the Andes have a life expectancy of 30–35 years. In India and Africa diseases of malnutrition such as kwashiorkor and marasmus cause thousands of deaths in children. Disease still accounts for a large percentage of early deaths. Sleeping sickness, elephantiasis, cholera and typhoid are still common. (See Unit 15.)

In Europe, vaccination, hygiene and control of microbial infections has saved many early deaths. Improved nutrition has also contributed to longer-lasting health. Recently very effective malaria control has greatly improved life expectancy in countries such as Mauritius and Ceylon, where over half the deaths were from that disease.

▶ **Question**

13.54 From Fig 13.22, what deduction can you make about the effect of the increased life expectancy in Mauritius?

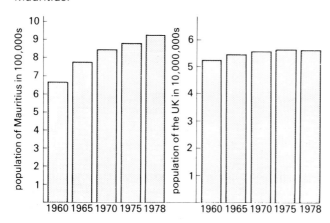

13.22 Population increase in Mauritius and the UK in recent years

▷ **Homework**

Discuss the effect of increased life spans on world population.

7 Demography

Demography is the study of populations. Using population statistics, it estimates future needs of a country in relation to its population, and indicates possible problems in the event of too great or too little an increase in population.

Statistics are based on censuses carried out at regular intervals in every country.

The censuses include:

1 crude birth rate = $\dfrac{\text{no. of live births per year} \times 1000}{\text{total population}}$

2 crude death rate = $\dfrac{\text{no. of deaths per year} \times 1000}{\text{total population}}$

These two sets of statistics give a very clear picture of population trends in a country.

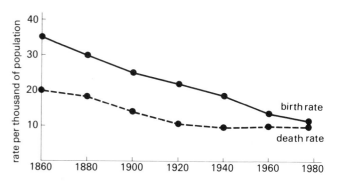

13.23 Birth rates and death rates for recent years in a country in Western Europe

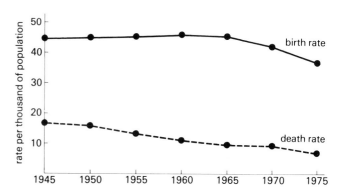

13.24 Birth rates and death rates for recent years in another country

Activity 13.2   Investigating population increase

1   In Fig 13.23 find the death rate in 1960.
2   Find the birth rate in 1960.
3   Calculate the difference between these two rates.
4   Decide whether this difference indicates an increase or a decrease in the population.
5   Repeat steps 1, 2, 3 and 4 for Fig 13.24.
6   The difference between the birth rate and death rate of a country is called the natural rate of population increase. Tabulate your data by copying and completing the table below.

	Crude birth rate (1960)	Crude death rate (1960)	Natural rate of population increase
Country A			
Country B			

In general, developing countries have much higher birth rates, death rates and population increase rates than developed countries.

▶ **Questions**

13.55 What changes have there been to the birth rate in

the country in Fig 13.24 since 1945? What changes have there been to the death rate?

13.56 Can you account for these changes, if any?

13.57 Into which group, developing country or developed country would you place the countries in Figs 13.23 and 13.24?

Table 13.5 shows the number of births and deaths per 1000, population increase rate, and number of years it will take the population to double, for six countries. The present population of each country is also stated in millions.

Table 13.5 Population statistics for six countries

Country	Population in millions	Births /1000	Deaths /1000	Population increase rate/1000	Years to double population
China	759.6	34	15	19	39
India	554.6	42	17	25	27
Latin – America	283.0	38	9	29	24
Sweden	8.0	12.2	10.8	1.4	96
UK	56.0	17.1	11.9	5.2	66
USA	205.2	17.6	9.6	8	70

▶ **Questions**

13.58 Account for the marked diference in increase of the populations of China and Latin America.

13.59 Which country has the biggest 'population explosion' ?

13.60 Which country has the slowest increase and how many years will it take to double its present population?

Fig 13.25 illustrates the 'demographic transition'. The situation at X is regarded as ideal to aim for in a developing country. At point X a low death is matched by a much reduced birth rate. This will reduce the natural increase of the population.

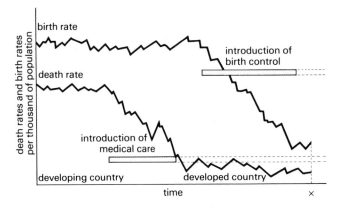

13.25 The demographic transition

Other statistics include:

3 fertility rate (net reproductive rate)
= no. of live births per year x 1000

no. of women aged 15–44

4 infant mortality
= no. of deaths under 12 months per year

no. of live births per 1000

Activity 13.3   Finding out the local net reproductive rate

1 Working as a class, question a sample of 100 children from different families to determine how many brothers and sisters they have, who were born in 1970.

2 Record the results and work out the fertility rate as follows:

no. of brothers and sisters born in 1970 x 1000

100 (number of different families)

▶ **Question**

13.61 The population of a remote Scottish island includes 640 women between the ages of fifteen and forty-four and there are 80 live births in one year. What is the net reproductive rate of the island?

The structure or composition of a population may be summarised diagramatically in an age-sex pyramid such as those illustrated in Fig 13.26.

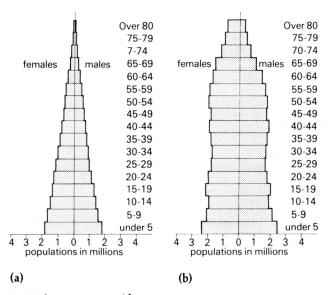

(a)   **(b)**

13.26 Age-sex pyramids

▶ **Questions**

13.62 What percentage of the population is under twenty years old in (a) and in (b)?

13.63 What percentage of the population is over sixty years old in (a) and in (b)?

13.64 Suggest a country which could have a population composition such as (a). What are the problems of this population structure?

13.65 Suggest a country which has a population composition such as (b). What are the problems of this population structure?

13.66 How do the male and female components of these population pyramids differ from each other in (a) and (b)?

▷ **Research project**

Construct an age-sex pyramid for your own community, by the following method:

1 Concentrate on your street, estate or village and estimate the total population.

2 Determine the number of males and females in each five-year age group. You will have to guess at some of these – you can't ask everyone their age. If you have time you could duplicate a polite questionnaire and deliver it to each house asking the householder to tick one of the following boxes:

Male	0–5	6–10	11–15	16–20	21–25	26–30
Female	0–5	6–10	11–15	16–20	21–25	26–30

3 Work out the percentage of the total population each group represents and construct an age-sex pyramid.

4 Compare your age-sex pyramid with those of other class members and note any significant differences. Does the composition of a population vary between village and town? There will be many possibilities for discussion.

8 Overpopulation and its control

13.27 Overpopulation leads to crowded towns and cities

13.28 Projected increase in world population

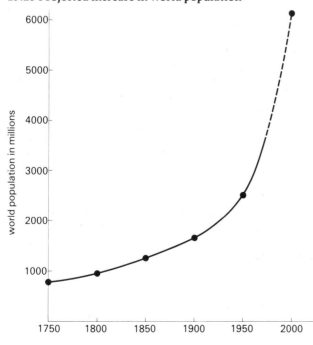

Thomas Robert Malthus, (1766–1834) predicted in the early 19th century that the consequences of an increased population were 'misery and vice'. He worked out that unchecked population growth would outstrip food production (see Fig 13.29).

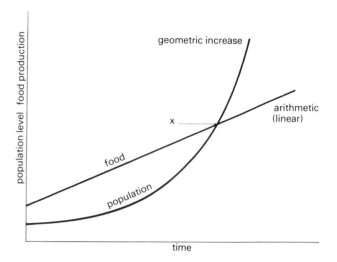

13.29 The predictions of Malthus

▶ **Questions**

13.67 What are the possible consequences of overpopulation?

13.68 What will happen at point X in Fig 13.29? Is it likely to happen in the near future?

Other consequences of overpopulation include pollution and exhaustion of fuels. These will be discussed in Unit 20.

Population control

With the recent fall in death rates, the only way to stabilise population growth is to control the birth rate (see Fig 13.25). Birth control has been practised for hundreds of years, but it is only within recent years that reliable medical methods have been discovered. Fig 13.30 is a condom which fits over the erect penis and prevents sperm from entering the vagina. This method has been in use for a long time and is about 80% reliable.

13.30 A condom

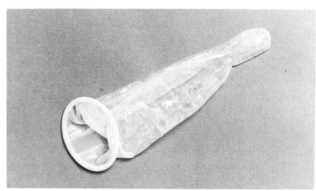

Fig 13.31 shows a diaphragm which may be fitted just before intercourse as shown. It forms a barrier preventing the sperms from entering the uterus. Diaphragms come in many sizes and a family planning clinic or general practice doctor has to discover the correct size for a woman. If the diaphragm is too big it will be useless. Spermicidal cream is used with the diaphragm to increase its reliability. It is about 90% reliable.

13.31 (a) A diaphragm

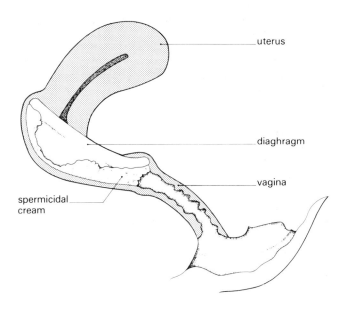

13.31 (b) A diaphragm in position

Fig 13.32 shows a variety of intra-uterine devices which have been found to be very effective contraceptives. It is believed that they interfere with the implantation of the zygote. They are about 98% reliable. They must be fitted by a doctor, and they stay in place for up to five years. A few women cannot tolerate them and eject them from the uterus. In other women they cause severe bleeding and their use should be discontinued.

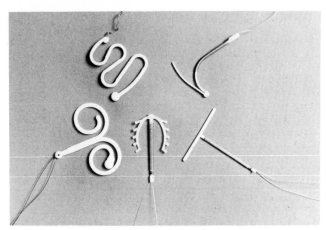

13.32 Some intra-uterine devices (IUDs)

Contraceptive pills such as those shown in Fig 13.33 are the most reliable of these forms of birth control. They are over 99% reliable.

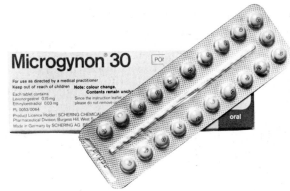

13.33 Contraceptive pills

▶ **Question**

13.69 A contraceptive pill works by suppressing ovulation and the normal menstrual cycle. What kind of substance might it contain? (See Unit 12.)

Some women are not able to take the pill because of contra-indications such as varicose veins or high blood pressure. There is evidence to suggest that circulatory problems are made worse by the hormones contained in the pill. A very low-oestrogen pill has been manufactured in an attempt to overcome this drawback. Scientists are now working on a 'morning after' pill which would be taken after sexual intercourse and would interfere less with the hormone balance of the body.

More permanent contraceptive devices are sterilisation of men and women. Male sterilisation or vasectomy is the simpler operation. The vas deferentia are severed and sealed off so that no sperms can reach the penis.

▷ **Homework**

Try to find reliable figures which indicate the number of people in this country who use each method of contraception discussed here.

Answers and discussion

1 Early growth and development

13.1 The predominant part of a two month foetus is the head. This is massively developed to house the brain, which grows more rapidly than other tissues.

13.2 The head grows very little after about the age of two years as compared with the remainder of the body. The head of a newborn baby represents a quarter of its height, of a two-year-old a fifth of its height, of a twelve-year-old a sixth of its height, and of an adult about an eighth of its height.

13.3 The legs increase proportionally more than the head or trunk after birth. At birth the legs represent about one third of the total height, while in the adult they may represent almost half of the total height. Longer legs bring increased mobility which enables parents to take better care of their young. (In early man, long legs helped in hunting for food.)

13.4 In Fig 13.1, reproductive organs are apparent externally in the newborn baby. They begin to increase in proportion at around the age of twelve.

13.5 1 The newborn baby has a cranium (see Unit 1) which occupies half of the total height of the skull. In an adult, the cranium is substantially below half of the total skull height.
2 The skull bones of the newborn baby are not fused. Those of the adult are fused.
3 A full set of teeth is present in the adult skull, while the newborn baby is toothless.

13.6 (a) A five year old has a brain which is 85–90% the size of an adult brain.
(b) A five year old has a skeleton which is 50% the size of an adult skeleton.
(c) The reproductive organs of a five year old are only 15% the size of mature reproductive organs.

13.7 The muscles of a one year old are only 15% the size of adult muscles. This is reflected in the lack of co-ordinated movements in an infant of this age. Most infants are not able to walk unaided at this age.

13.8 Late development of the reproductive organs ensures that the remainder of the body has had sufficient time to mature before reproduction can occur. A more mature parent is better able to care for the young.

13.9 When the newborn baby is held in a sitting position his head drops right forward and his back is rounded, showing that his neck muscles are not able to hold up his head, nor his back muscles able to straighten his back. By four months, however, his neck muscles are strong enough to hold his head upright, and his back is held straight, although he still needs support so that he does not overbalance. By eight months his co-ordination and balance has improved so that he can sit upright by himself.

13.10 In Fig 13.4(b) the baby has learned to walk. His legs and back have developed from being able to just hold his weight with supporting hands to help him balance, to being able to walk with a little assistance, to being able to walk independently. This requires good muscle co-ordination of the legs and back, and a fairly well developed sense of balance.

13.11 It takes about one year for the precision grip to become fully developed. At six months the simple palmar grasp is shown; at eight months an intermediate type of

grasp where the thumb is partially opposed has developed; at one year the proper precision grip is shown.

13.12 Other skills which develop during the first year of life are talking, feeding oneself with solid foods, learning to dress, and communicating with parents. All of these skills depend on quite sophisticated muscular co-ordination.

13.13 A baby begins to explore his environment at about the age of one year. By this time he may be able to walk, to use a lot of words, to hold objects in his hand and examine them, and to find out a lot from his parents. Many babies will begin their exploration much earlier than this if their muscular development is advanced.

13.14 (a) 126 cm (b) 142 – 146 cm (c) Between the ages of six and ten, growth in height is virtually linear – height increase with time is nearly constant. There is a steady increase.

13.15

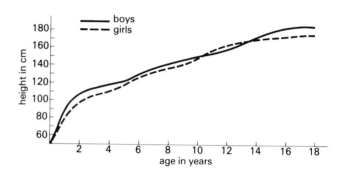

13.16 Increase in height from birth to six years is faster than from six to ten years in both sexes.

13.17 (a) In girls the rate of increase in height is greater from 10 – 14 years than 6 – 10 years.
(b) In boys the rate of increase in height from 10 – 14 years is less than from 6 – 10 years, but it becomes most rapid from 12 – 16 years.

13.18 The difference in average height between an 18-year-old boy and girl is 10cm (boys are 10cm taller).

13.19 (a) 26.3 kg (b) 31 kg (c) 37 – 38 kg
(d) The weight increase gets faster and faster towards the age of ten. There is also great variation in weight over short periods and the final weight at ten years old is lower than the boy's weight on his tenth birthday (37 kg compared with 38 kg).

13.20

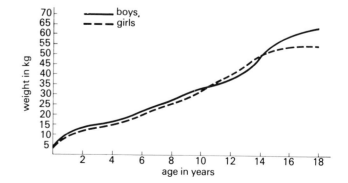

13.21 Weight increase is greater before the age of two in both boys and girls.

13.22 Between ten and fourteen years weight increase is greater in girls than in boys.

13.23 The difference in average weight between boys and girls at eighteen is 10 kg (boys are 10 kg heavier).

13.24 (a) The modal height is 162 cm.
(b) 22% of the group are this height.
(c) 80% of the group are between 156 and 164 cm.
(d) The range in height of the group is from 150 – 172 cm or 22 cm.

13.25 (a) The commonest weight is 45 kg.
(b) 20% of the group are this weight.
(c) 80% of the group are between 41 – 53 kg.
(d) The range in weight of this group is from 37 – 63 kg or 26 kg.

13.26 Height should be used as the main indicator of growth. There is a definite relationship between height and age as seen in Figs 13.5 and 13.7. There is a wide variation in weight at a given age as seen in Figs 13.6 and 13.8. Weight can go down before growth is complete. Also, when growth is complete, weight may still vary. A man of thirty-five years may weigh 64 kg one month, 72 kg the next, then return to 68 kg. His height will not be altered during this time.

2 Eruption of the teeth

13.27 Deciduous teeth are shed because of the erosion of their roots. They are no longer able to remain stable within their sockets.

13.28 Teeth erupt some time after birth because the early diet of a baby is solely milk. Sharp teeth would damage the nipples during suckling from the mammary glands.

13.29 Some suckling may continue for a number of months during weaning of the baby on to solid foods. At first only finely ground foods are suitable for the baby's digestion. The larger teeth are not required until the baby is able to digest more substantial, fibrous food, at the age of 18 – 24 months.

13.30 1 enamel; 2 dentine; 3 pulp cavity; 4 root.

13.31

Boys	Time (years and months)	
Teeth	Upper jaw	Lower jaw
First molars	6.4	6.2
First incisors	7.5	6.5
Second incisors	8.7	7.7
First premolars	10.4	10.8
Lower canines		
Second upper premolars	11.2	10.8
Upper canines		
Second lower premolars	11.7	11.5
Second molars	12.7	12.1

Girls	Time (years and months)	
Teeth	Upper jaw	Lower jaw
First molars	6.2	5.9
First incisors	7.2	6.3
Second incisors	8.2	7.3
Lower canines		
First premolars	10.0	9.9
Lower first premolars		
Second upper premolars	10.9	10.2
Upper canines		
Second lower premolars	11.0	10.9
Second molars	12.3	11.7

3 Bone growth and development

13.32 Most bone is derived from cartilage.

13.33 At A in Fig 13.12 (a) the epiphyseal plate is clearly visible, at at B in Fig 13.12 (b) the plate has become fully ossified and has merged into the texture of the bone shaft.

13.34 In (a) the bone shafts are thick and solid, but at (b) they have become thinner and longer.

13.35 The three main centres of ossification in a long bone are in the shaft (diaphysis) and the two heads (epiphyses plural; epiphysis singular).

13.36 The continuously-growing areas of cartilage between the epiphyses and the diaphysis are called the epiphyseal cartilages.

13.37 Growth in length of the long bone takes place by the epiphyseal cartilage extending, then becoming ossified.

13.38 The footprints of the two-year-old show a flat, total print, those of the five year old are incomplete, showing only the heel, ball of the foot and toes. The five year old has developed an arch to the foot, which improves leverage for walking. The two year old is still flat footed.

13.39 B is correct, since it leaves some room for growth of the foot bones. Shoes should not be too loose – this could cause rubbing and soreness as the shoes move against the skin.

13.40 C is probably the best shoe. It has a small heel and offers more support for a growing foot than any of the other shoes. Shoes with high heels such as A can cause misalignment of the bones and heavy heels such as B could result in the straps cutting into the foot causing discomfort.

4 Growth at adolescence

13.41 Secondary sexual characteristics develop under the influence of testosterone in the male and oestrogen in the female.

13.42 There is usually a general increase in body size at adolescence.

13.43

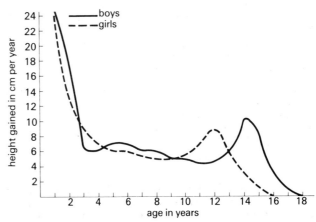

13.44 Girls suddenly gain in height at the age of eleven to twelve years.

13.45 Boys suddenly gain in height at the age of fourteen to fifteen years.

13.46 These height spurts coincide with the development of secondary sexual characteristics in both instances. The sex hormones may, therefore, initiate increased bone growth.

13.47 In males the shoulder: hip ratio is around 1.3:1, in girls 0.8:1

5 Senescence – ageing

13.48 1 very wrinkled skin; 2 sagging facial contours; 4 white hair; 5 bad eyesight; 6 impaired hearing; 7 toothless; 8 hunched-up appearance (dowagers' hump); 9 tottering gait; 10 thin legs and swollen ankles (muscular wasting); 11 excess clothing (cannot maintain body temperature).

13.49 Individuals can help the aged by understanding their problems and being tolerant. Deafness is trying, but with patience it is possible to communicate well with the deaf. Anticipating problems of a short-term memory will also help. Old people living with younger members of their family should be kept warm and allowed ease of movement within the house so that they won't fall. The community can help the aged by providing good medical care and recreational facilities (see Unit 18).

6 Growth of populations

13.50 'Three score years and ten' applies only to 1960. It is now nearer 73 years (1980).

13.51 Improved knowledge of disease control, including vaccination against infectious diseases and antibiotics has reduced premature deaths. Improved nutrition and hygiene has also contributed.

13.52 (a) 72 (b) 60 (c) 49 years

13.53 In Argentina and India there is shortage of food to feed very large populations and many die of starvation. Diseases are rife, many thousands dying from typhoid, cholera, elephantiasis and other infections which result from poor hygiene.

13.54 Increased life expectancy in Mauritius has produced a rapid rate of population increase.

7 Demography

13.55 Since 1945 the birth rate has remained fairly level at about 45 per 1000 population, although it has been falling recently. The death rate, on the other hand has fallen considerably since 1930 from about 25 per 1000 to around 11 per 1000 in 1973.

13.56 The falling death rate is probably due to improved medical care, better hygiene and living conditions and better diet. The steady birth rate shows that there has been no major change in the size of families or the numbers of people producing children over the last thirty years, although this may be changing now.

13.57 The country in Fig 13.23 is a developed country as its birth rate, death rate and population increase rate are small. It is in fact Sweden. The country in Fig 13.24 is a developing country. This example is Mexico.

13.58 The natural increase in China is only 19 as compared with 29 for Latin America mainly because of the much higher death rate in China (15/1000 compared with 9/1000). The birth rate in Latin America is 4/1000 higher.

13.59 Latin America, with a growth rate of 29 will take only 24 years to double its present population.

13.60 Sweden has the slowest natural increase at 1.4 per year and will take 96 years to double its present population.

13.61

$$\text{Net reproductive rate } = \frac{80}{640} \times 1000$$
$$= 125 \text{ live births/1000 females}$$

13.62 (a) 45% (b) 29%

13.63 (a) 8% (b) 16%

13.64 (a) is probably a less developed country where life expectancy is still low. The very large young population is not productive and is dependent on the relatively small young adult population. This chart is for the UK in 1871.

13.65 (b) has a substantial population in the older age groups which suggests that it is a developed country. As the population of the elderly increases, it becomes an increased burden on the younger producers. The UK is an example of this type of country. This chart is for the UK in 1966.

13.66 (a) In (a) there is little difference between male and female populations, but in (b) more females are alive in the older age groups than males.

8 Overpopulation and its control

13.67 Overpopulation could lead to exhaustion of food supplies and mass starvation. Physical overcrowding causes mental stress, disease and pollution.

13.68 The food supply becomes inadequate at point X. This is already happening in some parts of the world.

13.69 Progesterone suppresses ovulation during pregnancy, so the pill may contain this hormone. Most contraceptive pills in fact contain measured levels of oestrogen and progesterone.

14 Variation and heredity

1 Examples of variation

All living things vary. Collect hundreds of empty shells of the same type of periwinkle on the sea shore and no two will be exactly alike. Look around a crowded street. You are unlikely to see any two people who could be mistaken one for the other even though they possess the same basic features. Look at your brothers and sisters. Even very closely related members of the same species vary in detail. To what extent do people of the same age vary?

Activity 14.1   Finding out the variation in height in a class

1   Work in pairs and use a height measurer or a metre rule to record the height of every pupil in the class.
2   Construct a histogram from the class results.

▶ Questions

14.1   Does the histogram differ very much from the height histogram, Fig 13.7 in Unit 13?
14.2   What is the range of heights in your class?
14.3   Use the histogram to plot a graph to illustrate variation in heights. Use the same axes as for the histogram.
14.4   What can you conclude about variation in height in a given age group?

Repeat Activity 14.1, to find the range for head circumference, arm length, middle finger length and so on.

14.1 Fingerprint types

loop   arch   double loop   whorl

Fig 14.1 illustrates the four basic patterns of fingerprints found in man – the Malpighian layer is folded in such a way that whorls, loops, double loops or arches are produced.

Activity 14.2   Examining fingerprint types

1   Take an ink pad and roll your thumb and then each one of the finger tips of your left hand on the pad in turn.
2   Place each newly-inked digit on a piece of clean, white paper before inking the next one.
3   Number each print as it is made on the paper: L1 (thumb), L2, L3, L4 and L5.
4   Repeat using the digits of the right hand, recorded as R1, R2, R3, R4 and R5.
5   Identify each print, using Fig 14.1 as your guide.
6   Construct a table on the blackboard with the following columns.

Name	L1	L2	L3	L4	L5	R1	R2	R3	R4	R5
Brian	W	L	DL	A	W	L	DL	W	A	L
Claire	L	DL	L	L	L	W	DL	A	L	L

W = whorl; L = loop; DL = double loop; A = arch

▶ Questions

14.5   Have any two members of the class got exactly the same combination of fingerprint types? How may fingerprint records be useful?
14.6   What other factors can be used to identify people?

In addition to the ABO blood groups and Rhesus factors, there are twenty other known blood groups – M, S and Lewis factors are examples. The chance of one person having the same combination of all these blood groups as someone else is only one in several million. Another variable is intelligence (see Fig 14.2).

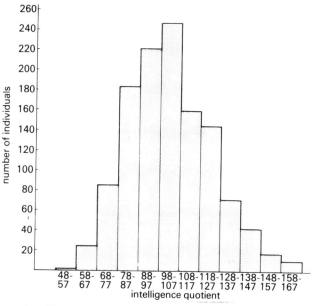

14.2 Intelligence quotient in 1000 11 year olds

▶ Questions

14.7 What is the commonest (modal) intelligence quotient of an eleven year old?

14.8 What is the range of intelligence in eleven year olds?

14.9 Suggest other advantageous variations which have resulted in the evolution of man as he is now. (Refer to Unit 1.)

14.10 Study the examples of the four human races in Fig 14.3. Which part of the world did each individual originally inhabit?

14.11 Explain how variation in physical features has equipped each race to live efficiently in its particular environment.

▷ **Homework**

Observe your parents and list the variable features you appear to have inherited from (a) your mother and (b) your father. Observe any brothers and sisters you have and list the features they have inherited from your mother and father. What can you conclude from this?

14.3 (a) Negroid

14.3 (b) Australoid

14.3 (c) Mongoloid

14.3 (d) Caucasoid

2 The genetic basis of variation

Most of the variable features of individuals of the same species are inherited. Family likeness, as seen in the homework above is a testimony to this fact – daughters and sons resemble their parents and have a mixture of maternal and paternal features. How do these mixtures come about? The answer lies in the DNA of the nuclei of the gametes. The DNA (see Unit 2) is found in the chromosomes which are visible in dividing cells. Fig 14.4 shows how the long thread-like chromosomes coil up during cell division. These chromosomes are magnified many thousands of times, but it is still not possible to see much of their structure.

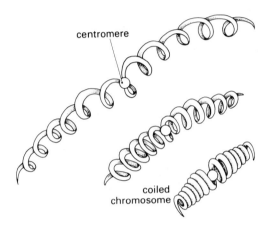

centromere

coiled chromosome

14.4 Coiled chromosomes

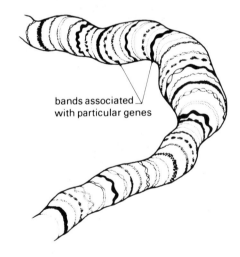

bands associated with particular genes

14.5 A giant chromosome from the fruit fly, *Drosophila*

The dark bands on the chromosome in Fig 14.5 represent areas of DNA which are organised to form genes. The electron microscope has made it possible actually to examine the structure of a gene. A gene is a number of active sections of a DNA molecule which are able to instruct the development of a particular characteristic.

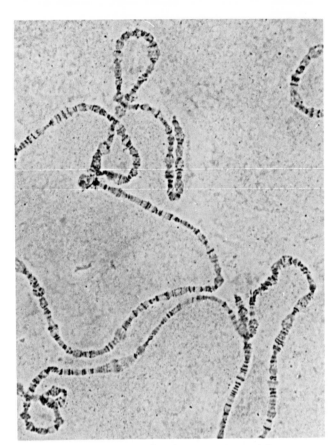

14.6 Photo micrograph showing *Drosophila* **giant chromosomes**

Figure 14.6 is a photo micrograph showing giant chromosomes from *Drosophila* (the fruit fly). The chromosomes consist of alternating dark 'bands' and light 'interbands'. The genes may be located in the DNA of the 'bands'. When active bands swell up to form 'puffs'.

The zygote contains two genes for each protein or group of proteins to be formed to produce a particular characteristic. One of these genes is contained in the chromosome from the female parent and the other is contained in the equivalent (homologous) chromosome from the male parent. Every characteristic in the developing zygote is therefore controlled by a pair of genes. A pair of genes is called an allelomorphic pair, or **alleles** for short. Often each gene of a pair affects a character differently. For example, in humans one allele may produce blue eyes, and the other allele brown eyes. Every cell in your body contains pairs of genes carried on pairs of chromosomes. The genes appear in definite positions on the chromosomes called loci (singular: locus). How are genes sorted into the gametes (ova and sperms) prior to fertilisation?

▶ Questions

14.12 What happens to the chromosome number during gametogenesis? (Refer to Unit 12.) What, therefore, happens to the alleles?

14.13 What is the name of this special type of reduction cell division?

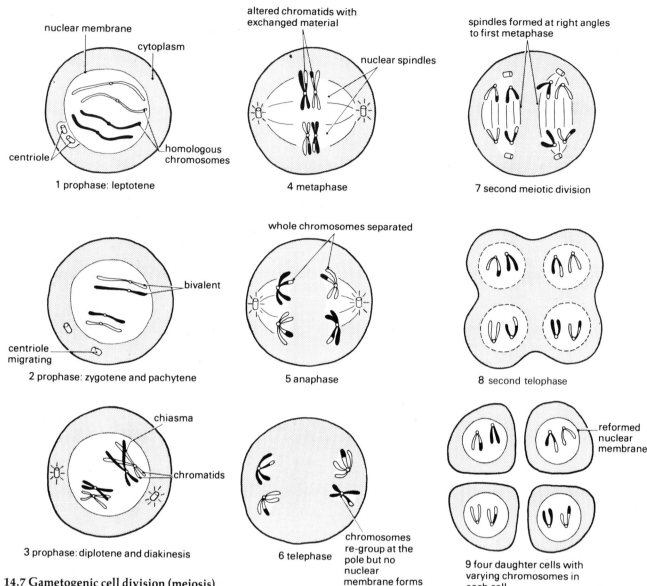

nuclear membrane
cytoplasm

centriole

homologous chromosomes

1 prophase: leptotene

altered chromatids with exchanged material

nuclear spindles

4 metaphase

spindles formed at right angles to first metaphase

7 second meiotic division

bivalent

centriole migrating

2 prophase: zygotene and pachytene

whole chromosomes separated

5 anaphase

8 second telophase

chiasma

chromatids

3 prophase: diplotene and diakinesis

chromosomes re-group at the pole but no nuclear membrane forms

6 telophase

reformed nuclear membrane

9 four daughter cells with varying chromosomes in each cell

14.7 Gametogenic cell division (meiosis)

14.8 Crossing over during meiosis

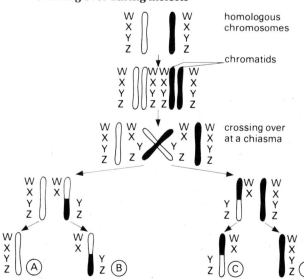

homologous chromosomes

chromatids

crossing over at a chiasma

Fig 14.7 illustrates the events which occur during meiosis. For the sake of simplicity it is assumed that the diploid number of chromosomes is four (see Unit 12). Follow the changes which occur in the chromosomes very carefully. Fig 14.8 shows simply what happens at each cross-over point when the chromatids of homologous chromosomes wrap around each other. These cross-over points are called **chiasmata**.

▶ Questions

14.14 Describe what happens to the chromosomes between the third stage of prophase and metaphase in Fig 14.7.

14.15 In Fig 14.8 how many varieties of chromosome are present in the gametes?

14.16 What proportion of genes do A and B have in common? What proportions do B and C, C and D and A and D have in common?

172

▷ **Homework**

Write a brief essay explaining to a non-scientist why two children of the same parents may inherit a different assortment of characteristics from their parents.

3 Inheritance of single characteristics

Most of our characteristics, such as our height and intelligence quotient, are probably controlled by very many genes combining to produce a particular result. There are a few characteristics which we know are controlled by a single pair of allelomorphic genes. Where a single pair of genes is involved, it is possible to work out probabilities of inheritance of a particular characteristic. This is called monohybrid inheritance.

Activity 14.3 Finding out the probability of inheriting a particular eye colour using coloured beads

1 Take two bottles filled with an equal number of red and yellow beads. The red and yellow beads represent pairs of alleles controlling eye colour inheritance. One bottle represents genes in the female, the other bottle, genes in the male.
2 Allow one bead at a time to fall out of both bottles simultaneously.
3 Record every combination of yellow and red beads as they fall out. These represent alleles coming together in fertilisation.
4 Add up the number of YR (yellow/red) combination, RR (red) combinations and YY (yellow) combinations.

▶ **Question**

14.17 What is the proportion of RR:YR:YY?
14.18 What are the chances of one combination being YR?

Activity 14.4 Finding out the proportion of the class who can roll their tongue

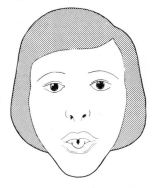

14.9 Can you roll your tongue like this?

Another characteristic controlled by a single pair of alleles is the ability to roll your tongue.
1 Check that you are able to roll your tongue like the girl in Fig 14.9. It may be as well to get a partner to confirm that you can!

2 Record your result under a positive or negative column on the blackboard.

14.19 What proportion of the class is able to roll their tongues?
14.20 How does the result of both Activity 14.4 compare with that of Activity 14.3?

The most likely result for Activity 14.4 is that three-quarters of the class will be able to roll their tongues and a quarter will not be able to. The ratio of ability to inability is 3:1. At first sight this appears to be very different from the result using probability beads, where the proportions were one quarter yellow, one half orange and a quarter red – a ratio of 1:2:1, yellow: orange: red. The apparent difference is due to the fact that of a pair of alleles, one usually expresses itself more strongly than the other. If that particular gene is present, the expression of the other gene is masked. This is easier to understand if symbols are used. For the characteristic of tongue-rolling, the two alleles involved are *T* for tongue-rolling and *t* for no tongue-rolling. Imagine you have two bottles containing equal numbers of *T* and *t* alleles. The probabilities of resulting combinations will be as follows.

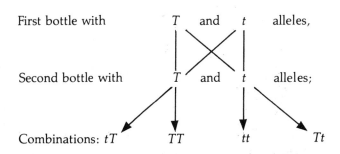

These are the four possible combinations of alleles, and they are all equally likely to be formed. Note that *tT* and *Tt* will both be tongue-rollers because the *T* allele masks the effect of the *t* allele.

▶ **Question**

14.21 What is the ratio of tongue-rollers to non-rollers in this diagram?

In the original experiment with the probability beads, the beads representing alleles were of similar dominance, so that both beads were expressed in the offspring. In tongue-rolling, one gene, for rolling, is **dominant**, while the other gene, for non-rolling, is **recessive**. The recessive gene is only expressed in the absence of a dominant one.
  In man, many dominant and recessive allelomorphic pairs are present, controlling recognisable characteristics. Dark hair is dominant to blonde hair, curly hair is dominant to straight hair, pigmentation is dominant to lack of pigmentation (albinism) and one eye colour is known to be dominant to another.

Activity 14.5   Finding out whether blue or brown eyes are dominant

1   For the purposes of the experiment, hazel eyes (with brown flecks) count as brown and pure green eyes count as blue (or grey) eyes.
2   Look at your neighbour's eyes. Decide whether they belong to the brown group or the blue group.
3   Place a tick under the appropriate column on the blackboard headed 'brown eyes' or 'blue eyes'.

▶ **Question**

14.22   What is the proportion of brown eyes to blue eyes in the class? Which colour is dominant?

Not all people with brown eyes possess the same alleles. Refer back to the diagram illustrating the possible combinations of tongue-rolling alleles.

▶ **Question**

14.23   If *B* stands for the brown eyes allele and *b* stands for the blue eyes allele, what possible combinations of alleles could a brown-eyed person possess?

A person may possess two identical genes for a characteristic, for example *BB*, in which case they are said to be homogzygous for that characteristic. If they mate with a person who is also homozygous for that characteristic, all their offspring (progeny) will have the same alleles.

Similarly, a person with two identical genes for blue eyes, *bb*, will always produce blue-eyed offspring is they mate with another blue-eyed person.

If an individual possesses a dominant and a recessive gene for a particular characteristic, for example *Bb*, they are said to be heterozygous. Two individuals with these alleles could produce blue-eyed children.

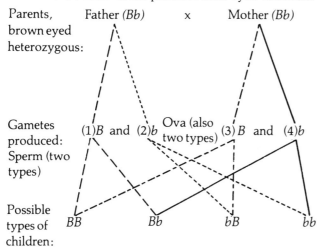

Parents, brown eyed heterozygous: Father *(Bb)*   x   Mother *(Bb)*

Gametes produced: Sperm (two types)   (1)*B* and (2)*b*   Ova (also two types)   (3)*B* and (4)*b*

Possible types of children: *BB*   *Bb*   *bB*   *bb*

Note that there are four possible types of children, all equally likely. Gamete (1) can combine with either gamete (3), to form *BB*, or gamete (4) to form *Bb*. Also gamete (2) can combine with either gamete (3), to form *bB*, or with gamete (4) to form *bb*. Because *B* is dominant to *b*, all of these children will be brown eyed,

except for *bb*, which will have blue eyes. Another way of working out this cross result is as follows.

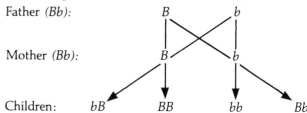

Father *(Bb)*:   *B*   *b*

Mother *(Bb)*:   *B*   *b*

Children: *bB*   *BB*   *bb*   *Bb*

Brown-eyed individuals are all said to have the same **phenotype**. They look alike as far as eye colour is concerned, but they are not all genetically the same. There are two genetic possibilities, *BB* and *Bb*. This is called the **genotype**. It is sometimes possible to discover the genotype of an individual by studying their progeny (if they have enough children).

▶ **Questions**

14.24   How many genotypes of blue-eyed individual are there?
14.25   Using symbols, work out the ratios of brown-eyed: blue-eyed progeny in the following combinations, indicating which offspring are homozygous and which are heterozygous: Homozygous brown-eyed male x blue-eyed female.
14.26   Heterozygous brown-eyed male x blue-eyed female
14.27   Given that dark hair is dominant to blonde hair, use symbols to work out the ratios of dark hair; blonde hair in the progeny resulting from the following matings.
(a) Heterozygous dark-haired male x heterozygous dark-haired female
(b) Homozygous dark-haired male x blonde-haired female.
(c) Heterozygous dark-haired male x blonde-haired female. State how many genotypes result from (a), (b) and (c). Identify the genotypes in each case. What phenotypes are produced in each cross?

In certain cases, more than two alleles may operate from the same point (locus) of a chromosome. Thus more than two allelomorphic genes may control a characteristic, though one individual will only possess two of the possible alleles. The best known example is the ABO blood groups, which are determined by three alleles conveniently called *A*, *B* and *O*. *A* and *B* are equally dominant to each other and *O* is recessive to both of them.

▶ **Questions**

14.28   What are the possible genotypes of a group A individual?
14.29   What are the possible genotypes of a group B individual?
14.30   What are the genotypes of group O and group AB individuals?
14.31   Using appropriate symbols, work out all the possible blood groups possessed by the progeny of a mating between a group A person and group B person. (Try combinations of all the possible genotypes of the parents.)
14.32   Is it possible for two AB parents to have any offspring with blood group O? What types of blood group could their children have?

Inheritance of the Rhesus factor is totally independent of inheritance of ABO blood groups. Several pairs of alleles are concerned in the inheritance of the Rhesus factor, but one pair is particularly important. These are designated *D* (Rhesus positive) and *d* (Rhesus negative).

▶ Questions

14.33 Considering the proportions of Rhesus positive to Rhesus negative blood groups in the population (refer to Unit 7) which characteristic would you expect to be dominant?
14.34 What are the possible genotypes of a Rhesus positive individual?
14.35 Which Rhesus positive genotype in a father is less likely to cause a Rhesus negative mother to produce antibodies against her foetus?

▷ Homework

Carry out a survey on hair colour in your school and determine which colour appears to be dominant. Is the result what you expected?

4 Inheritance of more than one characteristic

When homologous chromosomes are sorted into separate gametes, they are not exactly the same in their gene content as they were at the start of gametogenesis (see section 2). During crossing over in the early part of meiosis, some alleles pass over into the other chromosome of the pair. Because of this it is not certain that a batch of genes occupying neighbouring positions (loci) on the chromosome will be inherited together and the further apart their loci, the less likely that they will be inherited together. Thus most pairs of characteristics are inherited more or less independently of each other. See Fig 14.10.

The likelihood of different alleles being inherited together is even less when you consider that they may be on separate chromosomes. The following example illustrates this. In the nineteenth century some Scandinavian sailors were shipwrecked on a Caribbean island. They settled and married some of the local females. Fig 14.11 shows the phenotypes.

14.10 Detail of crossing over during meiosis

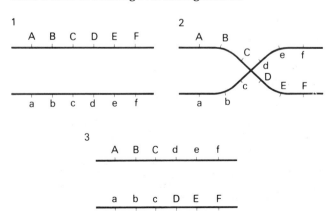

14.11 Blond Scandinavian sailors with dark Caribbean girls

▶ Questions

14.36 Using the symbols *D* and *d* for dark hair and blonde hair, and *B* and *b* for brown eyes and blue eyes, suggest (a) the genotype of the sailors for hair colour and eye colour. (b) the genotype of the Caribbean girls for hair colour and eye colour.
14.37 All the first generation progeny of the sailors and the Caribbean girls are dark-haired and brown-eyed. Explain why. What is their genotype?

The first generation, called the **first filial** generation, gives the impression that dark eyes and dark hair are inherited together. This can be checked by studying the second filial generation resulting from matings between individuals of the first filial generation.

The second filial generation of the hybrid children on this Caribbean island included about 90 dark-haired, dark-eyed individuals, 30 dark-haired, blue-eyed individuals, 30 blonde-haired, brown-eyed individuals and 10 blonde, blue-eyed individuals. The example used here, where two pairs of alleles are involved, is called dihybrid inheritance.

▶ Questions

14.38 What can you conclude from this result?
14.39 What combinations of alleles were possible in the gametes of the first filial generation?
14.40 Copy the following grid, which illustrates all the possible crossings of those gametes and fill in all the gaps.

gametes

		DB	*Db*	*dB*	*db*
gametes	*DB*	DDBB			
	Db		DDbb		
	dB			ddBB	
	db				ddbb

D = dark hair   *B* = brown eyes
d = blonde hair   *b* = blue eyes

14.41 What are the phenotypes of the four combinations shown in Question 14.40?

14.42 Are these individuals homozygous or heterozygous for hair colour and eye colour?

14.43 State the ratio of all the resulting phenotypes. How does this theoretical ratio compare with the actual second filial generation on the Caribbean island?

14.44 What can you conclude about the inheritance of more than one characteristic from this exercise?

▷ **Homework**

Albinism (lack of pigment) is recessive to normal pigmentation and straight hair is recessive to curly hair. Using appropriate symbols, work out the probability of two normally pigmented, curly-haired heterozygous parents producing a straight-haired albino.

5 Sex-linked inheritance

Though linkage of characteristics on non-sex chromosomes (autosomes) is not very common, certain characteristics are linked with the sex chromosomes. There is a marked tendency for some characteristics to be mainly confined to the male sex. The reason for this lies in the differing structure of the X and Y chromosomes (see Unit 12). Fig 14.12 shows the X and Y chromosomes of a male and the X and X chromosomes of a female. A number of gene loci are included. Study the diagrams carefully, then answer the following questions.

▶ **Questions**

14.45 How many alleles are present for blood clotting in a female?

14.46 How many alleles are present for blood clotting in a male?

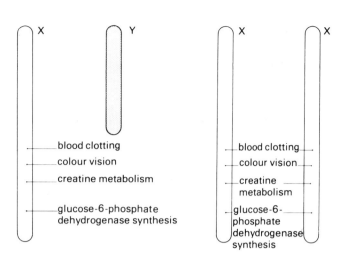

14.12 XY and XX chromosomes

Once in about 40 000 mitotic divisions, it appears that an allele may suddenly change its nature. This is called **mutation**. This is usually a change for the worse. In the case of Queen Victoria, one of her alleles for blood clotting changed so that it could not instruct the production of one of the blood clotting factors. Fig 14.13 shows the effect of this mutated allele when it was passed on to her children, grandchildren and great grand children. Two of her great grandchildren bled to death after accidents.

▶ **Questions**

14.47 What was the sex of the great grandchildren who bled to death?

14.48 Why were Alexandra, Alice and Victoria Eugenie free from any ill effects of this defective allele?

14.13 Family tree of Queen Victoria

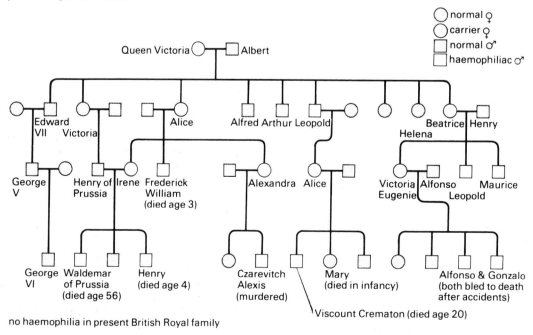

no haemophilia in present British Royal family

The defective gene which prevents blood from clotting properly is recessive to the gene for normal blood clotting. Provided a person possesses one normal gene, the effect of the defective gene is masked. A female carrying the defective gene is, however, a danger to her future sons. They will only possess a single allele for blood clotting, which will be on the X chromosome they inherit from their mother. If they receive the defective gene, they will suffer from haemophilia. Each time they cut themselves they will be in danger of bleeding to death. If they knock themselves, internal blood vessels will leak blood into their joints which will swell and become extremely painful.

If XH stands for a normal blood clotting allele on an X chromosome, Xh stands for a haemophiliac allele on an X chromosome, and Y stands for the Y chromosome with no allele of either type on it, then a cross between a female carrier and a normal male would be as follows.

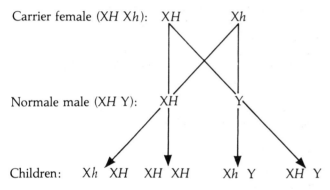

Carrier female (XH Xh): XH Xh

Normale male (XH Y): XH Y

Children: Xh XH XH XH Xh Y XH Y

▶ Questions

14.49 Identify the sex and state of the four progeny shown here.
14.50 What are the chances of a female carrier having a son who suffers from haemophilia?
14.51 Work out what the offspring of a marriage between a haemophiliac male and a normal female are likely to be.
14.52 Under what exceptional circumstances could a haemophiliac female be born?

Another relatively common sex linked condition is red-green colour blindness.

▶ Questions

14.53 Of the alleles for normal sight and colour blindness, which is likely to be dominant?
14.54 Using appropriate symbols, work out the genotypes and phenotypes of the progeny of matings between (a) a female carrier for red-green colour blindness and a normal male and (b) a man suffering from red-green colour blindness and a normal woman.
14.55 What parental genotypes would produce a red-green colour blind daughter?

Other sex linked conditions include one type of the muscle wasting disease called muscular dystrophy (Duchenne type), one type of water diabetes and a number of enzyme deficiency diseases.

▷ **Homework**
Using reference books, list all the sex linked disorders you can find.

14.14 Two-toed Zambesi valley Africans

6 Mutation

Minor variations within a species are controlled by the independent assortment of alleles during gameto-genesis. Larger, abrupt variations (discontinuous variations) are caused by sudden changes in either the alleles or the chromosomes which carry them. A spontaneous change in an allele may result in a disorder such as haemophilia, or a more visible variation such as brachydactyly (short fingers) or two-toed feet (see Fig 14.14).

The condition in Fig 14.14 is called 'lobster-claw syndrome' and though it looks very strange, a large proportion of a tribe living near the Zambesi river in Africa possesses the mutant gene, and the flexible webbed feet do not affect the mobility or survival of these people. They can even use their feet as an extra pair of hands. Chromosome mutations usually have a more serious effect on an individual, since more than one characteristic is normally affected.

Fig 14.15 is the karyotype (see Unit 2) of a male suffering from Down's syndrome. He is mentally retarded, physically weak with a failing heart, and his features are mongoloid. All these defects are caused by an irregularity in the meiosis which occurred during gametogenesis in the cells of his mother. Study the karyotype very carefully and compare it with the karyotype of a normal male in Unit 2.

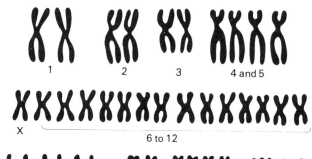

14.15 Male Down's syndrome karyotype

▶ **Question**

14.56 What is the chromosomal abnormality causing this type of mongolism?

The vast majority of mutations are harmful to the individual and tend to be bred out of the population. Occasionally a mutation arises which gives those members of the population possessing it a positive advantage over those who do not possess it. Fig 14.16 shows two views of two forms of a moth called *Biston betularia*. The original form of the moth had a peppery wing colouration. A mutation of one gene produced a black form, called a melanic mutant. Study the diagram carefully and pick out both forms of the moth on both the sooty bark and the natural bark.

▶ **Questions**

14.57 (a) Which form is easier to pick out on the sooty bark?

14.16(a) *Biston betularia* **types on sooty bark**

(b) Which form is more easily detected on the natural bark?
14.58 What advantage has one moth over another if it is less easily visible?
14.59 From Fig 14.17 describe the type of areas in which the melanic form does better than the typical form? Explain why.

Industrial melanism, as shown by *Biston betularia* is an excellent example of evolution in action. The melanic forms were selected in preference to the typical forms in blackened, industrial areas since their colour camouflaged them from would be predators. More recent surveys of some areas which are becoming less industrial have shown an increase in the population of typical forms over melanic forms. Thus the environment determines which form is more likely to survive. Examples of advantageous mutations in man are less dramatic, since it takes far longer for their effect to spread in a population whose generation time is so

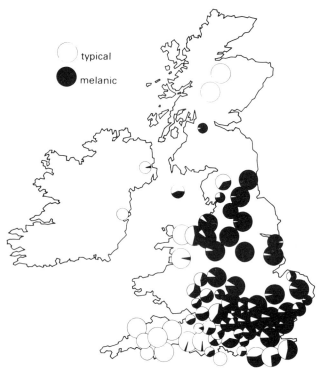

14.17 Distribution of typical and melanic forms of *Biston betularia* **in the UK**

14.16(b) *Biston betularia* **types on a bark with lichen**

much longer than that of a moth. In Africa as much as 40% of the population carry a recessive mutant gene which can cause the red blood cells to distort to a sickle shape.

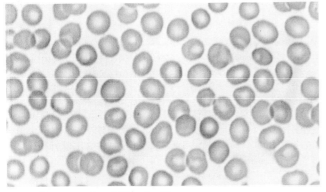

14.18 (a) Normal red blood cells

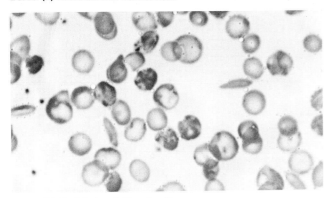

14.18 (b) Sickled red blood cells

▶ **Question**

14.60 What effect would you expect the sickling of red blood cells to have on the health of an individual?

Individuals who carry one of the sickling genes are heterozygous and have an *AS* genotype. (*A* is for normal haemoglobin, not the A blood group, which is a quite different system. *S* is for sickling haemoglobin.) A proportion of their circulating haemoglobin is abnormal, but it still carries oxygen satisfactorily and does not normally cause any ill effects, so that heterozygous individuals may even be unaware that they carry the sickle cell gene. Homozygous individuals (*SS* genotype), however, have all abnormal haemoglobin and this tends to make the red blood cells sickle and rupture whenever there is a temporary shortage of oxygen. This makes them anaemic, listless, prone to infections and they often experience severe pain in their joints when the circulation becomes blocked by distorted cells. Many die young. Why, then, does this mutant gene persist in the population? Fig 14.19(a) shows a map of the distribution of populations of the *Anopheles* mosquito throughout Africa. This mosquito is the vector (transmitter) of malaria. The second map shows the percentage of the human population carrying the sickling gene in the same areas. Study the maps carefully.

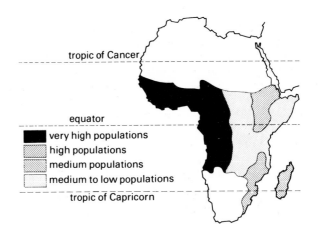

14.19 (a) *Anopheles* **distribution in Africa**

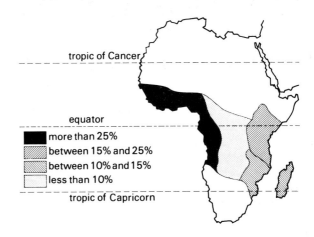

14.19 (b) Distribution of population carrying sickling genes

▶ **Questions**

14.61 (a) What percentage of the human population carries sickling genes in areas with very high populations of the *Anopheles* mosquito?
(b) What percentage of the human population carries the sickling gene in areas with very low populations of the *Anopheles* mosquito?

It seems that the sickling gene in some way gives the carrier resistance against malaria. Many people die from malaria, so immunity from malaria is of greater survival value than a lack of anaemia. The malarial parasite, *Plasmodium*, spends part of its life cycle in red blood cells. It is not able to survive in sickled red blood cells.

▶ **Question**

14.62 What is the selecting factor in this example?

▷ **Homework**

The selection of certain significant mutations is thought to be the basis for the emergence of all the main groups of plants and animals, including man. (See Unit 1.) Bearing this in mind, suggest useful mutations which could have been selected leading to the evolution of reptiles from amphibia, birds from reptiles, and mammals from reptiles.

7 Heredity or environment?

Evolution may be summarised as the interaction of heredity and the environment. The environment selects the fittest inherited characteristics for survival. Can the environment go even further? Can it actually affect the physical and mental make-up of an individual during that individual's lifetime?

Many people agree that diet, education and wealth can alter basic inherited traits such as height, intelligence quotient and weight. The best way to investigate such assertions is to study twins. Comparisons of identical and non-identical twins are particularly useful.

▶ Questions

14.63 (a) How genetically alike are identical twins? (Refer to Unit 12.)
(b) How genetically alike are non-identical twins?
14.64 How may the genetic differences between identical and non-identical twins be used to assess the significance of the roles of heredity and environment in the physical and mental make-up of a person?

Table 14.1 Correlation coefficients* in twins reared apart

Characteristic	Identical twins	Non-identical twins
Height	0.93	0.65
Weight	0.96	0.76
Intelligence quotient	0.98	0.63

*A correlation coefficient of 1.0 means a totally identical result.

Table 14.1 was constructed from a study of thirty pairs of non-identical twins reared apart and nineteen pairs of identical twins reared apart. The latter are more difficult to trace because there are fewer born. In some cases the twins had been reared in different countries. In nearly all cases the environment over the fourteen to twenty years of their various lives was very different for each twin.

▶ Question

14.65 From these results, would you deduce that environment or heredity is the more significant factor determining height, weight and intelligence?

Twin studies have been used to assess whether tendency to certain diseases is inherited or environmental. The following table summarises the results of some of these studies.

Table 14.2 The percentage of co-twins likely to suffer from the same illnesses

Disease	Percentage risk to co-twin Identical	Non-identical	Percentage risk to general population
Sugar diabetes	50%	10%	2%
Gastric ulcers	45%	22%	1%
Tuberculosis	30%	13%	0.1%
Schizophrenia	80%	15%	1%
Epilepsy	80%	20%	3%
Club foot	23%	2%	0.001%
Influenza	30%	28%	25%

▶ Question

14.66 From a careful study of Table 14.2 list those diseases which have a high inherited predisposition, those which probably have some inherited predisposition and those which affect anyone regardless of their genetic make-up.

▷ Homework

Write a brief essay discussing the relative effects of heredity and environment on the phenotype.

Answers and discussion

1 Examples of variation

14.1 The class histogram should basically resemble the histogram obtained for a group of students in Unit 13.

14.2 The ranges of height will probably be about 145 cm to 185 cm (40 cm).

14.3 The curve should be bell-shaped, as shown in Fig 14.20.

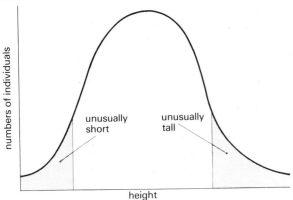

14.20 Distribution curve for height

14.4 In a given age group the majority of the individuals have a height falling within a narrow range. The small numbers at the extremes of the range – the very short and the very tall – will probably be at a disadvantage in some respects. This is an example of continuous variation, with individuals representing each intermediate height between the extremes. Such variation has probably been important in the slow changes occurring over a long period of time in the evolution of a species. Man, *Homo sapiens*, is a good example of this – he has gradually become taller over the centuries.

14.5 No two members of the class are likely to possess exactly the same combination of fingerprints. This variation is very useful in crime detection. Many criminals have been convicted as a result of leaving a set of fingerprints at the scene of the crime.

14.6 As well as physical features, such as hair colour and face, blood can now be used for identification. Individuals can be recognised by the possession of particular blood groups.

14.7 The commonest intelligence quotient of these eleven-year-olds is between 98 – 107.

14.8 The intelligence quotient ranges from 48 – 167.

14.9 Advantageous variations resulting in the evolution of modern man include an opposable thumb, walking on two legs, long legs, a large cerebrum and a long infancy.

14.10 (a) lived in tropical areas such as Africa; (b) lived in the cold parts of central and eastern Asia; (c) lived in the Australian continent and (d) lived in the temperate regions of Europe.

14.11 (a) and (c) both have a very dark skin. This contains a lot of melanin, a pigment which protects the skin and tissues from damage by the hot sun. (a) is also very tall and thin, giving him a large surface area to volume ratio which helps him to lose heat. (b) has a pale skin to enable as much sunlight as possible to penetrate the skin and help with the manufacture of vitamin D from ergosterol (see Unit 4). (b) is very stocky and solid, enabling him to conserve as much heat as possible. (d) also has a pale skin, enabling him to manufacture vitamin D using what little sun is available. He is neither thin nor stocky. In a temperate climate neither heat loss nor heat conservation is a prime consideration for survival.

2 The genetic basis of variation

14.12 The chromosome number is halved during gametogenesis. Body cells contain twenty-three pairs of chromosomes. These are matching pairs called homologous chromosomes. When the gametes are formed, one of each of the chromosomes of a homologous pair passes into one gamete. When this happens, allelomorphic pairs of genes carried on these chromosomes are also sorted into separate gametes. Each gamete therefore contains only twenty-three chromosomes – the haploid number. On fertilisation each of these chromosomes will have its pair restored.

14.13 This reduction division is called meiosis.

14.14 During prophase the chromatids of the homologous chromosomes coil around each other. When they uncoil, they appear to have exchanged segments. This is called crossing over. The resulting chromosomes will contain different alleles.

14.15 Four different chromosomes are present in the gametes illustrated in Fig 14.8. They all contain a different assortment of genes – they are all different alleles.

14.16 (a) A and B have 50% common genes; (b) B and C 50% common genes; (c) C and D 50% common genes and (d) A and D have no genes in common.

3 Inheritance of single characteristics

14.17 $\frac{1}{4}:\frac{1}{2}:\frac{1}{4}$

14.18 The chances of one combination being YR are 50:50.

14.19 About three-quarters of the class should be able to roll their tongues.

14.20 The results of Activity 14.3 include three possibilities of offspring in the ratio 1:2:1. Activity 14.4 shows two possible expressions of a character in the ratio 3:1.

14.21 The ratio of tongue-rollers:non-tongue-rollers is 3:1.

14.22 There will probably be about three-quarters brown eyes to one-quarter blue eyes in the class. Brown-eyedness is therefore dominant to blue-eyedness.

14.23 A brown-eyed person could either possess the alleles *BB* or *Bb*.

14.24 There is only one genotype for blue eyes: *bb*.

14.25

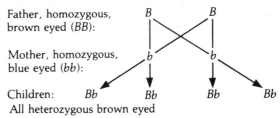

Father, homozygous, brown eyed (*BB*):

Mother, homozygous, blue eyed (*bb*):

Children: *Bb* *Bb* *Bb* *Bb*
All heterozygous brown eyed

Two other ways of working out the offspring from this

particular cross are shown below. The first is similar to the diagram on page 174; the second is called a Punnett square. See which of these three methods you find the easiest to understand, and use it to help you answer the other questions in this unit.

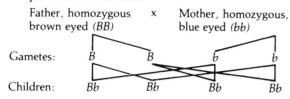

Father (BB) gametes	B	B
Mother (bb)	b	Bb	Bb
gametes	b	Bb	Bb

14.26

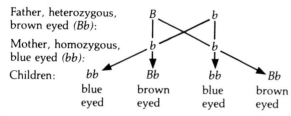

There should be an equal probability of blue eyed and brown eyed children, that is they will be in a ratio of brown:blue, 1:1. All the brown eyed children from this cross are heterozygous.

14.27

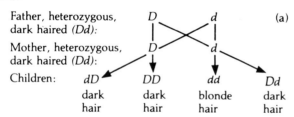

There is a ratio of dark:blonde, 3:1. Two of the dark haired progeny are heterozygous and the third is homozygous.

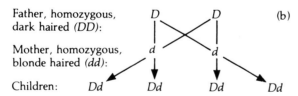

All the children are heterozygous and dark haired.

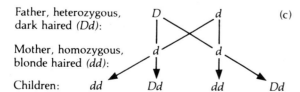

Half of the children are darked haired and half of them are blonde haired. They are dark:blonde in a 1:1 ratio.

In (a), three genotypes are produced. DD, Dd; dd, in(b) one genotype: Dd and in(c) two genotypes: Dd and dd.

In (a), two phenotypes are produced: dark-haired and blonde-haired, in (b) only one phenotype: dark-haired and in (c) two phenotypes: dark-haired and blonde-haired.

14.28   Possible genotypes of a group A individual are: AA or AO.

14.29   Possible genotypes of a group B individual are: BB or BO.

14.30   Group O genotype is always OO and group AB genotype is always AB.

14.31   Possible results of group A x group B matings:

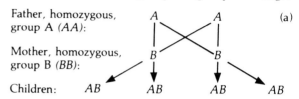

All the children are blood group AB.

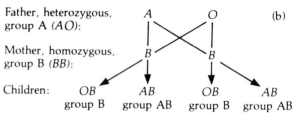

There are equal numbers of B and AB individuals.

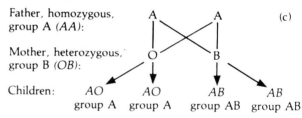

There are equal numbers of A and AB individuals.

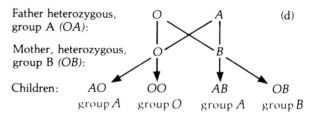

There is one of each type of blood group, A, B, AB and O. All these groups have equal chances of appearing.

14.32   To discover whether or not it is possible for group AB parents to have a group O child, use the following cross.

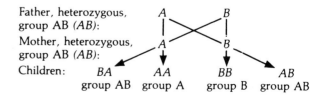

Groups A:B:AB are in the ratio 1:1:2.

The phenotypes of the cross are group A, group B or group AB. It is not possible for group AB parents to have a group O child. Even if only one parent has blood group AB, none of the progeny will be group O. See Table 14.3, which summarises the possible progeny from all possible combinations of ABO crosses. Such information is useful when establishing a disputed paternity.

Table 14.3 The inheritance of ABO blood groups

		Mother's group			
Father's group		O	A	B	AB
	O	O	O or A	O or B	A or B
	A	O or A	O or A	O or A or B or AB	A or B or AB
	B	A or B	O or A or B or AB	O or B	A or B or AB
	AB	A or B	A or B or AB	A or B or AB	A or B or AB

14.33 Rhesus positive blood is possessed by 85% of the population and is most likely to be the dominant characteristic.

14.34 The possible genotypes of a Rhesus positive individual are DD or Dd.

14.35

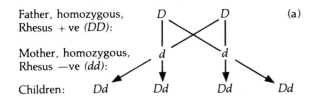

Father, homozygous, Rhesus + ve (DD):

Mother, homozygous, Rhesus — ve (dd):

Children: Dd   Dd   Dd   Dd   (a)

All the foetuses will be heterozygous and Rhesus + ve.

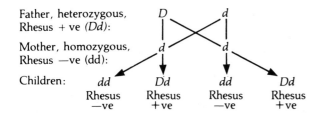

Father, heterozygous, Rhesus + ve (Dd):

Mother, homozygous, Rhesus — ve (dd):

Children: dd   Dd   dd   Dd
          Rhesus   Rhesus   Rhesus   Rhesus
          —ve   +ve   —ve   +ve

Half the foetuses will be Rhesus + ve and half of them will be Rhesus —ve.

If the father is heterozygous, Dd, half the foetuses are likely to be negative. If the foetus is negative, the mother will not produce antibodies since no Rhesus bodies will be present to sensitise her blood.

4 Inheritance of more than one characteristic

14.36 (a) The genotypes for the sailors will be dd and bb (recessives), or ddbb.
(b) The genotypes of the Caribbean girls will be DD and BB (dominant alleles), or DDBB.

14.37 All the first generation progeny will be dark-haired

and brown-eyed since these are the dominant alleles. Their genotype will be DdBb.

14.38 Hair colour and eye colour alleles are not linked together in the gametes, otherwise all the second filial generation would also be dark-haired and brown-eyed. There must be some separate assortment of different alleles into the gametes.

14.39 Possible combinations of different alleles in the gametes are DB, Db, dB or db.

14.40

	DB	Db	dB	db
DB	DDBB	DDBb	DdBB	DdBb
Db	DDBb	DDbb	DdBb	Ddbb
dB	DdBB	DdBb	ddBB	ddBb
db	DdBb	Ddbb	ddBb	ddbb

4 dark-haired, brown-eyed

2 dark-haired, brown-eyed
2 dark-haired, blue-eyed

2 dark-haired, brown-eyed
2 blonde-haired, brown-eyed

1 dark-haired, brown-eyed
1 dark-haired, blue-eyed
1 blonde-haired, brown-eyed
1 blonde-haired, blue-eyed

14.41 The four phenotypes are DDBB dark-haired brown-eyed; DDbb, dark-haired, blue-eyed; ddBB, blonde-haired brown-eyed; ddbb, blonde-haired, blue-eyed.

14.42 All four individuals are homozygous for both hair colour and eye colour.

14.43 The ratio of the four phenotypes is: 9 : 3 : 3 : 1.
9 dark-haired/brown-eyed : 3 dark-haired/blue-eyed : 3 blonde-haired/brown-eyed: 1 blonde-haired/blue-eyed. This is exactly the ratio found in the Caribbean island second filial generation.

14.44 Where more than one pair of characteristics are inherited, they are passed on independently of each other. Genes are not inflexibly linked together on the chromosomes.

5 Sex-linked inheritance

14.45 There are two alleles for blood clotting in the female.

14.46 There is only a single allele for blood clotting in the male.

14.47 Both great grandchildren who bled to death were male. Another male great grandchild died at age four and another great grandson died at age twenty.

14.48 The females are protected from the effects of this defective gene by their allele for normal blood clotting.

14.49 $XhXH$ stands for carrier female; $XHXH$ stands for normal female; XhY stands for haemophiliac male and XHY stands for normal male.

14.50 A female carrier has a 50% chance of having a son who suffers from haemophilia.

14.51

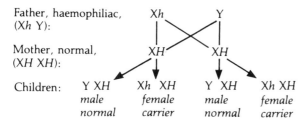

Father, haemophiliac, (Xh Y):

Mother, normal, (XH XH):

Children: Y XH / male / normal   Xh XH / female / carrier   Y XH / male / normal   Xh XH / female / carrier

All the sons of this marriage will be normal and all the daughters will be carriers.

14.52 A haemophiliac male who unwittingly marries a carrier female has a 50% chance of a haemophiliac daughter. In the rare event of this conception, miscarriage is likely, since two defective alleles will probably produce a more serious condition than a single defective allele. At least two female haemophiliacs have survived to adulthood in the USSR.

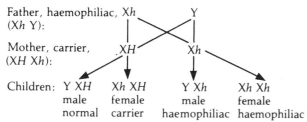

Father, haemophiliac, Xh (Xh Y):

Mother, carrier, (XH Xh):

Children: Y XH / male / normal   Xh XH / female / carrier   Y Xh / male / haemophiliac   Xh Xh / female / haemophiliac

14.53 Normal sight is probably dominant to colour blindness.

14.54 (a)

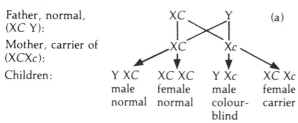

Father, normal, (XC Y):

Mother, carrier of (XCXc):

Children: Y XC / male / normal   XC XC / female / normal   Y Xc / male / colour-blind   XC Xc / female / carrier

There are four different genotypes here, but only three phenotypes: two females with normal vision, one male with normal vision and one colour-blind male.

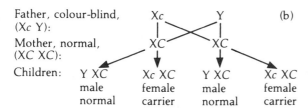

Father, colour-blind, (Xc Y):

Mother, normal, (XC XC):

Children: Y XC / male / normal   Xc XC / female / carrier   Y XC / male / normal   Xc XC / female / carrier

Phenotypes: 2 males with normal vision, 2 females with normal vision.

14.55 The parental genotypes which would produce a colour-blind female are: XcY x XcXC

6 Mutation

14.56 There are three chromosomes 21 in the Down's syndrome karotype instead of two. The homologous pair, 21, failed to separate during gametogenesis in the mother.

14.57 (a) The peppery variety is more easily picked out on a sooty bark.
(b) The melanic form is more easily seen on a natural bark.

14.58 If a moth is well camouflaged it is less likely to be eaten by passing predators such as birds.

14.59 The melanic form of moth has taken over from the typical form in industrial areas. This is because the surfaces of trees and buildings become blackened in industrial areas so that the melanic form is better camouflaged than the peppery form. In rural areas the typical form is still better camouflaged than the melanic form, so the melanic form does not become established there.

14.60 Sickled red blood cells will not be able to carry oxygen to the tissues as effectively as normal red blood cells and they tend to break up more quickly. The individual will become listless, have painful joints and be lacking in energy, with all the symptoms of anaemia.

14.61 (a) More than 25% of the human population carry the sickling gene in areas with a high population of the *Anopheles* mosquito.
(b) Less than 10% of the human population carry the sickling gene in areas with a low population of the *Anopheles* mosquito.

14.62 The selecting factor in this example is the *Anopheles* mosquito. It carries malaria to those individuals who do not have the sickling gene, causing their premature death. This reduces the proportion of those without the sickling gene in the population. Incidence of the sickling gene amongst negro populations in the United States is much lower than in Africa. Malaria is not endemic in the USA, so more negroes will die from anaemia, taking the sickling gene out of the population.

7 Heredity or environment?

14.63 (a) Identical twins are 100% alike genetically. They contain identical genes for every characteristic.
(b) Non-identical twins have as many genes in common as ordinary brothers and sisters, probably about 50%.

14.64 These genetic differences between identical and non-identical twins are the basis for the comparison of a range of characteristics. One would expect identical twins to display identical characteristics if these characters are entirely genetic. Even identical twins reared apart should show very close correlation if the factor under consideration is genetic. Non-identical twins should show less similarity if the characteristics are inherited, but there should still be a fairly significant correlation.

14.65 Heredity is the significant factor determining height, weight and intelligence quotient in Table 14.1. Despite the fact that they were reared apart, the identical twins show almost 100% correlation and the fraternal twins also show a considerable correlation.

14.66 Diseases with a high inherited predisposition are schizophrenia and epilepsy. Those with some inherited predispositions are sugar diabetes, gastric ulcers and tuberculosis. Club foot may have been the result of being cramped in the uterus by the co-twin. Influenza has no inherited predisposition.

15 Disease and its control

1 The causes of disease

The word 'disease' means simply 'dis-ease'. Any factor which results in the body no longer being 'at ease' or normal, is an agent of disease. Fig 15.1 shows the factors which can make the body 'dis-eased'.

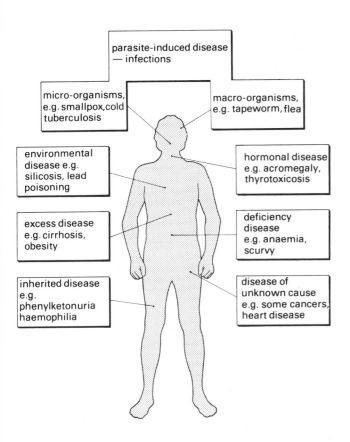

15.1 Causes of disease

Question

15.1 List the agents of disease and suggest two examples of diseases caused by each agent which are not shown on Fig 15.1.

Table 15.1 The ten major diseases causing death, taken from the *Weekly Bill of Mortality 1723*

Causes of death	Percentage of all causes
1 Convulsions (fever from infections)	30
2 Smallpox	14
3 Consumption (tuberculosis)	13
4 Ague (fever – probably influenza)	12
5 Griping in the guts (typhoid?)	3
6 Teeth	2.9
7 Measles	1
8 Stillborn	0.8
9 Dropsy (fluid retention)	0.7
10 Rickets	0.6

▶ Questions

15.2 Suggest a reason for the high proportion of deaths from convulsions.
15.3 Which type of disease shown in Fig 15.1 was the most common cause of death in 1723?
15.4 Why should nearly 3% of the population die from 'teeth'?
15.5 Suggest what could cause 'dropsy'.
15.6 Which categories of disease shown in Fig 15.1 were not a common cause of death in 1723 according to the table?

15.2 The ten major diseases causing death in England and Wales in 1965

Causes of death	Percentage of all causes
1 Heart disease	21
2 Cancer	19.5
3 Vascular disease affecting the central nervous system (stroke)	14
4 Diseases of the respiratory system	12
5 Accidents (including suicide)	4.5
6 Diseases of the digestive system	2.5
7 Diseases of the urinogenital system	1
8 Congenital malformations	1
9 Diabetes mellitus	1
10 Tuberculosis	0.5

15.7 Which type of disease shown in Fig 15.1 was the most common cause of death in 1965?
15.8 Suggest some common diseases of the respiratory system which can cause death.
15.9 Which type of disease shown in Fig 15.1 was not a very common cause of death in 1965?
15.10 Summarise the basic differences in disease incidence leading to death in 1723 and 1965. Suggest some of the factors which have brought about the changes evident in 1965.

▷ **Homework**

Construct a questionnaire to discover the five most common diseases experienced by children of your age. Ask you teacher for advice on the most suitable questions to ask.

2 Microbial diseases – bacteria

In the bad old days, parasite-induced diseases were major killers. Black Death, or bubonic plague accounted for one-third of all deaths in England and Wales at the beginning of the 18th century. In many developing countries infectious diseases are still a significant cause of death.

Most infectious diseases are caused by micro-organisms, such as bacteria, viruses, fungi and protozoa.

Activity 15.1   Cultivating bacteria present on different parts of the body

1   Your teacher will prepare an agar plate for you as shown in Fig 15.2.

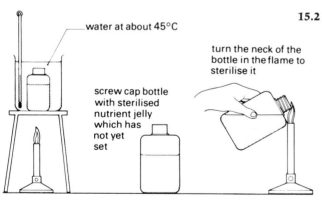

15.2

water at about 45°C

turn the neck of the bottle in the flame to sterilise it

screw cap bottle with sterilised nutrient jelly which has not yet set

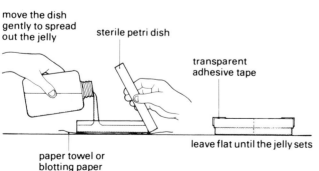

move the dish gently to spread out the jelly

sterile petri dish

transparent adhesive tape

paper towel or blotting paper

leave flat until the jelly sets

2   When you receive your plate, do not open it until instructed, and replace the lid as quickly and deftly as possible when you carry out your part of the experiment.
3   As instructed, carry out one of the following treatments to your agar plate.
(a) Using tweezers, place a nail paring in the centre of the agar.
(b) Cough into the plate.
(c) Add saliva to the plate.
(d) Place a newly-washed hair on the agar.
(e) Place an unwashed hair on the agar.
(f) Make a light impression on the agar with a dirty finger and thumb.
(g) Make a light impression on the agar with a newly washed finger and thumb.
(h) Add a piece of clothing fluff to the agar.
(i) Put the plate on a table top and leave the lid off for 10 minutes but add nothing to the agar.
4   One plate will be left untreated as a class control.
5   Seal the plates and incubate them at 37°C for twenty-four hours. The plates are best stacked upside-down to avoid condensation falling onto the agar.
6   Examine your plate carefully *without opening it* and write your result in a table on the blackboard. Examine an example of each other treatment. NEVER OPEN A SEALED INCUBATED PETRI DISH.

► **Questions**

15.11   What is the purpose of the class control?
15.12   Briefly describe the results of each treatment
15.13   What can you conclude from this experiment?

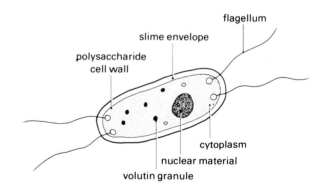

flagellum

slime envelope

polysaccharide cell wall

cytoplasm

nuclear material

volutin granule

15.3 Structure of a typical bacterium

Bacteria are only visible to the naked eye when they have multiplied to produce a colony. The smallest colonies visible on an agar plate will contain hundreds of millions of bacteria. Bacteria are measured in microns.

Fig 15.3 shows a single bacterium. It consists of a single cell with a rigid wall containing cytoplasm and nuclear material consisting of DNA. It is covered with a layer of slime which causes neighbouring cells to stick together in a colony following cell division. Bacteria vary in shape and size. The largest bacterium, *Bacillus megatherium*, is about 7μm (microns) in length.

186

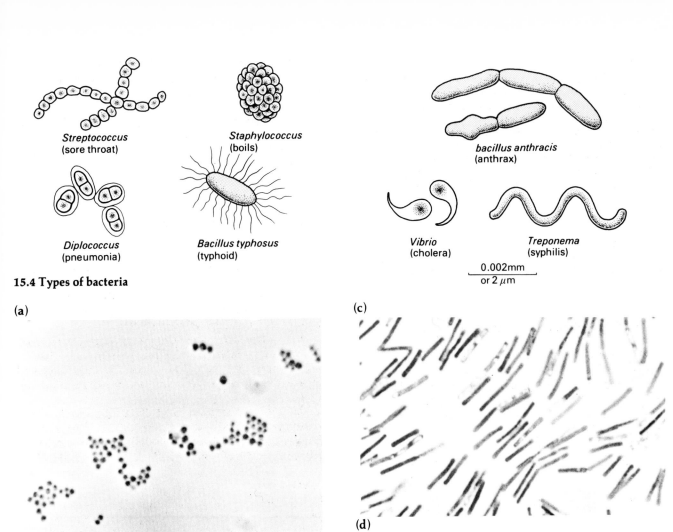

Streptococcus
(sore throat)

Staphylococcus
(boils)

Diplococcus
(pneumonia)

Bacillus typhosus
(typhoid)

bacillus anthracis
(anthrax)

Vibrio
(cholera)

Treponema
(syphilis)

0.002mm
or 2 μm

15.4 Types of bacteria

(a)

(c)

(b)

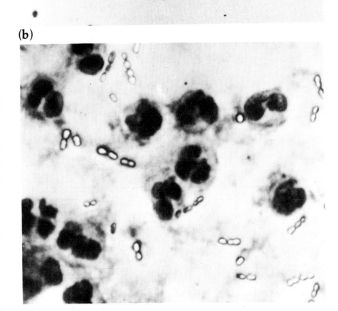

(d)

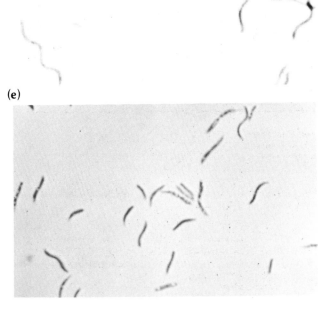

(e)

15.5 Photomicrographs of bacteria

▶ **Question**

15.14 Use Fig 15.4 to identify the numbered photo micrographs in Fig 15.5.

187

Bacteria are classified into three groups by shape. These are rounded-shaped, rod-shaped and spiral. The three groups are called cocci (*Staphylococcus; Streptococcus; Diplococcus*); bacilli (*Bacillus anthraci; Salmonella typhi; Vibrio*) and spirilli (*Treponema*).

As living organisms, bacteria have a number of requirements. All bacteria need food in order to grow, though the individual food requirements of bacteria vary enormously. A few bacteria are even able to photosynthesise. Some bacteria manufacture most of their food from simple inorganic chemicals such as sulphur. Most bacteria obtain their food ready-made – putrefying bacteria obtain their food from humus, parasitic bacteria from their hosts and milk bacteria from milk. The majority of bacteria require oxygen for respiration, though a few dangerous bacteria which cause food poisoning can respire anaerobically.

▶ Question

15.15 Apart from food and oxygen, what else must bacteria have in order to grow and multiply?

Most bacteria only take about twenty minutes to grow to their maximum size. They then divide into two and the process is repeated. This rapid reproduction rate may result in the production of 490 000 000000 000 bacteria from one parent cell in twenty-four hours! Fig 15.6 shows the growth of a population of bacteria in a large flask containing a culture medium kept at 40 °C.

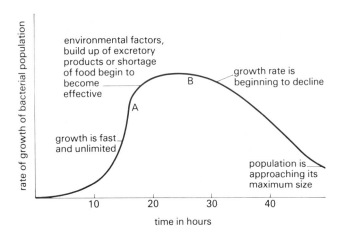

15.6 Growth of a bacterial population

▶ Questions

15.16 When is the period of most rapid growth?
15.17 What happens to the growth rate between A and B?
15.18 Suggest reasons for the decline in growth rate which begins at B.

As bacteria use up food to grow, they produce waste products. In some bacteria these waste products are stored in their cytoplasm, while in others, the waste products are discharged into the surrounding medium. It is these waste products, or toxins, which

may produce symptoms of disease in man. The toxins may accumulate and destroy the bacteria themselves.

When conditions become unfavourable – when food or oxygen is scarce, the temperature too low, or toxin level too high – bacteria produce a resistant wall around their cell contents and form spores. The spores may be formed inside the cell wall, **endospores**, or at the end of a cell, **exospores**. The number and type of spores formed is constant for each species of bacterium. Spores are resistant to high temperatures and to total absence of moisture. Steam heat and pressure or ultra-violet light are the best means of destroying these resistant bodies.

Tuberculosis

Most of the population in this country is infected by the tubercule bacillus, *Mycobacterium tuberculosis*, at some time in their life. Most people are sufficiently healthy to produce body defences (see section 5) to combat the bacteria and they become immune to the effects of the disease. People living in dusty, over-crowded conditions, eating a poor diet and in poor general health will not be able to defend themselves against constant infection by *Mycobacterium tuberculosis*. Improvements in living conditions and basic diets

15.7 Spread, diagnosis and sites of a attack of the TB bacterium, *Mycobacterium tuberculosis*

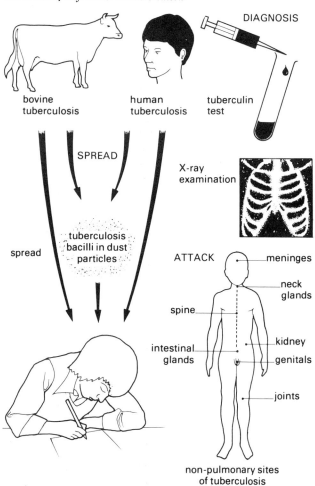

have reduced the incidence of the disease enormously in this country (see section 1), but it is still common in developing countries.

Pulmonary tuberculosis is the most common form of the disease. Early symptoms may go unrecognised. Loss of appetite and loss of weight are an indication of the disease. The bacteria form lesions in the lungs which can be detected in early stages, before they become large cavities, by X-ray examination. The sufferer develops a persistent cough and may cough up blood. The high temperature induced by the bacteria causes night sweating. Every schoolchild is tested at the age of twelve or thirteen to ensure that they have acquired immunity against tuberculosis. A small amount of serum containing toxin from dead tubercule bacilli is injected into the arm using a Heaf gun which has several small needles on one head.

If a child has developed immunity to tuberculosis, his antibodies will produce a reaction to the injection. It will appear red and blistery.

If there is no reaction against the injected toxin, a vaccine is administered to the child. The BCG vaccine (so named after French scientists Camille and Guerin) contains weakened tubercule bacilli (the 'B' stands for 'bacilli') which will induce the blood to produce antibodies, without harming the body. About 10% of the twelve-thirteen year olds tested are TB-positive.

▶ **Questions**

15.19 Why might some of this 10% be sent for X-ray examinations?

15.20 Apart from inhaling infected air droplets, what was the other common source of tubercule bacilli? Why is this source almost non-existent in this country now (See Fig 15.7)?

In the comparatively rare event of an individual contracting tuberculosis, the following measures are taken to treat the individual and to prevent the disease from spreading to other members of his family.

1 The patient is transferred to an isolation hospital (sanatorium).

2 Members of the patient's family are screened to ensure that they are free of the disease.

3 The patient is prescribed good food, rest and limited exercise.

4 Antibiotics such as streptomycin, neomycin and aureomycin are administered to halt the growth of the tubercule bacilli (see section 5). Isoniazid, one of the effective drugs, is also an anti-depressant drug which helps the patient's attitude.

5 In extreme cases, surgery is used if a lung is severely damaged.

Pneumonia

Pneumonia is an inflammatory condition of the lung caused by an infection with one of a number of bacteria or viruses. The alveoli become filled with inflammatory cells (white blood cells, some red cells) and fibrin (see Fig 15.8). The lung becomes consolidated.

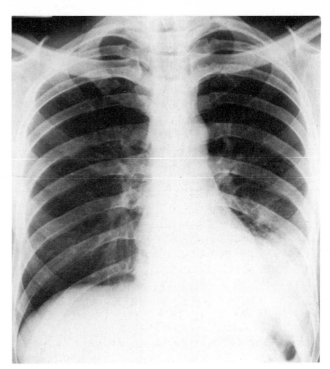

15.8 Consolidation of part of a lung in a case of bacterial pneumonia. Compare this with Fig 16.1(b)

▶ **Question**

15.21 What effect will this condition have on gaseous exchange in the alveoli? How can it be rectified?

The most common form of pneumonia is broncho-pneumonia, where patches of all the lobes of the lungs become consolidated. It is caused by bacteria, the most important being *Diplococcus pneumoniae*. It is unusual for a healthy person to inhale sufficient numbers of these bacteria to become infected. Pneumonia is most common as a complication of existing respiratory infections. If a person is already weakened by the effects of the viruses of influenza, measles or the common cold, or by the bacteria which cause bronchitis or tuberculosis, he is more likely to succumb to the pneumonia bacteria already present in the lung tissue.

Individuals at risk of pneumonia include babies and small children with infectious diseases such as measles or whooping cough; elderly, frail people during winter who are not able to keep warm enough, alcoholics and people who are undernourished.

Onset of the disease is sudden, with a high fever (39–40 °C), accompanied by shivering attacks. A severe chest pain is caused by the consolidation of part of the lung, which makes breathing difficult. The short, sharp cough after a number of days produces a nasty sputum, which contains the consolidation material. In common with all other respiratory infections, pneumonia bacteria are carried by tiny water droplets.

Deaths from pneumonia used to be frequent, but with penicillin, ampicillin, amoxcyillin, and other antibiotics, the disease is now easy to treat.

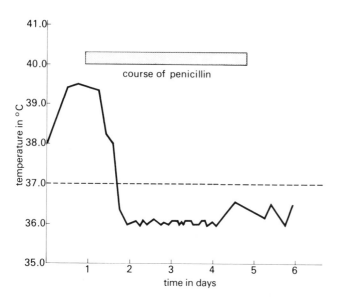

15.9 Temperature chart of a patient suffering from lobar pneumonia

▶ **Questions**

15.22 (a) What was the temperature of the patient described in Fig 15.9 on the afternoon of the first day?
(b) What has brought about the rapid drop in temperature on the second day?
15.23 List the ways in which spread of an infectious disease such as pneumonia may be prevented.

Typhoid

Typhoid fever is a highly infectious disease of the digestive system caused by a bacillus, *Salmonella typhi*. It is associated with insanitary conditions and was a common cause of death in the Middle Ages in this country. It is still relatively common in tropical countries where water supplies are untreated.

15.10 Spread, incubation and course of typhoid fever

Complications which can cause death from typhoid include perforation of the intestines, bleeding (haemorrhage) or dehydration. These are all caused by the excessive diarrhoea.

▶ **Questions**

15.24 List the ways in which a person may become infected with typhoid.
15.25 How long does it take for the symptoms to appear following infection?
15.26 For how long does the high temperature persist?

Treatment of typhoid with the antibiotic chloramphenicol was very successful until recent times. In 1979, 14 000 people in Mexico died in a terrible outbreak of the disease. The patients were given chloramphenicol, but it was ineffective against the typhoid bacilli.

The typhoid bacilli had become resistant to the effect of chloramphenicol. Each time chloramphenicol was administered, a few bacteria were not killed because they possessed a particular variation which made them resistant to the antibiotic (possibly a thicker slime layer). Over a period of time as more and more of these bacteria survived, the population of typhoid bacilli would contain a higher proportion of the resistant variety. Other antibiotics such as ampicillin are now being used to combat typhoid bacilli.

Certain people may be infected with *Salmonella typhi* and show no symptoms of the disease. These people are called carriers. A famous example is 'Bloody Mary' who worked as a cook in London in the 18th century.

▶ **Questions**

15.27 Explain why this cook was given such an unflattering nickname.

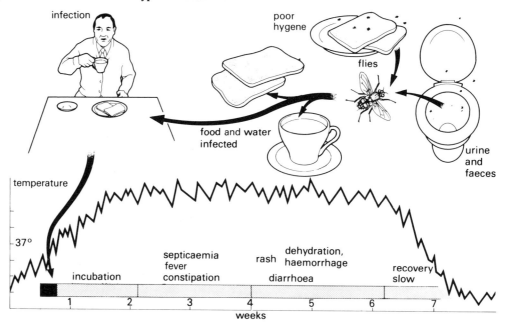

190

15.28 How may the problem of carriers be overcome?
15.29 List all the methods which may be used to control typhoid.

Venereal diseases

Venereal diseases are spread by contact during sexual intercourse. They are mainly caused by bacteria. Gonorrhoea and urethritis are the most common diseases, but syphilis is by far the most dangerous and is often fatal. Syphilis is caused by the spirillum, *Treponema pallidum*. The disease develops in three stages.

1　The primary stage occurs about a month after the infective intercourse. A painless ulcer called a chancre may appear on the penis in the male or the labia in the female. In some cases the chancre appears on the lip, on a finger or on the breast. It takes a few weeks to heal.

2　The secondary stage follows some weeks after the disappearance of the chancre if no treatment is given. The lymph glands swell, there is a mild fever and a rash appears on the trunk.

3　The tertiary stage follows some years after the original infection. The spirillum now attacks the circulatory system and the aorta may be blown out to form an aneurism. Involvement of the nervous system may result in deafness, blindness or insanity.

If syphilis is diagnosed in the primary stage it can be treated with penicillin. The secondary and tertiary stages will then be eliminated.

An infected mother may give birth to a baby such as that illustrated in Fig 15.11. This baby has congenital syphilis and is likely to have disorders of growth, of the eyes and the nervous system.

15.11 Baby with congenital syphilis

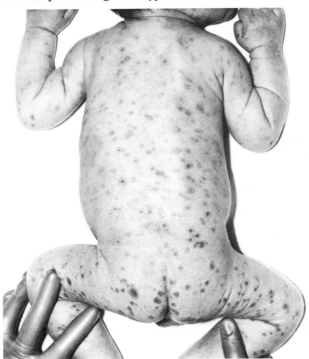

► **Question**

15.30　How could the tragedy of such a birth have been avoided?

Gonorrhoea is due to infection with *Gonococcus*, a bacterium causing acute inflammation. Symptoms of gonorrhoea are:

1　Acute inflammation of the urethra in the male and of the cervix in the female. In both cases a thick, yellowish purulent discharge is produced. Micturition is painful in the male.

2　The infection may spread to the prostate gland in the male and to the fallopian tubes in the female. Peritonitis (acute inflammation of the membrane covering the intestines) may result in the female.

3　The bacteria may spread to the blood, producing septicaemia, to the nervous system, producing meningitis, and to the eyes, producing iritis and conjunctivitis.

Treatment with penicillin is effective, particularly in the early stages of infection.

There is the danger of babies being born blind if their mother is infected. The gonococci in the cervix may attack the babies' eyes.

Non-specific urethritis is another common venereal disease which has some symptoms in common with gonorrhoea. The causative organism is not a bacterium but is thought to be an organism called *Chlamydia*.

▷ **Homework**

Venereal diseases have reached epidemic proportions in this country. Find out why they are so common these days and suggest what could be done to help eradicate them.

3 Microbial diseases – viruses

Viruses are agents of disease which are very much smaller than bacteria. A really large virus may be as long as $0.2\,\mu$m, but the majority are less than half this size. A bacterium is visible under the high power magnification of a school microscope, but a virus can only be seen with the help of an electron microscope. The virus in Fig 15.12 is a virus which parasitises bacteria. The micrograph magnifies it 360 000 times. It is called a T4 bacteriophage or T4 phage.

15.12 Electron micrograph of T4 bacteriophage attached to a cell wall

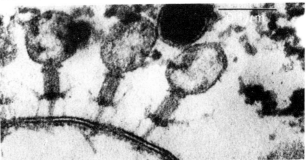

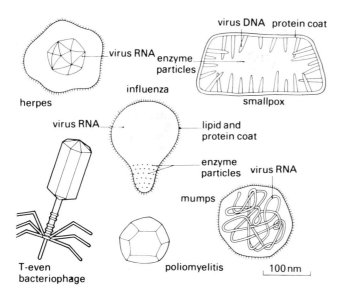

influenza

herpes

smallpox

T-even
bacteriophage

mumps

poliomyelitis

100 nm

15.13 Some common viruses

▶ **Questions**

15.31 What is the actual length of the T4 bacteriophage virus in Fig 15.12?

15.32 In what respects other than size do viruses differ structurally from bacteria?

Viruses are only able to reproduce in the cell of a living host. They are obligatory parasites. They cannot be grown on a nutrient culture medium in the laboratory. Their method of reproduction is unusual. It is outlined in Fig 15.14.

1 The tail plate of the T4 phase becomes attached to the potential host cell (a bacterium called *Escherichia coli*).

15.14 Reproduction of a T4 bacteriophage

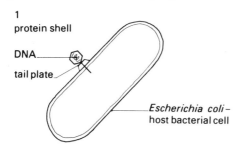

1
protein shell

DNA

tail plate

Escherichia coli –
host bacterial cell

2 The DNA coil contained within the protein shell is discharged into the cytoplasm of the bacterium. The protein shell remains outside.

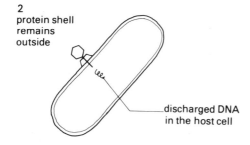

2
protein shell
remains
outside

discharged DNA
in the host cell

3 The bacterial cell is organised by the phage DNA to produce new protein shells, then new DNA coils.

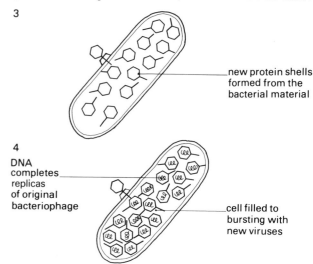

3

new protein shells
formed from the
bacterial material

4
DNA
completes
replicas
of original
bacteriophage

cell filled to
bursting with
new viruses

4 The bacterial cell bursts, liberating a mass of new phages which will infect more cells.

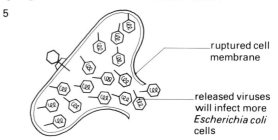

5

ruptured cell
membrane

released viruses
will infect more
Escherichia coli
cells

Viruses are able to survive for long periods outside their host cells. They will not undergo any activity and may even become crystallised for a time. They are only able to replicate in one particular type of host cell – they are host-specific.

Because of their rapid replication, viral diseases are highly infectious. As you study the following examples of viral diseases, see if you can detect any common factors apparent in all the examples.

▶ **Questions**

15.33 What process occurring in every living cell is similar to the replication of viruses?

15.34 List the ways in which viruses differ from bacteria in their mode of existence.

Influenza

Influenza is the name given to a group of diseases which have very similar symptoms, but which are actually caused by different, though closely related viruses. These diseases are all characterised by a running nose and sore throat, followed by a high temperature, headache, backache and sometimes vomiting. Severity of the symptoms varies depending on the strain of the infective virus. Fig 15.15 shows the course of a case of the Hong Kong variety of influenza.

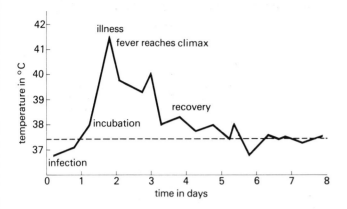

15.15 Influenza infection

▶ **Question**

15.35 (a) How long is the incubation period?
(b) How long is the fever period?
(c) How long should the patient be in quarantine?

Influenza is a social problem in this country. More working days are lost through influenza than any other disease. Many industries now offer a vaccination service to their staff. Vaccination in early autumn with a mixed culture of various strains of influenza viruses gives about 60% protection against the disease through the winter period when the disease is most infective. Apart from rest and confinement to a constant environmental temperature, treatment of influenza consists primarily of ensuring that complications such as bronchopneumonia do not occur. Broad spectrum antibiotics which are active against a broad band of micro-organisms, are prescribed to prevent secondary infections.

▶ **Question**

15.36 If a girl in your class develops influenza, what steps can be taken to to prevent the rest of the class from catching the disease?

Common cold (coryza)

On average, every person in Britain is infected by viruses causing the common cold seven times a year. Five of these times, symptoms do not develop, possibly because of a substance present in the blood called interferon(see next page). The remaining two attacks produce a running nose, watery eyes, sore throat, sometimes a cough and inflammation of the upper respiratory tract. There may be a slight fever. The symptoms generally subside after two to three days. Rest in a constant environmental temperature is the best treatment. Some people at risk may be prescribed antibiotics to prevent the development of secondary bacterial infections.

▶ **Question**

15.37 Describe the sort of people who will need antibiotic prescriptions.

Poliomyelitis

Poliomyelitis, also called infantile paralysis, is caused either by inhalation of droplets containing the infective virus, or by ingesting the virus in food or water. Seven to fourteen days after infection there is a sudden onset of fever, backache, headache and a running nose. Three or four days after this there may be paralysis of some muscles in the body, particularly the legs. Some patients do not develop paralysis, which only occurs if the virus invades the motor area of the cerebrum.

▶ **Question**

15.38 Why are some victims of poliomyelitis placed in an iron lung?

Treatment of paralysis is only possible by physiotherapy to encourage other muscles to take over the role of the immobilised muscles. The disease is now rare in this country due to the thorough vaccination campaign. All babies are encouraged to receive a series of oral vaccines to give them immunity against this crippling disease.

Measles

Measles is now one of the most virulent of all the infectious diseases. The nature of the infection is such that dangerous complications are likely. The disease is spread by droplet infection and the first symptoms

15.16 Boy with measles

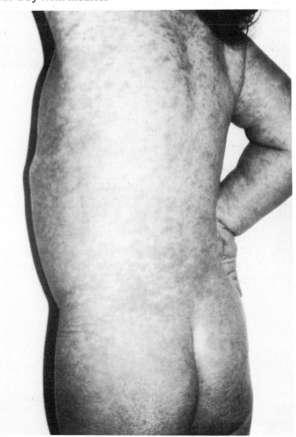

appear ten to fourteen days after infection. The onset is abrupt, and starts with extreme coryza - running nose, sneezing, inflamed running eyes, coughing and a sore throat. Small white spots, called Koplik's spots appear inside the mouth. These disappear when about four days later, the rash appears. This starts on the forehead, then behind the ears and spreads throughout the face and body. The temperature rises to about 39.4 °C as the rash appears. Both the rash and the temperature subside after about a week.

▶ Question

15.39 From the description of the symptoms, what complications would you expect could develop?

Other complications which occur are acute gastroenteritis, middle ear infection and encephalomyelitis (inflammation of the membrane around the brain and spinal cord).

In addition to the prescription of antibiotics to prevent the development of complications, care must be taken to exclude bright light from the patient when the eyes are inflamed and exuding. The patient should remain in bed until a normal temperature is attained, and remain in quarantine for two weeks after the onset of the infection.

If an injection of anti-disease serum (containing gamma globulin antibodies) is given to a person within five days of exposure to measles, they will not develop the symptoms of the disease. The antibodies will destroy the measles virus.

▶ Questions

15.40 How is measles best prevented?
15.41 What characteristics would you list as being common to all these viral diseases?

Susceptibility to viral diseases does vary in individuals. In 1957 a protein called interferon was isolated from human cells attacked by viruses. This substance has been shown to prevent the replication of viruses. Work has been undertaken to find a way to stimulate interferon production in humans. Attempts are now being made to synthesise interferon by genetic engineering of bacteria. If successful, it could mean an end to the miseries of viral infections, but at the moment it is very expensive and its action is not fully understood.

Viral infections spread more quickly than other types of disease if proper control is not observed. A disease outbreak among a population with little immunity is called an epidemic. There was an epidemic of smallpox in the UK in 1965, when an infected man travelled into Heathrow. Several people on the aeroplane caught the disease and transmitted it to many others. If a disease outbreak reaches worldwide proportions, a pandemic results. Asian, Hong Kong and Mao influenza outbreaks are examples from recent years. The virus responsible in each case was a new strain, so no one had immunity.

Endemic diseases are those which occur regularly in a population without undue spreading. Most of the population has some immunity to these diseases.

▶ Question

15.42 Give some examples of endemic diseases in this country.

▷ Homework

The World Health Organisation has recently claimed that smallpox is now eradicated from the world. Find out all you can about the basis of their claim.

4 Microbial diseases – fungi

Fungi are a group of plants which are not able to manufacture their own food because they lack chlorophyll. Instead they either obtain their food from dead or decaying organic matter, or they become parasitic and obtain food from a living host. A majority of fungi fall into the first category. These are called saprophytes. Examples include mushrooms, toadstools, and some moulds.

Activity 15.2   Growing some mould

1   Take a piece of stale bread and moisten it.
2   Place the bread on a saucer on a window ledge in a warm place.
3   After exposing the bread to the air for about half an hour, invert a jam jar over the saucer.
4   Observe the bread twenty-four hours later. Record your observations.
5   Using a mounted needle, remove a small amount of the growth from the surface of the bread and place it on a microscope slide.
6   View under the low and high power of a microscope. If possible, draw what you see, identifying and labelling the structures shown in Fig 15.17 (a) and (b) if possible.

15.17 (a) *Pencillium* **mould**

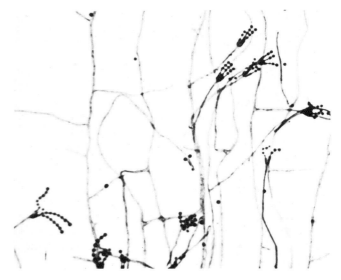

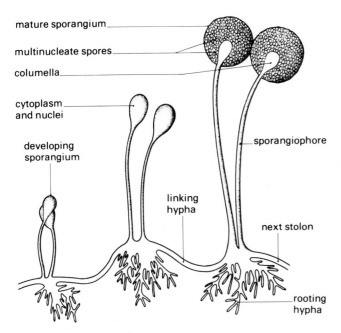

mature sporangium

multinucleate spores

columella

cytoplasm and nuclei

developing sporangium

linking hypha

sporangiophore

next stolon

rooting hypha

15.17 (b) *Mucor* **mould**

Moulds consist of a tangle of threads called **hyphae** which look rather like cotton wool. Enzymes are passed out from the hyphae into the substrate on which the mould is living. The enzymes digest the substrate and soluble products of digestion diffuse into the hypha enabling it to grow. Soon vertical hyphae are produced, at the tip of which, reproductive bodies are formed. These may be chains of spores called conidia as in *Penicillium*, or they may be large spore cases (sporangia) containing hundreds of individual spores as in *Mucor*. When conditions are suitably damp, the spores are released into the air. Many of these spores perish, but any spore which lands on a suitable, damp substrate will germinate and shoot out a hypha.

Certain moulds infect man. They are able to live in the hair, skin or lungs of man. In each case a network of hyphae, called a mycelium, will be formed.

▶ **Question**

15.43 Suggest a way in which a man might become infected by a mould.

Ringworm

Fig 15.18 illustrates a characteristic lesion on the arm produced by the growth of the mould *Microsporum*. This disease, ringworm, causes a lot of irritation. It also affects the scalp, growing in the shaft of hairs which become weakened and fracture near their bases. Skin ringworm is frequently found in the groin, where moisture and warmth provide ideal conditions for growth. Inflammation in this region may be acute, with blistering as a result of scratching. Ringworm is common amongst schoolchildren from five to fifteen years old. It is highly contagious. Treatment is mainly by the use of an antibiotic called griseofulvin which destroys the fungus.

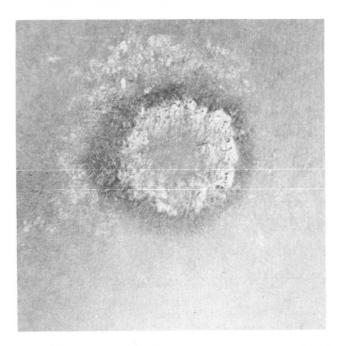

15.18 Ringworm on a man's arm

▶ **Questions**

15.44 Suggest how the disease may be transmitted among schoolchildren.
15.45 How may spread of the disease be prevented?

Athlete's foot

The most common fungal disease in this country is athlete's foot. The pathogenic mould causing the disease is *Tinea*.

15.19 *Tinea* **mould growing on a toe (athlete's foot)**

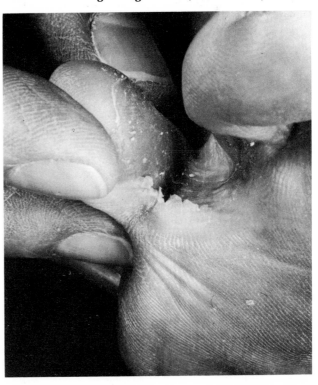

Tinea grows between the toes. The skin peels and cracks and appears sodden. The disease is not confined to athletes, but is particularly common amongst people using communal changing and bathing facilities. Sweating of the feet may aggravate the condition.

▶ Questions

15.46 Explain why athlete's foot is common amongst individuals sharing bathing facilities.
15.47 Suggest how the spread of athlete's foot may be limited.

Fungicides such as nistatin, zinc cream or zinc powders are used in treating fungal diseases. Other fungal diseases include thrush, which infects the mouth cavity and the vagina, and aspergilliosis which infects the lungs.

▷ Homework

Make a check of your local swimming pool and of your school's changing rooms to see how they prevent the spread of fungal diseases.

5 Microbial diseases – protozoa

Protozoa are one-celled animals which are found living in many diverse places. They include free-living aquatic and terrestrial types and a large number of parasites. Some of these parasites infect man, the best known and possibly the most dangerous ones being species of *Plasmodium*, an organism which lives in the blood and causes malaria.

Malaria is a malignant fever, produced as a result of the destruction of red blood cells by the plasmodial parasite. Fig 15.20 shows some of these parasites dividing in red blood cells. The word 'malaria' means 'bad air'. The disease was commonly found in marshy areas where the air was damp and it was believed that the bad air rising from the marshes carried malaria. Later it was found that the disease is transmitted by the bite of the *Anopheles* mosquito (see section 7). *Plasmodium* spends part of its life cycle in man and part in mosquito.

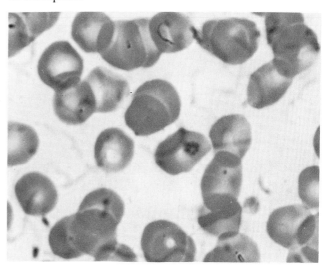

15.20 Blood smear showing *Plasmodium*

15.21 Life cycle of *Plasmodium* **parasite**

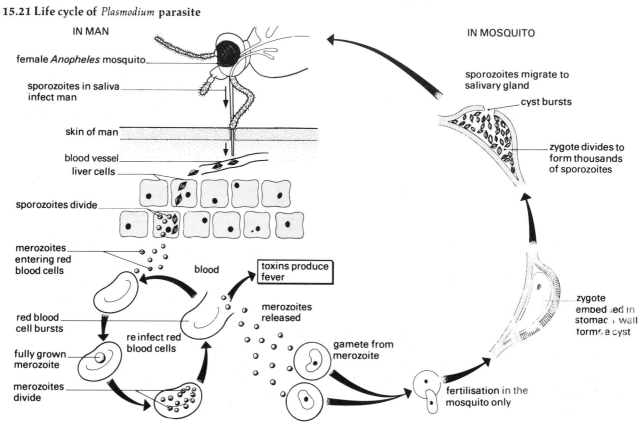

15.48 Where do the infective *Plasmodium* sporozoites travel to in man?
15.49 Where does multiplication of the parasite take place in man?
15.50 In what form is the parasite taken into the mosquito?
15.51 Where does the parasite multiply inside the mosquito?
15.52 How do the sporozoites enter the mosquito's proboscis?
15.53 What is the best method of preventing the spread of malaria?

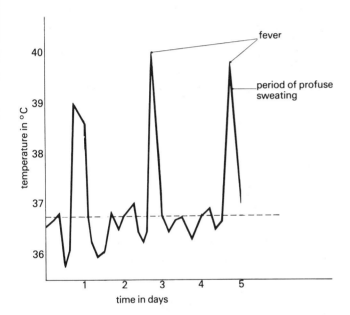

15.22 Temperature chart of a malarial patient

▶ **Questions**

15.54 The patient of Fig 15.22 has malaria. How frequently does the fever return?
15.55 Suggest an event in the blood which could cause the fever.

▷ **Homework**

Find out about two other protozoan diseases which infect man.

6 Internal and external parasites

In addition to microscopic parasites, man is also beset by larger parasites. These fall into two groups, those living inside man, and those which cling to the outside of the body.

Nearly all the macro-organisms which parasitise the inside of man are worms. In the tropics, worm infestation is very serious and blood fluke is one of the commonest diseases. In the United Kingdom tapeworm, threadworm and roundworm are the most common parasites.

15.23 *Taenia saginata,* **the beef tapeworm**

Tapeworm

Tapeworms are flat, ribbon-like worms composed of hundreds of **proglottids**. The most common tapeworm occurring in man is *Taenia solium*, the pork tapeworm.

Tapeworms are similar to *Plasmodium* in that they require two hosts in order to complete their life cycle. In *Taenia solium* man is the primary host and pig is the secondary host. The adult worm grows in the intestine of man. It has a head which is dominated by a circle of hooks and a number of suckers.

15.24 (a) Head or scolex of *Taenia*

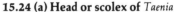
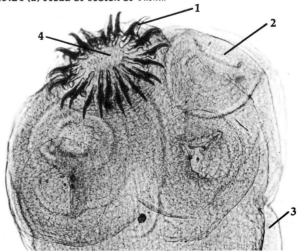

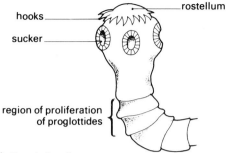

15.24 (b) *Taenia* **head**

▶ **Question**

15.56 Using Fig 15.24 (b) as a guide, identify the structures numbered in Fig 15.24 (a).

New proglottids are constantly being produced in the neck region of the worm. Mature proglottids are shed in the faeces of the host. *Taenia* feeds by absorbing the soluble products of digestion from the intestine of the host. The host loses weight because he is being deprived of food.

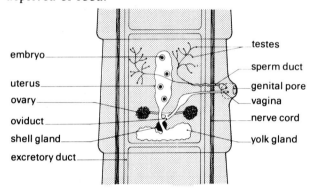

15.25 (a) Immature proglottis of *Taenia*

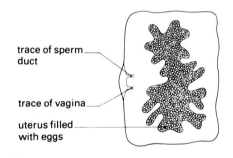

15.25 (b) Mature proglottis of *Taenia*

▶ **Questions**

15.57 (a) What are the dominant structures visible in an immature proglottis?
(b) What is the dominant structure visible in a mature proglottis?
(c) What is the sex of this worm?
(d) What structures are missing from both the head and the proglottids?
15.58 How is the shape of *Taenia* an aid to food absorption?
15.59 List the features of *Taenia* which make it an ideal parasite.

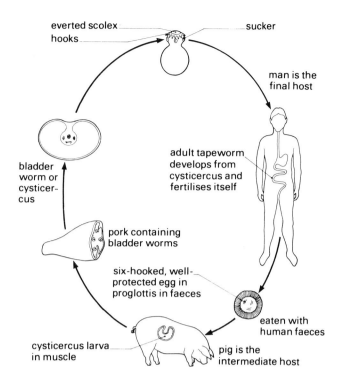

15.26 Life cycle of *Taenia solium*

▶ **Questions**

15.60 What helps the egg to survive until it is eaten by a pig?
15.61 In what way does the larva (bladder worm or cysticercus) in the pig muscle resemble an adult tapeworm?
15.62 How does man become infected with cysticerci?
15.63 How many tapeworm infestation be prevented?

Tapeworm infestation is not usually dangerous, but the hooks and suckers of the adult can damage the intestine wall. A real danger is the cysticercus becoming lodged in the brain, but this only usually occurs if a bladderworm from beef, *Taenia saginata*, is ingested. The normal treatment is by drugs such as mepacrine which can dislodge the adult worm so that it is passed out.

15.27 Thread worms, *Enterobius vermicularis*

Thread worm

Thread worms are common in children, causing irritation around the anus. The adult male and female worms live in the colon. The male is 2–5 mm long and the female 10 mm. When the female is full of fertilised eggs, she migrates to the anus and deposits her eggs. Children re-infect themselves because they scratch the area covered with the irritating eggs, the eggs stay under their fingernails and re-enter the mouth when the child puts his fingers there. Eggs can also be transmitted in dust and may settle on food. Drugs such as gentian violet and piperazine can be used to destroy the worms.

▶ Question

15.64 What other measures may be taken to prevent thread worm infestation?

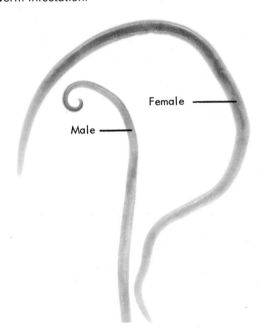

15.28 Male and female roundworm, *Ascaris lumbricoides*

Roundworm

Ascaris lumbricoides is one of the largest roundworms, being up to 30 mm in length and up to 4 mm in diameter. It can live in the small intestine of man. A large number of these worms can cause an obstruction in the alimentary canal. The adult female liberates eggs which are passed out in the faeces. Vast numbers of eggs with resistant shells are produced. They are able to live for long periods and can reinfect man.

If an egg containing an infective larva is swallowed by man, the shell is digested and the larva is released and bores its way through the wall of the intestine into the blood stream. Many larvae settle down in the blood vessels of the lungs, before breaking out into the alveoli. They then wriggle their way up the air passages, find their way to the back of the throat and are swallowed into the stomach and intestine. *Ascaris* can be killed by various drugs such as piperazine.

▶ Questions

15.65 Which part of this life cycle would you expect to produce the most damage?
15.66 What other means of control could eradicate roundworm?

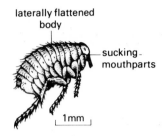

laterally flattened body

sucking mouthparts

1mm

15.29 A flea, *Pulex*

Fleas

A variety of insects are equipped to live on the external surfaces of man. These include fleas, lice and bedbugs.

The human flea, *Pulex*, is flattened from side to side and has claws for clinging on to the hairs of man. It can leap considerable distances due to the length of its legs. It has sucking mouthparts which enable it to suck the blood of its host.

Apart from causing irritation, fleas are the carriers of disease micro-organisms such as the plague bacilli, typhus fever and leptospirosis. They pick these bacteria up from rats. The Black Death was caused by the transmission of plague bacilli from rats to man.

▶ Questions

15.67 How do fleas spread from one human host to another?
15.68 How can man avoid infestation with fleas?

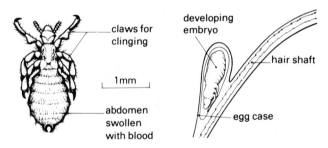

claws for clinging

1mm

abdomen swollen with blood

developing embryo

hair shaft

egg case

15.30 (a) *Pediculus*   **(b) Egg case of** *Pediculus*

Louse

Fig 15.30 shows a body louse, *Pediculus*. The head louse is very similar in structure, but the pubic louse is much squatter. It is also called the crab louse because of its shape. A louse egg or nit is also shown.

Like the flea, the louse can cause extreme irritation as it withdraws blood from the host. Head lice are particularly contagious amongst schoolchildren.

▶ Questions

15.69 What features of the louse equip it for living on a human body?

15.70 (a) Suggest a reason why head lice are easily caught by young schoolchildren.
(b) What measures are taken to reduce the incidence of head lice?
(c) What precautions can an individual take to reduce the chances of catching head lice?

15.31 A bedbug, *Cimex*

Bedbug

Bedbugs cause inflammation of the skin as they bite the surface and cause irritation. These parasites are only rarely found these days in this country. They used to live in the bedding of humans.

▶ **Question**

15.71 Why has the bedbug become a rare parasite in recent years?

15.32 Fourteen ways in which diseases are transmitted

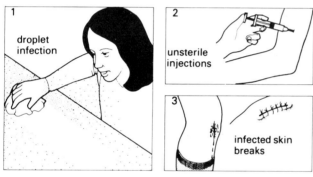

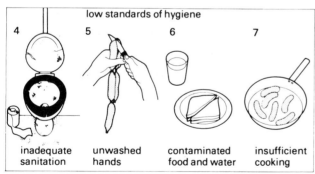

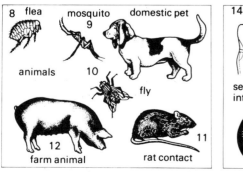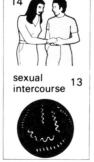

▷ **Homework**

Consider every disease mentioned in sections 2–6 and place them in one of the fourteen methods of transmission illustrated in Fig 15.32.

7 Vectors

Many fleas and lice transmit disease organisms (pathogens) without showing any symptoms of disease themselves. In this instance, fleas and lice are said to be vectors of the particular diseases caused by the pathogens they transmit. Vectors frequently determine the distribution of a disease. Malaria is not endemic in this country because the vector of malaria, the female of the *Anopheles* mosquito, does not survive in this country. *Anopheles* is a tropical mosquito.

Mosquito

As early as 1880 in France, Laverain (1845–1922) discovered the plasmodial parasite in the blood of malaria sufferers. Years later Sir Ronald Ross (1857–1932), after dissecting hundreds of possible vectors, detected the sporozoites in the stomach of the female *Anopheles* mosquito. Mosquitoes breed in stagnant water, where their larvae and pupae are also found. If you examine any old water baths or stagnant ponds in summer, you should be able to find larval stages of the *Culex* mosquito, which are very similar to the *Anopheles* forms.

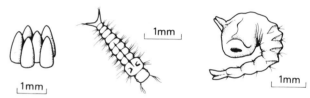

15.33 *Culex* **mosquito eggs, larvae and pupae**

▶ **Question**

15.72 Study Fig 15.33 carefully and list the ways in which each of the three stages in the life cycle are particularly well-adapted to living in water.

The eggs normally hatch into larvae about three days after they are laid. The larval stage is an actively growing phase. Plankton in the water is swept into the mouth by the mouth brushes. After moulting twice

15.34 Adult (imago) *Anopheles* **mosquito**

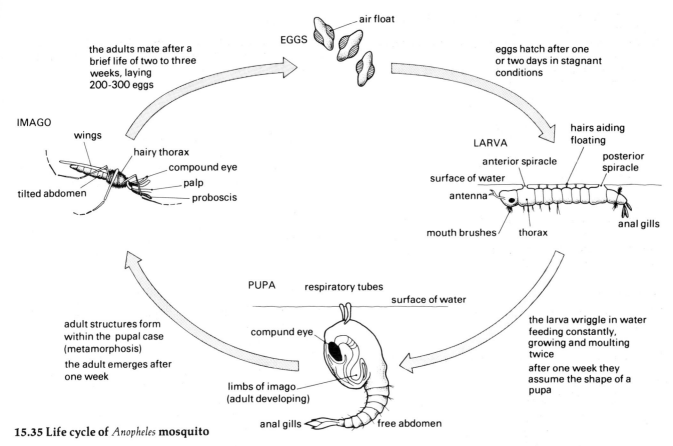

15.35 Life cycle of *Anopheles* **mosquito**

during the course of a week, the larva changes into the pupa. Inside the pupa metamorphosis takes place. The larval tissues are broken down and the adult tissues are formed. A week later a fully formed adult emerges from the split casing of the pupa. See Fig 15.34.

Adult mosquitoes look something like small flies. We call them gnats. *Anopheles* may be recognised because it projects its abdomen up into the air. The female *Anopheles* mosquito sucks up blood from humans using a needle-like proboscis (see Fig 15.21). Saliva containing an anti-clotting substance is poured down the proboscis. An *Anopheles* mosquito containing *Plasmodium* parasites infects a person with malaria in this way. Male *Anopheles* mosquitoes are not dangerous. They suck up plant juices. They may be recognised by their feathery antennae.

▶ **Question**

15.73 Suggest ways in which man could eradicate the various stages of the life cycle of *Anopheles*. How can these mosquitoes be prevented from attacking man?

Housefly

The most dangerous and common vector in Britain today is the housefly. Housefly eggs are creamish in colour and the size of the clusters shown in Fig 15.36. You may have seen them on old meat or on rotten food in dustbins. The larvae of blowflies, which are similar to houseflies, may be purchased from fishing tackle shops. They are commonly called maggots. See Fig 15.36.

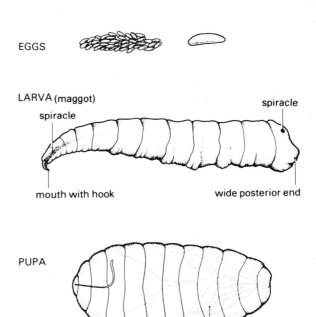

15.36 Housefly eggs, housefly larva and pupa

▶ **Question**

15.74 Suggest how these larvae move and feed.

After a week in favourable conditions, having moulted twice, the fully-grown cream maggot (about 1·5 cm long), becomes encased in a thick, brown case. The barrel shaped pupa, unlike the pupa of the mosquito, is immobile. Inside the pupa the adult structures form and after about a week the fully grown fly forces the top segment of the pupal case open and emerges. As shown in Fig 15.37 the adult housefly is a very hairy creature. It soon becomes covered with bacteria which it picks up from filthy places. It has disgusting feeding habits which make it an extremely dangerous vector. Study the mouthparts of the housefly shown in Fig 15.37. The housefly feeds by discharging salivary juice onto faeces or meat. The food is broken down into a liquid form and is then sucked up into the gut. Houseflies are important vectors of dysentry, diarrhoea, typhoid and cholera – all intestinal diseases.

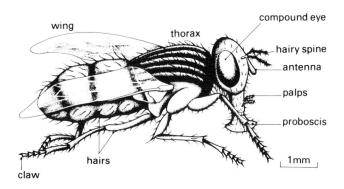

15.37 Housefly adult

▶ Questions

15.75 What could happen if a housefly, after feeding on faeces, alighted on a piece of meat you are about to eat?
15.76 List all the methods you would use to prevent the housefly from contaminating the people in your household.

▷ Homework

List all the insect and rodent vectors and the diseases they transmit.

8 Defence against disease

The best method of combating disease is undoubtedly the complicated defence mechanism of the body. If an individual is fit, he is far less likely to contract disease than an undernourished, unhealthy person. It is only when all the various defences of the body break down that medical help becomes necessary. Even before a disease organism (pathogen) enters the bloodstream, it has to overcome a battery of defences. These include the skin, the mucous membranes, gastric juice, and a substance called histamine. The sebum produced by the sebaceous glands which lubricate the hairs is slightly antiseptic. Gastric juice contains dilute hydrochloric acid, which destroys a large number of bacteria.

Pollen, dust and feathers may invoke a reaction in the mucous membranes. The nose runs with excess mucus and the eyes become red and puffy. People suffering such a reaction are said to be allergic to pollen or dust. The condition is sometimes called hay fever because it occurs when there is a lot of pollen around at hay-making time. The cause of this reaction is the release by body cells of a hormone-like chemical called histamine. Histamine is released in response to a recognised foreign body or antigen. It causes inflammation by dilating blood vessels in the region under attack. Dilation of blood vessels in the nose results in more mucus production. An angry reaction to an insect bite is caused by histamine.

▶ Questions

15.77 How do the mucous membranes lining the nose help to defend the body against micro-organisms? (Refer to Unit 6.)
15.78 How can histamine over-reaction be treated?

The most significant forms of natural defence are in the blood. The white blood cells are able to detect foreign bodies (antigens) and react accordingly to bring about their destruction.

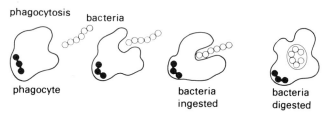

15.38 Polymorph reacting to an infection with streptococci by phagocytosis

▶ Question

15.79 Describe how the polymorph prevents the streptococci from producing symptoms in the body.

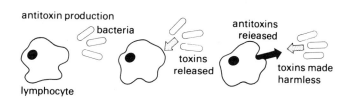

15.39 Anti-toxin production

Some bacteria produce symptoms in the body by releasing waste products of metabolism, **toxins**, into the blood. Certain lymphocytes react against these toxins by producing chemicals called **antitoxins** which make the toxins harmless. See Fig 15.39.

Each bacterial toxin is neutralised by one particular antitoxin. Only diphtherial toxin will be acted upon by one type of lymphocyte and only tetanus toxin will be destroyed by another lymphocyte.

Many other bacteria and all the viruses provoke a reaction by various lymphocytes because of the antigens they carry on their surfaces (see Unit 7). This is an antigen-antibody reaction. The antibodies produced are specific for each antigen. See Fig 15.40. Some antibodies act by precipitating the antigens together and making them coagulate. The serum protein, gamma globulin, also produces antibodies.

antibody production

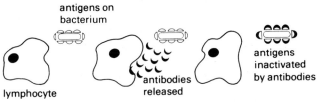

15.40 Antibody production

▶ **Question**

15.80 When the antitoxins or antibodies have destroyed all the invading antigens, what happens to any remaining antitoxins or antibodies?

People exposed to a particular disease will develop an immunity against that disease so that they will not be infected again. Antibodies remaining in the blood after the first infection will quell any subsequent infection. Babies are born with a limited amount of immunity which they gain from antibodies from their mother's blood. These antibodies crossed the placenta. This protects them in their first vulnerable year of life.

Unit 19 describes how Edward Jenner, without understanding the true implication of what he was doing, made a young boy immune to smallpox. Since that time the practice of making people artificially immune to disease has saved millions of lives. There are two methods of conferring immunity on an individual, active immunity and passive immunity.

In active immunity a weakened form of the disease organism, or an extract of the toxin of the disease organism, is injected into the blood. This is called a vaccine. The blood cells react to the injection as they would to the normally occurring form of the organism and produce either antibodies or antitoxins. The person does not suffer the disease because the antibodies can easily combat weakened micro-organisms. The antibodies remain in the blood, but in order to cope with an active form of the disease, a higher level of antibodies may be needed. In such cases a second injection is given and more antibodies are produced.

In passive immunity, serum containing antitoxins or antibodies is injected into the blood. The antitoxins or antibodies are obtained from animals which have been infected with the disease organism.

Children in this country receive a number of recommended vaccinations. Vaccinations against diphtheria and whooping cough have virtually eradicated these diseases, though the particular vaccine used against whooping cough has been implicated in a few cases of fits and brain damage.

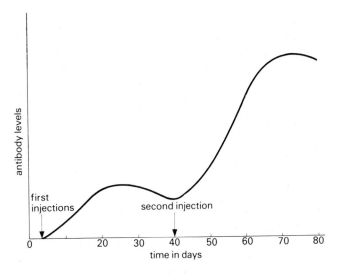

15.41 Antibody levels following two injections

The following table lists the vaccines given in this country.

Table 15.3 Vaccination in Britain

Disease	Type of vaccine	Number of injections	Age when first dose given
Polio-myelitis	Attenuated (weakened) viruses	3 oral doses plus a booster at 5 years	6 months
Tetanus Diphtheria Whooping cough	'Triple' vaccine containing toxins of bacteria	3 injections plus a booster at 5 years	6 months
Smallpox	Attenuated viruses	1 injection plus a booster in the teens	1 year
Measles	Attenuated viruses	1 injection	1 year
Rubella	Attenuated viruses	1 injection	12 years (girls only)
BCG	Attenuated bacteria	1 injection	12–13 years

▶ **Question**

15.81 (a) Why are some boosters given at five years of age?
(b) Why are only girls given the rubella vaccine?

In recent years the antigen-antibody reaction has produced problems in the transplantation of organs. Heart transplant and kidney transplant patients are given **immunosuppressive** drugs to depress the activity of the lymphocytes. This is shown in Fig 15.42.

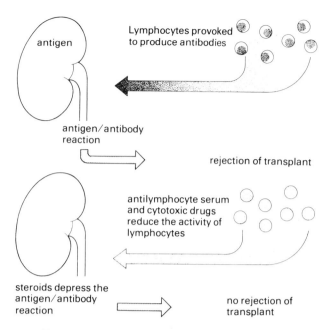

15.42 Prevention of rejection after a kidney transplant

A transplanted organ is 'foreign', so it is recognised as an antigen by the body's defence mechanisms. Immunosuppressive drugs make transplant patients very vulnerable to infection. One British heart transplant patient died from aspergilliosis despite the sterile conditions maintained in the hospital.

Antibiotics

The immune response is not always enough. Since the Second World War the introduction of the 'miracle drugs' – antibiotics – has revolutionised the fight against many infectious diseases. Antibiotics are substances produced by fungi or bacteria which have an inhibiting effect on the growth of a wide variety of bacteria. Sir Alexander Fleming (1881–1955) was the first person to observe the effect (see Unit 19). The agar plate used in this experiment (see Fig 15.43) is the same type of apparatus as that on which Fleming made his original discovery.

15.43 Results of an experiment with the mould *Penicillium chrysogenus*

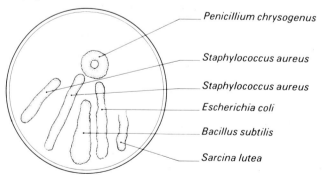

- *Penicillium chrysogenus*
- *Staphylococcus aureus*
- *Staphylococcus aureus*
- *Escherichia coli*
- *Bacillus subtilis*
- *Sarcina lutea*

▶ **Question**

15.82 Which bacteria is *Penicillium chrysogenus* most effective against?

The active substance extracted from *Penicillium* is called penicillin. It is not effective against all bacteria, but many other antibiotics are now available to deal with most common bacteria.

Activity 15.4 Testing the action of penicillin and streptomycin on some common bacteria.

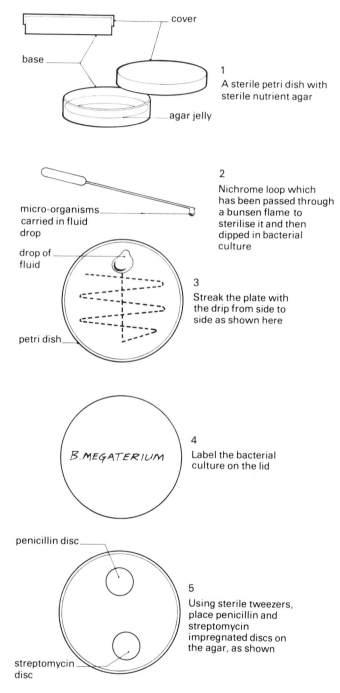

cover

base

agar jelly

1 A sterile petri dish with sterile nutrient agar

micro-organisms carried in fluid drop

2 Nichrome loop which has been passed through a bunsen flame to sterilise it and then dipped in bacterial culture

drop of fluid

3 Streak the plate with the drip from side to side as shown here

petri dish

B.MEGATERIUM

4 Label the bacterial culture on the lid

penicillin disc

5 Using sterile tweezers, place penicillin and streptomycin impregnated discs on the agar, as shown

streptomycin disc

15.44

1 Take a sterile petri dish containing sterile nutrient agar.
2 Flame a nichrome loop and drop it into one of four prepared suspensions of bacteria in distilled water.

3 Streak the loop across the surface of the agar in two zig-zags as shown in Fig 15.44. Do not cut into the agar.

4 Mark the name of the bacterial culture on the lid of the petri dish with a chinagraph pencil.

5 Using sterile tweezers, place one paper disc impregnated with penicillin and one paper disc impregnated with streptomycin in the positions shown in Fig 15.44.

6 Incubate the plate at 37 °C for thirty-six hours.

7 Draw the results of your experiment. Compare it with that of other members of the class who used different bacterial cultures.

8 Construct a table of the class results and write down what this experiment shows you.

There are restrictions on the use of pathogenic bacteria in laboratory experiments, so your results will depend very much on what bacterial cultures your teacher is able to prepare safely. Fig 15.45 shows the results of a similar experiment carried out using *Salmonella typhi*.

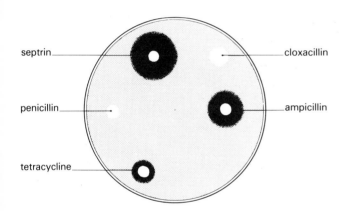

15.45 **Effects of antibiotics on** *Salmonella typhi*

▶ **Questions**

15.83 Which antibiotics tested here would be effective against typhoid?

15.84 Why are many of the older antibiotics becoming less effective against some bacteria?

Disease incidence can be reduced by the destruction of micro-organisms in our immediate environment. This is done by the use of disinfectants, which are normally used on articles such as sinks, baths and lavatories, and antiseptics which are applied externally to the body (on cuts for example). The efficiency of either of these substances can be tested using the following experiment.

Activity 15.5 Comparing the efficiency of common disinfectants in preventing the growth of soil bacteria

1 Working in groups of four, take three test tubes containing equal dilutions of Savlon, Dettol, Jeyes

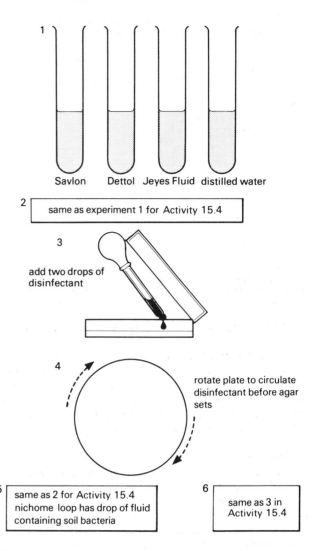

15.46

Fluid and one test tube containing distilled water. You will be given a sterile container with 10 ml of freshly prepared nutrient agar.

2 Each member of the group is responsible for one agar plate.

3 Pour in 2 ml of nutrient agar to cover the base of the petri dish. Take care to avoid contamination.

4 Before the agar sets, add two drops of the test disinfectant with a dropper pipette. Rotate the petri dish to circulate the disinfectant.

5 Take a nichrome loop, and when the agar has set, flame the loop and streak the plate with a suspension of soil bacteria in distilled water. Make zig-zags at right angles to each other.

6 Label the plate and incubate at 35 °C for thirty-six hours.

7 Compare and record the results of the four plates.

8 Write down what this shows you.

▶ **Question**

15.85 What happens to the plate with distilled water? What is the purpose of this plate?

Joseph Lister (1827–1912) was the first person to use antiseptics to combat post-surgery infections. An account of his work is given in Unit 19. Though the use of carbolic acid as an antiseptic greatly reduced deaths following surgery, even more effective is the method of entirely eliminating the presence of micro-organisms by the use of sterile techniques. This is called **asepsis**. In modern operating theatres, all the surgical instruments and the surgeons' and nurses' clothing are sterilised in a pressurised steam oven called an autoclave. This heats objects up to 300 °C under pressure and destroys even the most obstinate bacterial spores.

▷ **Homework**

Write a brief essay outlining the methods you would use to minimise possible infections in your home.

Answers and discussion

1 The causes of disease

15.1 The main causes of disease (with examples) are as follows.
(a) Parasite-induced disease (i) Micro-organisms: measles; typhoid. (ii) Macro-organisms: roundworm; head louse.
(b) Deficiency disease: rickets; anaemia.
(c) Excess disease: paralysis (nicotine excess); fluorosis (calcification of soft tissues).
(d) Hormonal disease: diabetes mellitus; dwarfism.
(e) Environmental disease: asbestosis; radiation sickness.
(g) Inherited disease: sickle cell anaemia; mongolism.
(h) Diseases of unknown cause: migraine; epilepsy.

15.2 'Convulsions' are a complication of many infectious diseases and are caused by a very high temperature during the fever stage. In 1723, treatment of infectious diseases was not very effective and it was common for the temperature to go up to a dangerous level.

15.3 The most common cause of death in 1723 was infectious diseases or resulting complications. 73% of the deaths were from these causes (1, 2, 3, 4, 5 and 7 in the table).

15.4 Death from 'teeth' was probably from blood loss and infection following barbarous methods of tooth extraction! Fillings were rarely used in the 18th century.

15.5 'Dropsy' or fluid retention could be caused by a failure of the kidneys to excrete enough water, or failure of the heart to pump fast enough to keep fluid circulating.

15.6 Environmental disease and inherited disease did not appear to be common causes of death in 1723.

15.7 The first five major causes of death in 1965 were associated in some way with the environment. Heart disease, cancer, strokes, chronic bronchitis and accidents are all thought to be caused in part by environmental factors (see Unit 16).

15.8 The most common fatal respiratory disease in Britain is bronchitis. Causes include smoking, industrial smoke and a damp environment. Emphysema (see Unit 16) is another serious respiratory disease sometimes associated with bronchitis.

15.9 Very few infectious diseases appear in Table 15.2. Tuberculosis is the only definite parasite-induced disease listed, and incidence of that is comparatively low. A majority of the diseases of the digestive system are not infectious, but environmental, for example, gastric and duodenal ulcers.

15.10 The basic difference in disease incidence 250 years ago and now is that the infectious diseases which were rife in 1723 have now been largely controlled by the use of vaccination, antibiotics and improved hygiene. The biggest killers today are diseases caused by stress such as coronary thrombosis, stroke and accidents, and the environment such as some cancers, chronic bronchitis and ulcers.

2 Microbial diseases – bacteria

15.11 One agar plate must be left untreated to show that the agar itself is sterile and free from bacteria. Any bacteria which grow on the agar in the other plates must, therefore, have come from the additional treatments.

15.12 (a) Small cream blobs appear clustered around the nail cutting.
(b) A splattering of small, slimy blobs appear from the cough.
(c) The plate is covered with minute blobs varying in colour.
(d) One or two small cream blobs (colonies) grow near the hair.
(e) A mass of cream colonies grow along the length of the hair.
(f) One or two tiny blobs (colonies) appear in the areas of the prints.
(g) A mass of large colonies, running into each other, appear in the areas of the prints (see Fig 15.47).
(h) A number of colonies appear near the clothing fluff.
(i) A variety of different coloured colonies grew all over the agar.

15.13 Bacteria are present all over the body, in the saliva and clothing. More bacteria are present in dirty conditions (compare (d), (e), (f) and (g)).

15.14 (a) *Staphylococcus* (b) *Diplococcus* (c) *Bacillus* (d) *Treponema* (e) *Vibrio*

15.15 Bacteria require an optimum temperature in order to grow and multiply. Bacteria which live on the human body grow best at 37 °C, while soil bacteria thrive at around 30 °C.

15.16 The period of most rapid growth of the bacterial population is between fifteen and twenty hours.

15.17 The rate of growth levels off and begins to decline.

15.18 The decline in growth rate which begins at B may be due to exhaustion of food supplies in the culture medium, or all the oxygen may have been used up, or there could be a toxic by-product of bacterial metabolism present. Bacteria produce waste products, and accumulation of these substances could inhibit growth.

15.19 Some of the TB-positive children are sent for X-ray examinations to ensure that they are not suffering from active tuberculosis.

15.20 The other most common source of tuberculosis was cow's milk. Many cows used to be infected with tubercule bacilli, but now all herds are tuberculin tested to ensure that they are free from the disease. Milk is pasteurised and any tubercule bacilli present would be destroyed in this process. (See Unit 19.)

15.21 The inflammatory products filling the alveoli will exclude air so that gaseous exchange will be reduced. If the patient manages to cough these substances out in phlegm, the condition will be relieved. Physiotherapy is an aid to removal of phlegm. The physiotherapist is trained to beat the back and chest in such a way that the phlegm is detached from the walls of the bronchioles.

15.22 (a) The patient's temperature after the first day was 40 °C.
(b) Penicillin was probably responsible for the rapid lowering of temperature on the second day.

15.23 Diseases such as pneumonia are spread by droplet infection. Spread may be prevented by isolation of the patient, use of handkerchieves, covering and destruction of all sputum of the patient and good ventilation. Pneumonia may be prevented from developing by careful nursing of children with infectious diseases and of people suffering from other chest complaints. Elderly people should be kept warm and should eat properly.

15.24 Typhoid may be contracted by eating infected food and by drinking or bathing in infected water.

15.25 The symptoms of typhoid appear ten to fourteen days after infection. This is the incubation period.

15.26 The fever persists for over two weeks.

15.27 'Bloody Mary' was so called because she infected thousands of people with typhoid. Such carriers are highly dangerous, since they are a constant source of typhoid bacilli.

15.28 The problem of carriers may be overcome by tracing such people and treating them with an effective antibiotic to rid them of the typhoid bacilli.

15.29 Typhoid may be controlled by treating water supplies so that they are free from typhoid bacilli, ensuring that sewage disposal is hygienic and kept away from water supplies, excluding houseflies from access to human excreta and food, ensuring that hands are washed after visiting the toilet and before eating food, and isolating sufferers and tracing and treating carriers. Vaccination is given to people at risk, such as visitors to tropical countries who have no natural immunity to the disease. Europeans are not allowed to enter certain countries without an International Certificate of Vaccination against typhoid.

15.30 Two ways of avoiding the tragedy of a baby born with congenital syphilis are to seek treatment during the primary stage of syphilis, and to refrain from having indiscriminate sexual intercourse. Tests before marriage would identify infected potential parents, and these are required in some parts of the USA.

3 Microbial diseases – viruses

15.31 0.000 458 33 mm or 0.45 μm

15.32 Viruses have a protein shell; bacteria a polysaccharide cell wall. Viruses have no cytoplasm; bacteria have cytoplasm. Viruses have RNA or DNA; bacteria have nuclear material containing RNA and DNA. Viruses are not true cells; bacteria are true cells.

15.33 Replication of DNA during cell division is basically similar to replication of viruses. It is the DNA or RNA of the viruses which instruct the host cell to produce the new viruses.

15.34 Viruses are obligatory parasites; bacteria are free-living, saprophytic, parasitic and autotrophic (make their own food). Viruses reproduce by replication; bacteria reproduce by fission of the cell. Viruses can be crystallised and will later replicate in favourable conditions, whereas bacteria reproduce by fission of the cell. Bacteria cannot be crystallised. Viruses cannot be cultivated in the laboratory, whereas bacteria can be. Viruses do not grow before replication, whereas bacteria grow before cell division. Viruses do not need oxygen. They do not respire, but bacteria do respire. Viruses do not behave like living organisms. Many people believe that they are genes which have wandered away from their parent cell. This would explain why they will only replicate in one particular type of host cell.

15.35 (a) 1–2 days (b) 2 days (c) 6 days

15.36 First, send the girl home. Then open the windows to circulate air containing the viruses out of the room. It would be ideal to vacate the room until the air has recirculated.

15.37 People requiring antibiotics when suffering a common cold include babies, elderly people and those who have chronic chest complaints.

15.38 Some unfortunate victims of poliomyelitis suffer paralysis of their respiratory muscles. An iron lung is a mechanism which raises and lowers the chest to maintain breathing.

15.39 Extreme inflammation of the upper respiratory tract could lead to bronchitis or bronchopneumonia. Inflammation of the eyes in severe cases has resulted in blindness.

15.40 A vaccine is now available which is effective in giving immunity against measles. It is given to children over one year old.

15.41 All the examples described begin with common cold type symptoms or coryza. There are followed by fever, plus the specific symptoms of each disease. All the diseases are spread by infected droplets and are best contained by quarantine procedures.

15.42 Endemic diseases in the UK include mumps, measles, chickenpox, common cold, German measles and influenza.

4 Microbial diseases – fungi

15.43 Man becomes infected by a mould when one or more spores of that mould, carried in the air, alight on his body. The spore will germinate in the presence of warmth and moisture, both of which are present on the human body.

15.44 Ringworm is transmitted among schoolchildren by direct contact and by the sharing of combs, brushes, hats and other items of clothing.

15.45 Spread of ringworm may be prevented by training children to stop sharing each others' combs, brushes and towels.

15.46 Athlete's foot is common amongst communal bathers since they may share towels infected with *Tinea* spores. Inadequate drying of the feet between the toes will encourage germination of the spores.

15.47 Strict limitation of the use of towels will reduce the spread. Each person should have their own towel. Rigorous drying of the feet between the toes will reduce the possibilities of germination. Hygiene of the feet and regular changing of socks to reduce the effects of excessive sweating will also limit the disease. Public swimming pools often have disinfectant footbaths to prevent the spread of spores.

5 Microbial diseases – protozoa

15.48 *Plasmodium* travels first to the liver cells of man.

15.49 Multiplication of the parasite takes place first in the liver cells, then repeatedly in the red blood cells.

15.50 *Plasmodium* is sucked into the mosquito in the gamete form. Further development occurs inside the mosquito.

15.51 The zygote burrows into the stomach wall of the mosquito and multiplies to form thousands of sporozoites.

15.52 The sporozoites invade the salivary glands and are poured down the proboscis in the saliva.

15.53 Destruction of the *Anopheles* mosquito is the best method of preventing the spread of malaria (see section 7).

Destruction of the parasite in the blood and liver of man is possible using various anti-malarial drugs such as quinine, Paludrine and Daraprim. These drugs may be taken as a prevention. Daraprim only has to be taken once a week.

15.54 The fever returns every 48 hours. In some forms of malaria, fever occurs every 72 hours.

15.55 Fever recurs after each time the red blood cells burst to release merozoites into the blood. The length of time it takes the merozoites to multiply varies according to the *Plasmodium* species, which explains the different types of malaria.

6 Internal and external parasites

15.56 1 hooks; 2 suckers; 3 proglottids; 4 rostellum.

15.57 (a) In an immature proglottid, the dominant structures are the male and female reproductive organs.
(b) In a mature proglottid, the dominant structure is a uterus laden with eggs.
(c) The worm is both male and female, that is it is hermaphrodite.
(d) There are no digestive organs in the head or the proglottids.

15.58 The very flat, long structure of *Taenia* provides a huge surface area to volume ratio for rapid absorption of food.

15.59 *Taenia solium* is an excellent parasite for the following reasons.
(a) Its hooks and suckers secure it to the wall of the intestine.
(b) It is hermaphrodite, so is not dependent on a mate. A single worm will be able to perpetuate itself.
(c) It has a massive development of its reproductive organs and produces hundreds of thousands of eggs. Some of these eggs at least are sure to find a suitable secondary host.
(d) It has an excellent shape for maximum absorption of food from the host.

15.60 The very thick protective coat around the egg helps it to survive extremes of temperature as does the covering of faeces.

15.61 The cysticercus has an inverted head which resembles the head (scolex) of the adult.

15.62 Man becomes infected with cysticerci by eating raw or undercooked pork.

15.63 Tapeworm infestation may be avoided by:
(a) cooking all pork and pork products thoroughly,
(b) depositing faeces in flushable lavatories,
(c) keeping pigs away from sewage.

15.64 Thread worm infestation may be prevented by:
(a) regular changing of underwear,
(b) regular washing of the anal region,
(c) washing hands before meals and after using the toilet,
(d) cutting nails short so that thread worm eggs are less likely to lodge in them,
(e) washing bedclothes regularly, and
(f) keeping food covered.

15.65 Passage of the larvae of *Ascaris* through the lungs will probably cause the most damage. Inflammation of the alveoli, coughing and breathlessness may be caused.

15.66 Roundworm infection may be reduced by hygienic disposal of faeces, and by washing hands after using the toilet and before eating or preparing food.

15.67 Fleas are able to leap from one person to another.

15.68 Infestation with fleas may be avoided by eradicating rats, keeping the body and the clothes clean, and by using flea powders to kill the fleas.

15.69 The claws of the louse enable it to cling on to its host. The eggs are cemented onto hairs so that the larva will hatch on a suitable host.

15.70 (a) Head lice are easily caught by young children who frequently have their heads together while working or playing.
(b) The school nurse regularly examines the hair of schoolchildren to ensure that they are free of nits and lice.
(c) Individuals can avoid catching head lice by regular washing of the hair and by refraining from borrowing other people's combs. If lice are contracted, an application of paraffin oil about two hours before shampooing will kill both nits and lice.

15.71 The bedbug was associated with unclean bedding. These days most people change bed linen every week.

Homework question

1 Tuberculosis, pneumonia, *Streptococcus*, poliomyelitis, common cold, influenza, measles.
2 *Streptococcus* (septicaemia).
3 *Streptococcus*, ringworm, athlete's foot.
4 Typhoid, tapeworm, roundworm, threadworm.
5 Roundworm, tapeworm, typhoid, threadworm.
6 Typhoid, thread worm.
7 Tapeworm.
8 Plague, typhus fever, leptospirosis.
9 Malaria.
10 Typhoid, poliomyelitis.
11 Fleas.
12 Tapeworm
13 *Streptococcus* (impetigo), measles, ringworm, athlete's foot, fleas, lice, bedbugs.
14 syphilis; gonorrhoea.

7 Vectors

15.72 (a) The eggs of the mosquito have air floats to keep them close to the surface of the water so that they can obtain sufficient oxygen.
(b) The larvae have spiracles with tubes which open on to the surface of the water so that they can obtain oxygen from the air, and anal gills to enable them to extract oxygen from the water if they are disturbed and lose contact with the surface.
(c) The larvae have hairs to help them to float near the surface.
(d) The pupa has respiratory tubes for air breathing and anal gills for water breathing.

15.73 (a) The eggs, larvae and pupae can be destroyed by the introduction of predatory fish which will eat them.
(b) If stagnant water is drained, there will be no place for the eggs to be laid.
(c) If stagnant water is channelled to flow, the eggs will not develop into larvae.
(d) Oil sprayed on the surface of stagnant water blocks the respiratory tubes of the larvae and pupae and lowers the surface tension so that larvae and pupae sink.
(e) Spraying stagnant water with DDT has cleared many swamps of mosquitoes, but a lot of other life has been destroyed in the process (see Unit 20).
(f) Breeding grounds (long grass by stagnant water) and

buildings are sprayed with insecticide to destroy the adult mosquitoes.

(g) Mosquitoes may be prevented from attacking man by the use of mosquito netting over beds, windows and by using insect repellants.

15.74 Maggots 'wriggle' along. The hook at the anterior end sinks into the substrate to give anchorage, then the back of the body is drawn up by longitudinal muscles contracting. The hook is then released and circular muscles contract at the anterior end, propelling the maggot forward. Maggots are only able to suck. They pass digestive juices onto the substrate and suck up the soluble, liquid products.

15.75 If a housefly lands on a piece of meat after visiting and feeding on faeces, it will infect the meat with intestinal bacteria from the faeces which will be present in the saliva.

15.76 Houseflies may be prevented from contaminating food by:
1 keeping all food covered and away from houseflies,
2 keeping dustbins covered so that flies cannot feed on debris,
3 keeping dustbins well away from the kitchen,
4 covering compost heaps and flushing toilets so that houseflies will not alight on faeces,
5 killing houseflies with insecticide which will not harm people, for example pyrethrum.

8 Defence against disease

15.77 The goblet cells produce mucus which entangles the micro-organisms and the cilia waft them out of the nostrils.

15.78 Anti-histamine tablets or injections reduce the secretion of histamine.

15.79 A polymorph engulfs the *Streptococci*, then digests them, thus effectively removing them from the blood.

15.80 Following destruction of all the antigens, any remaining antitoxins or antibodies remain in the blood indefinitely and provide a lasting immunity to further attacks of the same type.

15.81 (a) At five years of age children go to school and are exposed to many more pathogens than when they are at home. A boost to their immunity at this stage could give them the extra protection they need.
(b) The rubella virus can damage a foetus during pregnancy, but only has a mild effect on children and adults. (See Unit 12.)

15.82 *Penicillium chrysogenus* is most effective against *Staphylococcus aureus (not R)*, *Bacillus subtilis* and *Sarcine lutea*. *Staphylococcus aureus R* is a resistant strain of the bacterium. Such resistance is causing great problems in hospitals. It may arise from over-prescription of penicillin and other antibiotics.

15.83 Septrin and Ampicillin should be most effective against typhoid.

15.84 Bacteria are resistant to many of the older antibiotics through overuse. See 15.82 and section 2 (typhoid).

15.85 The plate with distilled water showed profuse growth of bacterial colonies. This proves that bacteria were present to be acted against!

16 Non-infectious diseases

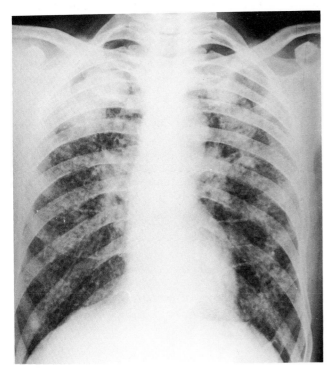

16.1 (a) X-ray photograph of the chest of a 60 year old coal miner

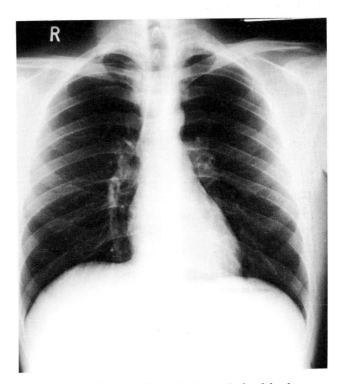

16.1 (b) X-ray photograph of the chest of a healthy farmer

This unit discusses a variety of diseases which are not caused by micro-organisms or larger parasites. For our purposes, these diseases may be classified into three broad categories:
(a) environmental diseases,
(b) organic diseases, and
(c) inherited diseases.
Diseases caused by deficiencies or excesses in the diet will be considered as a type of environmental disease.

1 Environmental diseases

In section 1 of Unit 15, lists of the major killer diseases in 1723 and 1965 were contrasted.

▶ Question

16.1 What are the major fatal diseases of the 20th century shown in Table 15.2?

Many of the diseases common today are contracted in part as a result of our way of life. Many occupations produce hazards which can cause disease; the food we eat can induce disease and the stress of competition in an acquisitive society is a factor contributing to two of today's lethal diseases – coronary thrombosis and cerebral haemorrhage (stroke).

Silicosis

For hundreds of years, people working in a dusty atmosphere, such as quarry and mine workers, have suffered from a debilitating lung disease called silicosis. Deposition of particles in the lung scars and damages the tissue. Many small nodules are visible on the lung in Fig 16.1(a). Fibrous tissue is formed by the lung in an attempt to seal off the particles. This will interfere with gaseous exchange.

▶ Question

16.2 Describe the ways in which the lung shown in Fig 16.1(a) differs from the healthy lung shown in Fig 16.1(b).

211

The condition becomes progressively worse, with the sufferer literally fighting for breath. Miners often develop chronic bronchitis and have a greater tendency to pulmonary tuberculosis than other people. The non-mining members of a mining community are also liable to silicosis.

Asbestosis

Another chronic lung disease caused by exposure to particles is asbestosis. Like silicosis, it takes a long time to develop, but it may occur years after a person has ceased to work with asbestos. There are several varieties of asbestos, which is the name given to fibrous mineral silicates. Blue asbestos, crocodilite, is the worst hazard. Its fibres cause extreme scarring of lung tissue and thickening of the surrounding pleural membranes. The symptoms are similar to those of silicosis: breathlessness and a cough, caused by emphysema. 50% of asbestosis sufferers later contract lung cancer. Continuous inspiration of the minute fibres of asbestos can eventually lead to the formation of an 'asbestos body' in many sufferers of pulmonary fibrosis (asbestosis). A number of fibres unite to form a 'talc crystal' which obviously impairs breathing.

Apart from people working in the manufacture of asbestos, individuals using asbestos building materials may also contract the disease. Ordinary talcum powder contains 10% asbestos – so take care with the talc!

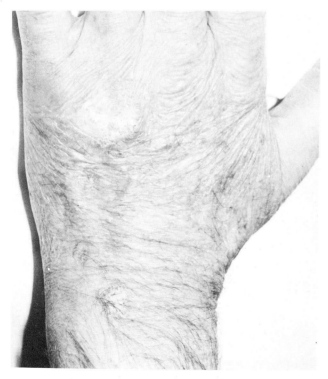

16.2 The scarred tissue on this man's hand is due to everyday contact with oil.

16.3 Suggest what occupation might give rise to the damage shown in Fig 16.2.

Radiation

A relatively recent environmental hazard is radioactivity resulting from the use of nuclear power. This will be discussed more fully in Unit 20. A disease associated with nuclear power workers is leukaemia or blood cancer. The white blood cells begin to divide erratically as a result of radiation-induced mutations (changes to a chromosome). As yet there is no effective cure for adult leukaemia. The men who used to paint the luminous figures on watch faces used to develop mouth cancer. Luminous paint contained a radioactive ingredient which contaminated the painter if he licked the brush.

▶ **Question**

16.4 Why has the incidence of this type of mouth cancer decreased in recent years?

Cancer

Cancer is the second major killer in Britain today. It is caused by the erratic uncontrollable division of cells. There are numerous forms of cancer and the possible 'triggers' of cancer at present seem almost as numerous. Though both heredity and micro-organisms were ruled out as causes of the disease at one time, they have both re-entered the list of possibilities. Certain viruses have been associated with a few cancers such as 'Birkett's lymphoma', a cancer of the face common in East Africa. Some scientists claim that they have proof that certain people inherit a tendency to develop cancer.

Table 16.1 Occurence of certain forms of cancer

Type of cancer	Countries where it is common
Lung cancer	UK, Western Europe, USA
Stomach cancer	Japan
Skin cancer	Tropical countries
Cancer of the colon	UK, Western Europe, USA*
Cancer of the oesophagus	China (Lin Xian Valley)

*Cancer of the colon has never been seen in some African countries.

▶ **Question**

16.5 Suggest a reason why certain types of cancer should be more common in some countries than in others.

In many instances, a contributing cause of a cancer can be traced to something in the environment. The environment contains many agents which can trigger off cancers. These agents are called carcinogens. Examples include a wide variety of chemicals such as hair dyes, aerosol propellants, paints, food ingredients (especially preservatives), tars, radiation and sunlight. Cigarette smoke as a carcinogen involved in lung cancer will be discussed in Unit 17.

Cancer of the colon is now associated with a lack of roughage in the diet. Lack of roughage can result in constipation and certain bacteria accumulating in the colon are thought to produce carcinogens which cause the disease. The high-roughage diet of Africans protect them from this form of cancer. The ultra-violet radiation in sunlight is thought to be the reason for the high incidence of skin cancer in tropical countries.

In parts of the remote Lin Xian Valley in China, one in four of the population contracted cancer of the oesophagus. It was then discovered that chickens feeding on the food scraps of these people were also developing cancer of the oesophagus. The people's diet included pickled cabbage on which moulds grew – a prized local delicacy. A team of local scientists discovered that these moulds produced a potent carcinogen – nitrosamine – and this was the prime cause of the high incidence of oesophageal cancer.

Coronary heart disease

The biggest killer of the 20th century in developed countries is disease associated with the heart and blood vessels. Of these diseases, **coronary thrombosis** is the most significant. A thrombus is a clot of blood. If a clot becomes lodged in the coronary artery, which supplies the heart muscle with blood, and therefore food and oxygen, the heart muscle will be damaged or destroyed.

16.3 (a) Cross-section of normal artery

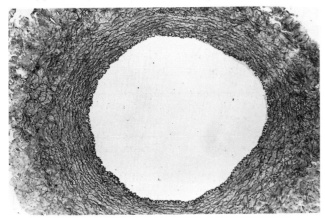

16.3 (b) Cross-section of a diseased artery partially blocked by an atheroma or fatty deposit

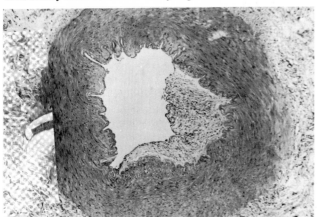

One of the main causes of heart disease is the hardening and thickening of the artery walls, known as atherosclerosis. The deposits which silt up the artery contain cholesterol. Cholesterol is a substance found in animal fats.

Research has shown that all the factors in Fig 16.4 contribute to coronary thrombosis.

Stroke is also caused by these factors. A clot lodging in the brain where blood vessels are constricted can produce a haemorrhage, destroying the brain cells. Death or paralysis may result, though recovery from minor strokes is usually good.

▶ Question

16.6 What test is carried out regularly by doctors to ensure that their patients are not developing hardened atherosclerotic arteries?

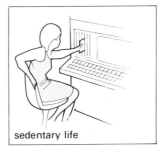
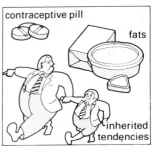

16.4 Factors contributing to coronary thrombosis

▶ Questions

16.7 What effect will the thickening of the artery walls have on blood flow?

16.8 List all the factors associated with coronary thrombosis. Describe the sort of person who is likely to suffer the disease.

16.9 Suggest ways of avoiding a heart attack or stroke.

Dietary diseases

Fig 16.5 is a photograph of a baby suffering from a protein deficiency disease called **kwashiorkor**. In this disease the skin peels and pigment becomes broken down causing patches to form on the skin. The abdomen becomes enormously distended. This disease is virtually confined to tropical countries,

213

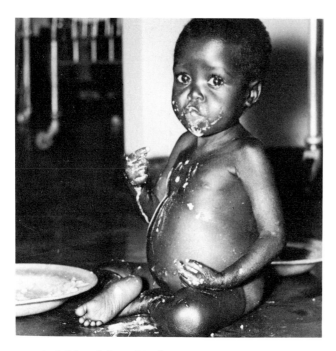

16.5 A child with kwashiorkor

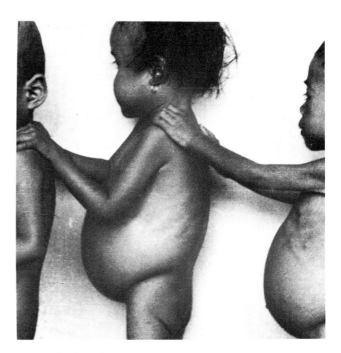

16.6 A child with marasmus

particularly parts of the African continent.

The child in Fig 16.6 is suffering from **marasmus**. This disease is characterised by muscular wasting and the general appearance of starvation.

▶ **Questions**

16.10 Why is kwashiorkor found in tropical countries?
16.11 Suggest the cause of marasmus.

In Unit 4, the roles of the various vitamins in the body were discussed. Listed below are six diseases which result from a deficiency of a particular vitamin.
1   Easy bruising, slow healing of wounds, susceptibility to infection and eventually scurvy. In scurvy there is extensive internal bleeding and the teeth very often drop out from damaged gums.
2   Rickets. The bones become soft and are unable to support the weight of the body, so the legs bend. Deficiency of this vitamin also increases the likelihood of tooth decay.
3   Lack of resistance to respiratory infections, poor night vision and a disease of the eyes called xerophthalmia or 'dry eye' are all due to a deficiency of one vitamin.
4   Beri-beri, a disease of the nerves, is common in people whose staple diet is 'polished' rice.
5   Pellagra, an acute form of dermatitis, is produced by a deficiency of a vitamin closely related to that needed to prevent 4.
6   Sterility, abortion and lack of sexual drive may be due to another vitamin deficiency.

▶ **Question**

16.12 From your knowledge of the role of vitamins in the body, identify the vitamin which is deficient in each of the diseases 1–6. Refer to Unit 4.

Lack of mineral salts in the diet will also produce symptoms of disease. Refer to Unit 4 to revise the function of the more important minerals in the body. Symptoms of mineral deficiency diseases are listed below.
1   Constant tiredness, a pale appearance characteristic of anaemia.
2   A tendency to excessive tooth decay.
3   Brittle bones.
4   A goitre (swelling) in the neck.
5   Slow blood clotting.

▶ **Questions**

16.13 Which minerals are necessary to relieve the symptoms in 1–5?
16.14 Suggest some of the consequences of overeating.

▷ **Homework**

Using newspapers and magazines make a list of as many suspected carcinogens as you can find.

2 Organic diseases

Many diseases are caused by a malfunctioning of the various organs or systems of the body. Here we will consider the results of the faulty production of some of the hormones of the endocrine system.

The goitre which is produced when there is a lack of iodine is due to the enlargement of the thyroid gland which is attempting to produce more thyroxin. Thyroxin is a hormone manufactured from iodine in the thyroid gland. Some people are not able to manufacture enough thyroxin even if sufficient iodine is available.

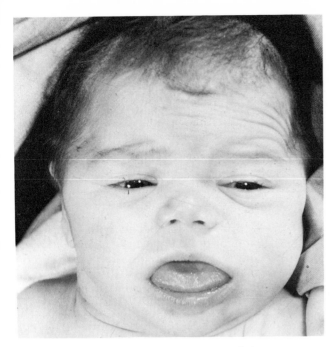

16.7 (a) 8 month old baby who is thyroxin deficient

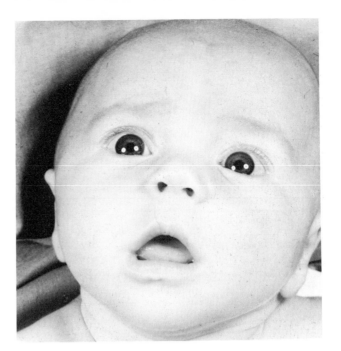

16.7 (b) The same baby after 3 months of thyroxin treatment

In Unit 11, the effects of a deficiency of insulin are discussed, and in Unit 12, the effects of a deficiency of the sex hormones are discussed.

16.8 Man suffering from abnormal phyone production

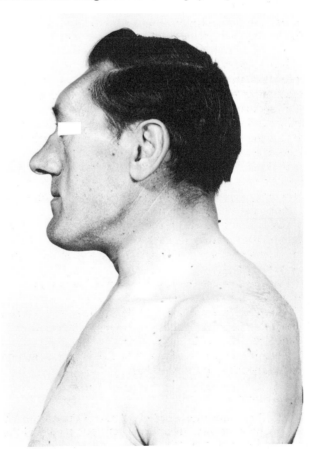

▶ **Questions**

16.15 What is the role of thyroxin in the body? Refer to Unit 9.
16.16 What are the results of a deficiency?
16.17 Describe the difference in the child in Fig 16.7(a) and (b) before and after treatment.

If the baby had been left untreated, she would have become a cretin. Lack of thyroxin slows down mental and physical growth. Even when fully physically grown, this girl might only have been the mental and physical age of a five-year-old. If an adult suffers from a defective thyroid later in life, myxodoema is the result. A lack of thyroxin makes the person sluggish and subject to cold because their basal metabolic rate drops. Mental processes are retarded, hair growth slows down and the skin thickens. If the thyroid becomes over-active in later life, the person suffers from thyrotoxicosis or exophthalmic goitre. This condition is characterised by bulging eyes and constant, restless over-activity.

The growth hormone, phyone, found in the anterior lobe of the pituitary gland, may be deficient. The result of this deficiency is a perfectly proportioned dwarf who never grows more than about three feet tall. In contrast to dwarfism, over-secretion of phyone produces giantism. Giants seven or eight feet tall are known in many parts of the world. They are in perfect proportion, but their bones have been stimulated to grow too fast by excess phyone.

▶ **Question**

16.18 Fig 16.8 shows a man, who is not a giant, but who is displaying an abnormal condition which is due to abnormal phyone production. Suggest how the abnormalities have occurred.

16.19 Construct a summary table of the following hormones under the following headings:

Hormone	Result of deficiency	Result of excess
Thyroxin		
Phyone		
Insulin		
Sex hormones		

▷ **Homework**

Find out about the effects of faulty production of the hormones cortisone, adrenalin and oxytocin.

3 Inherited diseases

Certain inherited diseases have already been outlined in Unit 14. One of these is caused by errors in the chromosomes. Many inherited diseases are caused by mutant genes on the autosomes (non-sex chromosomes). One such disease is mentioned in Unit 14 in connection with a hidden advantage.

▶ **Questions**

16.20 What are the inherited diseases discussed in Unit 14, and how are they inherited?
16.21 What is the disease caused by chromosome errors?
16.22 Name the disease with a hidden advantage.

Diseases caused by dominant mutant genes
Mutant genes on the autosomes causing disease may either be dominant or recessive in their effect.

16.9 A woman with achondroplasia

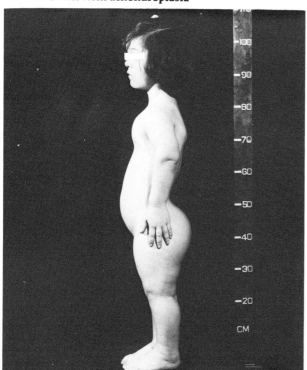

The individual in the photograph suffer from achondroplasia. These dwarfs are the typical circus dwarfs, with very large heads in proportion to their bodies. The upper parts of their arms and legs are particularly short. They are mentally normal, but physically not very fit. Many achondroplasic dwarfs die young, so that the frequency of the disease occurring is only 1 in 40 000.

▶ **Question**

16.23 Using appropriate symbols, work out the probabilities of the woman in Fig 16.9 giving birth to an achondroplasic child. Assume that the father is normal.

A relatively rare but very serious inherited disease due to a dominant mutant gene is a form of insanity caused by deterioration of brain tissue, Huntington's chorea. Onset of the disease is usually in the 30's, by which time the individual will possibly have already had children.

▶ **Question**

16.24 What will be the chance of the children of an affected individual developing the disease? Assume the other parent is normal.

Diseases caused by recessive mutant genes
The most common inherited disease is one which is caused by a recessive mutant gene. It is called cystic fibrosis and probably affects 1 in every 2000 individuals. It is caused by abnormally viscid (thick) mucus. The duct of the pancreatic gland becomes blocked by this mucus so that digestion of fats and proteins is incomplete. The smaller bronchioles become blocked and infection develops in the blocked ducts. At one time no sufferers survived to adulthood, but now with the introduction of penicillin, survival is common.

▶ **Questions**

16.25 What are the probabilities of a sufferer giving birth to a child with the disease (a) if married to a non-sufferer, and (b) if married to a carrier? Use suitable symbols to work out your answers.
16.26 What are the probabilities of a child being born with the disease if two carriers marry?

Carriers of one cystic fibrosis recessive gene appear to be normal, but tests are being developed to detect carriers. Sufferers have particularly high salt levels in their sweat, and it is possible that carriers have levels of salt above normal in their sweat.

One child in every 40 000 suffers from a disease called phenylketonuria. Tests on children in mentally handicapped institutions have shown that 1 in every 100 children who are mentally subnormal is suffering from phenylketonuria. The disease is due to a lack of the enzyme phenylalanine hydroxylase which breaks phenylalanine down to tyrosine. See Fig 16.10. A lack of tyrosine reduces the amount of melanin (pigment) production, so sufferers are usually fair-haired and have fair skin. The excess phenylalanine in the bloodstream produces lesions in the brain causing mental deficiency.

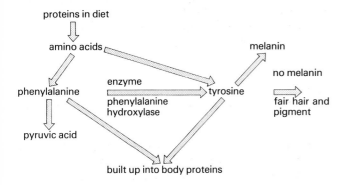

16.10 Action of phenylalanine hydroxylase

▶ **Question**

16.27 Refer back to Unit 4 and explain how the disease may be arrested in sufferers.

The disease may be detected by adding ferric chloride to a specimen of the baby's urine. A green colouration indicates phenylalanine derivatives which means that the individual has phenylketonuria. In recent years, attempts have been made to detect carriers of one recessive gene by testing the level of phenylalanine in the blood before breakfast.

▶ **Question**

16.28 Using appropriate symbols, work out the probabilities of a phenylketonuriac being born from a union of the following:
(a) a phenylketonuriac and a normal individual,
(b) two carriers.

Answers and discussion

1 Environmental diseases

16.1 The major killer diseases are coronary thrombosis, cancer, strokes, respiratory diseases and accidents.

16.2 The lung shown in Fig 16.1(a) shows cloudy areas where the lung tissue is tough and fibrous. The lung in Fig 16.1(b) is clear and healthy and much more effective at gaseous exchange.

16.3 This man worked as a motor mechanic and had oil on his hands all day. Not all people react to oil in this way.

16.4 Non-radioactive forms of luminous paint have been developed, and in any case many watches are now illuminated by light-emitting diodes (digital watches).

16.5 It could be argued that heredity is responsible for the distribution of cancers in the world, but if a European lives in Africa he is less likely to contract lung or colon cancers and more likely to contract skin cancer or Birkett's lymphoma. This being the case, there must be environmental reasons involved in the distribution of these types of cancer.

16.6 The patients' blood pressure is measured. High blood pressure is one sign of hardened arteries.

16.7 Thickening of the artery walls will increase the resistance of the artery wall to blood flow. This will make the heart work harder to pump blood around the body, and increase the blood pressure.

16.8 Coronary thrombosis is associated with overeating, lack of exercise, mental stress, cigarette smoking, too much sugar and animal fat in the diet, high levels of blood cholesterol, the contraceptive pill and an inherited tendency to the disease. Males are five times more prone to coronary heart disease than pre-menopausal females. Oestrogen is thought to protect women in some way. A typical candidate for a coronary is a businessman who drives to work, sits at his desk all day, works under great pressure, has a rich business lunch and smokes and drinks a lot.

16.9 To prevent a stroke or heart attack, avoid overeating, particularly sweet and rich (animal fat) food, take regular exercise, find time to relax, avoid smoking, and only take the contraceptive pill if there are no cases of thrombosis in your family.

16.10 Consumption of protein is very low in many tropical countries. The staple diet is largely carbohydrate – yams, cassava, rice and maize. Some legumes are eaten such as cowpeas and soyabeans, but very little meat. Children are often the first to go without food and thousands of children have kwashiorkor. They usually develop the disease after weaning from mother's milk.

16.11 Marasmus is caused by a generally inadequate intake of food. It is sometimes called protein-calorie deficiency, since neither enough protein nor carbohydrate is consumed.

16.12 1 vitamin C; 2 vitamin D; 3 vitamin A; 4 vitamin B_1; 5 vitamin B_5 (niacin); 6 vitamin E.

16.13 1 iron; 2 calcium and phosphorus; 3 calcium and phosphorus; 4 iodine; 5 calcium.

16.14 General overeating leads to obesity (overweight) which is often associated with the major diseases apart from cancer. In addition to increasing the likelihood of disease,

217

obesity can cause social problems, difficulty in dress and exercise, and increased inclination to sweating. Excess sugar and cholesterol in the diet may be contributing factors to coronary heart disease.

2 Organic diseases

16.15 Thyroxin controls the basal metabolism.

16.16 A deficiency of thyroxin will reduce the basal metabolic rate.

16.17 Before treatment the baby had protruding eyes and a protruding tongue. Her eyes looked dull. After treatment her eyes look normal and bright and her tongue no longer protrudes. Her skin is no longer flabby and loose.

16.18 The man in Fig 16.8 has very large hands and an abnormally heavy brow and large nose. This suggests that the bones have begun to grow again, to alter his body proportions. Excess phyone must have been produced after maturity. This condition is called acromegaly.

16.19

Hormone	Results of a deficiency	Results of an excess
Thyroxin	Cretinism (retarded mental and physical growth), myxoedema	Exophthalmic goitre
Phyone	Dwarfism (limited bone growth)	Giantism, acromegaly
Insulin	Sugar diabetes; coma	Coma
Oestrogen Testosterone	Underdevelopment of secondary sexual characteristics	Overdevelopment of secondary sexual characteristics

3 Inherited diseases

16.20 These diseases are haemophilia, red-green colour blindness, duchenne muscular dystrophy and diabetes insipidus. They are sex-linked diseases caused by a recessive mutant gene on an X chromosome.

16.21 Mongolism is the disease caused by defective chromosomes.

16.22 Sickle cell anaemia is an example of a disease caused by a recessive mutant gene on the autosomes which has a hidden advantage.

16.23 Let A stand for achondroplasia, a stand for normal growth.

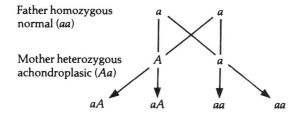

Father homozygous normal (aa)

Mother heterozygous achondroplasic (Aa)

The probability of mother giving birth to an achondroplasic dwarf is 50%.

16.24 There will be a 50% chance of the children developing Huntington's chorea.

16.25 (a) An individual with cystic fibrosis will have two recessive genes, cc, a normal individual two normal genes CC

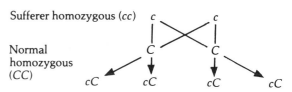

Sufferer homozygous (cc)

Normal homozygous (CC)

None of these offspring will have cystic fibrosis. They will all be carriers.

(b)

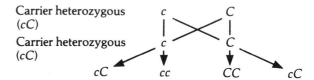

Sufferer homozygous (cc)

Carrier heterozygous (cC)

50% of these offspring will have cystic fibrosis and 50% will be carriers.

16.26

Carrier heterozygous (cC)

Carrier heterozygous (cC)

25% of these offspring will have the disease, 50% will be carriers and 25% normal.

16.27 Phenylketonuria may be controlled by use of a phenylalanine-free diet.

16.28 (a) A pheynlketonuriac will have two recessive mutant genes, pp. A normal individual will have two normal genes, PP.

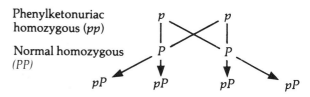

Phenylketonuriac homozygous (pp)

Normal homozygous (PP)

None of these individuals will be phenylketonuriacs. They are all carriers.

(b)

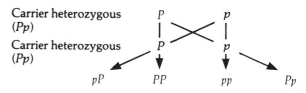

Carrier heterozygous (Pp)

Carrier heterozygous (Pp)

25% of these offspring will be phenylketonuriacs, 50% carriers and 25% normal.

17 Personal health care

17.1 A girl who cares for her personal health . . .

17.2 . . . and a man who is less concerned

1 Good and bad habits

You yourself have more influence over your own health than any other single factor. Care of your body, clothing, eating habits, sleeping habits and daily activities are all under your control. Good health is largely a question of learning good habits early in life.

▶ **Question**

17.1 List all the ways in which the girl illustrated in Fig 17.1 looks after herself better than the man in Fig 17.2. What bad habits are suggested by Fig 17.2?

Make a list of the good habits you have which help to keep you healthy. Then try to find at least two bad habits you have.

2 Care of skin and hair

The surface of the skin is covered with sebum from the sebaceous glands, sweat which contains salts, urea and other organic substances, and bacteria and other parasites.

▶ **Questions**

17.2 Which experiment in Unit 15 demonstrates the presence of bacteria on the skin? In what conditions did appreciably more bacteria than usual appear to be present on the skin?
17.3 Explain why bacteria and fungi can live successfully on the skin.

If sebum, sweat and dirt are not regularly washed off the skin, then substances accumulate in the pores and become visible as blackheads. These may become the centre of skin infections. Impetigo and erysepelas are two infections of the skin caused by *Streptococcus*.

Pimples and boils are usually caused by bacterial infections. Some pimples are produced by *Streptococcus* bacteria and some by *Staphylococcus* bacteria. Boils are caused by *Staphylococcus*.

Washing in water alone is not sufficient because it does not remove accumulated sebum. Sebum is an oil and soap is needed to dissolve and remove it. Shampoo for washing hair is basically a liquid soap which dissolves the sebum in the hair and removes it. Some oil is necessary to lubricate the hair, but excess oil makes the hair greasy and encourages parasites.

▶ **Questions**

17.4 When is it particularly important to wash your hands?
17.5 Name a common parasite which lives in hair.

17.3 (a) Some people have skin which is sensitive to their clothing.

If possible it is advisable to have a bath every day. Sweat and sebum collect and bacteria flourish where skin surfaces meet, such as in the groin.

In addition to washing it may be helpful to use a deodorant. A deodorant disguises the odour produced by the organic substances in sweat. Particularly in hot conditions, with profuse sweating, body odour can be unpleasant and embarrassing. Care should be taken when selecting a deodorant. Some preparations also claim to be anti-perspirant.

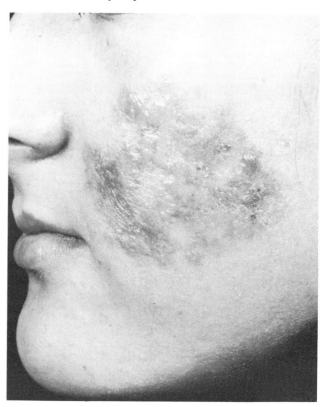

17.3 (b) An allergic reaction on the face

▶ **Questions**

17.6 Why is it not advisable to use an anti-perspirant?
17.7 Suggest the possible causes of the allergic reactions illustrated in Fig 17.3. How may such reactions be avoided?

A cosmetic in common use today is hair dye. Some individuals are allergic to the bleach, present in permanent hair dyes (lasting for up to six months). It can cause extreme irritation. Even more serious is the recent evidence to suggest that both permanent dyes and toners (also called rinses, semi-permanent dyes) may be carcinogenic.

▶ **Question**

17.8 What does a carcinogen do? Refer to Unit 16.

▷ **Research project**

Carry out a survey to discover the different types of shampoo available on the market. Note their contents. Find out about the role of a conditioner in hair care.

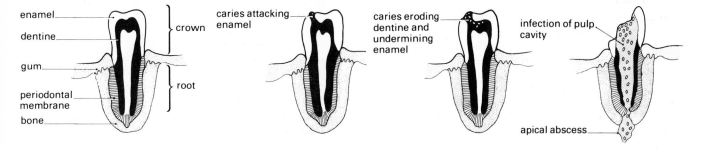

enamel

dentine

gum

periodontal membrane

bone

crown

root

caries attacking enamel

caries eroding dentine and undermining enamel

infection of pulp cavity

apical abscess

17.4 Progress of dental decay due to caries

3 Care of the teeth

The internal structure of a tooth is discussed in Unit 5. Teeth are living structures growing in an environment where numerous bacteria flourish. Though enamel is the hardest substance in the body, it is not totally immune to digestion by the acid produced when the bacteria digest sugar left in the mouth.

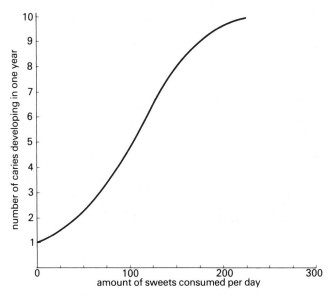

17.5 Incidence of dental caries in a group of young children

▶ **Questions**

17.9 How many dental caries were found on average in children who did not eat any sweets?
17.10 How many dental caries were found on average in children who consumed 100 g of sweets in a week?
17.11 What can you deduce from the graph?
17.12 Name the substances from which enamel is constructed.
17.13 Which foods in the diet will supply these substances?

Strong enamel is a good deterrent to tooth decay. There is evidence to suggest that enamel on teeth in well-exercised jaws is stronger than enamel which is not. Eskimos do not suffer from tooth decay for this reason, and because they have a very low-sugar diet.

▶ **Questions**

17.14 What is the diet of eskimos and how does it help to strengthen enamel?
17.15 List the components of a diet which could help to prevent tooth decay.
17.16 (a) What is the number of decayed teeth per 100 children with 0.5 ppm fluoride in the water in Fig 17.6?
(b) What is the number of decayed teeth per 100 children with 1 ppm of fluoride in the water?
17.17 What can you deduce from the graph?

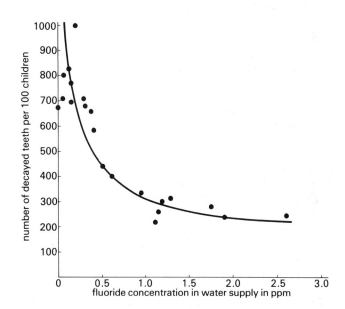

17.6 Effect of fluoride concentrations in the water on tooth decay

Periodontal disease, or disease of the gums and fibrous (periodontal) membrane accounts for most of the teeth lost later in life. Gums become soft and inflamed and shrink away from the teeth. The fibres in the fibrous membrane become damaged, break and the tooth becomes loose in its socket. **Plaque** is the main cause of periodontal disease.

Activity 17.1   To show the beginning of plaque

Suck an erythrosine tablet, then look in a mirror.

▶ **Question**

17.18 Describe what you see.

Plaque is a hard deposit which builds up on the teeth. It consists of a mixture of mucus, food debris, insoluble carbohydrates, bacteria and enzymes. Build-up of plaque on the base of a tooth causes destruction of the fibrous membrane. Plaque is also a contributory factor in tooth decay.

Cleaning the teeth
Regular cleaning of the teeth with toothpaste and water reduces the amount of tooth decay and periodontal disease.

▶ **Questions**

17.19 Why should brushing the teeth reduce tooth decay and periodontal disease?

17.20 Describe the best way of cleaning your teeth, using Fig 17.7 as a basis.

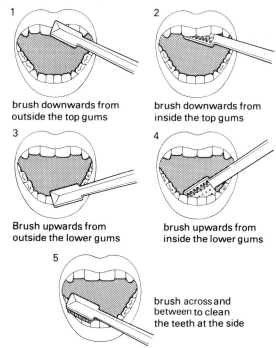

1 brush downwards from outside the top gums

2 brush downwards from inside the top gums

3 Brush upwards from outside the lower gums

4 brush upwards from inside the lower gums

5 brush across and between to clean the teeth at the side

17.7 Correct brushing of the teeth

The toothbrush used is important. Very soft bristles will not dislodge food particles and hard bristles could damage the gums and make them bleed. A good compromise is a brush which has medium strength bristles on the outside and harder bristles in the middle.

Toothpaste contains an abrasive substance which helps to remove the film which may produce plaque. Over-abrasive toothpaste could damage the enamel. Some toothpaste contains fluoride which could be of help in areas where there is no fluoride added to the water supply. Toothpaste also contains a mild antiseptic to help remove bacteria from the mouth.

Treatment
A very important part of caring for the teeth is to visit the dentist regularly. A careful look at Fig 17.4 will show the basic reason for this.

▶ **Question**

17.21 How can regular visits to a dentist prevent tooth loss?

In addition, many dentists employ a dental hygienist who removes dental plaque regularly. This particularly helps to keep the gums healthy by reducing the likelihood of infection.

Tooth decay may damage the general health. When decay reaches the root, toxins liberated by the bacteria may set up an abscess at the base of the root. If the abscess bursts, there is a chance that the bacterial toxins will enter the bloodstream. In some circumstances septicaemia (blood poisoning) may be the result and frequently the digestive system will be affected.

▷ **Homework**

Write a summary of all the things you can do to ensure that your teeth are kept in a healthy condition.

4 Sensible use of clothes

Good grooming involves care with clothes. Care begins with regular cleaning and pressing of clothes. Just as the skin carries millions of bacteria, so do our clothes (see Activity 15.1). Washing clothes with recommended washing powders removes dirt and bacteria. It is very important to rinse clothes thoroughly, particularly since some washing powders may cause allergic reactions.

▶ **Question**

17.22 Apart from improving the appearance of clothes, suggest another function of pressing (ironing) the clothes.

One of the main functions of clothes is to help us to maintain a constant body temperature (see Unit 11).

Table 17.1 Properties of clothes

Property	A	B	C
1 Colour	Very dark	Bright	Very light
2 Material	Cotton	Wool	Nylon
3 Layers and thickness	One thick layers	Several layer	One thin layer
4 Fit	Tight	Loose	Close

▶ **Question**

17.23 Colours, material, number and thickness of layers and the fit of clothes are all-important when considering what to wear in different climates. Table 16.1 lists the possible choices under A B and C.
(a) Select the combination of properties you would choose in a very hot climate and explain your choice.
(b) Select the combination of properties you would choose in a very cold climate and again explain your choice.

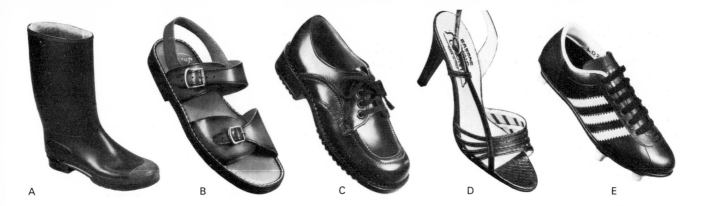

A   B   C   D   E

17.8 Various types of footwear

Footwear is a very important item of clothing and we are fortunate in being able to obtain a very wide range of shoes and boots to suit our every need. The importance of correctly fitting shoes has already been discussed in Unit 13.

▶ **Question**

17.24 Suggest a suitable occasion for wearing each of the types of footwear illustrated.

▷ **Research**

Deep-sea divers working in the North Sea, and astronauts working in the space shuttle, wear special clothes. Find out what their clothes are like and explain how they help overcome some of the problems of the divers and astronauts.

5 Exercise, rest and sleep

The importance of exercise in the maintenance of bodily health has already been emphasised in Unit 3.

▶ **Question**

17.25 List all the reasons you can remember why exercise is important for the body.

Exercise is also a form of relaxation. As a total change from a routine which may involve a lot of mental activity, exercise can help to clear the mind and relieve stress.

Rest is essential for health of body and mind. Rest does not necessarily mean stretching out in the sun or in front of the television. It can be a gentle stroll in the country or pottering in the garden or enjoying a drink of coffee with a group of friends. Again it is a break from routine.

Sleep is a state of lowered metabolism which practically everyone must undergo regularly in order to survive. During sleep, when the conscious part of the brain is inactive, many vital processes such as repair and growth are able to proceed unhindered. The reason for our need of sleep is still something of a mystery, but the results of lack of sleep give a clue. Individuals vary greatly in their sleep requirements, but very young people need more sleep than older people. An average adult sleeps one-third of his life away, but the quality of the remaining two-thirds is undoubtedly better for it.

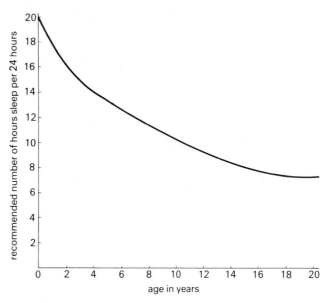

17.9 Sleep requirements in hours per 24 hours according to age

▶ **Questions**

17.26 How can you tell that a person is suffering from a lack of sleep?

17.27 Using Fig 17.9 give the sleep requirements in terms of hours per twenty-four hours of the following:
(a) a newborn baby,
(b) a two-year-old,
(c) a four-year-old,
(d) a ten-year-old,
(e) a twelve-year-old,
(f) a fourteen-year-old,
(g) an adult.

▷ **Homework**

Compile a questionnaire to discover how much sleep each of the following takes on average, every twenty-four hours:
(a) a parent, (b) a brother, sister or friend aged 3–7 years,
(c) a brother, sister or friend aged 10–14 years.

223

6 The smoking habit

Every pack of cigarettes sold in Britain carries a Government health warning: 'Cigarettes can seriously damage your health'. Why should cigarettes damage your health and, if it is true, why do people continue to smoke?

Activity 17.2   Investigating the contents of a cigarette

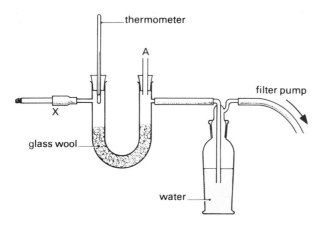

17.10

1   Set up the apparatus as shown in Fig 17.10.
2   A second apparatus without a cigarette should also be set up.
3   Allow the filter pump to run gently and place a finger periodically over 'A' causing air to be drawn through the cigarette.

▶ Questions

17.28   What is the purpose of the apparatus without a cigarette?
17.29   What is the difference in the appearance of the glass wool in the two U-tubes?
17.30   How would you use this experiment to compare the levels of tar obtained from plain and filter-tipped cigarettes?

Tar is one of several substances present in cigarette smoke which are thought to be carcinogenic. Because of this, manufacturers have developed special low tar brands. However, many smokers turning to the low tar brands in the interest of their health find that they smoke more cigarettes, so that their total exposure to tar is the same.

There is direct evidence to suggest that it is the combustion products of sugar in cigarettes which are the most dangerous carcinogens. This has been demonstrated in experiments exposing rats to smoke from cigarettes of different types. Indirect evidence is that French cigarettes have a very high tar content and a low sugar content, while English cigarettes have low tar and high sugar. This is due to the different methods used for curing the tobacco. Lung cancer deaths in England are four times as frequent as comparable deaths in France.

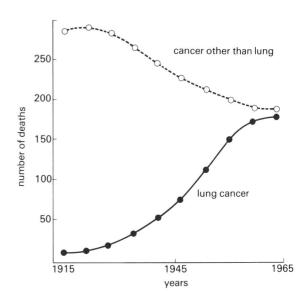

17.11 Incidence of deaths from lung cancer and from other forms of cancer per 100 000 men between 45 and 64

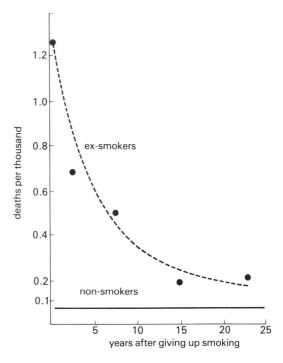

17.12 Incidence of deaths from lung cancer in ex-smokers and non-smokers

▶ Questions

17.31   Why can Fig 17.11 be used as evidence to suggest that lung cancer is associated with the smoking habit?
17.32   From Fig 17.12 how much more likely is someone who has just given up smoking to get lung cancer compared with a non-smoker?
17.33   How much more likely is an ex-smoker who gave up smoking ten years ago to contract lung cancer compared with a non-smoker?
17.34   What can be deduced from this graph?

The heavy smoker who continues to smoke forty cigarettes a day has a much greater risk of contracting lung cancer than a smoker who limits himself to about five a day. Lung cancer is almost invariably a fatal disease.

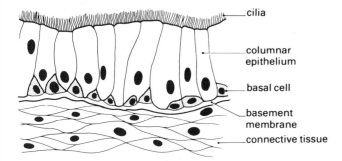

17.13 (a) normal epithelium of a lung

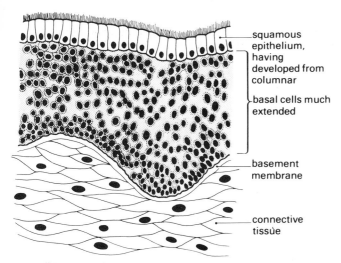

7.13 (b) diseased epithelium of a smoker's lung

17.13 (c) diseased epithelium developing a tumour

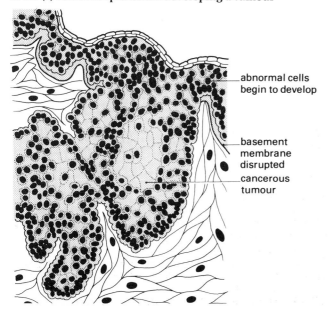

▶ **Questions**

17.35 (a) What change has occurred in Fig 17.13(b)?
(b) What change has occured in Fig 17.13(c)?
17.36 How would the health of a smoker with bronchial epithelium like that shown in Fig 17.13(c) be affected?
17.37 In what way is the epithelium in Fig 17.13(c) more abnormal than that shown in Fig 17.13(b)?

Chronic bronchitis and emphysema are diseases commonly associated with smoking. They are contracted as a result of continuous respiratory infections bombarding the lungs in the absence of cilia.

▶ **Question**

17.38 What is the effect shown in Fig 17.14 of air pollution on respiratory disease in ageing smokers compared with ageing non-smokers?

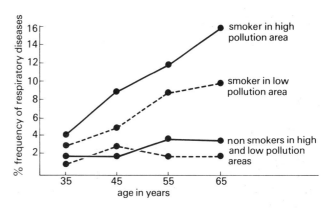

17.14 Respiratory disease in smokers and non-smokers in areas of high and low air pollution

Apart from the carcinogens, carbon monoxide and nicotine are also present in cigarette smoke. Carbon monoxide has an even greater affinity for haemoglobin than oxygen. The carboxyhaemoglobin formed is a bright cherry red. It prevents oxygen transport by the blood and is the cause of death in many suicides when car exhaust fumes are used.

Nicotine is a drug which slows down transmission of impulses at synapses and motor end plates. It is a sedative and mild nerve poison. It is this nicotine which gives the smoker a feeling of relaxation.

It is the combined effect of carbon monoxide and nicotine which is thought to increase the risk of coronary thrombosis in smokers. Smokers aged about fifty are roughly three times more likely to suffer from coronary thrombosis than non-smokers. This is partly because nicotine increases the demand of the heart for oxygen, while carbon monoxide reduces available oxygen.

▶ **Question**

17.39 Smokers are said to give birth to smaller babies than non-smokers and it is even claimed that babies born to smokers are less intelligent. Suggest which ingredients of cigarette smoke could cause this.

A smoker runs the risk of suffering from the following diseases: cancer of the lung, mouth and oesophagus, bronchitis, emphysema, recurring respiratry infections, gastric and peptic ulcers, coronary thrombosis, paralysis, undersized, less intelligent babies and a reduced sex drive. The smell of smoke in the hair and clothes of a heavy smoker may also be a social handicap, as may nicotine-stained fingers and teeth.

7 The alcohol habit

Whereas smoking has recently become socially unacceptable to many people, there is still widespread tolerance of alcohol consumption. Many social gatherings are for drinks and teenagers are becoming more and more drawn towards pubs.

Alcohol is a dangerous drug. It has a powerful effect on the central nervous system. It slows down reactions, giving the consumer a feeling of well-being. It dulls perceptions and lowers people's inhibitions – a drinker becomes less conscious of himself and will do things which he would not normally consider doing. The hangover experienced after an evening of heavy drinking has become a social problem. Many working days in this country are lost through sickness and headache following a night out. Even more serious is the effect of drink on driving. Fig 17.15 compares a driver who has not consumed any alcohol with a driver who has consumed three pints of beer.

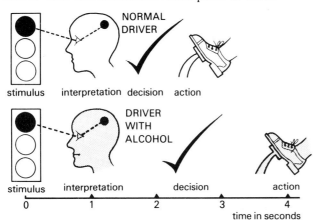

stimulus | interpretation decision action

NORMAL DRIVER

stimulus | interpretation | decision | action

DRIVER WITH ALCOHOL

0 | 1 | 2 | 3 | 4
time in seconds

17.15 Reaction times for a normal driver compared with those for a driver with a high blood alcohol level (80 mg/100 ml) (from the Transport Canada publication "Smashed").

▶ Questions

17.40 How much longer does the driver with alcohol take to react to the red traffic light by applying his brakes?

17.41 If both drivers are in cars travelling at 15 metres per second (33½ mph) how much further will the driver with alcohol travel before he even begins to apply his brakes?

17.42 If both cars need 60 m to stop in after the brakes are applied, and if the red traffic light comes on when both cars are 100 m from the road junction, travelling at 15 ms⁻¹, will both drivers be able to stop in time?

17.43 Under what conditions is it particularly dangerous to drink and drive?

Until the introduction of the breathalyser test in this country, hundreds of individuals were killed or injured as a result of the slow reactions of drivers who had consumed alcohol. Few people now risk consuming above the allowed limit for driving. Anyone found to have above 80 mg of alcohol in 100 ml of blood while driving is commiting an offence. A blood test is taken from anyone whose breath turns the crystals in the breathalyser green. 80 mg/100 ml in a young 150 lb man is roughly equivalent to 1½ pints of lager or cider, two pints of draught bitter, two schooners of sherry or three single whiskies. Wine is particularly difficult to assess, but three glasses of table wine would put you over the limit. Blood alcohol levels depend on weight, age, sex and individual tolerance as well as the amount you drink.

Habitual drinkers are at greater risk than casual drinkers. Research has shown that people whose blood contains 80 mg of alcohol/100 ml of blood at least once a day are in danger of developing cirrhosis of the liver. Alcohol is absorbed in the stomach and much of it passes straight to the liver. It literally pickles the liver, which becomes hardened and the cells no longer function. Many habitual drinkers die from cirrhosis. Habitual drinking also leads to deterioration of brain cells. The British Medical Association recently published evidence of a decline in memory and reasoning over a long period in drinkers which was not paralleled in non-drinkers.

Addiction to alcohol is on the increase. Several thousand individuals in this country succumb to alcoholism every year. One professional group which has a particularly large proportion of alcoholics is the medical profession.

An alcoholic becomes so dependent on the drug that he experiences severe physical withdrawal symptoms if alcohol is witheld. Hospital treatment may be necessary. An organisation called Alcoholics Anonymous arranges meetings of alcoholics where they attempt to talk each other through their problems.

▷ Homework

Find out about Alcoholics Anonymous.

8 The drugs habit

A drug is a substance which modifies the way in which the body operates. So called dangerous drugs all affect the functioning of the central nervous system. Of these drugs, only alcohol, nicotine, barbiturates and other sleeping pills are 'socially acceptable'. It is illegal to use any of the drugs mentioned in this section unless they are on prescription.

Drug dependence can often begin as a social habit in the same way that alcohol consumption starts.

Cannabis

In the early 1970s it was estimated that about a third of the student population in the UK had smoked 'pot' or marihuana. Extracted from Indian hemp, this drug gives an effect of well-being, alters the appreciation of time and space and in some subjects may even produce hallucinations. Large doses produce mental confusion and there is some evidence to show that a pregnant woman who habitually smokes cannabis has an increased risk of a deformed baby being born to her.

The effect of cannabis wears off in a similar time span to alcohol, but instead of being excreted in the urine, it accumulates in the fat reserves of the body.

Pressure groups have campaigned hard for the legalisation of cannabis which is not physically addictive as are the 'hard' drugs.

▶ **Question**

17.44 Do you consider that there is a case for the legalisation of cannabis? Justify your answer.

LSD

Lysergic acid diethylamine is a notorious hallucinatory or mood-disturbing drug. A person taking LSD is said to 'go on a trip'. Perceptions are drastically altered and the subject sees bright colours and patterns and may even imagine that they have the power of flight. The drug acts on the synapses and nerve endings.

▶ **Question**

17.45 What is the immediate danger of taking such a drug?

It has happened that an individual has experienced a repeat performance of the trip much later, without taking any more LSD. The drug is a proven mutagen – it damages chromosomes causing the birth of deformed babies to mothers who habitually take the drug. Physical dependence on the drug is not the rule, though psychological dependence may develop.

Sedatives

There is an increasing tendency amongst people who cannot sleep and who are prescribed barbiturates, to become dependent on these drugs. Barbiturates depress activity in the cerebral cortex and slow reaction time by depressing the cerebellum. A serious withdrawal symptom if barbiturates are witheld is convulsions.

▶ **Question**

17.46 What other drug produces similar effects to barbiturates and why must the two drugs never be taken together?

Stimulants

Amphetamines are drugs which maintain alertness and increase energy, wakefulness and drive. They are usually mood-elevating and were often taken by pop groups who needed to keep awake and active for long periods at pop festivals. Individuals have been known to go without sleep for two or three days on amphetamines, but this is followed by fatigue, irritability and depression. Any underlying tensions

or anxieties will be exaggerated by use of these drugs and in some cases schizophrenic symptoms have been produced. Physical dependence may result.

Tranquillisers

The most widely consumed drugs today are undoubtedly the tranquillising drugs prescribed by doctors to millions of anxious patients. These drugs, the benzodiazepines, include Librium, Valium and Medezepam. They act on the limbic system, a part of the cerebrum concerned with emotional reactions. They reduce muscular tension and relieve anxiety. Unfortunately they can induce dependence and many people who habitually take tranquillisers appear less alert than formerly. Strong tranquillising drugs such as chloropromazine are used with good effect to treat schizophrenia.

▶ **Question**

17.47 Suggest an alternative to tranquillising drugs for people suffering from anxieties.

Narcotics

By far the most dangerous of all the drugs are the so-called 'hard' drugs. These include opium and its derivatives – morphine and heroin, and cocaine. All these drugs are occasionally used as analgesics (pain-killers) by the medical profession. They operate on

▶ **Question**

17.48 Explain how this act may be the cause of death of an addict rather than the actual effects of addiction.

17.16 Heroin addict injecting himself

centres in the brain which perceive pain and as a result perception is dulled, anxiety relieved and a state of euphoria (well-being) achieved. If taken regularly, the body becomes tolerant to these drugs so that increased amounts are necessary to produce the same effect. Withdrawal symptoms from large doses are extreme, with sweating, cramps, nausea and vomiting. Addiction to heroin is extremely difficult to stop. Clinics are in operation where addicts are gradually weaned off heroin onto a substance called physeptone, a synthetic opiate which is less addictive. Cure rates are not encouraging, and a heroin addict becomes uncaring about his general health, loses his appetite for food and sex and lives only for his next fix.

▷ **Homework**

Use references to find out information about the more common dangerous drugs in use. For each drug record the effect the drug has on the body and try to find out what long-term problems may be associated with dependence.

Answers and discussion

1 Good and bad habits

17.1 The girl in Fig 17.1 has developed the following good habits.
(a) She takes care of her clothes. They are clean, well-pressed and neat.
(b) She regularly washes her hair and keeps it tidy.
(c) Her teeth are well-brushed and in good condition.
(d) Her clean, clear skin is regularly washed.
(e) She keeps her nails clean and reasonably short.
(f) Her posture is good, which will help to maintain general health (see Unit 3).
(g) She eats a balanced diet and does not overeat.
(h) Her alert expression suggests that she has adequate sleep.
Bad habits suggested in Fig 17.2 are: inadequate washing of hair, skin and clothes, and poor posture.

2 Care of skin and hair

17.2 Activity 15.1 on growing bacteria included agar plates of finger prints. Far more colonies are produced from dirty finger prints than from clean finger prints, which suggests that bacteria are associated with dirt.

17.3 Bacteria and fungi thrive on reasonably clean skin because it is warm, moist (insensible perspiration) and some bacteria can feed on the sebum.

17.4 Hands must be washed after visiting the toilet to avoid intestinal infection. It is also advisable to wash hands before eating.

17.5 Head louse, *Pediculus* is a parasite in hair.

17.6 An anti-perspirant, by reducing perspiration, could interfere with the cooling process in very hot conditions.

17.7 The allergy in Fig 17.3(a) is a reaction to the elastic rubber waistband of the man's underpants, and that in Fig 17.3(b) on the face is a reaction against cosmetic face creams.

As more and more special additives are being used in the preparation of washing powders and cosmetics, so the possibility of certain people reacting against some of these substances increases. Since there are so many different brands of both detergents and cosmetics on the market, it should be possible for most people to find one to which they are not allergic. A few extra sensitive people cannot use any detergents and some individuals cannot tolerate any cosmetics. Now 'pure' cosmetics are produced for such people. A lot of research is carried out to ensure that all such products are free of irritants.

17.8 A carcinogen is a cancer-producing agent.

3 Care of the teeth

17.9 Children not eating sweets had an average of one dental carie in a year.

17.10 Children eating 100 g of sweets per day had four or five dental caries in one year.

17.11 Incidence of dental caries increases with consumption of sweets. Sugar, as a soluble carbohydrate, is a major contributing factor in tooth decay. Fizzy soft drinks, which contain a lot of sugar are especially likely to cause tooth decay.

17.12 Enamel is made from calcium and phosphorus salts. It is principally calcium phosphate.

17.13 Dairy products such as milk, butter, cheese and eggs supply these substances, together with vitamin D which is essential for the assimilation of calcium and phosphorus into enamel.

17.14 Eskimos live mainly on fish, seal and deer meat, which is tough and which exercises their jaws. In some individuals the teeth are worn short by the abrasive action of the raw flesh. They do not eat sweets, and use very little sugar, treacle, chocolate, syrup or fizzy soft drinks.

17.15 A diet which helps to prevent tooth decay should include dairy products, hard foods such as celery and raw carrots, and very few sweet, sticky or sugary foods.

17.16 (a) With 0.5 ppm fluoride in the water supply, there were about 450 decayed, missing or filled teeth per 100 children.
(b) With 1 ppm fluoride in the water supply, there were 300 decayed, missing or filled teeth per 100 children.

17.17 As fluoride concentration is increased up to 1 ppm, there is a dramatic reduction in the incidence of dental caries in children. Above 1 ppm, the benefit is less apparent. 2 ppm of fluoride does not cause much more reduction than 1 ppm.

Many people oppose the addition of fluoride to water supplies. There is evidence that excess fluoride causes damage to the teeth – mottling called 'fluorosis' occurs. Fluorine helps calcification, but in excess may cause the calcification of organs other than teeth and bones (soft tissues such as areolar connective tissue). However, its help in preventing dental disease at concentrations up to 1 ppm is clear.

17.18 Deeply-stained pink areas appear on the teeth. The pink areas indicate where plaque will build up unless the teeth are well cleaned. It is a good idea to clean your teeth thoroughly, then repeat the experiment. You will learn from this how well you clean your teeth.

17.19 Brushing the teeth reduces tooth decay by removing food particles which could produce acid and build up plaque. Gentle brushing of the gums keeps blood circulating in them and helps to reduce inflammation.

17.20 1 Clean the outside of the upper set of teeth from top to bottom, brushing from the gum on to the teeth.
2 Clean the inside of these teeth the same way.
3 Clean the biting surfaces of the upper molars.
4 Repeat 1 – 3 on the lower set of teeth, starting from the base of the teeth and brushing upwards.

17.21 Regular visits to the dentist will enable him to detect the very beginning of a carie when it is still only attacking the enamel. This can be easily removed and the cavity filled with an amalgam (metal mixture). If a carie is allowed to extend into the softer dentine, the rate of decay is much more rapid and could soon lead to loss of the tooth.

4 Sensible use of clothes

17.22 Pressing is another way of destroying bacteria – by the use of heat.

17.23 (a) Hot climate: 1C, 2A, 3C, 4B.
Very light colours will reflect heat. Cotton is a poor insulator which does not impede heat loss. One thin layer will not reduce heat loss. Loose fitting clothes will allow free circulation of air to encourage heat loss by convection.
(b) Cold climate: 1A, 2B, 3B, 4C.
Very dark colours absorb heat. Wool is a good insulator which traps the warm air given off by the body. Several layers will trap several layers of warm air. Close-fitting garments will cut down convection currents.

17.24 A – boots are ideal for snowy or wet weather to keep the feet and legs dry.
B – sandals are suitable for hot weather, enabling air to circulate to the toes and evaporate sweat which would otherwise accumulate.
C – low-heeled lace-ups give ideal support for walking long distances.
D – elegant shoes are suitable for dancing.
E – football boots have reinforced toe caps to protect the toes when kicking a football violently.

5 Exercise, rest and sleep

17.25 Exercise is important for maintaining muscle tone and posture, improving breathing, maintaining a good circulation, particularly of the lymph, and helping to keep the bowels working.

17.26 A person who is suffering from a lack of sleep is pale, lacking in energy, irritable, and unable to concentrate. Electrical activity in the brain (cerebrum) is very limited during sleep and it is possible that a recuperating process is necessary at regular intervals.

17.27 The sleep requirements are as follows:
(a) 20 hours, (b) 16 hours, (c) 14 hours, (d) 11 hours, (e) 10 hours, (f) 9 hours, (g) 7–8 hours.

6 The smoking habit

17.28 The apparatus without a cigarette acts as a control. It is preferable to place a source of heat at X so that both sets of apparatus involve warm air.

17.29 A dark brown sticky substance remains on the glass wool in the U-tube with a cigarette. This is tar. The glass wool in the control remains clean.

17.30 Levels of tar in plain and filtered cigarettes may be compared by using clean glass wool for each cigarette, and comparing the wools after the experiment.

17.31 Smoking, particularly in men, has increased in very much the same way as lung cancer from 1916–65. The fact that other cancers have reduced in incidence over this period, possibly due to improved health care, is another indication that lung cancer must be associated with a modern habit.

17.32 About 0.07 non-smokers per 1000 will get lung cancer compared with about 1.24 smokers who have just given up. They are about eighteen times more likely to get lung cancer than a non-smoker.

17.33 After ten years, an ex-smoker is about four times as likely as a non-smoker to get lung cancer (0.32 per 1000).

17.34 A smoker who gives up the habit greatly reduces his chances of getting lung cancer. After fifteen years he is only twice as likely to get the disease as is a non-smoker. The sooner he gives up the better, whereas if he continues smoking he is about twenty times as likely to get lung cancer as a non-smoker.

17.35 (a) The basal epithelial cells in (b) have divided excessively.
(b) The cilia have all been destroyed in (c) and the columnar epithelium has been replaced by squamous epithelium. Smoke destroys cilia by literally burning them away.

17.36 Lack of cilia will make the smoker more liable to

droplet infections, particularly respiratory infections such as influenza and pneumonia. Cilia normally help to expel micro-organisms.

17.37 The epithelium in (c) shows the appearance of abnormal cells. This could lead to cancer.

17.38 Air pollution increases the likelihood of an ageing smoker contracting bronchitis significantly (from 10% – 16% of the tested sample). High pollution only marginally increases the likelihood of an ageing non-smoker contracting bronchitis (from 2% – 4% of the tested sample).

17.39 Carbon monoxide probably reduces the amount of available oxygen to cross the placenta. The developing foetus, receiving sub-optimal oxygen, may suffer reduced mental and physical growth.

7 The alcohol habit

17.40 $1\frac{1}{2}$ seconds

17.41 $22\frac{1}{2}$ metres

17.42 The normal driver will be able to stop in $97\frac{1}{2}$ metres – he will be safe. The driver with alcohol will take 120 m altogether, and may well stray into cross-traffic at the road junction.

17.43 It is particularly dangerous to drink and drive at high speeds, at night, on wet roads or where there is a lot of other traffic. Remember that the drinker is usually unaware of how much his ability is impaired.

8 The drugs habit

17.44 Legalisation of cannabis is not a good idea because it can cause birth of deformed babies and mental confusion. Storage of cannabis in the fat reserves over a period of time could have damaging effects.

17.45 If sensations are greatly altered under the influence of LSD, an individual may try to do something which is actually impossible. It is also possible that permanent damage may be done to the brain by the wild mental activity under the influence of LSD.

17.46 Alcohol has similar depressing effects to barbiturates. If these drugs are taken together, nervous transmission can be depressed to such an extent that death results. Both accidental deaths and suicides have happened this way.

17.47 People suffering from anxieties sometimes only need a sympathetic ear. If friends and relatives had more time to listen, fewer tranquillisers would be prescribed. Doctors are aware of this need and some are appointing counsellors in their group practices for just this purpose.

17.48 Heroin addicts do not keep themselves clean and they are unlikely to keep the syringe and needle used to inject the drug any cleaner. A large proportion of addicts die from septicaemia or blood poisoning resulting from the introduction of bacteria by unsterile syringe needles.

18 Health in the home

18.1 Two possible sites for building a house

1 Construction of a house

When constructing a home, many factors must be borne in mind. The house should be built so as to shelter effectively the inhabitants from the extremes of climate, such as wind, rain, hot sun, freezing temperatures and so on. It should be made from durable materials. It should be designed to keep out pests, and with an efficient system for hygienically disposing of waste. Size will depend on the number of people to be housed (and the amount of money available); if the house is intended for a growing family it may be necessary to add extra rooms. The site will influence the eventual form and size of the house.

▶ **Question**

18.1 The two possible sites for building a home shown in Fig 18.1 both have advantages and disadvantages. Explain which site you would choose to build on, and why.

The soil on which a house is constructed will affect the design of the foundations. For example, clay soils often require deep foundations, or even piles.

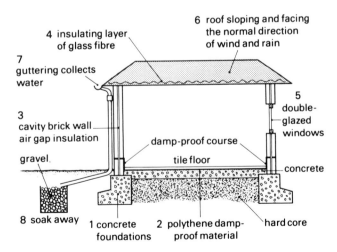

18.2 Section through a well-constructed house

▶ **Question**

18.2 Explain the importance of each of the numbered items on the diagram in Fig 18.2.

231

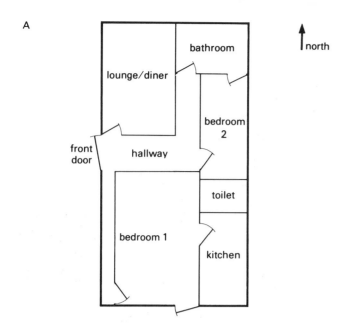

18.3 Plans for residential houses

The house plans illustrated in Fig 18.3 were drawn up for a family of four people: parents, a boy of ten and a girl of eight. The floor area of both bungalows is the same, but the rooms are of different dimensions.

▶ **Questions**

18.3 Which of the plans, A or B, will provide the best accommodation for the family? Explain your choice.
18.4 Which house has the better positioning and why?
18.5 List the other faults of the plan you rejected.

The first step to achieving a hygienic home is to ensure that the water supply and waste disposal system are well-planned. In most modern homes waste is disposed of through drains flushed with water.

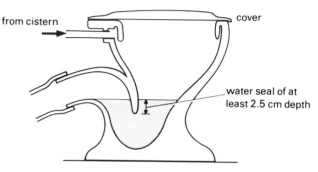

18.4 Section through a modern WC

▶ **Questions**

18.6 What is the purpose of the water seal in Fig 18.4 and why must it be maintained at a depth of at least 2.5 cm?
18.7 Suggest the role of the 'soil pipe'.
18.8 What is the function of the gully traps?
18.9 Why is an inspection chamber needed?

▷ **Homework**

Try to construct a diagram to illustrate the water carriage system in your house.

2 Lighting, heating and ventilation

In temperate countries, lighting, heating and ventilation in houses is controlled to ensure that a reasonably steady environment is maintained. Very low temperatures may produce serious lowering of the body

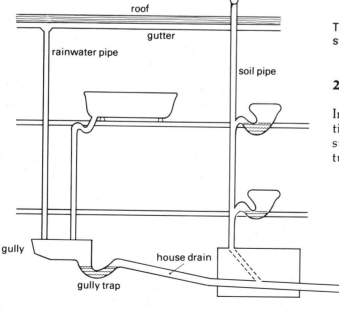

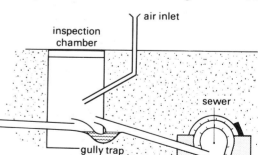

18.5 Domestic waste drainage system

temperature (hypothermia) in the very old or young. In hot countries ventilation and cooling become important as a means of preventing heat stroke (hyperthermia).

Lighting

Modern homes are an improvement on older homes in one important feature: the size of the windows. Very few contemporary houses exclude unnecessary amounts of light. In older properties many windows were smaller than the recommended fifth of the floor area of a room. This figure was recommended by the Parker-Morris commission after the Second World War as a minimum requirement for council housing. Light helps to destroy bacteria as well as making work easier and reducing the possibilities of accidents (see section 5). Artificial lighting has made it possible for people to continue their work and leisure activities after sunset. Early lighting, by candles and later by paraffin lamps and gas lamps, was dim and very bad for the eyesight if tasks like reading, writing or sewing were attempted. Use of electricity has revolutionised lighting in the home. A whole range of light intensities is available, with their power measured in watts. Conventional filament bulbs range from 20 watts to 250 watts, though most bulbs in home use are 60–100 watts.

▷ **Homework**

Examine the light bulbs in your bedroom, in a side light, a study light, over the dining room table and in the kitchen and bathroom. Record the wattage in each case. Did any of the wattages surprise you? If so, state which ones.

Fluorescent tubes frequently replace filament lamps in kitchens and bathrooms. They give out a very

18.6 Kitchen lighting

bright light, but are only rated at 40 – 60 watts. Most of the energy produced by a fluorescent tube is dissipated as light, whereas in a filament bulb a proportion is lost as heat. Fluorescent tubes are thus more economical to use because they give out more light and use less electric current than filament bulbs. Some people find fluorescent light very glaring and a strain on the eyes, particularly if the light flickers. Positioning of lights is all important.

18.7 Two ways of lighting a stairway

(a)

(b)

► Questions

18.10 Explain the good and bad points of the lighting in the kitchen in Fig 18.6.
18.11 Which example in Fig 18.7 shows the best overall lighting? Explain your choice.
18.12 How could the lighting in the less well lit stairway be improved?

Most light bulbs are pearlised rather than clear. This reduces glare. In the same way, good lighting is indirect rather than direct. The wall lights in Fig 18.7 are a good example of indirect lighting.

Heating
Even the earliest homes in Britain had provision for

18.8 An open fire

heating. A fire was lit in the centre of the floor and the smoke, after filling the foom, found its way out of a hole in the roof. Open fires today are built in specially constructed fireplaces of many designs (see Fig 18.8) which have a separate channel or chimney leading to the roof. Open fires are not so popular these days, because they are dirty to prepare, need constant attention and are said only to produce localised radiant heat.

Activity 18.1   Finding out the effect of a model fire on air currents

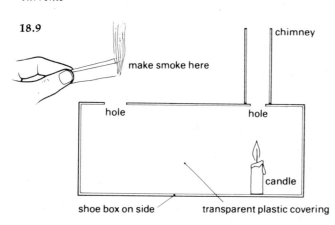

18.9

1   Construct a model room from a shoebox as shown in Fig 18.9. The candle represents an open fire and the toilet roll the chimney.
2   Use a piece of smouldering rope as a source of smoke and apply it close to the second hole as shown.
3   Note the direction taken by the smoke.
4   Repeat the experiment without the candle.
5   Note the direction taken by the smoke.

► Questions

18.13 What effect does the candle have on the smoke?
18.14 Suggest some advantages of an open fire.

18.10 Closed solid fuel stove

Coal, coke and anthracite are not only burned in open fires. Fig 18.10 illustrates a closed solid fuel stove which not only heats the room, but also heats hot water and a number of radiators in other rooms.

The most common form of modern heating is central heating, but some people prefer to use sources of heat such as those illustrated in Fig 18.11. These heaters warm air either by radiation from a visible source of heat, or by warming up the air by convection.

18.11 (a) An electric radiator

18.11 (b) A gas fire

18.11 (c) An electric radiant heater

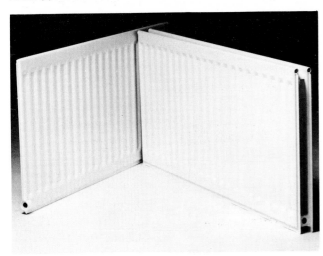

18.12 Typical central heating radiator

▶ Questions

18.15 Identify the method of transfering heat used by (a), (b) and (c) in Fig 18.11. What fuel is being used in each case?
18.16 Suggest any possible disadvantages of these forms of heating.

18.17 Why are radiators thin and ribbed?
18.18 By what methods does a radiator heat a room?
18.19 What are the advantages of central heating over other forms of heating?

Central heating is the best way of supplying uniform heat, but it has a tendency to dry the air. This can aggravate respiratory conditions such as bronchitis and sinusitis. Humidifiers are now on sale to help control the humidity of the environment.

▷ Homework

Make a study of the heating in your home. How efficient is it? Compare your findings with those of other members of the class.

Ventilation

As well as achieving an ideal temperature, air in a house needs to circulate. A constant supply of fresh air is essential. Stale air in an occupied room contains expired droplets possibly carrying pathogens. If these remain in a room, other people will inspire these droplets and become infected. Bodies radiate heat which warms up the surrounding air. If this air is not removed, the temperature will rise. Because the stale air is saturated with water droplets, sweat formed to reduce the body temperature will not evaporate.

Fig 18.13 illustrates natural methods by which the circulation of air is maintained through a building. (a) is simple cross-ventilation where currents pass straight through from the windward to the leeward side of the building.

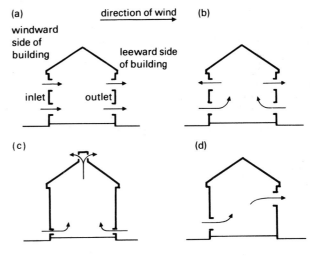

18.13 Methods of natural ventilation

▶ Questions

18.20 What is a possible result of continued lack of ventilation in a crowded room?
18.21 What physical process is bringing about the ventilation currents shown in (b), (c) and (d) in Fig 18.13?
18.22 What are the usual air inlets and outlets for ventilation in a home?
18.23 Which type of window gives the better regulated ventilation, a casement window or louvres? See Fig 18.14.

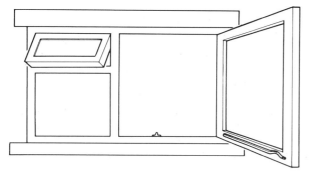

18.14 (a) Casement windows

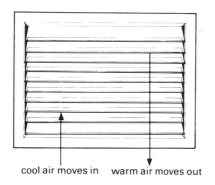

cool air moves in   warm air moves out

18.14 (b) Louvre windows

In some circumstances natural ventilation by a window may not be possible – for example in modern en suite bathrooms. In such cases, alternative

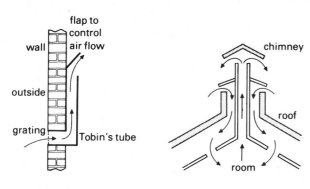

18.15 (a) Tobin's tube ventilation

18.15 (c) McKinnell's roof ventilator

18.15 (b) Ventilation bricks

18.15 (d) Artificial ventilation using an extractor fan

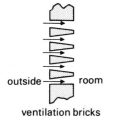

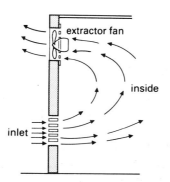

methods such as those illustrated in Fig 18.15 may be used. Many large buildings depend heavily on artificial methods of ventilation, such as the method where air is sucked in by a ventilation fan.

Excessive ventilation may produce draughts. Badly fitting doors and windows may be a contributing factor. Draught excluders may be used to cut down such problems. They consist of a strip of material which is fixed to the frame of the door or window.

▶ **Questions**

18.24 Where are the methods of ventilation shown in Fig 18.15(a) and (b) often used?
18.25 Describe two instances in which extractor fan ventilation is used in homes.
18.26 Why are draughts unwelcome?

▷ **Homework**

Study your house carefully and assess the efficiency of both lighting and ventilation. What improvements could be made?

3 Cleanliness in the home

Cleanliness in the home is essential to reduce the incidence of disease. Pathogens thrive in dirt, so dirt as far as possible must be excluded. This is particularly important where food is likely to be prepared.

Activity 18.2   Investigating the occurrence of bacteria on kitchen surfaces

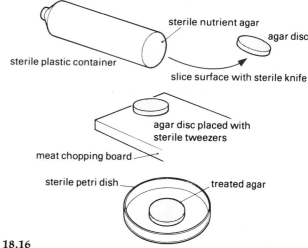

18.16

1   Place discs of agar gel (obtained from an agar 'sausage') on a variety of surfaces to be tested. Try a sink, a draining board, a working surface, a wooden preparation board and so on.
2   After five minutes, place each disc in a sterile petri dish and label with a chinagraph pencil.
3   Incubate for thirty-six hours at 37 °C.

▶ **Question**

18.27   What is the result of this experiment?

Activity 18.3 Investigating the effect of various detergents and disinfectants on bacterial populations on kitchen surfaces

1 Select a well-known liquid kitchen cleaner (such as Jiff) and a disinfectant (such as Dettol or Domestos).
2 Clean half the surfaces tested in Activity 18.2 with the cleaner and the other half with the disinfectant. Make a note of which substance you used for each surface.
3 Repeat Activity 18.2 using fresh discs of agar jelly.

▶ Questions

18.28 What are the results of this experiment?
18.29 What can you conclude from Activities 18.2 and 18.3?
18.30 How can a polished teak dining room table be protected from pathogens?

18.17 A professional cook

When preparing food it is vital that not only are the surfaces and utensils clean, but also that the person preparing the food is spotlessly clean. Fig 18.17 illustrates a chef suitably prepared for cooking.

▶ Question

18.31 In what ways is the chef well prepared for food preparation?

As far as possible it is better for a food preparer to be free of any sort of infection. All kinds of pathogens may be transmitted by food. Coughing on the food can spread colds and other respiratory infections. Any cuts on the hands should be covered with plaster and preparation such as pastry-making should not be undertaken by anyone with a wound on the hands.

Another very important aspect of cleanliness in the home is clean careful storage of food. Probably the best method of storing most food is in a refrigerator. Food not stored in a refrigerator or freezer must be in clean containers. No perishable food should be stored outside a refrigerator for more than a week – less than this in the summer.

▶ Question

18.32 Why is keeping food in a refrigerator a better storage method than storing food in a clean cupboard?

▷ Homework

List those places in your home which attract the most dirt. How may they be effectively cleaned?

18.18 Some commercially preserved foods

4 Food preservation

Not all food is suitable for storage in a refrigerator or freezer. An alternative way of storing perishable food is to preserve it. Fig 18.18 illustrates a variety of foods which have already been through a commercial preservation process before we buy them.

▶ Questions

18.33 Name the method of preservation used in each of the foods illustrated.

18.34 What other methods of food preservation are used which are not illustrated in Fig 18.18?

18.35 Why do these varied processes stop food from going bad?

A lot of food preservation may be carried out in the home. It would be instructive to carry out a class experiment on a variety of foods using as many methods of preservation as possible. A wide-ranging experiment of this sort requires very careful recording. One person will probably only carry out one of the procedures, but needs to know all of them. Every procedure requires an untreated control.

Activity 18.4   Preserving a variety of foods

1   Carry out one of the methods listed in the table and copy the table in your exercise book.

2   After two weeks, examine the experiments and controls and write up the results on the blackboard. If there is no evidence of bacteria or fungi to be seen, a swift smell will provide a clue.

3   Complete the table by writing in all the results from the blackboard.

▶ **Question**

18.36 Suggest how growth of bacteria was prevented in each of the seven methods used.

▷ **Homework**

List the ways in which the food stored in your kitchen at home is preserved.

Table 18.1 Methods of food preservation

Method	Suitable foods	Procedure	Results : Experiment Control
1 Freezing	Peas or beans	Fill two petri dishes with fresh garden peas. Place one in a freezer, leave the other in a cupboard.	
2 Heat treatment	Fresh fruit juice	Heat 5 cm³ juice in boiling tube at 65°C for 30 minutes in a water bath, add a sterile bung, cool rapidly. Store with 5 cm³ untreated juice in another boiling tube.	
3 Jam-making (preserving)	Fresh, clean fruit	Heat half fruit sample with an equal quantity of sugar in boiling tube. Allow to boil and simmer. Seal with greaseproof paper and rubber band. Heat other half without sugar.	
4 Bottling	Fresh apples	Fill a kilner jar to the brim with cut fruit, cover with boiling water containing a spoonful of sugar, screw top on and heat at 150°C for 30 minutes in the oven. Fill a second jar with cut fruit and leave.	
5 Dehydration	Apples	Cut apples into rings. Place a ring in one petri dish without a lid and a second ring in a petri dish with a lid in place.	
6 Pickling	Onions (small)	Remove skins and wash onions, leave in salt water overnight. Rinse, pack in a sterilised boiling tube, cover with vinegar and add a sterile bung. Place untreated onions in water in a boiling tube.	
7 Addition of preservative	Fresh orange juice	Fill a sterile boiling tube with fresh orange juice, add a drop of 5% sodium benzoate and stopper. Stopper a second boiling tube containing untreated orange juice.	

5 Accident prevention

Statistics show that most accidental deaths in this country are caused by transport (7944 in 1978), but that this is closely followed by accidents in the home (7145 in 1978). The total number of accidental deaths in 1978 was only 17,630, showing the domestic share to be nearly 45%. Of the women who die from non-transport accidents, 87% are killed in the home. 62% of women killed in the home and 45% of the men suffer fatal falls. A large proportion of these individuals are either elderly or very young. (Figures taken from *The Facts about Accidents*, published by RoSPA; source OPCS and GRO)

▶ Questions

18.37 What sort of accidents in the home could cause death?
18.38 Where are falls most likely to occur and how can they be prevented?

It is safer for elderly people to live in bungalows where there are no steps. Worn carpets also may be a hazard to them. If possible, wall-to-wall carpeting is preferable to rugs.

Poisoning and gassing account for about 20% of domestic fatalities.

A household is well-advised to have a medical cabinet in the kitchen, close at hand. Fig 18.19 shows two possible sites, X and Y, for such a cabinet.

18.19 Good and bad positions for a medicine cabinet

▶ Questions

18.39 Which cupboard would you use to keep medicines in and why?
18.40 What other substances kept in the kitchen should be out of the reach of children?

Fires are the next most important hazard. About 10% of all domestic fatalities are caused by fires. In addition, thousands of people are seriously injured and maimed by the effects of domestic fires. Children are particularly fascinated by fire, and it is essential to guard an open fire carefully when toddlers are around. There have been many cases of little girls wearing nylon nightdresses in front of a fire being set alight and seriously burnt.

A common cause of outbreak of fire in a home is the electricity supply. This may be due to faulty wiring or to overloading the electrical circuits with too many appliances. The latter causes overloading of wires which may begin to burn.

Electrocution is another serious danger. Normal dry skin has a fairly high resistance to the flow of current, but if the skin is wet, the resistance is drastically lowered and the chance of suffering a fatal electric shock if touching a 'live' object is greatly increased.

▶ Question

18.41 Bearing in mind the lowered resistance of wet skin, what special precautions must be taken to prevent the possibility of suffering a fatal electric shock in the bathroom?

▷ Homework

See if you can find any potential sources of accidents in your home.

6 First aid in the home

Everyone should know how to cope with the effects of an accident or sudden illness which may occur in or around the home. A basic requirement is knowledge of the simple methods of artificial respiration which can save the life of a person suffering from an electric shock or of someone who has been saved from drowning. As a class exercise carry out both the methods shown in fig 18.20 and fig 18.21. Do not practise the kiss of life, on each other. You must use a Manikin to practise.

Activity 18.5 Practising the kiss of life

1 Turn the subject on his back, lift the neck up and press the top of the head. Make sure any tight items around the neck such as a tie is loosened.
2 Hold the person's nostrils closed
3 Take a deep breath.
4 Place your mouth tightly over the subject's mouth, making a tight seal, then exhale into his mouth until his chest expands.
5 Remove your mouth and let the subject exhale (his

chest passively falls) while you take another deep breath.

6 As soon as the subject has breathed out, replace your mouth over his mouth, and repeat the procedure.

7 Repeat in time with your natural breathing rate until the subject starts breathing.

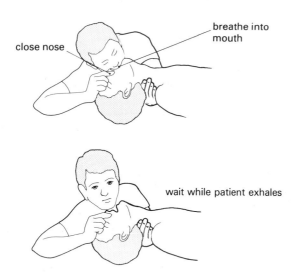

close nose

breathe into mouth

wait while patient exhales

18.20 Artificial respiration — kiss of life

▶ **Question**

18.42 What is the purpose of loosening the subject's collar?

Activity 18.6 Applying Holger-Nielsen method

1 Place the subject on his chest, face downwards.
2 Turn his head slightly to one side and place it on his hands.
3 Kneel in front of the subject's head, place your hands over his shoulder blades and spread the fingers out over the ribs. Rock forward until your arms are straight.
4 Rock backwards and slide your hands to the subjects armpits and along the upper arms and grasp them at the elbow, pulling them upwards. Let go of the subject's arms and kneel upright again with your hands over his shoulder blades.
5 Repeat the cycle ten to twelve times per minute.

Unconsciousness

A subject can become unconscious following an accident or sudden illness. This is when the functions of the nervous system and circulation are interferred with and the brains activities interrupted.
1 Ensure the mouth is clear of mucus and debris
2 Loosen tight clothing to the neck, chest and waist.
3 Place subject in the recovery position fig **18.21**

Question

18.43 What are the common causes of unconsciousness?

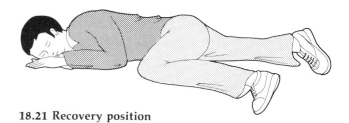

18.21 Recovery position

Cuts and haemorrhage

A small cut can be covered with an adhesive dressing (plaster). If the cut is dirty it should be cleaned with fresh clean water, adding antiseptic and washing away from the wound. Larger wounds may involve larger blood vessels than just capillaries. If an artery is damaged, blood loss (haemorrhage) will be serious. Grasp hold of the wound to stem bleeding, raise the effected limb (if not fractured). Apply a sterile dressing to cover the wound and bandage firmly, adding more bandage if blood loss is not stemmed.

18.22 Sterile dressing

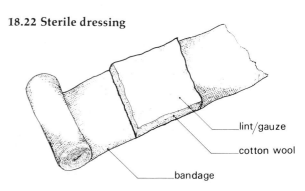

lint/gauze

cotton wool

bandage

Questions

18.44 How would you be able to tell if blood was coming from artery or a vein?
18.45 Why will haemorrhage be more serious from an artery than from a vein?

Scalds and burns

Scalds are caused by water and steam, burns by dry heat. Both can be serious. Place the area burnt under water to cool the tissue, remove any constriction (ring, belts) before the part swells. Leave in water until the pain ceases. Take the patient to hospital with moistened dressings held gently in place.

Fractures and dislocations

If a limb is fractured in a fall and no immediate assistance is available, the limb should be immobilised by securing it to the subjects body. A fracture is a broken bone and can occur in any bone within the body. A dislocation occurs at a joint and is the displacement of one or more bones. The joint becomes fixed and cannot be moved. The limbs affected should be placed in a comfortable position and immobilised.

▷ **Homework**

Practise treatment for fainting, cuts and haemorrhages and scalds and burns.

Answers and discussion

1 Construction of a house

18.1 Site A is on good, level ground which is not being used at the moment, close to possible employment (note the factory) and suitable for pleasant gardens (note the allotments). Site B would use valuable agricultural land, is more hilly and there may be more difficulty supplying electricity, gas or drainage. On the other hand site B is in a much more attractive area and in a less polluted environment.

18.2 1 Foundations provide a firm base for the house and prevent it sinking into the ground. This could lead to cracks in the walls which could make the house unsafe.
2 A damp-proof course is essential to prevent rising damp from the ground. Water is inclined to rise up bricks by capillary action because bricks are porous. The damp proof course is above ground level and is constructed of an impermeable substance such as heavy-gauge polythene, in the water or bituminised felt in the walls.
3 A cavity between two layers of bricks prevents the inner layer of bricks becoming damp when rain lashes against the walls. Also the cavity assists in insulating the wall against heat loss. The insulation can be improved by using special lightweight bricks for the inner layer or by filling the cavity with insulating foam.
4 About one-quarter of all the heat lost from a house is through the roof. To counteract this, most roofs are now insulated with a layer of glass fibre.
5 Double glazing traps a layer of air between the window panes to cut down heat loss.
6 The roof slopes to help the rainwater run off more easily. The steepness of the slope depends on the kind of tiles or slates being used — a felt roof needs only a shallow slope.
7 Rain is best channelled into gutters to prevent it, as much as possible, from running down the walls.
8 The soakaway prevents rainwater from flooding the garden.

18.3 House B offers better accomodation for a young family of four. The children will need separate bedrooms as they grow older.

18.4 House B has better positioning than A. The sun will shine into the living area in the afternoon, while the bedrooms and bathroom at the north side of the house will be kept cooler. In A, only the kitchen and a bedroom will receive the afternoon sun. The living area would not receive sunlight at all.

18.5 1 A is badly planned since the toilet is next to the kitchen. This is unhygienic, and it has no door.
2 The kitchen and bathroom are at opposite ends of the home, making plumbing difficult.
3 The kitchen is a long way from the dining room, and it can be reached only through the bedroom.
4 More space is used as hall in A, and the corridor to bedroom 1 is wasted space.

18.6 The water seal prevents bad smells from gases formed in the pipes reaching the bathroom. It must be maintained at a good level above the S-bend to function without any danger of gases getting through.

18.7 The soil pipe allows foul gas smells to escape into the air.

18.8 The gully traps act like water seals.

18.9 An inspection chamber is needed to trace pipe leakages or blockages.

2 Lighting, heating and ventilation

18.10 There are three spot lights which give a good light over the worktop, and the sink is placed in front of the window which makes use of the daylight. However there is no overall fluorescent light, nor any lower level lighting to illuminate the shelves.

18.11 B shows the better overall lighting. In particular the stairs are better lit, reducing the possibility of accidents.

18.12 Further lighting is required up the stairs and the glaring single bulb at the bottom could be replaced by two softer wall-lights.

18.13 The candle causes the smoke to rise and pass out through the toilet roll chimney. The fire sets up convection currents and the rising hot air is lighter than the surrounding cold air, so rises up the chimney.

18.14 (a) An open fire draws fresh air in from under doors and from windows, circulating the air so that stale air is replaced by fresh air.
(b) In addition to heating a room by radiation, an open fire also heats by convection, though much of this is lost up the chimney.
(c) Some people maintain that an open fire is a psychologically comforting focal point. It makes you 'feel' warm.

18.15 (a) heats by convection, (b) by both convection and radiation and (c) by radiation. (a) and (c) are electric and (b) is a gas fire. Both convector heaters and radiant heaters may be fuelled by oil. This did have the advantage of being cheap, but with rising oil costs these heaters are becoming obsolete.

18.16 None of these forms of heating can easily provide a uniform temperature throughout a good-sized room. (b) and (c) are dangerous in that they have very hot exposed areas which can cause burns.

18.17 A typical radiator is thin and ribbed so that it presents a high surface area to volume ratio for rapid transfer of heat.

18.18 A radiator heats a room principally by convection. If it is very hot it may radiate heat a little. A radiator may be placed beneath a window to heat incoming air.

18.19 (a) Central heating is the only form of heating which can supply uniform heat throughout a room.
(b) It is instant heat which can be programmed to switch on in the absence of the occupants of the house.
(c) It is safe. Some forms of central heating use ducted air, so there is no chance of a child being burned by touching a too-hot radiator.
(d) It is clean and involves little or no maintenance.
(e) It can be run on a variety of fuels – solid fuel, gas, oil or even electricity alone.
(f) It can be thermostatically controlled.
Absolutely uniform heat is not desirable through the whole house. It is usual for the sitting room to be at a slightly higher temperature (perhaps 20 °C) than the other rooms, where 15 °C is probably high enough. Some people dislike heat in the bedrooms. Radiators may be turned off in such cases. The ideal situation is to have a thermostat fitted to

every radiator. This is being done more frequently now.

18.20 If sweat cannot evaporate, the person will overheat and headache, nausea and fainting may result.

18.21 Convection currents are assisting natural ventilation in (b), (c) and (d).

18.22 Usual inlets and outlets for air currents in a home are windows, doors and chimneys.

18.23 Louvres give a more regulated ventilation by helping to draw in cold air at the bottom and send out warm air at the top.

18.24 Ventilation bricks are often found in pantries and storage cupboards to encourage air flow. Tobin's tubes may be seen in some toilets.

18.25 Extractor fans are fitted into kitchen windows to extract cooking smells and excessive steam from cooking. En suite bathrooms with no external wall frequently have an extractor fan which operates when the light is switched on.

18.26 Draughts cause heat loss and can cause people at risk to develop chills or rheumatic conditions.

3 Cleanliness in the home

18.27 A large variety of bacterial colonies may be expected to grow on every disc of agar.

18.28 Fewer bacterial colonies appeared on the agar discs from surfaces cleaned with a domestic detergent than in Activity 18.2. The agar discs from surfaces with disinfectant grew hardly any colonies at all.

18.29 All the various surfaces tested in Activity 18.2 are likely to be well-covered with bacteria, but most of the bacteria are destroyed by cleaning with a disinfectant.

18.30 Detergents and disinfectants cannot be used on teak or other polished woods, but regular polishing to maintain the shine will reduce the incidence of bacteria. This can be verified by using agar discs before and after polishing.

18.31 The chef is wearing a clean overall, covering his everyday clothes, his hair is tidy and away from his face, and he has clean hands and short fingernails.

18.32 Food is kept below the temperature at which bacteria can grow in a refrigerator. Spores will still be present, but they will not produce more bacteria until the temperature goes up. Thawed food should not be refrozen for this reason.

4 Food preservation

18.33 A pickling; B canning; C preserving; D freezing; E vacuum packing; F and G dehydration.

18.34 Methods not illustrated include pasteurisation, bottling, sterilisation (sterilised milk), food additives (preservatives such as nitrites, sulphur dioxide and benzoic acid) and radiation.

18.35 These processes prevent food from going bad by preventing the growth of bacteria in food. Bacteria are responsible for most of the decay (putrefaction) in food (see Unit 19). Moulds are a minor agent of food decay, though they can be particularly dangerous in producing carcinogens (see Unit 16).

18.36 Growth of bacteria was prevented in Activity 18.4 as follows:

1 Freezing – bacteria cannot grow in temperatures below freezing.
2 Heat treatment – most bacteria are destroyed at 65 °C. This method is pasteurisation. Rapid cooling prevents growth of spores at optimum temperature.
3 Preserving – sugar draws water out of bacteria by osmosis. Deprived of moisture, the bacteria cannot grow.
4 Bottling – the special Kilner jar top provides a vacuum seal excluding air from the bacteria. The weak syrup surrounding the apples again draws water out of the bacteria by osmosis. Canning operates on the principles of air and water exclusion.
5 Dehydration – bacteria deprived of water will not grow.
6 Pickling – vinegar is more concentrated than the cytoplasm of bacteria. Water is drawn out of the bacteria by osmosis. They fail to grow because of dehydration.
7 Preservatives are substances which are toxic to bacteria. These substances are used in minute quanitites, only a few ppm, and they will not harm humans. Use of nitrites is becoming limited because of their possible conversion to nitrosamines which are carcinogenic (see Unit 16).

5 Accident prevention

18.37 Possible fatal accidents in the home could include falling, gassing, poisoning, fire and electrocution.

18.38 The most likely place for falling is down the stairs. This may be prevented by siting the stairs well at the outset. A straight flight of stairs is preferable to one with a bend. Good natural and artificial lighting is essential. A handrail must be provided and if small children are around, a stair gate must be fitted across the top or bottom of the stairs to prevent the children from trying to climb or descend the stairs unaided.

18.39 The medicines should be kept in X out of the reach of young children. Aspirin, paracetamol and other 'mild' painkillers are highly dangerous if consumed in any quantity, particularly by small children. Prescribed medicines may be even more dangerous.

18.40 Other substances which children might try to consume and which will cause them harm include disinfectants, antiseptics, bleach, cleaning fluids, cosmetics such as nail polish remover or perfumes, dry cleaning fluid, adhesives, polishes etc. They must all be stored out of reach.

18.41 No hand switches should be installed in the bathroom. A cord is the usual method used to turn bathroom lights on and off. Heating in the bathroom should be well away from the bath. It is not advisable to have any sort of portable electric heater in a bathroom. A non-conducting material such as cork tiles on the bathroom floor will reduce the possibility of an accident. In the kitchen, the kettle must not be allowed to produce steam which could cover switches close at hand with moisture.

6 First aid in the home

18.42 The air passage must be clear if the mouth-to-mouth resuscitation is to succeed.

18.43 A stuffy atmosphere in the home is most likely to cause fainting. A family party with closed windows and the central heating full on could produce such conditions.

18.44 and 18.45 Haemorrhage from an artery is more serious than from a vein because the blood is under pressure in an artery and will spurt out with force. Blood from a vein will only trickle out since it is not under pressure.

19 Community health care

1 Town planning

As the human population has increased, so has the tendency for people to live together in large communities. With the advent of industry, there has been a mass migration from the country to the towns. The result of this is the sprawling conurbations, most of which have grown up without any long-term planning. During the last century this lead to slum dwellings and massive epidemics. In the latter half of the 19th century, many people became aware of the need for public health and welfare services and adequate town planning. Since the turn of the century, a number of **new towns** have been planned from scratch, such as Bracknell, Milton Keynes and Hemel Hempstead. In each case a village already existed on the site, but subsequent expansion has been completely planned.

▶ **Questions**

19.1 List the ways in which the town plan in Fig 19.1 (b) offers better living conditions to its community than Fig 19.1 (a).

19.2 Suggest any other facilities needed by a community not represented in Fig 19.1 (b).

▷ **Homework**

Make a study of your home town and list the good and bad points in its planning.

19.1 Two possible town plans (a) and (b)

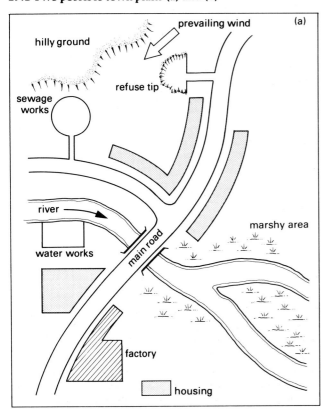

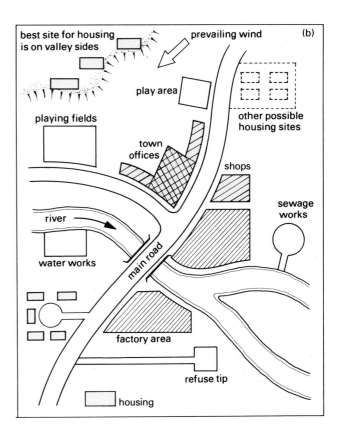

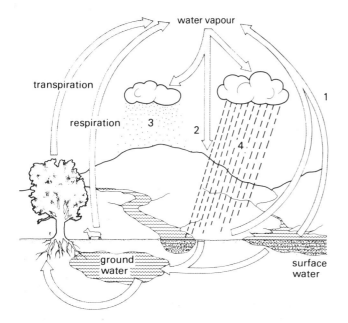

19.2 The water cycle

19.3 A village water supply in the tropics

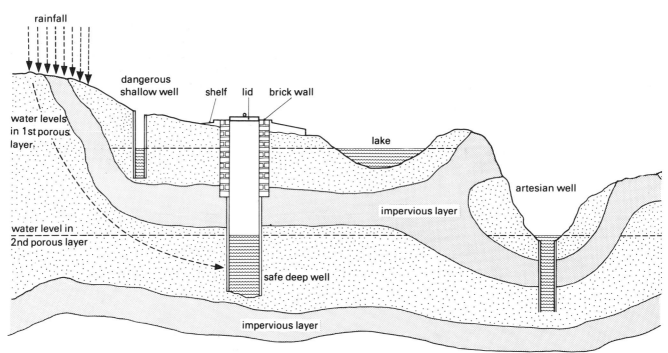

19.4 Sources of water

2 A pure water supply

The most essential resource for survival, apart from oxygen, is water. Man cannot live without water for more than a few days (see Unit 4). Water is made constantly available by the water cycle shown in Fig 19.2.

▶ Questions

19.3 List some of the reasons why man cannot survive without water.

19.4 Name the process at 1 in Fig 19.2.
19.5 By what means is water which has evaporated being replaced at 2, 3 and 4 in Fig 19.2?
19.6 What are the sources of water illustrated in Fig 19.2?
19.7 Would you be happy to use the village water supply shown in Fig 19.3? Explain your answer.
19.8 After studying Fig 19.4 explain why it is dangerous to drink water from a shallow well, but safe to drink water from a deep well.

In 1832 there was a world-wide pandemic of cholera. In Russia 50 000 people per million died from the disease and in the British Isles 7500 people per million died. Cholera is a bacterial disease of the lower digestive tract which is transmitted by water. London was the worst affected centre in England and the infection was traced to public water pumps. These pumps brought up Thames water, which was used for drinking and washing. The river was full of untreated sewage, containing contaminated human excreta, which drained into it, and this was the cause of the epidemic. The community became aware of the need to obtain clean water.

Domestic filters like those in Fig 19.5 worked on the same principle as natural rock filtrations. Those illustrated were filled with carbon particles. These were very small particles with minute spaces between them which prevented all but the smaller bacteria and viruses from draining through. They are not much used in this country now, as the public supply is much improved.

19.5 Advertising domestic water filters

19.6 A public water works

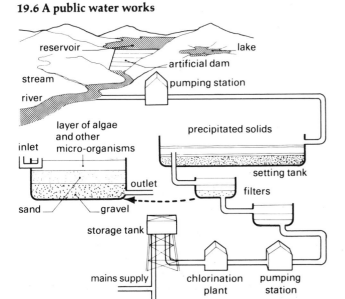

▶ **Question**

19.9 How can bacteria in water be destroyed in the home?

Following the cholera epidemic Public Health Acts were introduced, and the Public Health Act of 1875 forced local authorities to supply an 'adequate water supply'. Fig 19.6 illustrates a scheme for purification of a town water supply which is typical of many water works found today. Water is pumped to one or more settling tanks where it remains for about twenty-four hours.

From the sedimentation (settling) tank the water passes into a number of filters. The filters contain fine sand, coarse sand and gravel, as shown in Fig 19.6. A layer of algae, protozoa and other micro-organisms forms around the sand particles. The water trickles slowly through each filter bed. The protozoa and other micro-organisms in the film-like layer digest the bacteria in the water. This is similar to the action of certain bacteria in the soil (see Unit 20). From the filter beds, the water is conveyed to a chlorination plant, where a few parts per million (ppm) of chlorine are added to the water.

Regular tests are carried out on the water. One test is a coliform count. This estimates the number of 'coliform' bacteria in the water. These are intestinal bacteria, and a high number of coliforms is indicative of faecal contamination of the water supply. The amount of chlorine added to the water is governed by the results of the coliform counts.

A pumping station pumps the chlorinated water into storage reservoirs and tanks which are situated high up to maintain adequate water pressure in the pipes and taps. The storage reservoirs are always covered.

Water is conveyed to homes through non-corrodable pipes. Lead pipes are no longer used because of the harmful effects of lead (see Unit 20). Thick heavy-duty polythene is used for modern piping.

Some local authorities add a second chemical to the water before it is piped to homes.

▶ **Questions**

19.10 What happens to the water in the settling tank?
19.11 What is the purpose of chlorination?
19.12 Explain why the storage reservoirs are covered.
19.13 What is the second chemical sometimes added to water supplies? Why is it added?

▷ **Research project**

Investigate the sources of domestic water in your area.

3 Safe disposal of waste

The cholera epidemics in London were an important factor in the construction of the first sewage systems in the country. Before this, people emptied chamber pots out of upstairs windows into channels in the street below. These channels also collected rainwater

19.7 Early sewerage system near Marylebone station. The tunnel marked 2 is the newly built low-level sewer.

and street garbage and discharged eventually into the River Thames. By 1867, London had a well-constructed underground system of channels for collecting sewage. The sewage was initially channelled out to remote fields where it gradually percolated through the soil. Hence the term **sewage farm**. Fig 19.7 shows the 'sewerage' system near Marylebone station in 1867. The modern sewage farm is much more sophisticated than the 19th century version. Any sewage treatment plant you visit will either use the biological filter method (B in Fig 19.8) or the activated sludge process. Early treatment of the sewage is the same in both methods. Sewage contains domestic excreta and waste water with detergents and possibly some solid wastes. Large particles such as vegetable peelings are trapped by a metal screen or grid at the entrance to the plant. The grid leads into a deep grit pit into which heavy particles settle, then the water is channelled into sedimentation tanks for twenty-four hours.

▶ Questions

19.14 How is the entrance grid kept clear to allow the rest of the sewage through?

19.15 What happens to the sewage as it remains in the sedimentation tanks?

Solid matter which has accumulated at the bottom of the sedimentation tank is pumped out. This sludge is passed to a treatment plant where it may be converted into dried fertiliser pellets or into methane gas. Some dried sludge is even used as land fill (in land reclamation schemes). The liquid remaining either passes through a biological filter or an aeration tank. See Fig 19.9. The effluent trickles into the biological filter through a rotating arm or 'sprinkler'. The filter bed contains coke which is graded, with small particles at the top and coarser particles at the bottom. A micro-organism film grows over the particles of coke.

▶ Question

19.16 Describe how a biological filter purifies the effluent.

In the activated sludge process, the effluent, together with a small quantity of sludge containing some protozoa and bacteria is pumped into long channels or aeration tanks. Air is bubbled under pressure through a perforated pipe along the bottom of each tank. The air agitates and mixes the effluent and sludge together, helped by a mixing paddle. A high oxygen level in the water encourages aerobic micro-organisms which digest the harmful bacteria in the

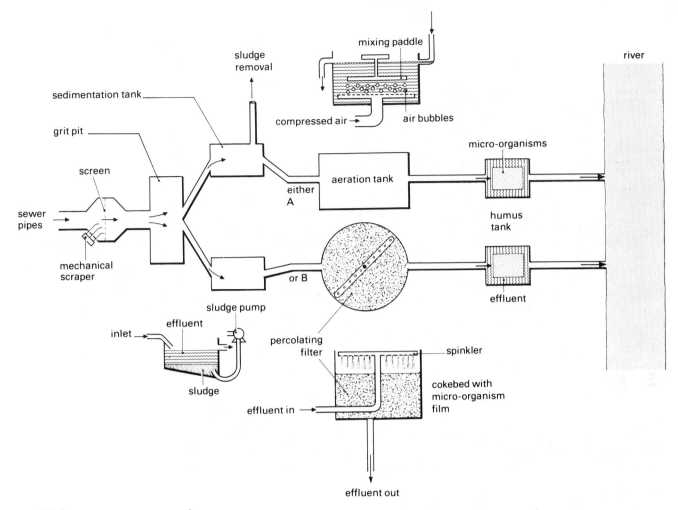

19.8 Modern sewage treatment plant

19.9 (a) Biological filter

19.9 (b) Aeration tanks

effluent. The process is faster than the biological filter method. Some sludge builds up, but this is recirculated. Any remaining sludge is digested, dried and used as fertiliser.

In both methods, the final treatment of the effluent is carried out in a humus tank. This tank separates out any micro-organisms remaining in the effluent. The liquid which is finally discharged into the river is fit for drinking, with all impurities removed.

Bacteria play a key role in both biological filters and aeration tanks. The putrefying and nitrifying bacteria which are active in the soil (in the nitrogen cycle – see

Unit 20) are similarly active in the biological filter. The filter is simply a means of hastening the normal process of decay which sewage underwent on the original sewage farms. Algae in the humus tank remove dissolved nitrates from the effluent before the water is passed into a river.

Solid waste from homes is another potential source of disease. Local authorities are compelled to provide a refuse collection service to take away solid waste and to dispose of it. Most householders provide themselves with a dustbin for storage of refuse until collection. Such dustbins must have tight-fitting lids. They are normally made of a non-corrodible substance such as galvanised zinc or hard plastic.

▶ **Questions**

19.17   Why must dustbins have tight-fitting lids?
19.18   Where should a dustbin be sited in relation to the house?

Some local authorities supply householders with a metal frame and cover into which disposable paper bags are fitted. A new bag is supplied by the authority each week. This modern method of storing household refuse is illustrated in Fig 19.10.

heavy rubberised cover

hinged door opens for easy removal of bag

disposable bag of heavy brown paper

19.10 Modern method of disposing of household refuse

▶ **Questions**

19.19   What are the advantages of the disposable bag system over the conventional dustbin?
19.20   Suggest two aspects of the design of the vehicle in Fig 19.11 which make it a hygienic means of transporting refuse to the tip.
19.21   What factors would you consider to be important in the selection of a site for a refuse tip?

Some local authorities have invested in re-cycling waste, and have elaborate systems to extract

19.11 Refuse collection van

different items (see Unit 20). Many authorities burn (incinerate) a large proportion of the waste. Nottingham has an incinerator which produces heat from the city's waste to provide central heating for hundreds of homes.

▷ **Research project**

Find out all you can about the re-cycling of refuse by local authorities in this country.

4 Communal food hygiene

Food can be a source of many diseases. Apart from typhoid, certain *Salmonella* bacteria cause a particularly violent form of food poisoning called salmonellosis. Sickness and diaorrhoea are common symptoms. *Staphylococcus* also causes food poisoning. Neither of these diseases, though quite severe for a short period, usually cause death. Death is the usual result of infection with *Clostridium botulinum*. This anaerobic bacterium thrives in the absence of oxygen and has been known to infect badly canned or potted meat. Anyone consuming such meat suffers from botulism, an extremely virulent infection which leads to paralysis and death if untreated within a few hours.

All these diseases may be contracted if food is inadequately prepared, or handled and stored without proper care. Water used to cool cans has been implicated in several outbreaks of typhoid or botulism. Untreated water may enter tiny undetectable holes in a defective can seal, causing pathogenic bacteria to enter the can.

Environmental health officers regularly visit all establishments concerned in the production, processing, preparation, handling and storage of food to ensure that all the regulations in the Food and Drug Act of 1955 are being complied with.

19.22 List the sort of establishments that will be visited by the environmental health officers.

19.23 Imagine that you are an environmental health inspector and list all the things that the cook in Fig 19.12 is doing wrong.

19.24 What basic facilities should a food shop possess in order to maintain a satisfactory level of hygiene?

19.25 The example shown in Fig 19.13 illustrates good food display in a shop. Explain how it maintains a hygienic standard.

19.26 What points would you look for in an assistant serving behind the counter of a bakery?

19.27 What would you expect an environmental health officer to look for in a hotel providing meals for non-residents?

19.28 What does a meat inspector look for in an abattoir?

19.12 What's cooking?

19.13 Meat on display in a supermarket

Clean milk

Milk is an excellent environment for the growth of bacteria. As a near-complete food, it provides bacteria with all the necessary nutrients. A very wide range of bacteria can thrive in milk. Bacteria which cause curdling of milk are called lactobacilli. These bacteria are harmless, but many potential pathogens are harboured in milk.

► Questions

19.29 Name two bacteria found in milk which were the cause of two major illnesses.

19.30 Why are these bacteria not prevalent today?

Very few herds of cattle in Western Europe today are not tuberculin tested. The test applied to cattle is very similar to that applied to man (see Unit 15). Cattle tested in this way will not produce milk containing tubercle bacilli. Other pathogens, such as the bacteria which cause brucellosis, are destroyed by various heat treatments. The most common of these is pasteurisation. Some dairy farmers have their own pasteurisation plants, but most milk in this country is pasteurised in large dairies.

The whole process of milk production is carefully controlled to avoid bacterial contamination. Most farmers in the UK use milking machines to obtain milk from their cattle. These are kept scrupulously clean and are disinfected daily, special attention being given to the metal teat cups of the machine

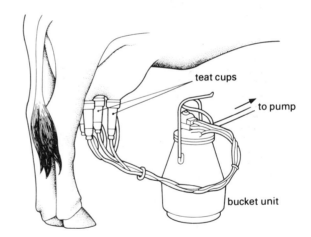

19.14 Milking machine

The milking shed is kept clean at all times and the milk is passed from the machine through pipes into a special refrigerated metal tank. This milk is collected within hours by a tanker which is also refrigerated. The tanker delivers the milk to the nearest dairy for pasteurisation. Several methods of pasteurisation are employed. In each case the milk is heated to a sub-boiling temperature for a set time, then cooled rapidly to 15 °C. The flash method of pasteurisation is most commonly used today. The milk is heated rapidly to 75 °C and kept at that temperature for thirty seconds before rapid cooling.

19.31 Since the aim of pasteurisation is to destroy bacteria, why are boiling temperatures not used?

19.32 How does this method of pasteurisation compare with the method you used to preserve fruit juice in Unit 18?

Following pasteurisation the milk is bottled in sterilised bottles and sealed with a foil cap. Within hours this milk is delivered to households, or stored in cool compartments in supermarkets. Milk treated in this way and kept cool will last for two to three days, before it begins to go off. In hot weather, badly stored pasteurised milk will only stay fresh for twenty-four hours.

Pasteurisation does not destroy bacterial spores, so after a few days the spores will germinate and produce new bacterial populations.

Sometimes it is necessary to keep milk for longer periods. Mountaineers and campers may be some distance from a source of fresh milk. Some milk is sterilised (heated under pressure to temperatures well over boiling) and bottled in air-tight containers (hermetically sealed). This milk will last for long periods, but is less pleasant in taste. An alternative is UHT milk (ultra-high-temperature). This milk is steam heated for a few seconds only, then rapidly cooled. As in the case of sterilisation, this destroys all the spores and the milk will remain fresh for long

19.15 Pasteurisation plant

periods. This 'long life' milk tastes more like fresh milk than completely sterilised milk. Recently, dried milk powder has become very popular. A tin of milk powder can be kept almost indefinitely, and when reconstituted with water it has a reasonable flavour.

A class experiment may be carried out to compare the bacterial populations in milk which has been treated in a variety of ways. An indicator, methylene blue is used. This blue dye is reduced by bacteria, which means that as bacteria use up oxygen in respiration, the dye becomes less oxidised. A moderate bacterial population will extract sufficient oxygen to change the dye to a pinkish colour. A heavy bacterial population will cause the dye to become totally colourless. An alternative dye is resazurin.

Activity 19.1   Comparing the numbers of bacteria in milk treated in a variety of ways

1   Set up a series of boiling tubes containing milk treated by the following processes: pasteurisation, laboratory pasteurisation (refer to Unit 18), boiling, sterilisation, UHT, dried milk, etc. Include a sample of untreated milk (raw), obtained from a farmer.

2   Add 1 cm³ of methylene blue to each sample and stir with sterile glass rod to mix.

3   Heat in a water bath maintained at 40 °C for thirty minutes, but examine the samples at regular intervals.

4   Observe the colour of each sample.

▶ **Questions**

19.33 What is the purpose of the sample of raw milk?

19.34 What results are obtained and what is your conclusion?

This experiment may be adapted to compare the methods of storage of a sample of commercially pasteurised milk, after using a cupboard, a refrigerator, a window sill, a doorstep, etc.

▷ **Homework**

Find out all you can about preservation of milk by drying processes.

5 Public health and welfare services

Following the drastic cholera epidemics in the mid 19th century, the first Public Health Acts were passed in Parliament. These began the trend towards awareness of the need to establish certain standards of public health and welfare. Important recent Acts include the National Health Service Act of 1946, the Health Services and Public Health Act of 1968 and the Local Authority Social Services Act of 1970. Though much administration of the National Health Service is carried out at a national level, the most immediate services are under the control of the District Health Authorities and the Family Practitioner Committees. Examine Fig 19.16.

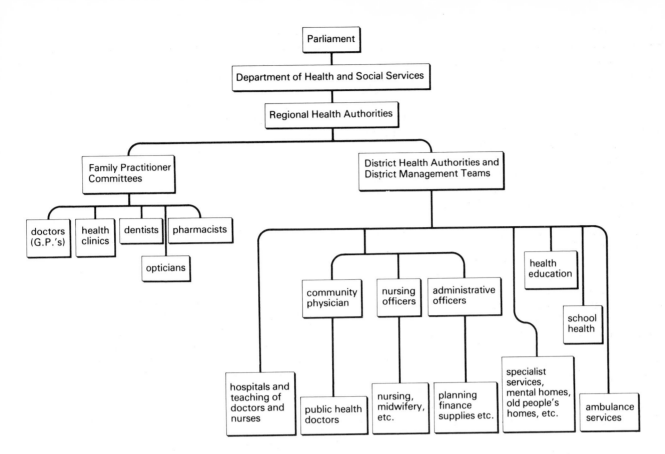

19.16 Structure of the National Health Service from 1982 when the District Health Authorities were made responsible for health care provision

▶ **Questions**

19.35 Which authority is responsible for school health programmes?
19.36 What sort of medical statistics are of particular importance to the Community Physician?
19.37 What are the roles of pharmacists and opticians?

Every district authority is responsible for providing ante- and post-natal clinics, child welfare clinics, family planning clinics and geriatric clinics (for looking after the aged). All these clinics may be held in the same building at different times in the week.

Many towns today have a joint practice run by a number of general practioners. Such an arrangement encourages the public to make use of medical facilities as they become familiar with the place and the people who run the clinics.

Provision of hospital beds is one of the functions of the National Health Service. Most large towns have a general hospital which offers a variety of treatments.

Local authorities are also responsible for providing leisure facilities to stimulate the physical and mental faculties of the community. Such facilities include sports centres where a swimming pool, squash courts and badminton courts may be provided, and playing fields and libraries.

World health is the concern of the World Health Organisation (WHO), an international body affiliated

19.17 Addenbrookes hospital, Cambridge

to the United Nations. It is concerned with the promotion of a healthy body and mind and satisfactory social relationships. Pandemics are monitored by WHO. Research into a wide variety of medical problems is also their concern. Statistics of diseases are compiled by WHO. A recent triumph of WHO is the virtual eradication of smallpox by a world-wide vaccination campaign.

Another body affiliated to the United Nations is the Food and Agriculture Organisation (FAO). The aim of this organisation is to ensure that no one is deprived of necessary nourishment. It seeks to educate developing countries in agricultural techniques to enable them to feed their populations more effectively. In times of famine the FAO issues milk powder and other high protein food to children. Experts advise on aspects of crop growing, animal husbandly, forestry and soil science.

▷ **Homework**

Investigate further the work of the WHO and the FAO. Select one aspect of their work and say whether you think it has lead to a better standard of living for some people, and why.

19.18 Dr Edward Jenner vaccinating Jimmy Phipps

6 Research for better health

Since the 18th century, a number of men have had a tremendous impact in the war against disease. One of these men was Dr Edward Jenner (1749–1823), a general practioner who lived in the village of Berkeley in Gloucestershire.

Smallpox was rife in Gloucestershire around 1780, but Dr Jenner noticed that people working with cows never seemed to contract the disease. He examined the hands of Sarah Nelmes, a milkmaid, and discovered pock marks very similar to those of smallpox. Further investigation revealed that the cows had similar marks. These were caused by a mild disease called cowpox. Jenner decided that the cowpox infection somehow made Sarah immune to smallpox. To test this idea, he scratched some pus from a cow pock into Jimmy Phipp's arm. Jimmy developed cowpox. Some weeks later Dr Jenner took a great risk and gave Jimmy a second inoculation which consisted of pus containing smallpox itself.

▶ **Question**

19.39 What would you expect the result of this inoculation to be if Dr Jenner's theory was correct?

Dr Jenner took a calculated risk, but his theory was supported, because Jimmy Phipps did not develop smallpox. It was some time before Dr Jenner could persuade the British Government to treat British soldiers in India with cowpox. Hundreds of them were dying from smallpox. He finally persuaded the government and hundreds more lives were saved. The technique became known as **vaccination** after the latin word *vacca* meaning 'cow'. Dr Jenner had no idea why vaccination worked. He knew nothing of micro-organisms or antibodies. It was left to a man who was born the year before Dr Jenner died in 1823 to work out this connection.

Louis Pasteur (1822–1895) was in many ways the father of bacteriology. Fig 19.19 illustrates a very famous early demonstration he carried out to disprove the prevailing theory of spontaneous generation. Scientists in Pasteur's time believed that food went bad because of the spontaneous formation of decay inside it. Study the swan-necked flask experiment in Fig 19.19 step by step.

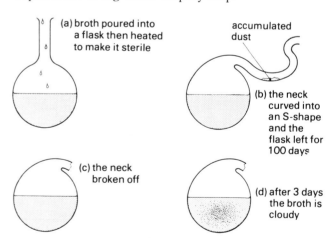

19.19 Pasteur's swan-necked flask demonstration

▶ **Questions**

19.40 Describe how the experiment disproved the theory of spontaneous generation.
19.41 What is the source of the decay seen in Fig 19.19 (d)?

Activity 19.2   Verifying Pasteur's swan-necked flask experiment

1   Pour equal quantities of sterile nutrient broth into four sterile test tubes.
2   Add a cotton wool plug which has been sterilised to one test tube.
3   Place a straight glass tube through a sterile cotton wool bung in another test tube.
4   Place an S-bend glass tube through a sterile cotton wool bung in the third test tube.
5   Leave the fourth test tube open and store all four tubes together.
6   Observe the state of the broth over a period of two weeks.
7   Record your results and conclusion.

▶ **Question**

19.42   Which test tubes finally contained cloudy broth and why?

Pasteur was soon asked to investigate the cause of wine going bad. Again he discovered that bacteria were the cause. He was asked to devise a method to prevent the wine going bad. It was very important that the flavour of the wine should not be impaired. He developed the method which is now used for keeping milk fresh (see section 4).

▶ **Question**

19.43   How did he prevent wine going bad?

19.20 Pasteur inoculating sheep against anthrax

Pasteur lost two of his daughters who died of typhoid. He became obsessed with the possibility that as well as causing food to go bad, bacteria could also cause disease (badness) in people and animals.

Fig 19.20 shows Pasteur inoculating a sheep

against anthrax. Anthrax was a serious disease of farm animals and men. Pasteur added a drop of the sheep's blood to a nutrient broth in the laboratory. Later he introduced some of the nutrient broth into another sheep, which contracted the disease. Robert Koch (1843-1910) at about the same time actually saw rod-shaped micro-organisms in the blood of an infected animal which he viewed under the microscope. Thus anthrax was shown to be caused by micro-organisms.

Pasteur thought that vaccination might be effective because the body produces resistance to the micro-organisms causing the disease. He spent many years producing vaccines against dangerous diseases. First he produced a vaccine against fowl cholera, using dead bacteria. Later he produced an effective vaccine against anthrax by using weakened anthrax bacilli. He kept bacterial cultures at sub-optimal temperatures to weaken or attenuate them. Probably his greatest achievement in this field was the vaccine he developed which was tested on a small boy who had been bitten by a dog.

▶ **Question**

19.44   What disease was this vaccine active against?

Sir Joseph Lister (1827–1912), a surgeon working in Glasgow in the late 19th century, was concerned at the high death rate following surgical operations. Most of these deaths were caused by blood poisoning and other infections which entered the body during the operation. Fig 19.21 illustrates the apparatus which Lister devised in an attempt to reduce this problem. Carbolic acid is a strong germicide (antiseptic). The spray was directed in the general direction of the incision. The number of post operative deaths from septicaemia or infection of the blood was drastically reduced after the introduction of this antiseptic.

19.21 Carbolic acid spray

19.45 What are the sources of infection in the operating theatre shown in Fig 19.22?

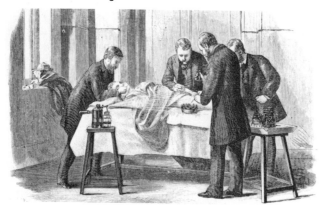

19.22 Carbolic acid spray in use during an operation

Ignaz Semmelweiss (1818–1865) had already noticed how infection could spread in hospitals as early as 1846 in Vienna. The death rate from puerperal fever, which attacked women after childbith, was so high in one particular hospital ward that they begged not to be placed in it. Semmelweiss realised that medical students often visited the ward after they left the dissecting room. The neighbouring ward, where midwives exclusively looked after the births, had far fewer deaths from puerperal fever. He suspected that the puerperal fever organisms were carried on the unwashed hands of the medical students who were allowed to participate at deliveries after dissecting bodies in the adjoining room.

He later instructed any doctor or student coming from the post mortem room to wash his hands thoroughly in the basin of chlorinated water placed at the entrance to the maternity wards. The death rate from puerperal fever dropped by 90% in two years.

19.23 Agar plate observed by Sir Alexander Fleming

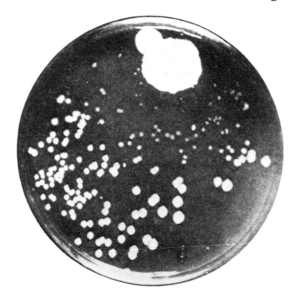

Later he waged a war against the continual use of dirty sheets, demanding clean sheets for each patient.

A significant contribution to disease control was made in this century by Sir Alexander Fleming (1881–1955). In 1928, Fleming, who was working on a series of experiments which required pure bacterial cultures of *Staphylococcus,* discovered that one plate was contaminated with the mould, *Penicillium notatum.* Fig 19.23 is a photograph of the contaminated agar plate which intrigued Fleming and led to his most important contribution to medical science.

▶ **Questions**

19.46 What do you notice about the distribution of the bacterial colonies in relation to the mould?
19.47 What may be deduced from this?

Fleming was quick to realise a possible use for the inhibiting agent in the mould. He named it an antibiotic. It was some years later that Ernst Chain and Howard Florey extracted a pure sample of this agent, which they called penicillin.

Penicillin proved to be much more effective than the existing sulphonamide drugs in arresting the growth of *Staphylococcus, Streptococcus, Treponema, Gonococcus,* and *Diplococcus.* It was not effective against *Salmonella,* nor against any of the pathogenic viruses. A wide variety of antibiotics are now available, some of which, the tetracyclines, are effective against most bacteria and some viruses.

▶ **Question**

19.48 What major current problems are associated with the use of antibiotics?

In recent years many more advances have been made in medical science. Have a class discussion on the subject, nominate possible candidates for the contribution they have made and take a vote to decide which nominee has contributed the most useful research for better health.

▷ **Homework**

List the top ten contributors to advances in medicine over the last 200 years and justify your choice in each case.

Answers and discussion

1 Town planning

19.1 1 The sewage works are on the leeward, lower side of the town, so that contamination of inhabitants is unlikely since the effluent is conveyed away from, not through the town. The works must be close to the river.
2 The refuse tip is on the leeward side of the town. This is important, since in (a) the prevailing wind could easily blow dust and other waste from the tip over the town.
3 The swamp has been drained and is now used for factories, the sewage works and the refuse tip. In the badly planned town the undrained swamp has housing built on it.
4 Housing is sited in healthy positions on high ground and away from factories, sewage works and the refuse tip.
5 Housing is well spaced. Where this is possible it is an advantage, since spread of disease is limited and it is psychologically beneficial.
6 Factory waste is discharged into the river at the lower end of the town after the river has flowed past housing. This is not the case in (a).
7 Recreation areas are provided for adults and children.
8 The water works in both plans are situated at a higher level in the town than most housing, but (b) has a better situation since the waterworks are situated well away from the sewage works. The waterworks in (a) could easily be contaminated by sewage.

19.2 1 Shopping facilities are not shown on Fig 19.1(b). They would probably be built near of the town offices.
2 A hospital and various clinics will be needed. They could be built beyond the play area.
3 All new towns have community centres where people can meet during their leisure time. Activities such as drama, indoor games and adult education classes are carried out in such centres.

2 A pure water supply

19.3 90% of protoplasm is water and 70% of the body total is composed of water. 2 All the body fluids, that is blood, lymph, digestive juices, and so on, are water based. 3 Water is necessary for all chemical reactions in the body. 4 Water is needed for excretion (urine formation). 5 Water is needed to cool the body (sweating).

19.4 Evaporation.

19.5 2 condensation; 3 snow; 4 rain.

19.6 River; lake; ground water; surface water (e.g. a lake or reservoir).

19.7 The water is piped, so there is a good chance that it comes from a hygienic and safe water supply. It would be best to take water direct from the pipe rather than from the trough in which the boys are bathing!

19.8 The water in a shallow well has not passed through many layers of soil or rock so that few impurities have been filtered out. A deep well contains water which has filtered through many layers of rock and has had almost all of its impurities removed (left behind in the rock particles).

19.9 Any bacteria remaining after filtration may be destroyed by boiling the water. 'Purifying' tablets are used in countries where water is untreated. These are usually sodium hypochlorite tablets which chlorinate the water.

19.10 Water in a settling tank sediments out. All the particulate matter settles at the bottom of the tank.

19.11 Chlorination destroys any remaining bacteria.

19.12 Storage reservoirs are covered to prevent any aerial contamination, such as dust, or the growth of algae, which appear as a green slime on the surface of the water.

19.13 Fluoride may be added to water supplied in areas where the element fluorine is in low supply. Fluoride helps to build strong tooth enamel. Excess fluorine can cause disease, so some local authorities forbid the use of fluoride.

3 Safe disposal of waste

19.14 A mechanical scraper, simply illustrated in Fig 19.8, regularly removes debris from the metal grid.

19.15 In the sedimentation tanks solid particles precipitate to the bottom of the tank, leaving a much clearer liquid above.

19.16 The micro-organisms in the film surrounding the coke digest the harmful intestinal bacteria in the effluent. Both bacteria and protozoa in this film are active in the digestion of effluent micro-organisms.

19.17 Dustbins need tightly-fitting covers to exclude houseflies. Houseflies will breed in dustbins if they gain entry. They carry numerous pathogenic bacteria and are a source of disease, particularly in summer (see Unit 15).

19.18 Dustbins should be sited well away from the kitchen. The smell of refuse attracts flies, so even if a dustbin has a tight lid, flies will buzz around it. Flies are particularly unwelcome in the kitchen, where they can infect uncovered food.

19.19 The disposable bag system helps to prevent the build up of rotten smells. Dustbins are difficult to clean, but the disposable bag system relieves the problem. It is more hygienic for the refuse collectors to handle bags rather than possibly dirty dustbins.

19.20 1 The vehicle is completely closed while the refuse is transported so that flies cannot gain access to it.
2 The method of tipping is hygienic – the refuse workers do not have to handle any of the refuse.

19.21 A refuse tip should be sited in a remote spot, some distance from buildings. It is important that it should be on the leeward side of a town, well away from dwellings. Flies are always attracted to refuse tips and if it is close to housing this could cause an epidemic. The underlying rock should be impervious. There have been cases where poisonous liquids have leaked out of containers collected as refuse. The liquid has seeped into water supplies in the country, causing widespread illness and damage.

4 Communal food hygiene

19.22 Food factories; canneries; bottling plants; freezing plants; slaughter houses (abattoirs); food warehouses; dairies; food shops; hotels; restaurants; factory, business and school canteens.

19.23 The cook is cutting up fresh meat close to cooked meat (the pork luncheon meat). This could cause cross-contamination. She is using a dirty wooden board and there is vegetable rubbish nearby. The cat might jump up and eat the meat, and the cook's hair should be tied back.

19.24 A food shop must have adequate washing facilities to ensure that the shopkeeper's hands are regularly washed. The toilet should be well away from the food. Storage must include refrigeration facilities. There are regulations which demand that dairy products and meats are stored below 15 °C at all times. All perishable foods must bear a sell-by date. All surfaces should be easy to clean.

19.25 Cooked and uncooked meats are separated so that cross-contamination is avoided. The meats are stored on clean plastic trays, wrapped in cling film and kept in a clean refrigerated unit.

19.26 An assistant in a bakery should wear clean overalls, have hair tied back and covered with a cap, have spotlessly clean nails and hands and no wounds on hands or arms. Tongs should be used to handle cakes and pastries.

19.27 The kitchen would be the first concern of an environmental health officer visiting a hotel or restaurant. Kitchen surfaces must be clean and free of cracks which could harbour bacteria. Utensils must be clean and unbroken. Storage facilities must be adequate. The chef must be spotlessly clean, free from disease or any wounds on his hands or arms. Food must be fresh. Disposal of waste must be hygienic. Rodents and insect pests must be absent. The dining room must have clean tablecloths or mats and utensils. Toilet facilities for guests must be adequate.

19.28 A meat inspector will ensure that the meat carcasses in an abattoir are free from disease organisms such as bacteria or tapeworms. He will inspect storage facilities and the cleanliness of the workers and the surroundings.

19.29 *Mycobacterium tuberculosi* – tuberculosis; *Streptococcus* spp. – scarlet fever (see Unit 15).

19.30 Tuberculin testing of cattle has helped to eradicate tuberculosis, and pasteurisation has reduced the number of both *Mycobacterium* and *Streptococcus*.

19.31 Boiling milk would impair its flavour.

19.32 This method of pasteurisation is more rapid than the laboratory method (thirty seconds as compared with thirty minutes) and a higher temperature is used (75 °C).

19.33 The raw milk acts as a control. One would expect it to go colourless first.

19.34 After thirty minutes the raw milk and possibly the laboratory pasteurised milk will have changed colour. The raw milk will be colourless and the laboratory pasteurised milk possibly pink. There is a chance that some commercially pasteurised samples will go pink if they are not very fresh. From these results the conclusion is that bacterial populations are very low in all forms of treated milk with the possible exception of pasteurised milk which may have moderate bacterial populations. Raw milk contains heavy bacterial populations.

5 Public health and welfare services

19.35 The District Health Authority.

19.36 The Community Physician must be notified of all diseases occurring in his area which could lead to an epidemic so that the necessary precautions may be taken. Notifiable diseases include chicken pox, measles, poliomyelitis, tuberculosis, diphtheria, whooping cough, tetanus, typhoid, paratyphoid, smallpox. The list of diseases varies depending on current medical knowledge. In the case of a really dangerous disease which is not endemic in this country, the victim must be strictly isolated and all contacts traced and placed in quarantine. Smallpox and typhoid are examples of diseases requiring this action.

19.37 Pharmacists stock and dispense the drugs and medicines which are prescribed for patients by doctors. Opticians examine eyes and assess eyesight and arrange for glasses if necessary.

19.38 Clinics likely to be found in most areas include antenatal clinics (where expectant mothers learn to care for themselves and their baby); post-natal clinics where the progress of babies is monitored; family planning clinics where couples are advised on contraception; geriatric clinics where the complaints associated with age are treated; psychiatric clinics for people who have mental problems and dental clinics.

6 Research for better health

19.39 If Dr Jenner was right, Jimmy Phipps would not develop smallpox after the second inoculation. The cowpox inoculation had somehow made him immune.

19.40 After 100 days, the broth in the swan-necked flask was still fresh. Three days after the neck was broken, the broth went bad. The broth did not therefore contain something inside it which went bad. The 'something' must have been particles in the air which came into contact with the broth after the neck was broken off. These particles were trapped in the S-bend during the first 100 days and only the air reached the broth.

19.41 The source of the decay in (d) must have been the particles in the air. Micro-organisms are present in the air and some of these must have produced the decay. It was these micro-organisms which were trapped in the S-bend.

19.42 The tubes containing cloudy broth were the one left open and the tube with the straight glass tubing. In both cases the air was able to enter the broth, together with contained micro-organisms which made the broth go bad.

19.43 Pasteur prevented the wine from going bad by heating it to sub-boiling temperatures for a set period then cooling it rapidly. This was the first time pasteurisation, named after its originator, was used. The flavour of the wine was not impaired.

19.44 Pasteur's most famous vaccine was active against rabies.

19.45 Sources of infection in Fig 19.22 are the surgeons' uncovered clothes; their uncovered hands; their breath (no masks were worn) and their unsterile instruments.

19.46 No bacterial colonies are growing in the vicinity of the mould.

19.47 The mould may contain an inhibiting agent which diffuses into the agar and stops the bacteria from growing.

19.48 As antibiotics are used so much, some mutant bacteria are becoming resistant to them. This is particularly true of various strains of *Staphylococcus* and *Vibrio* (cholera). The only solution, apart from restricting the use of antibiotics, is the continual production of new antibiotics. Some people are allergic to penicillin. Their skin peels off and the gut lining is shed. The results can be fatal.

20 Pollution and conservation

1 The interdependence of plants and animals

▶ **Question**

20.1 Consider the activities of living organisms discussed in Unit 1 and list what you believe to be the basic needs of living things.

Constant use of food and oxygen could, in theory, lead to their exhaustion. How are these resources maintained in the environment? Study the diagrams in Fig 20.1 carefully, then answer questions 20.2 to 20.6. At the beginning of the demonstration none of the nails appeared rusty. All the tubes contain boiled water which has been allowed to cool and they have been left for 24 hours.

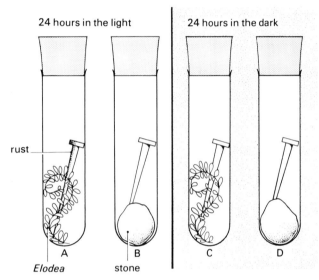

20.1

▶ **Questions**

20.2 In which tubes have the nails become rusted?

20.3 What two factors have operated in this boiling tube to produce rust on the nail?

20.4 What substance must be present in order that rusting occurs?

20.5 Refer to Unit 4 and explain the origin of the oxygen produced.

20.6 What is the significance to the living world of the production of oxygen?

▶ **Questions**

20.7 In Fig 20.2 what is the source of the carbon used to manufacture food by photosynthesis?

20.8 How is the level of carbon dioxide in the atmosphere maintained?

20.9 Outline briefly the cycle of carbon between plants and animals.

20.10 By what means is atmospheric nitrogen made available to plants in Fig 20.3?

20.11 What is the alternative source of plant nitrogen and how is it obtained?

20.12 Why do plants and animals need nitrogen?

20.13 Summarise the role of bacteria in the circulation of both carbon and nitrogen.

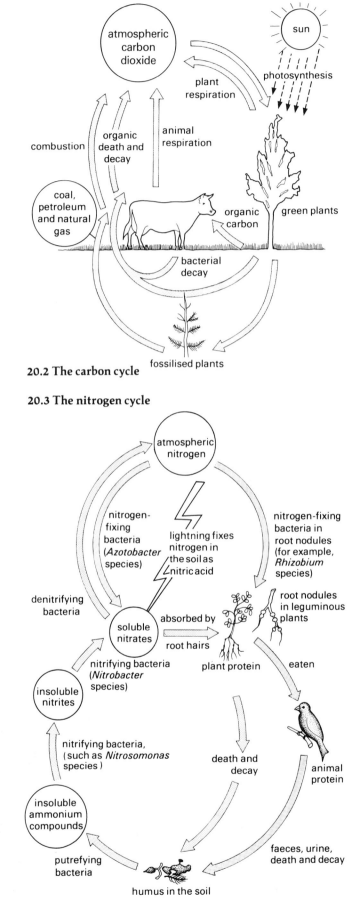

20.2 The carbon cycle

20.3 The nitrogen cycle

20.14 Summarise the interdependence of animals and plants in terms of basic requirements.
20.15 Complete Fig 20.4 which illustrates the interdependence of pond organisms.

▷ **Homework**

Study a habitat near your home – a forest, copse, hedgerow, meadow, pond or stream, and construct a diagram similar to Fig 20.4 to illustrate interdependence within that habitat.

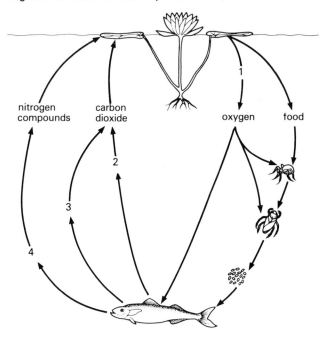

20.4 Interdependence of pond organisms

20.5 (a) Tree clearance

2 The interaction of man and the environment

Of all the animal species living in the world, man has probably had the biggest impact on the environment. His way of life has altered the soil, the water and the air. He has also interfered with other living species. All these acts have disturbed the balance of nature in one way or another. Figs 20.5 to 20.7 show a variety of ways in which man has modified the environment.

"Actually – I used to be a woodpecker!"

20.5 (b)

20.5 (c) Agricultural practices can sometimes cause soil loss

20.5 (d) Severe soil erosion. This gully will spread and carry away more topsoil with the next rain, unless plants are introduced.

► Questions

20.16 How is man interfering with the environment in Fig 20.5 (a)?

20.17 How has this act affected the wild life depicted in Fig 20.5(b)?

20.18 How has this act affected the soil in Fig 20.5(d)?

20.19 Suggest what man could have done to contaminate the ground on Gruinard Island.

20.20 Why has man transformed the landscape depicted in Fig 20.6(b) so drastically?

20.21 What is depicted in Fig 20.6(c)?

20.22 In your opinion, are any of these acts of man justified? Explain your answer.

20.23 What part of the environment is being polluted in the scenes in Fig 20.7?

20.6 (a) Notice about contamination on Gruinard Island

20.6 (b) Manhattan Island

20.6 (c) Common ground

20.7 (a) Smoke emission from factory chimneys

20.7 (b) Detergent foam on a river

Harm is often caused to living species, even to man himself by these disturbances to the environment. Fig 20.8 illustrates two animal species which have been seriously harmed by pollution. The fishes in Fig 20.8(a) are dead. The sea bird in Fig 20.8(b) is unable to fly.

20.8 (a) Dead fish in the River Derwent

20.8 (b) A razorbill covered in oil

▶ **Questions**

20.24 The fishes in Fig 20.8(a) have died as a result of the shortage of a vital substance in the polluted water which is normally present in unpolluted water. What might this substance be? (Refer to section 1.)
20.25 Can you suggest what is preventing the guillemot from flying? What might be the origin of the pollutant?

These examples are directly affected by pollution, but in many cases the effect on a species is indirect. The death of sea birds as a result of oil contamination may affect other species, as was shown in the following investigation. Between 1955 and 1968, the numbers of oil tankers using a port were counted, together with the numbers of shore crustaceans, such as barnacles, per square metre within a radius of 10 km of the port. The numbers of dead birds covered in oil, collected within the same radius of the port, were also noted, and the results expressed in the graphs shown in Fig 20.9.

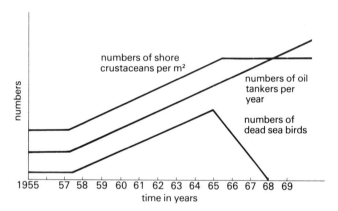

20.9 Increases in oil tankers, crustaceans and dead sea birds near a port

▶ **Questions**

20.26 What is the relationship between the number of dead birds and the number of oil tankers from 1955 – 1965?
20.27 Why do the number of shore crustaceans increase?
20.28 Suggest reasons why the numbers of dead sea birds decline from 1965 – 1968 despite the increase in the number of oil tankers.

Occasionally man has tried to modify the population of living things in a particular habitat for his own ends. A classic example was in Australia, where farmers were plagued with wallabies which ate their crops. To keep the wallabies out, the farmers planted prickly pear, a cactus, around the edge of their properties. The prickly pear grew so well that not only did it keep the wallabies out, but it spread into the fields and choked the crops. Farmers found they were producing an even smaller amount of crops than before.

20.10 Prickly pear cactus growing in Australia

▶ Questions

20.29 What was the anticipated result of planting prickly pear?
20.30 What went wrong with this plan? Explain why.
20.31 Suggest a natural method for eradicating a foreign species of weed.

With the increase in the world population of man, food reserves are under pressure (see Unit 13). In many parts of the world, food production is drastically reduced by the action of a variety of pests. Weeds, insects and rodents are responsible for the loss of as much as half the food crops in some developing countries. To counteract this loss, man has produced many chemical pesticides to destroy these pests. The aim of a good pesticide is simply to destroy the target organism only, but in practice this is rarely the case.

20.11 Damaged eggs of the Peregrine falcon

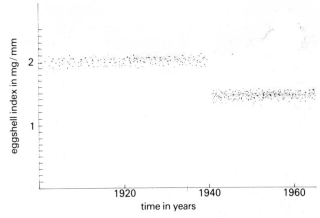

20.12 Scatter diagram of the eggshell index (relative weight) of the Peregrine falcon eggs from 1900 - 1960

▶ Questions

20.32 In what way are the falcon's eggs in Fig 20.11 deformed?
20.33 What effect would you expect this to have on the embryo inside?
20.34 At around what year was there a drastic reduction in the eggshell index shown in Fig 20.12?

During the Second World War, a very effective insecticide, **DDT**, was introduced. It was used to destroy lice in the trenches which transmitted the terrible trench fever. It was also used by farmers to destroy insect pests which damaged their crops, and in tropical countries to destroy the aquatic stages of the malaria vector, *Anopheles*. In low concentration, DDT does not harm vertebrates. Fig 20.13 is a food pyramid which illustrates the fate of DDT which has been sprayed in the environment to kill a primary consumer pest. It is a persistent compound, in common with all the organochlorines which form the basis of many insecticides. This means that it stays in the environment, in an unmodified form, for a long time.

20.13 Food pyramid from a freshwater lake

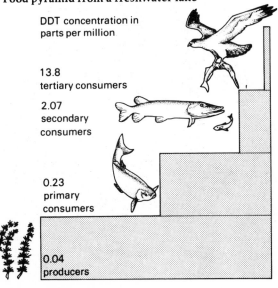

DDT concentration in parts per million

13.8
tertiary consumers

2.07
secondary consumers

0.23
primary consumers

0.04
producers

20.35 What is the concentration of DDT in ppm (a) in the producers, (b) the primary consumers, (c) the secondary consumers and (d) the tertiary consumers in Fig 20.13?

20.36 From these facts, and from the evidence in Fig 20.12, suggest what effect DDT has on the Peregrine falcon.

Many weedkillers in the past have caused human deaths. Arsenic was one of the first substances used, and more recently, paraquat has been the cause of a number of deaths. The search for non-toxic weedkillers produced the hormone weedkillers. These substances cause excessive growth of a plant, which 'outgrows' its strength and expires. Such herbicides are very effective for killing broad-leaved weeds in a lawn. The spray runs off the narrow grass blades, but remains on the broad leaves of the weeds. Such hormone weedkillers are called **selective weedkillers**.

Fig 20.14 is a photograph of a US plane which is spraying a Vietnamese jungle with a hormone weed-killer (a mixture of 2 – 4 D and 2 – 4, 5 T called Agent Orange). The aim of the spraying was to expose the enemy guerillas.

20.14 US planes spraying a Vietnamese jungle with the hormone weed-killer 'Agent Orange' to expose Vietcong guerillas

20.37 How can spraying a jungle with a hormone weed-killer expose enemy soldiers?

20.38 Agent Orange has recently been implicated in some very terrible diseases suffered by US Vietnam veteran soldiers and their children. The plant hormones are themselves harmless to humans. Suggest what may have happened to make the final product dangerous for the soldiers.

There are many substances which occur naturally in the rocks, water and air which are potentially harmful. In their natural concentrations they rarely cause harm, but if this concentration is increased artificially by the activities of man, they can and do bring about damage. Fig 20.15 is a graph illustrating the increase in lead pollution in the atmosphere as revealed by Greenland snow strata.

20.39 Try to think of some naturally occurring substances which could be harmful in large quantity.

20.40 Suggest a reason for the gradual increase in lead pollution shown in Fig 20.15 from 1750 – 1930.

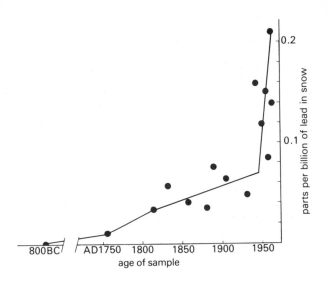

20.15 Levels of lead in Greenland snow

20.41 Why has there been such a steep increase since 1930?

20.42 Construct a table with the following headings, and using Fig 20.16 as a guide, complete the table.

Natural sources of lead	Lead produced by man's activities

20.43 Explain how lead from car exhausts, smelting works and ceramic glazes can increase the ppm of lead in food to dangerous levels.

▷ **Homework**

Find out all you can about the diseases which have been contracted by US Vietnam veterans and their children as a result of their exposure to Agent Orange.

20.17 Aerial view of Birmingham

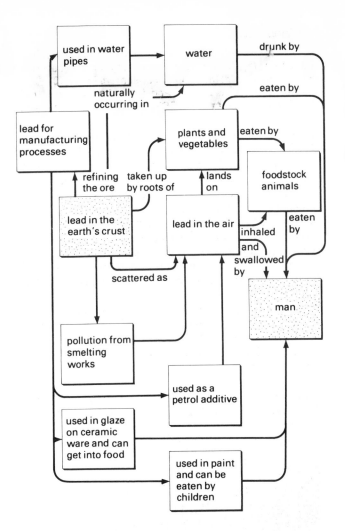

20.16 Sources of lead in air and in man

265

3 Air pollution

▶ **Question**

20.44 What two sources of air pollution are illustrated by Fig 20.17?

A typical London 'pea soup' smog of the 1950s is shown in Fig 20.18. Smog was smoke particles and other industrial pollutants trapped in river fog from the Thames. Fig 20.19 shows the number of deaths per day in London in 1952 during the killer smog, and the levels of some components of smog.

20.18 A 'pea-souper' in London

20.19 Analysis of the killer smog of 1952

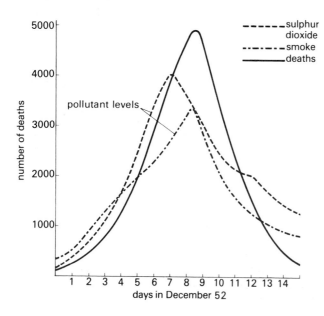

▶ **Question**

20.45 What two components of smog were isolated and measured during this period?
20.46 What is the relationship between these components and the number of deaths?
20.47 What was the highest number of deaths in one day?
20.48 Suggest the sort of diseases which could be caused by these components which could lead to death (see Unit 16).

Smoke particles are the cause of many respiratory diseases (see Unit 16). Destruction of the cilia allows the lungs to be bombarded with bacteria and viruses which cause pneumonia, bronchitis and influenza. The carbon particles lodged in the alveoli reduce the efficiency of gaseous exchange and cause breathlessness and emphysema. Sulphur dioxide is a soluble gas, which when dissolved in water produces a corrosive liquid.

▶ **Questions**

20.49 What usually fatal lung disease is also attributed to smoke?
20.50 Suggest what substances are formed when sulphur dioxide dissolves in water.
20.51 What effect do these substances have on buildings and statues in cities?
20.52 What effect would you expect these substances to have on lung tissue?

Most of the deaths during the two weeks of the smog were from bronchitis, pneumonia and emphysema. Elderly people were the major victims of the smog, as were those already suffering from chronic bronchitis.

Since the Clean Air Act of 1956 made the burning of smoky fuels by domestic users illegal in built up areas (see section 5), smog has not been suffered in London. There is still a problem of pollution from industrial effluents such as those emitted by the industries illustrated in Fig 20.20 and Fig 20.21. The result of these emissions is acid rain.

20.20 A coal power station emitting smoke laden with sulphur dioxide

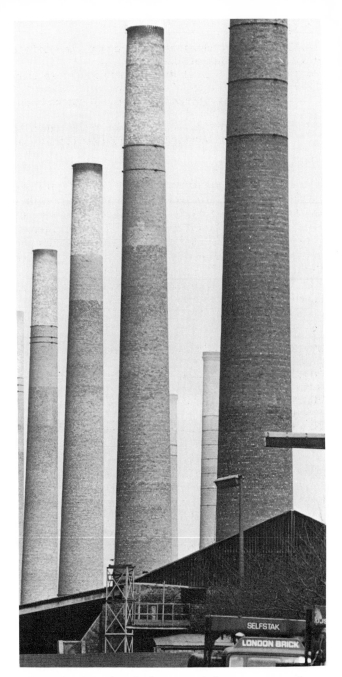

20.21 A brickworks which may emit large amounts of smoke

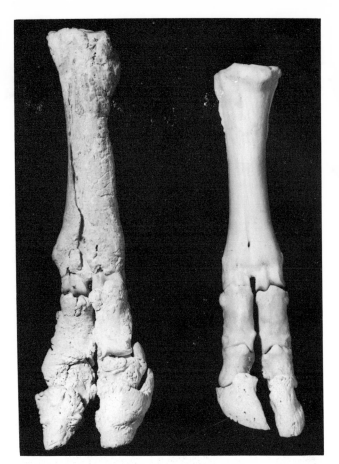

20.22 Foreleg bones from a calf with severe fluorosis

20.23 Foreleg bones from a healthy calf

▶ **Questions**

20.53 Suggest how acid rain may be formed.
20.54 Why do these factories have such tall chimneys?
20.55 Describe the defects brought about by excess atmospheric fluorine on the calf in Fig 20.22. How has the excess fluorine entered the calf?

Fluorosis in cattle used to be a serious problem in parts of Britain, but nowadays it is a very unusual condition. Tighter controls on the emission of fluorine from industrial processes have reduced the levels of fluorine in the air, and this has reduced the frequency of fluorosis.

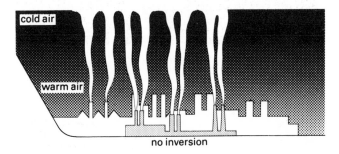

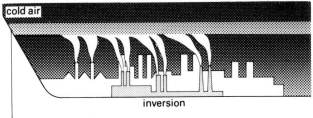

warm air inversion layer

20.24 Smog formation

▶ **Question**

20.56 Explain how the 'temperature inversion' illustrated in Fig 20.24 prevents the escape of pollutants from the city below.

267

The smog in Fig 20.24 is mainly caused by industrial effluents which are acted upon by sunlight. In Los Angeles and other American cities nestling in a valley, dangerous photochemical smogs are produced by the very high quantities of car exhaust gases. These gases, apart from carbon monoxide (see Unit 16), include nitrogen oxides, substances called PANs and ozones. Lead is also released in large amounts. Nitrogen oxides cause extreme eye irritation and mental defects. Los Angeles broadcasts warnings to mothers to keep children indoors in the event of a photochemical smog. PANs (hydrocarbon-nitrogen dioxide compounds) have a similar effect. Ozone also causes eye irritation, but may produce other damage.

WEST				EAST		
100m	50m	25m	wind →	25m	50m	100m distance
40	46	32		60	56	40 grass level
90	161	239		403	211	92 — 2cm
73	100	139		252	102	82 — 5cm	soil depth
61	93	63		121	74	60 — 10cm

20.26 Concentrations of lead in ppm near a major motorway

20.25 Spaghetti Junction near Birmingham

Lead pollution

In this country lead from car exhaust fumes is causing major pollution problems. At present, use of the car and of articulated lorries is continuously increasing and if this continues, engine exhaust pollution is also likely to increase. Legislation is now planned (1981) to reduce the amount of lead in petrol to avoid further pollution.

The World Health Organisation monitors the effects of poisonous substances in the environment and publishes permissible levels of these substances in the atmosphere. In Birmingham, lead levels close to Spaghetti Junction are five times over that permissible level.

▶ Questions

20.57 How many ppm of lead are present in the air (a) 25 m and (b) 100 m from the motorway on the east side in Fig 20.26?

20.58 How many ppm of lead are present in the soil (a) 25 m and (b) 100 m from the motorway on the east side?

20.59 What is the potential danger to a householder of the higher concentration of lead in the soil?

20.60 If you had to buy a house in this area, where would you choose your house and why?

The symptoms of lead poisoning are many and varied. Early symptoms are difficult to distinguish from many other diseases. Lethargy is the most pronounced early effect. For the synthesis of haemoglobin from iron, a specific enzyme, ALA-dehydrase must be active in the red blood cells. Its activity, however, is reduced by the presence of lead in the blood. See Fig 20.27.

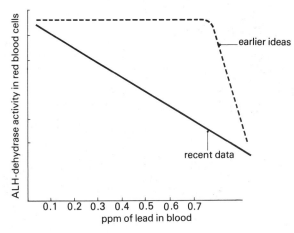

20.27 ALA-dehydrase activity in increasing blood lead levels. Earlier ideas and recent data

▶ Question

20.61 In what way were early ideas about the effect of lead on ALA-dehydrase misguided?

20.62 What will be the effect of reduced ALA-dehydrase on the body?

A study in the USA on lead poisoning in children with the 'pica' habit (eating dirt, including lead-containing paint from old buildings) showed the following effects of lead at different blood levels:

Over 20 micrograms/litre – hyperactivity (restlessness and irritability),

Over 40 micrograms/litre – changes in blood chemistry,

Over 80 micrograms/litre – acute digestive orders, lethargy,

Over 100 micrograms/litre – acute brain swelling.

The effects of lead on the brain have been shown to be irreversible and behavioural changes and inflexibility of learning result.

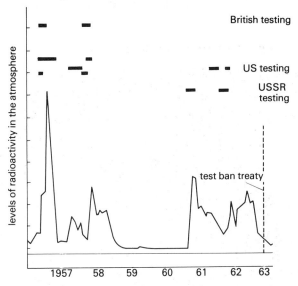

20.28 Effect of nuclear weapons testing on atmospheric radioactivity levels

Radioactivity

A dangerous air pollutant of this century is radioactive fallout.

▶ Questions

20.63 During which year did an atomic test produce the most radioactivity?

20.64 Why did subsequent explosions produce less radioactivity?

20.65 Suggest what happened to the radioactive substances produced in the late 1950s in 1960.

The main constituent of radioactive dust produced from the early atomic bombs was strontium 90. Fig 20.29 shows the annual deposition of strontium 90 in the atmosphere between 1958 and 1967, and the total cumulative strontium 90 in the environment (the total amount accumulated).

▶ Questions

20.66 How many megacuries of strontium 90 were deposited from the atmosphere in 1966?

20.67 How many megacuries of strontium 90 were released in the atmosphere in 1966?

20.68 How can you account for this difference?

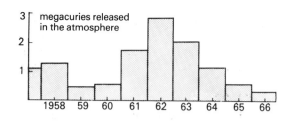

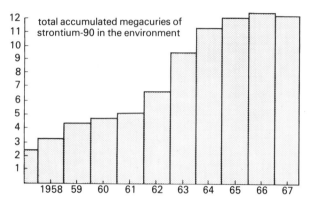

20.29 Strontium-90 in the environment

Many radioactive substances continue to be radioactive over many thousands of years. They are unstable and decay over a long period, producing radiation. Once an environment is contaminated by radioactivity, it may remain contaminated indefinitely.

Nuclear power stations sometimes leak their wastes into the environment. These may be classed as 'low activity leaks' by officials, but in fact the precise threshold levels of radioactivity which cause damage are very much in dispute and may be much less than is thought at present. Effects of radioactivity include leukaemia, cancers, premature ageing and the birth of deformed offspring.

▶ **Questions**

20.69 What possible sources of contamination of the environment by radioactive substances still exist today despite the Test Ban Treaty?

20.70 Suggest how radioactivity may bring about the diseases mentioned above.

20.71 Construct a table to summarise air pollution and its effects. Use the following headings: Pollutant, Sources, Damage, and Control.

▷ **Homework**

Find out all you can about the accident at the nuclear reactor in Harrisburg, Pennsylvania in 1979. What have been the effects of this accident?

4 Water pollution

A bridge near Blandford Forum, on the Dorset Stour, bears an ancient notice with this caution: 'Anyone found injuring the river is liable to be transported for life.' Pure water is an essential for life, but many sources of our water have been terribly 'injured'.

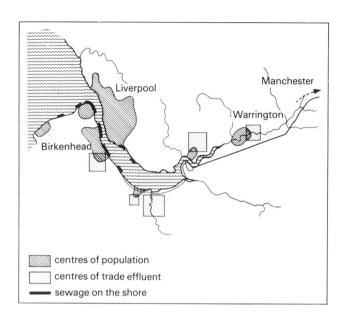

20.30 Effluents which pass into the River Mersey

▶ **Question**

20.72 What other effluents besides those shown in Fig 20.30 probably discharge into the River Mersey?

The Mersey is tidal as far as Warrington, which is the reason for the discharge of untreated sewage. In theory the tides remove the pollutants. But during twenty-four hours, several thousand million decilitres of sewage (about a quarter untreated) and a similar quantity of industrial effluents enter the river.

An indication of the seriousness of the pollution of a mass of water is the state of the fish in the water. Provided the amount of available oxygen is sufficient to sustain life in a river, the natural organisms will keep the river clean. The amount of oxygen needed to purify water is thus a measure of the degree of pollution. This is called the Biological Oxygen Demand (BOD). Rivers with a BOD of 12 or above are grossly polluted. Apart from the toxic substances they may contain, industrial effluents frequently have a high temperature. This has an adverse effect on the balance of life in the river, because less oxygen remains dissolved in the water as its temperature rises.

Heavy metals are one of the most dangerous contaminants introduced by industrial effluents. These include lead, mercury, cadmium, selenium and zinc. The effects of lead have already been discussed in section 3. Mercury has been found to be particularly dangerous. When released from a factory, mercury is in a relatively non-toxic inorganic form. This form is then taken up by fish. The fish convert inorganic mercury into highly toxic methyl mercury, an organic form. Not all these contaminated fish die naturally, and humans consuming these fish are liable to suffer from acute mercurial poisoning.

20.73 Why should humans consuming contaminated fish suffer more acute symptoms than the fish?

The worst known cases of industrial pollution occurred at Minamata, Japan. Methyl mercury compounds, formed during the manufacture of a paint solvent, were discharged into Minamata Bay. Local inhabitants who ate a large amount of fish soon began to suffer from slow and slurred speech, numbness in the limbs and lips, restricted vision, impaired hearing, disorientation, constant trembling, loss of consciousness, and in some cases, death. About 1000 people died. All these symptoms and deaths were caused by mercurial poisoning. At present over thirty tons of mercury are discharged into the North Sea each year, which is cause for concern.

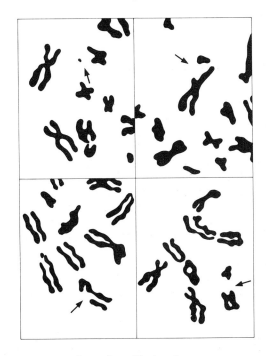

20.31 Karotypes of people suffering from mercury poisoning. Notice the broken chromosomes.

► Question

20.74 Why is mercury in the North Sea a potential hazard to people in the UK?
20.75 Fig 20.31 illustrates parts of human karyotypes which were taken from people suffering from mercurial poisoning. What defects are evident and what subsequent effects are likely?

Low activity liquid radioactive wastes are legally discharged into certain rivers and into the Irish Sea from nuclear power stations.

► Question

20.76 Is it possible to make regular tests to ensure that man cannot under any circumstances be contaminated by these wastes?

Treated sewage effluent will not harm river population and balance, provided the treatment has been effective. Fig 20.7(b) illustrates a problem which has affected a number of rivers in recent years.

► Question

20.77 What is the source of the foam in Fig 20.7(b)? How will it affect river life?

The problem was caused by 'non-biodegradable' detergents. These detergents could not be broken down by the bacteria in the percolating filters or aeration tanks, so they passed through the sewage treatment plant unaltered. Modern detergents are of the so-called 'soft' variety which can be broken down by bacteria. Some sewage treatment plants, if not well maintained, discharge large numbers of bacteria and salts into the river in the effluent. Fig 20.32 shows the concentration of dissolved oxygen, ammonium salts and bacteria along a certain distance of a river.

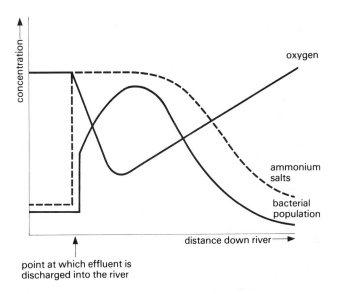

20.32 Concentration of oxygen, ammonium salts and bacteria in an effluent-receiving river

► Questions

20.78 What components are at high concentrations just below the point of discharge of the effluent?
20.79 Which substance is at a low concentration just below the point of discharge of the effluent?
20.80 Why has this substance become reduced?
20.81 Explain the drop in concentration of ammonium salts and numbers of bacteria some distance from the point of discharge.
20.82 Copy the axes of Fig 20.32 and draw a curve to represent the numbers of (a) protozoa and (b) algae in the river.

You may have expected in question 20.82 that the numbers of both protozoa and algae would decline with reduction in available oxygen. Ammonium salts, however, act like fertilisers. They contain nitrogen and they stimulate plant growth.

20.33 A tributary of the Cam in East Anglia, badly clogged with river weeds.

▶ Questions

20.83 What effect has the fertiliser had on the river in Fig 20.33?

20.84 How will this eutrophication (over-growth) affect the rest of the life in the river?

Farmers use a lot of nitrogenous fertiliser, some of which may run off and affect rivers like the one in Fig 20.33. Farm wastes also contain pesticides, including herbicides (weedkillers) and insecticides. Commonly-used insecticides on farms include dieldrin and DDT, both of which are persistent organochlorides (see section 2).

▶ Question

20.85 Explain why fish are in danger of serious contamination by these insecticides while protozoa and small crustaceans and insects are in less danger.

20.86 Construct a table to summarise the main water pollutants and their effects. Use the headings Pollutant, Sources, Damage and Control.

▷ Homework

Make a study of the nearest river, pond, lake or stream and investigate possible sources of pollution.

5 Conservation

Conservationists aim to change the living world as little as possible – to conserve the environment in every aspect. This does not only mean the air, water and soil, but also the balance of the living species in the physical environment. A national organisation exists which is devoted to preserving the environment. This is the Nature Conservancy. It looks after the ten National Parks in England and Wales, as well as the 119 National Nature Reserves in England, Scotland and Wales. Most of us live fairly close to one of the National Parks, such as Dartmoor, Snowdonia or the Lake District.

▶ Question

20.87 Why is a National Park less likely to suffer pollution than other areas of the country?

Maintenance of the soil is another important aspect of conservation if erosion is to be avoided. Activity 20.1 demonstrates how this may be done.

Activity 20.1   Investigating soil erosion

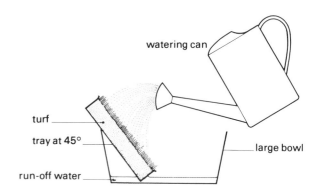

20.34

1   Fill one metal or plastic tray with tightly packed soil (A).
2   Fill a second identical tray with a rectangle of turf (B).
3   Pour water on both trays until the contents are saturated.
4   Place each tray in a large bowl at an angle of 45°.
5   Let one person water the tray containing soil from a watering can with a fine rose for thirty seconds, while another person treats the tray with turf in the same way.
6   Compare the water in the two bowls.

▶ Questions

20.88 Describe the appearance of the water in each case.
20.89 How may soil erosion be prevented?

Farmers use more sophisticated methods to avoid erosion. One excellent method is contour farming on hillsides as shown in Fig 20.35.

20.35 Strip contour farming

▶ **Question**

20.90 Why is this method preferable to planting crops down the slope of the hillside?

The problem of disposal of solid waste produced by man may be partly solved by recycling. Activity 20.2 shows how kitchen waste may be recycled.

Activity 20.2   Making a compost heap

1   Prepare a base for the compost heap, well away from the house, as shown in Fig 20.36(a).
2   Chop up kitchen waste such as potato peelings into small portions.
3   Mix kitchen waste with grass and leaves.
4   Add a generous sprinkling of solid ammonium salts.
5   If available, add some wood ash.
6   Spread a layer of topsoil over the mixture.
7   Continue to build up the compost in layers as shown in Fig 20.36(b).
8   Using a stick, make air holes in the compost heap.
9   Occasionally stir the compost by placing a stick in an airhole. You may expect to see steam being given off.

▶ **Questions**

20.91 What is the purpose of ammonium salts?
20.92 What important element is present in wood ash?
20.93 Why is topsoil added to the compost heap?
20.94 Why must air be present in the compost heap?

20.95 Why should steam be produced in the centre of the compost heap?
20.96 What natural process is being concentrated in the compost heap?
20.97 How does compost help plants to grow better?

20.36

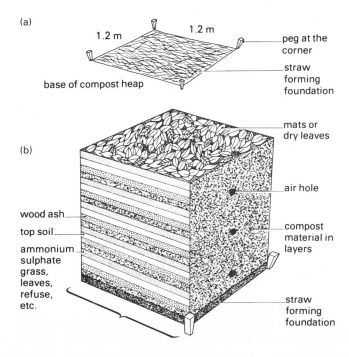

273

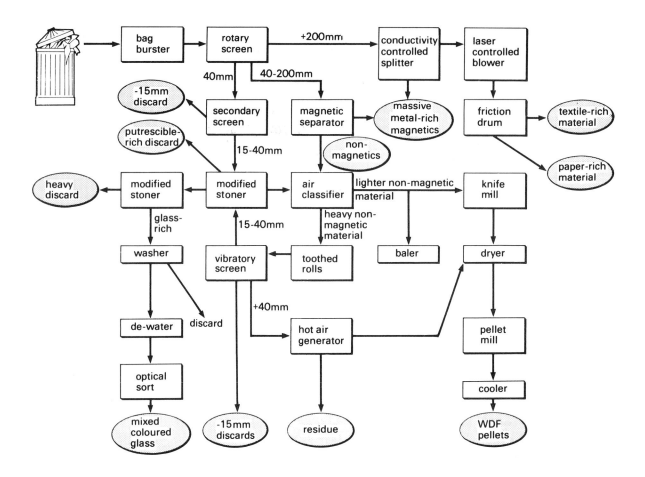

20.37 A local authority recycling process

Some local authorities re-use a proportion of the kitchen refuse they collect. Fig 20.37 is a diagram of a sophisticated process that one local authority has adopted for reclaiming useful substances from domestic refuse. WDF pellets contain plastics.

▶ **Questions**

20.98 On what basis are items in the refuse initially separated?
20.99 List the possible useful substances that are reclaimed at the end of the process.

20.38 (b) An electric milk float

Many serious problems arise from substances emitted in car exhausts. One method of reducing the problem is to fit heat reactors in exhausts which will cut down the amount of dangerous gases – PANs, nitrogen oxides, ozone and carbon monoxide in exhausts. Fig 20.38 illustrates two other answers to the problem.

20.38 (a) Many people in towns and small cities use bicycles to get around

► Questions

20.100 Explain how Fig 20.38(a) and (b) could answer the problem of pollution by car exhausts.
20.101 Suggest a simple remedy for the emission of lead from exhausts.

Since the middle of the 20th century, the extent of pollution has become so serious in Britain that the Government has stepped in to prevent further damage to the countryside as we know it. The first direct action to protect the environment came in 1956.

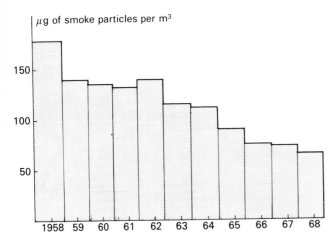

20.39 Micrograms of smoke particles per cubic metre of air in London from 1958 – 1968

► Questions

20.102 How many micrograms of smoke particles per cubic metre were present in the atmosphere in 1958 from Fig 20.39?
20.103 How many micrograms of smoke particles per cubic metre were present in the atmosphere in 1968?
20.104 What sort of Government action could have resulted in such a drastic reduction in the concentration of smoke particles?

The Clean Air Acts of 1956 and 1958 were the beginning of the national concern for the environment. There is now a Government Department of the Environment, and in 1974 the very important Control of Pollution Act was passed. This Act covers all forms of potential pollution and fixes standards which must be observed when disposing of all types of waste. International agreement on pollution control is now required, so that the balance of life in the sea may be conserved.

A continuing pollution problem is that of waste products formed from the production of energy. Fossil fuels such as oil, gas and coal, all produce hydrocarbons, carbon dioxide and carbon monoxide in their combustion. Even the smokeless fuels such as coalite and anthracite produce waste gases. Nuclear fuel produces dangerous nuclear waste.

Scientists in this country have been working for a long time on the possibility of solidifying nuclear waste so that the radioactivity will not leak into the environment. The glassified wastes could be stored in underground caves or mines. The photograph at the beginning of this Unit suggests a possible alternative to the problem of the production of dangerous wastes from fuels.

► Questions

20.105 What are the alternative methods of generating power shown in the photograph at the beginning of this Unit?
20.106 What other natural sources of energy could be harnessed by man?

The utilisation of tidal energy in the UK is promising. We are surrounded by large tides, and some, such as the Severn Bore, could yield large amounts of energy. Another possible source of energy is illustrated in Fig 20.40.

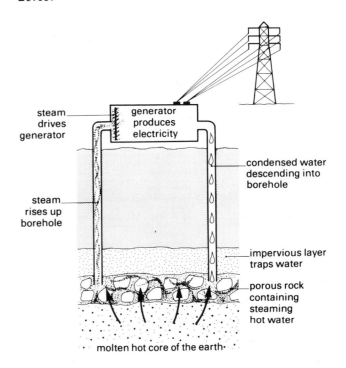

20.40 Generating power from geothermal energy

► Questions

20.107 Describe simply how a geothermal heating plant works.
20.108 What are the advantages of geothermal energy over existing energy sources?

Solar energy is beginning to be used to good effect in many tropical countries, but it is not so popular in this country. Expense is one drawback. A small proportion of homes in Britain have solar heating panels in the roof. The roof must face south to catch the maximum of the sun's rays. The amount of energy absorbed is usually only sufficient to heat the water and a supplementary form of energy is required.

Fig 20.41 illustrates a 'self-sufficient' house which has been built in this country. No pollutants will escape from this house to mar the environment.

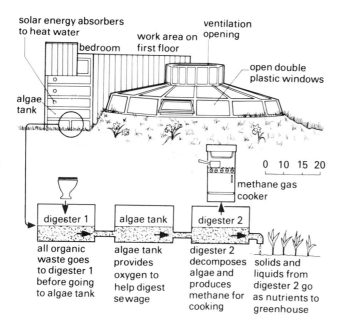

solar energy absorbers to heat water
bedroom
work area on first floor
ventilation opening
open double plastic windows
algae tank

0 10 15 20

methane gas cooker

digester 1 | algae tank | digester 2

all organic waste goes to digester 1 before going to algae tank

algae tank provides oxygen to help digest sewage

digester 2 decomposes algae and produces methane for cooking

solids and liquids from digester 2 go as nutrients to greenhouse

20.41 A self-sufficient house

▶ Questions

20.109 Suggest a second drawback to the development of solar energy as a major energy source in this country.
20.110 List all the ways in which the house in Fig 20.42 cuts down air pollution.
20.111 What useful products are gained from recycling in this house?

▷ Homework

List all the conservation measures suggested in this section. What possible problems could be presented by each measure?

Answers and discussion

1 The interdependence of plants and animals

20.1 Food, oxygen and water are requirements of all living things. In addition, green plants need carbon dioxide and light.

20.2 Only the nail in tube A is rusted.

20.3 Tube A is the only tube exposed to light which contains a green plant.

20.4 Oxygen must be present in order for rusting to occur.

20.5 There is no oxygen in boiled water, so the oxygen must have been produced by the green plant. No oxygen has been evolved in the dark, therefore light must be necessary for the formation of oxygen by *Elodea*. Green plants produce oxygen as a waste product in the process of photosynthesis. In this process, carbon dioxide and water are combined, using light energy, to produce carbohydrates. Light energy is converted into chemical energy in the process and this energy is stored in the carbohydrate molecules. It is later released by respiration.

$$CO_2 + H_2O \xrightarrow[\text{chlorophyll}]{\text{light energy}} CH_2O + O_2$$

Photosynthesis only occurs in green plants, since chlorophyll, their green pigment, is necessary to absorb the light. This characteristic makes green plants the sole source of carbohydrates for all living organisms.

20.6 Oxygen evolved as a waste product of photosynthesis replenishes the oxygen used up by all living things in respiration, particularly animals because of their faster respiration rate.

20.7 Carbon used in photosynthesis comes from atmospheric carbon dioxide (see section 5).

20.8 Respiration of animals and plants and decay of organic matter replenishes carbon dioxide in the atmosphere. Fossil fuel combustion may even raise carbon dioxide levels above the usual 0.03 – 0.04%.

20.9 Atmospheric carbon dioxide is used in photosynthesis by green plants to form carbohydrates (organic carbon). Some plants are then eaten by animals and the carbohydrates are broken down in the respiration of both plants and animals to produce carbon dioxide which is released to the atmosphere.

20.10 Atmospheric nitrogen is made available to plants by the nitrogen-fixing bacteria (*Rhizobium* spp) present in the nodules of leguminous plant roots or in the soil and by lightning.

20.11 The alternative source of nitrogen for plants is from the decay or breakdown of plants and animals by nitrifying bacteria (*Nitrosomonas* and *Nitrobacter* spp) and from similar breakdown of the urine and faeces of animals. Putrefying bacteria effect initial decay of all these substances to ammonium compounds and the nitrifying bacteria convert these compounds into soluble nitrates.

20.12 Plants and animals need nitrogen in order to produce proteins from carbohydrates.

20.13 In both cycles, bacteria are essential in bringing about decay. Plants and animals are either decayed rapidly to produce carbon dioxide, or sometimes delayed bacterial action over a long period of time results in the production of fossil fuels.

20.14 Animals depend directly on plants for carbohydrates and oxygen and indirectly on bacteria (simple plants) for proteins (from nitrogen). Plants depend on animals for carbon dioxide and for the urea present in urine, which is a prime nitrogen source for protein manufacture.

20.15 1 photosynthesis; 2 respiration; 3 death and decay; 4 excretion.

2 The interaction of man and the environment

20.16 Man is felling trees. Years ago most of this country was covered with trees. These have been felled to clear areas for growing crops and building, and to provide paper.

20.17 The woodpecker has nowhere to perch, so it has joined the ducks in the pond. Woodpeckers will not survive in the pond – they cannot swim. Felling trees deprives many birds of nesting places and shelter.

20.18 Trees act as windbreaks and their roots help to bind the soil together. Extensive felling may lead to serious soil erosion.

20.19 The Government might have used the island to test some kind of weapon. Some people might assume that the ground is contaminated with radioactivity and that nuclear weapons were under test. In fact, the ground is full of anthrax bacteria and the experiment was concerned with germ warfare.

20.20 The drastic change in the natural landscape is due to man's tendency to herd together in large communities. This is urbanisation. Houses and buildings are crammed together and none of the original land is visible.

20.21 Fig 20.6(c) shows an area of open land near a town which man has used to dump his wastes.

20.22 (a) The contamination of any land for whatever purpose can rarely be justified. In this case anthrax bacteria may remain in the soil in the form of spores indefinitely and the island will probably never be habitable again.
(b) Industrial society as it exists today could not function without cities. Care can be taken to avoid overcrowding and many modern cities (e.g. Brazilia) conserve parks and open spaces. Such action can be justified.
(c) Dumping waste as in this photograph, creating a potential source of infection, an eyesore and an immediate source of destruction of the land, is hard to justify.

20.23 Fig 20.7(a) illustrates air pollution by smoke and Fig 20.7(b) illustrates water pollution by detergent foam.

20.24 The fishes probably died of shortage of oxygen. All the debris on the surface of the water will exclude light, so reducing photosynthesis by water plants.

20.25 The guillemot is covered in crude oil, which weighs it down and prevents it from flying. The oil probably came from a leaking or discharging oil tanker.

20.26 As the numbers of oil tankers increased, so did the numbers of dead sea birds covered with oil.

20.27 Sea birds feed on crustaceans, so with fewer sea birds alive more crustaceans survive.

20.28 From 1965, measures to prevent oil pollution must have been taken. Oil tankers stopped discharging the remnants of their oil into the sea. Oil booms to contain oil slicks were put to use, and detergents were used to disperse the oil.

20.29 It was hoped that the prickly pear would form a hedge around the farms to help keep the wallabies out.

20.30 The prickly pear grew very quickly and eventually crowded out all the existing plants, including the farmers' crops! Prickly pear grew very fast because none of its natural predators were present in Australia, so it grew unchecked.

20.31 A natural way to control prickly pear is to locate its natural predators and introduce them in the new location. Scientists tested 156 species of insects from the part of America where prickly pear grows naturally. They found one species of moth, called *Cactoblastis*, whose caterpillars fed only on prickly pear. When *Cactoblastis* was introduced to the areas infested by prickly pear, it rapidly reduced what had been an economically disastrous weed. No other plants were attacked by the caterpillars.

20.32 The irregular shape of the eggs could be due to soft and fragile shells.

20.33 A soft eggshell will be poorly calcified and will not protect the embryo properly. Very few embryos will survive to hatch. The peregrine falcon has become very rare in this country because of these soft-shelled eggs.

20.34 The eggshell index fell from 1.8 – 2.3 mg/mm to 1.3 – 1.8 mg/mm in 1940. From that time it has continued to fall slightly.

20.35 (a) 0.04 ppm, (b) 0.23 ppm, (c) 2.07 ppm, (d) 13.8 ppm.

20.36 The evidence suggests that the accumulation of DDT in the peregrine falcon has affected the quality of the birds' eggshells.

20.37 The hormone weedkiller will make the broad leaves on the trees grow very fast, die and drop off. This will expose the undergrowth and the enemy will have no cover. This tactic was called defoliation.

20.38 If the hormones themselves are harmless, a contaminant must have been introduced during the manufacture of Agent Orange. The toxic contaminant is called dioxin and is one of the most potent poisons known to man. It caused widespread damage to people in Italy when a factory accident at Seveso liberated dioxin into the atmosphere.

20.39 1 radioactive elements; 2 sulphur dioxide; 3 mercury; 4 lead; 5 chloride; 6 fluorine.

20.40 The Industrial Revolution started around 1750. As more industries were set up, so more lead was released into the atmosphere in manufacturing processes.

20.41 Since 1930 lead has been added to petrol to improve performance. As the number of cars has also rapidly increased, the amount of lead emitted into the atmosphere through car exhausts has caused a sharp increase in atmospheric lead.

20.42

Natural sources of lead	Lead produced by man's activities
Water	Used in water pipes
Plants and animals	Smelting works
Foodstock animals	Glaze on ceramic ware
Soil	Used in paint
Air	Used as a petrol additive

20.43 Lead from car exhausts and smelting works enters the atmosphere, falls on the soil and is taken up by the roots of plants. Lead from a ceramic glaze in a water jug may gradually dissolve into the water.

3 Air pollution

20.44 Two sources of air pollution in Fig 20.17 are industrial smoke and exhaust fumes from cars using the major highway.

20.45 Smoke and sulphur dioxide were measured during December 1952.

20.46 The increase in smoke and sulphur dioxide is paralleled by the increase in deaths.

20.47 The highest number of deaths in one day was 5000.

20.48 The types of diseases were probably respiratory – bronchitis, emphysema, pneumonia etc.

20.49 Lung cancer is a fatal disease associated with smoke.

20.50 When sulphur dioxide dissolves in water, sulphurous and sulphuric acids are formed. In fact, weak sulphurous acid is a component of smog.

20.51 Acids in the atmosphere will corrode and wear away buildings and statues. Look out for statues with featureless faces – sulphurous acid is probably to blame.

20.52 Acids will also have a corrosive effect on lung tissue. In the lung, even more sulphur dioxide will dissolve in the moist bronchial tract forming sulphurous acid. This acid will cause irritation and inflammation of the lung tissue which could produce bronchitis and eventually emphysema.

20.53 Sulphur dioxide and fluorine pass up into the clouds by convection. Here they dissolve, and form acids which will fall in the rain. Sulphur dioxide dissolves to form sulphurous acid and fluorine forms hydrofluoric acid.

20.54 The very tall factory chimneys help to keep polluting smoke away from ground level.

20.55 The foreleg bones have become heavy and swollen with large deposits of calcified tissue. The excess fluorine probably entered the calf after being deposited on the grass it eats and the water it drinks.

20.56 Normally, warm air from a city rises, carrying pollutants with it, but when temperature inversions occur, a layer of warm air traps pollutants beneath it.

20.57 (a) 60 ppm, (b) 40 ppm.

20.58 (a) 403 ppm, (b) 92 ppm.

20.59 Lead in the soil will be taken up by any edible plants grown in the garden and thus gain access to the occupants of the house.

20.60 A house 100 m west of the junction would be preferable. Here there are only 21 ppm of lead as compared with 40 ppm of lead the same distance to the east of the junction.

20.61 Early ideas indicated that the ALA-dehydrase was unaffected by concentrations of lead below 0.8 ppm. Current data indicates that ALA-dehydrase activity is reduced even at 0.1 ppm lead concentration and that ALA-dehydrase activity continues to decrease with every 0.1 ppm.

20.62 Reduced ALA-dehydrase will result in reduced haemoglobin synthesis. This will produce anaemia and characteristic lethargy.

20.63 1957

20.64 Subsequent tests were carried out with greater safeguards after the high levels of fallout were recorded in 1957. Later tests were underground.

20.65 The radioactive substances released in 1957, 1958 and 1959 may have entered the seas and the soil by 1960, or have been dissipated from the atmosphere into space.

20.66 0.5 megacuries

20.67 12.2 megacuries

20.68 Strontium 90 must accumulate in the environment. Each annual deposition since 1958 has been stored up in the sea or soil.

20.69 Nuclear power is also used to produce energy for peaceful purposes. Scarcity of fossil fuels (coal, oil, etc.) has increased reliance on nuclear energy. Nuclear power stations are a possible source of danger. At Three Mile Island in Pennsylvania in 1979 a melt down of the core of the nuclear reactor at this large power station was only just averted. Towns were evacuated in anticipation of a major release of radioactivity.

20.70 Radiation is mutagenic (see Unit 16). It causes mutations in the genes and chromosomes leading to cancers and birth deformities.

20.71 See the table opposite. All forms of combustion produce carbon dioxide. Though the quantities of carbon dioxide in the atmosphere are unlikely to cause any damage directly to man, there is concern by some scientists that overheating of our planet may be produced by the so-called 'greenhouse effect'.

4 Water pollution

20.72 Other effluents will include radioactive waste from nuclear power stations, treated sewage and farm wastes.

20.73 Humans consuming contaminated fish will receive a more concentrated dose than the fish because they will perhaps consume a number of fish at one time.

20.74 The North Sea is one of the principal European fishing grounds. Most fish consumed in the UK comes from the North Sea.

20.75 Chromosome breakages are evident in the karyotypes taken from patients with mercurial poisoning. These will cause cell division abnormalities which may produce cancer or possibly malformed foetuses if an affected female conceives.

20.76 Regular tests of the water alone for radioactivity will not be enough. Any species living in the water which are consumed by man must be monitored. In south Wales, laverbread, an edible type of seaweed which accumulates a high level of radioactivity, is closely scrutinised. Radioactivity must not exceed a certain threshold level, and monitoring authorities assume that every Welshman consumes an inordinate amount of laverbread.

20.77 The foam in Fig 20.7(b) is detergent foam which has been released into the river in sewage effluents. It reached the sewage treatment plants in the waste water from ordinary houses. It will exclude light from the water, reducing photosynthesis, and reduce the chance of oxygen dissolving in the water.

20.78 Ammonium salts and bacteria are in high quantities just below the point of discharge of the effluent.

20.79 Oxygen is at low concentrations just below the point of discharge of effluent.

Index

Magnifications of histological photographs

2.6	× 800
2.10	× 200
2.11	× 6000
2.13(a)	× 1200
2.23 (all photos	× 800
3.15	× 100
3.17	× 200
3.30	× 300
3.31	× 200
3.33(a)	× 300
3.33(b)	× 450
3.33(c)	× 450
3.33(d)	× 20 000
5.13(a)	× 4
5.15	× 8
6.4	× 20 000
6.13	× 50
7.10	× 125
7.23	× 2500
8.2	× 8
8.10	× 3000
9.6	× 8
9.11	× 17 000
12.5	× 500
12.9	× 8
12.10	× 80
12.18	× 10 000
12.20	× 12000
12.22	× 12000
14.6	× 600
14.8(a) and (b)	× 800
15.12	× 300 000
16.3(a) and (b)	× 300

Acknowledgements

The authors and publisher are grateful to the following for permission to use their photographs:
Nigel Luckhurst: 1.1(a), 1.1(c), 1.1(d), 1.1(e), 1.7, 4.28(a), 4.28(c), 4.28(e), 4.28(f), 6.22, 8.13, 12.29, 13.8, 13.27, 13.30, 13.31(a), 13.32, 13.33, 14.3(d), 17.1, 17.2, 18.1, 18.6, 18.7(a), 18.7(b), 18.17, 18.18, 19.9(a), 19.9(b), 19.11, 19.12, 19.17, 19.18, 20.5(a), 20.5(c), 20.6(c), 20.7(b), 20.33, 20.38(b).
Dr. Paul Wheater: 2.6, 2.10, 2.11, 2.13(a), 2.23, 3.15, 3.17, 3.30, 3.31, 3.33(a), 3.33(b), 3.33(c), 3.33(d), 5.13(a), 5.15, 6.4, 6.13, 7.10, 7.23, 8.2, 8.7, 8.10, 9.6, 9.11, 12.5, 12.9, 12.10, 12.18, 13.10, 14.18(a), 14.18(b), 16.3(a), 16.3(b).
Mike Creasy: 4.3, 5.18, 7.27, 9.5, 12.25, 12.31, 13.12(a), 13.12(b), 15.8, 15.16, 15.18, 15.19, 16.1(a), 16.1(b), 16.2, 17.3(a), 17.3(b), 17.16.
Tony Duffy, All-Sport: photo at the beginning of Unit 1, 3.34, 4.1, 6.21. Bahamas Tourist Office: 1.1(b). Camilla Jessel FRPS: 1.1(f). Philip Coffey, Jersey Wildlife Preservation Trust: 1.4(b), 1.4(d). The Zoological Society of London: 1.4(a), 1.4(c), 1.4(e). F.B.C. Ltd: 1.6. Institute of Geological Sciences: 1.8. British Museum (Natural History): 1.13. Mansell Collection: 1.14. Philip Harris Biological: 2.1. Professor M.H.F. Wilkins, Wilkins, Biophysics Department, King's College, London University: 2.14. Griffin and George Ltd., Gerrard Biological Centre: 3.1, 3.8, 3.10, 3.12, 5.11, 7.19, 8.4. Syndication International: 4.2(a), 4.2(b), 4.27, 13.19, 20.8(a). Save the Children: 4.4(a), 4.4(b). ILEA — Learning Materials Service: 4.28(d). FAO: 4.30, 4.31, 4.35, 20.5(d), 20.35. John Cleare — Mountain Camera: 6.1. Supplied by M.I.S.S. Ltd: 6.8. Chris McLeod: 6.23, 20.38(a). Department of Medical Illustration, University of Aberdeen: 7.9. Dr. Nick Barnes: 8.1. British Airways: 11.1, 11.2. Canadian High Commission: 11.14(a). Royal Commonwealth Society: 11.14(b). Dr. J. Aitken, MRC, Edinburgh: 12.20, 12.22. BSC Footwear Supplies Ltd: 13.16, 17.8. Clarks Ltd: 13.16. Tony Seddon: 14.3(a). Australian Information Service, London: 14.3(b). Dr. M. Ashburner: 14.6. Frank Spooner Pictures: 14.14. Dr. H.B.D. Kettlewell: 14.16. Science Photo Library: 15.5, 15.12, 15.17(a). Medical Illustration Dept., St. Bartholomews Hospital: 15.11. C. James Webb: 15.23, 15.24(b), 15.27, 15.28. Shell: 15.34. Oxfam: 16.5, 16.6. National Coal Board: 18.8, 18.10. Berry Magical/John Mills Photography: 18.11(a). Dimplex: 18.11(c). Thorn Gas Appliances Ltd: 18.11(b), 18.12. Oxfam: 19.3. By courtesy of the Wellcome Trustees: 19.7, 19.18, 19.20, 19.23. Tesco Supermarkets: 19.13. Milk Marketing Board: 19.15. The Royal College of Surgeons, Edinburgh: 19.21. Richard McBride: photo at the beginning of Unit 20, 20.7(a), 20.20, 20.21. Denis Waugh/Sunday Times: 20.6(a). World Wildlife Fund: 20.8(b). Ardea, London: 20.11. Popperfoto: 14.3(c), 20.14. Aerofilms Ltd: 20.17, 20.25. BBC Hulton Picture Library: 20.18. Crown copyright: 20.22, 20.23. Keystone Press Agency: 20.6(b). Mary Evans Picture Library: 19.5. Anthea Sieveking/Vision Internation: 12.35. Department of Audio-Visual Communication, St. Mary's Hospital Medical School: 16.7(a), 16.7(b), 16.8, 16.9.

The following illustrations are based, with permission, upon already published sources as follows:
10.9 and 10.10(c) and (d); *Introduction to Biology* 5th Edn. D.G. MacKean (John Murray).
20.2 and 20.3; *Macmillan Biological Drawings for Tropical Schools* 1977 (Macmillan Education).
17.5; *Smashed* 1978 Transport Canada.